D1217721

THE PARTIAL CONSTITUTION

CASS R. SUNSTEIN

THE PARTIAL CONSTITUTION

HARVARD UNIVERSITY PRESS

Cambridge, Massachusetts, and London, England

1993

This book is printed on acid-free paper, and its binding materials
have been chosen for strength and durability.

Library of Congress Cataloging-in-Publication Data

Sunstein, Cass R.
    The partial Constitution / Cass R. Sunstein.
        p.   cm.
    Includes index.
    ISBN 0-674-65478-1 (acid-free paper)
    1. United States—Constitutional law—Interpretation and construction.
    I. Title.
    KF4549.S86   1993
    342.73'03—dc20
    [347.3022]

    92-32492
        CIP

Preface

Americans revere their Constitution. The four cornerstones of the system—checks and balances, federalism, individual rights, judicial review—are admired and emulated throughout the world. In periods of crisis, the constitutional system has helped America to avert tyranny, chaos, and oppression. In calmer times, the document has worked against less catastrophic but still serious difficulties. We should understand the framers' overriding goal as the creation of a deliberative democracy. In this system, public officials would be accountable to the people, but also in a position to avoid interest-group power, and thus to deliberate broadly about the public interest. More than two hundred years later, it is safe to report that this goal has often been realized. There is much to celebrate.

As it is currently interpreted, however, the American Constitution is partial. As so interpreted, it is partial, first, in the sense that it is biased. (I speak of current judicial interpretations of the Constitution, not of the text of the Constitution. For reasons that will be set out in detail, I do not believe that the Constitution itself is biased or that it must be interpreted in a biased way.) In contemporary constitutional law, the status quo—what people currently have—is often treated as the neutral and just foundation for decision. Departures from the status quo signal partisanship; respect for the status quo signals neutrality. When the status quo is neither neutral nor just, reasoning of this kind produces injustice. Sometimes the injustice is produced in the name of the Constitution. This is unnecessary and unfortunate.

In its current interpretation, the Constitution is partial, second, in the sense that it serves as part of what should be a whole. The largest problem here is that people tend to identify the meanings and workings of the Constitution with the decisions of the Supreme Court. In fact the Constitution was originally intended for the nation in general. The President and members of Congress are also sworn to uphold the Constitution. State officials and ordinary citizens also have obligations to the founding document. The Constitution does not mean only what the judges say it means. On the contrary, the Constitution has often served as a catalyst for broad public deliberation about its general terms and aspirations. Its meaning to Congress, the President, state government, and citizens in general has been more important than its meaning within the narrow confines of the Supreme Court building.

It is now critical to revive this broader understanding of the role of the Constitution. That understanding was an inextricable part of the original commitment to deliberative democracy. It is far from anachronistic today. Public deliberation about the meaning of the Constitution should in turn be freed from a principle of neutrality based on the status quo. The status quo, like everything else, should be subject both to deliberation and to democracy. These, at any rate, are the principal themes of this book.

For valuable comments on the manuscript, I am especially grateful to Bruce Ackerman, Jon Elster, Abner Greene, Don Herzog, Elena Kagan, Larry Lessig, Martha Nussbaum, Richard Posner, Frederick Schauer, David Strauss, and Mark Tushnet. Of the many friends and colleagues who provided helpful discussion and comments on individual chapters, I single out for particular thanks Akhil Amar, Mary Becker, Gerhard Casper, Joshua Cohen, Frank Easterbrook, Richard Epstein, Richard Fallon, Stephen Holmes, Martha Minow, Michael McConnell, Frank Michelman, Geoffrey Stone, Kathleen Sullivan, Lloyd Weinreb, Robin West, and James Boyd White. Michael Aronson was a supportive editor who also provided extremely valuable suggestions on the manuscript. Excellent research assistance was provided by Bart Aronson, Jason Cronic, Gabriel Gore, and Richard Madris. Marlene Vellinga helped with a wide range of secretarial tasks.

In this book I have drawn upon nearly ten years' work on the general subject of neutrality in constitutional law. Some of this work has been published elsewhere, though in significantly different form. I am grateful for permission to reprint portions of the following: "Naked Preferences and the Constitution," 84 *Columbia Law Review* (1984); "Lochner's Legacy," 87 *Columbia Law Review* 873 (1987); "Preferences and Politics," 20 *Philosophy & Public Affairs* 3 (1990); "Neutrality in Constitutional Law," 92 *Columbia Law Review* 1 (1992); "Free Speech Now," 59 *University of Chicago Law Review* 255 (1992); "What Judge Bork Should Have Said," 23 *Connecticut Law Review* 205 (1991); "Why the Unconstitutional Conditions Doctrine Is an Anachronism," 70 *Boston University Law Review* 593 (1990); "The Limits of Compensatory Justice," *NOMOS XXXIII: Compensatory Justice* (John W. Chapman ed., New York University Press 1991).

Contents

"[O]pinions were so various and at first so crude that it was necessary they should be long debated before any uniform system of opinion could be formed. Meantime the minds of the members were changing, and much was to be gained by a yielding and accommodating spirit. . . . [N]o man felt himself obliged to retain his opinions any longer than he was satisfied of their propriety and truth, and was open to the force of argument."

—James Madison in *The Records of the Federal Convention of 1787* (1911)

"If the artificial is not better than the natural, to what end are all the arts of life? To dig, to plough, to build, to wear clothes, are direct infringements on the injunction to follow nature. . . . All praise of Civilization, or Art, or Contrivance, is so much dispraise of Nature; an admission of imperfection, which it is man's business, and merit, to be always endeavoring to correct or mitigate. . . . In sober truth, nearly all the things which men are hanged or imprisoned for doing to one another, are nature's every day performances. . . . [I]t remains true that nearly every respectable attribute of humanity is the result not of instinct, but of a victory of instinct; and that there is hardly anything valuable in the natural man except capacities—a whole world of possibilities, all of them dependent upon eminently artificial discipline for being realized. . . . [T]he duty of man is the same in respect to his own nature as in respect to the nature of all other things, namely not to follow but to amend it. . . . Conformity to nature, has no connection whatever with right and wrong. . . . That a thing is unnatural, in any precise meaning which can be attached to the word, is no argument for its being blamable."

—John Stuart Mill, *Nature* (1874)

"[B]e the evils what they may, the experiment is not yet played out. The United States are not yet made; they are not a finished fact to be categorically assessed."

—John Dewey, *The Public and Its Problems* (1927)

Introduction

In the last generation, the terms of American constitutional law were set by the Warren Court and its successor in the first few years under Chief Justice Burger. An aggressive Supreme Court, acting on the basis of new ideas about civil rights and civil liberties, tried to bring about significant social change in the name of the Constitution. The Court invalidated segregation in the schools and elsewhere; created new protections for criminal defendants; imposed a rule of one person–one vote on state elections; recognized broad rights of freedom of speech, including not merely political discussion but commercial advertising, advocacy of crime, sexually explicit materials, and libel as well; removed prayer from the public schools; recognized a right of privacy, including the right to choose abortion; and created something like a flat rule against race discrimination, a strong presumption against sex discrimination, and barriers to discrimination on the basis of alienage and legitimacy.

All this amounted to a constitutional revolution. For defenders and critics of the Supreme Court, the debate, in the last generation, centered on these cases. That debate sparked a broad discussion of the role of the judiciary in social reform and of the Court's approach to constitutional interpretation in general.

The Emerging Constitutional Controversy

The discussion generated by the Warren Court and its successor is over. The terms of the earlier debates are increasingly anachronistic.

1

A new debate, with new terms and alliances, is emerging. Its contours remain indistinct. But it raises a new set of questions, very general in character, about the relationship between liberty and equality; the principle of free speech; the whole notion of judicial restraint; the role of property rights and freedom of contract; the connection between constitutional law and democratic deliberation; the nature of a well-functioning constitutional democracy. The new debate raises some more particular questions as well, about the power of our government to grant dollars, licenses, or jobs on "conditions" that might be thought to invade constitutional rights; about the meaning of freedom of speech in new areas involving advanced technologies, campaign finance regulation, government efforts to ensure quality and diversity on the airwaves, hate speech, and pornography; about legal treatment of reproductive rights, including abortion and surrogacy arrangements. The legacy of the Warren Court—the positions laid out by its defenders and detractors—is increasingly unhelpful to the resolution of these questions.

Above all, perhaps, the emerging alignments test the meaning of what we might well understand as the most basic organizing principle of American constitutional law. That principle requires the government to be impartial. Under the American Constitution, government should not single out particular people, or particular groups, for special treatment. Neutrality is its first obligation.

Ideas of this kind play a large role in political discussion. They help shape our views about what government may properly do. Some version of them can be found in nearly every political speech and party platform. Criticisms of governments not only in America but all over the world—in Russia and England, South Africa and Israel, Romania and Iraq, El Salvador and Peru—echo these ideas.

Such ideas also help account for much of American constitutional law. Many provisions of the Constitution are understood to require neutrality and prohibit partisanship. If the government takes property, discriminates between people, interferes with a contract, or abridges liberty, it must show that its decision reflects some effort to protect the public good rather than mere favoritism. The basic principle is extraordinarily widespread. It unites a striking range of seemingly disparate constitutional guarantees. It can even be seen as the heart of antiauthoritarianism, or as (what may be the same thing) the core of the impulse toward the rule of law.

Indeed, the most important contemporary disputes about the meaning of the Constitution reflect disagreement about the meaning of this principle. The power of government over private property; the status of affirmative action for blacks and women; the duty of the government to provide food, or housing, or protection against criminal violence; the relationship between government and the arts; the relationship between government and religion; the legal treatment of the handicapped; the distinction between "negative" and "positive" rights; governmental power to spend taxpayer money as it sees fit; the problems of pornography and abortion; government efforts to regulate campaign finance and access to the media—all these debates, and many more, are organized around competing views of the constitutional prohibition on partisanship and the constitutional obligation of neutrality.

Status Quo Neutrality

In discussing current problems in American constitutionalism, I will deal above all with that prohibition and that obligation. One of my principal goals is to identify and challenge an extremely pervasive understanding of the neutrality requirement. That understanding plays an important role in political debate. It also accounts for both reasoning and results in many areas of constitutional law.

In brief, the understanding that I mean to challenge defines neutrality by taking, as a given and as the baseline for decision, the status quo, or what various people and groups now have: existing distributions of property, income, legal entitlements, wealth, so-called natural assets, and preferences. A departure from the status quo signals partisanship; respect for the status quo signals neutrality. When government does not interfere with existing distributions, it is adhering to the neutrality requirement, and it rarely needs to justify its decision at all. When it disrupts existing arrangements, it is behaving partially, and is thus subject to constitutional doubt. Current rights of ownership are not seen as a product of law at all.

Even more than this, the very categories of government "action" and "inaction" are given their content by the status quo. Courts answer the question whether government has acted by reference to existing practices and existing distributions. Decisions that upset those practices and distributions are treated as "action." Decisions that do not are perceived to stay close to nature and thus to amount to no action at all. In constitutional law, then, we should understand the prevailing conception of neutrality to be one that treats as legally uncontroversial any decision to respect existing distributions, and as legally suspect any decision to disrupt them.

For the moment this description must remain unhappily abstract. The real argument lies in the details, where we will find many surprises. The surprises take the form of the courts' constant use of the status quo—to mark out the boundaries between neutrality and partisanship, or inaction and action—in cases in which something other than the status quo seems, at first, to be at work. Indeed, we will find that status quo neutrality lies at the heart of some of the most important legal principles involving free speech, use of government funds, property rights, and equality.

To be sure, few people actually proclaim that they take the status quo as the baseline for distinguishing between partisanship and neutrality. Most lawyers and judges would be extremely puzzled by any such proposition. But this conception of neutrality is in fact widely held, so much so that it operates reflexively rather than self-consciously. It is largely because of its reflexive character that it accounts for so many understandings about the meaning of the Constitution. And although my focus is on courts and the Constitution, the discussion bears on treatment of important issues outside the courtroom.

Status Quo Neutrality as a Mistake

I want not only to identify this understanding of neutrality, but also to argue that in many areas it is a mistake, and one that produces serious injustice. Most narrowly: Status quo neutrality disregards the fact that existing rights, and hence the status quo, are in an important sense a product of law. It is a matter of simple fact that people own things only because the law permits them to do so. Without law, no one can "own" anything, at least not in the sense that we understand the notion of ownership. Status quo neutrality is a mistake precisely to the extent that it overlooks the fact that our rights, including our rights of ownership, are creations of law. Often important constitutional decisions do indeed overlook this fact.

The point is especially important if our rights are seen, as they should be, to include the many entitlements that the law confers.[1] These entitlements are not easily visible as legal creations. We tend to take them for granted. But they are nonetheless a product of legal rules. The law allows people not merely to own land, or newspapers, or cars, but also to act within a legally specified territory: to go certain places, to hire and fire certain people, to control their bodies, to enter into agreements, to say things, to allow certain people (and not others) access to their property, to do certain things with what they own. Without legal protection, no such rights would be secure.

The state always stands ready to defend our rights of free action and free mobility (very broadly defined) against invasions by private people as well as government. We need the law of trespass, for example, to prevent people from coming onto or taking our land. We need the law of contract to protect our rights to enter into (or to refuse to enter into) agreements. We need the law of tort to allow us to engage in a protected sphere of action, accompanied by legal safeguards when we do as we are permitted, and insulated from liability for such offenses or harms as the law allows us to impose on others. And the state eliminates people's right to "self-help"—use of their own coercive powers—when they are unhappy with some outcome, like a discharge from a job, or an eviction from a home.

I offer all this as a simple description of our legal and social world. It is of course possible to argue that some rights are "natural" or a product of the correct theory of justice. But if we are trying to describe why we are allowed to do what we do, or why our world looks the way it does, it is important to understand the pivotal and omnipresent role of legal rules.

In general, it is surely good—for reasons of liberty and prosperity—that the law gives people these various entitlements. But it is not so good, indeed it may turn out to be very damaging, if we forget that these entitlements have been conferred by law in the first place. In thinking about the meaning of the Constitution, we often do forget that fact. We act as if the relevant entitlements come from nature, and are not a legal product at all.

To take a familiar and important example: Many people think that they oppose government regulation, or that we have all learned that government regulation "fails." But no one really thinks this. Markets are made possible only by government regulation, in the form of the law of tort, contract, and property. Such law is, among other things, coercive, in the sense that it stops people from doing what they want to do. For example, the law of property stops some people from getting food or shelter; the law of contract prevents some people from keeping their jobs. It is perfectly possible to think that markets are a desirable system of human ordering. But it is not possible to think that markets are not a product of law, or that they represent something called "laissez-faire."

More broadly: A decision to use the status quo as the baseline would be entirely acceptable if the status quo could be independently justified. In many contexts, however, the status quo should be highly controversial as a matter of both principle and law. Respect for existing distributions is neutral only if existing distributions are themselves neutral.

When the status quo—between, say, rich and poor, or blacks and whites, or women and men—is itself a product of law and far from just, a decision to take it as the baseline for assessing neutrality is unjustifiable. The status quo might well be a target of law, and not taken as an inevitable or natural precondition for law. It is the law (to take an extremely important current example) that confers rights of exclusive ownership on the broadcasting media. Let us suppose that the resulting system of free expression offers little discussion of public issues and little diversity of view, and produces instead sensationalist anecdotes, attention to "horse race" issues rather than substance, and watered-down versions of conventional morality rather than a wide range of positions. If this is so, the entire problem is created by law. We do not have to complain about "private power" in order to see that the system of broadcasting is a creature of legal rules, and that these legal rules, like all others, should be assessed for conformity to the Constitution.

The basic problem with status quo neutrality is that it shuts off, at the wrong stage, the American system of deliberative democracy. It refuses to subject existing legal practice to democratic scrutiny. It does not see legal practice as legal at all. It refuses to treat current distributions, or ownership rights, as a subject or object of deliberation.

In fact my challenge to the prevailing conception of neutrality is far from novel to American law and government. Some such challenge can be found in both the founding generation and the period following the Civil War, and it played a central and explicit role in Franklin Roosevelt's New Deal. For the New Dealers, the status quo was a product of law and frequently unjust; they thought it was a mistake to see the New Deal programs as "government intervention" into an otherwise voluntary and law-free private sphere. In this respect, the New Deal deepened and strengthened the original constitutional commitment to deliberative democracy. The New Dealers saw the status quo as no longer immune from that commitment. I attempt here to recover this aspect of the New Deal, to trace its profound effects on the legal and political culture, and to bring it to bear on current controversies.

Nor is my challenge to status quo neutrality novel to the study of American law. The legal realists, most prominently Robert Hale and Morris Cohen, paved the way for the New Deal reformation. Along with the American pragmatists, especially John Dewey, the realists insisted that existing distributions were a product of law and that these distributions should be evaluated in terms of their human consequences. (See Chapter 2.) More recently, Bruce Ackerman has emphasized the foundational importance of the New Deal to American constitutionalism; Ackerman has also identified the New Dealers' insistence that the law inevitably created the so-called "private sphere." Laurence Tribe has similarly stressed the New Deal attack on status quo neutrality, and he has shown in detail how pre–New Deal assumptions play a prominent role in many areas of contemporary constitutional thought. Others have worked on closely related ideas.[2]

The views presented here will depart in important respects from those of the realists, Ackerman, Tribe, and others.[3] But I will be trying to build on their insights, making them part of a general inquiry into the issue of neutrality in constitutional law.

Interpreting the Constitution

My subject is not only the substance of constitutional law but also the problem of constitutional interpretation. With respect to that problem, a distinctive conception of neutrality also turns out to be widespread. On that conception, the decision about constitutional meaning is at least to some extent a mechanical process, one of discerning the commands of a superior—the people who ratified the Constitution.

This process, it is often thought, does not authorize interpreters to use their own values, commitments, or principles. Neutrality in interpretation consists precisely in the abandonment of the interpreter's own views. Some people think that this abdication of personal responsibility—in favor of a principle of obedience to others—reflects the distinctive morality of law.

This conception of neutrality contains an important truth. Judges do owe a duty of fidelity to the founding document. The Constitution (like other legal texts) cannot reasonably be said to mean whatever the judges think that it should mean. Moreover, any sensible system of interpretation must attempt both to limit the discretion of the interpreters and to constrain the power of judges over democratic processes.

As I have described it, however, this conception of neutrality in interpretation is implausible. It is built on a conceptual mistake; it aspires to a form of neutrality that is literally impossible. The meaning of any text, including the Constitution, is inevitably and always a function of interpretive principles, and these are inevitably and always a product of substantive commitments. The problem with the prevailing conception of interpretive neutrality is that it denies the role of interpretive principles in giving meaning to texts, and thus hides the inevitability of judicial reliance on substantive commitments.

There is simply no such thing as preinterpretive meaning, or meaning without resort to interpretive principles. Personal responsibility, in this particular sense, should not be denied—which is not at all, however, to say that legal thought is "subjective," or that law is simply politics.

Although I spend considerable space in identifying and challenging these ideas about neutrality in law, my claims here will not be solely negative. Indeed, I will be arguing for a large number of general propositions and for particular resolutions of current legal disputes. I will claim that a certain form of objectivity in law is a salutary ideal, and that there are good reasons for judicial restraint in the area of social reform. I will also contend that the Constitution neither forbids nor requires affirmative action; that government restrictions on pornography and campaign expenditures do not offend the First Amendment; that government has very substantial discretion to fund, or not to fund, artistic projects; that the equal protection clause (if not the right to privacy) protects women's right to have an abortion, and indeed compels governmental funding of that right in cases of rape and incest; that our present educational system violates the Constitution, and that the President and Congress are under a constitutional duty to remedy the situation; that there is no constitutional problem if government creates a right of private access to the media or otherwise imposes obligations of diversity and public affairs programming on broadcasters; and that the Constitution does not create a judicially enforceable right to welfare or other forms of subsistence. My argument will bear as well on the foundations of regulatory law, above all in the context of environmental protection.

The Constitution outside the Courts

I also suggest that there has been far too much emphasis, in the last generation, on the role of courts in the American constitutional system. This court-centeredness is a continuing problem for constitutional thought in the United States. It has helped to weaken the sense of responsibility of other officials and indeed ordinary citizens, and it has distracted attention from nonjudicial strategies. Rooted in the overwhelming symbol of *Marbury v. Madison*, which established judicial review, the notion that the Constitution is directed to judges was dramatically fueled by our experience under the Warren Court. But the Constitution is aimed at everyone, not simply the judges. Its broad phrases should play a role with legislators, executive officials, and ordinary citizens as well.

Nor is this understanding novel. It receives strong support from the original views of the founders, who were hardly obsessed with the judiciary. James Madison, the most important voice behind both the Constitution and the Bill of Rights, came to advocate the bill primarily because of its effects on political deliberation. In his crucial letter to Jefferson on October 17, 1788, Madison asked, "What use, then, it may be asked, can a bill of rights serve in popular Governments?" His first response was that the "political truths declared in that solemn manner acquire by degrees the character of fundamental maxims of free Government, and as they become incorporated with the National sentiment, counteract the impulses of interest and passion."[4] Hence Madison hoped not for legal protection through courts, but for educative effects on the citizenry at large.

Madison's second response was that when oppression came from the government itself, "a bill of rights will be a good ground for an appeal to the sense of the community." Here as well, the judiciary was not the principal vehicle for constitutional protection. The Bill of Rights was to appeal more broadly to the "sense of the community." Three years later Madison wrote in the same vein: "In proportion as Government is influenced by opinion, must it be so by whatever influences opinion. This decides the question concerning a bill of rights, which acquires efficacy as time sanctifies and incorporates it with public sentiment."[5] The central point here is that "public sentiment," not only the Supreme Court, is to concern itself with constitutional protections.

Too little attention has been paid to the possible role of the Constitution outside the judiciary and in the democratic process.[6] For the next generation, a shift to administrative and legislative bodies, and to democratic arenas generally, is necessary. Such a shift would amount to a recovery of the original constitutional goal of creating a deliberative democracy, one that would benefit from widespread discussion among representatives and the citizenry at large. Hence many of the constitutional proposals set out here are intended not for the judges at all, but for others thinking about constitutional liberties in the modern state.

I will claim more generally that despite the persistence of an inadequate conception of neutrality, the aspiration to neutrality is far from an outmoded or empty one. On the contrary, a number of conceptions of neutrality are indispensable parts of our legal system. To say that neutrality should not be founded in the status quo is hardly to say that there is no room for neutrality at all. Interpretation may rest on interpretive principles, but this does not mean that judges should feel free to choose whatever principles they prefer. One of my major goals is to say something about the nature of truth and objectivity in law, and to challenge the view that the failure of mechanical interpretation is a reason to give up on notions of neutrality altogether.

This book is organized into two parts. The first deals with general questions of both constitutional substance and constitutional method. The second applies the general conclusions to specific areas.

In Chapter 1, I describe the original aspiration to deliberative democracy, the American Constitution's distinctive conception of political life. I identify commonalities among many provisions of the Constitution, arguing that all of them are taken as embodying a general principle of neutrality, one that I describe as "impartiality." The impartiality principle requires reasons, or justifications, for the distribution of social benefits and burdens. The impartiality principle is part and parcel of one of the founders' creation of what we might think of as a republic of reasons.

In Chapter 2, I introduce the principle of status quo neutrality by exploring three of the most important Supreme Court cases decided in the late nineteenth and early twentieth centuries. I show how a controversial and indeed implausible conception of neutrality was thought to justify racial segregation, sex discrimination, and "laissez-faire" in the economy. This conception of neutrality was based on a status quo, then taken as prepolitical and just, that now seems conspicuously state-created and unjust. Most of all, I argue that very much the same conception of neutrality operated in all three areas.

Chapter 3 deals with contemporary cases. I attempt here to show that current constitutional law is pervaded by a conception of neutrality identical with the one that infected the law at the turn of the century. Status quo neutrality is hardly a thing of the past. By showing the pervasiveness of that conception, I intend to set the stage for the more particular discussions in Part II.

Chapter 4 deals with the problem of constitutional interpretation, with special emphasis on the commitment to interpretive neutrality. I claim that constitutional interpretation inevitably calls for reliance on interpretive principles, external to the Constitution itself and requiring some kind of justification independent of the founding document. For this reason, many conventional views about interpretive neutrality are unacceptable. At the same time, the contemporary skepticism that legal reasoning is even possible, and the contemporary belief that legal decisions are based on intractable social "conventions," are both inadequate. I explore as an alternative a different conception of constitutional interpretation, one that sees the process as an exercise in practical reason rather than deduction. This process, I argue, can claim appropriate neutrality.

Chapters 5 and 6 are the heart of the book. In them I develop the notion of deliberative democracy and connect it to constitutional law. Here I emphasize the foundations of good interpretive practice in the overriding commitment to a certain conception of democracy. This commitment entails serious limits on the appropriate role of the courts. But it also suggests that constitutionalism does not entail unlimited majoritarianism, and that courts do have an important, though secondary, part to play.

Chapter 6 discusses the foundations of deliberative democracy, principally by criticizing the widely held view that a democracy should always respect the preferences of its citizenry, and base its decisions on existing desires and beliefs. In some cases, I argue, the claim that preferences should be the foundation for policy is unacceptable precisely because preferences have been created by legal rules. Here the preferences turn out to depend on the status quo. For example, some women may not seek equality because the law has made it unavailable to them, and they have adjusted to their fate. I also claim that in some cases, a government that departs from existing private preferences can reflect the democratic aspirations of its citizenry.

Part II applies these general claims to some specific controversies. In Chapter 7, I argue that our current system of free expression depends on status quo neutrality and to this extent is seriously flawed. There is far too little attention to public issues and far too little diversity of view. Indeed, current approaches to the problem of free speech closely resemble approaches to the problem of property before the New Deal. In both cases, existing distributions and the status quo are taken as neutral, natural, just, or in any case as the baseline for decision; in both cases, government "intervention" is disfavored. The current approach has seriously harmed the system of freedom of expression. Thus it is that a "free market" in speech distributes the opportunity to speak to those people whom other people are willing to pay to hear— hardly an attractive conception of free expression in a democracy. In particular, I claim that the First Amendment should be understood as a guarantee of a deliberative democracy among political equals. This view argues in favor of large shifts in current understandings and practices—involving government regulation of broadcasting, including above all television, and greater campaign regulation, to reduce the distorting effect of financial expenditures and to counteract the "soundbite" phenomenon that currently threatens democratic deliberation in America.

In Chapter 8, I argue that the free speech principle should be viewed through the lens of democracy. Political speech is at the core of the principle, and it may be regulated only on the basis of the strongest showing of harm. Nonpolitical speech—including violent pornography, scientific speech, libel of celebrities, and commercial speech— may be regulated more easily. Government can control nonpolitical speech, not on a whim, but on the basis of a showing of lesser harm.

Chapter 9 discusses the closely linked problems of pornography, abortion, and surrogacy. Here I challenge both the view, popular in law and politics, that "freedom of choice" should be the prevailing principle in all three areas, and the also-popular but competing view that government should be allowed to intrude on "choice" when necessary to protect sexuality and reproduction from the harms produced by all three practices. Both of these views, I claim, share a version of status quo neutrality, one that takes existing distributions of authority as between men and women as the baseline for decision. I argue instead that in all three areas, the focus of the law should be on ensuring that women's sexual and reproductive capacities are not turned into objects for the control and use of others. I therefore argue against constitutional arguments based on privacy and freedom of choice, on the ground that these arguments have missed the ways in which control of women's sexual and reproductive capacities has been connected with inequality on the basis of sex. The problems of pornography, abortion, and surrogacy are fundamentally ones of inequality.

Chapter 10 discusses an increasingly important question: the government's use of its own resources to affect what some people consider constitutional rights. The government might decide, for example, to fund some art but to withdraw funding from others; or to pay for public but not private schools; or to hire employees of a certain political view; or to exclude abortion from Medicaid programs. I challenge the dominant approach to this problem—the "unconstitutional conditions doctrine"—on the ground that it depends on status quo neutrality. I also propose an alternative approach, focusing on the question whether government has constitutionally legitimate reasons for intruding on the relevant interests. Under this approach, government may fund public but not private schools; has broad discretion to allocate funds to different artistic projects; but must fund abortion in cases of rape or incest, at least if it is funding childbirth in such cases. These conclusions have broad implications for the analysis of government's power to use taxpayer money as it chooses. They argue for a large-scale reformulation of current law.

In Chapter 11, I argue that a principle of compensatory justice—embodying status quo neutrality—has organized legal thought in both regulatory law (including environmental protection) and the law of equality under the Constitution. In both places, I suggest, this conception of neutrality is misplaced. Instead of compensatory justice, we need two novel foundations for law: the first rooted in the management of social risks, the second in the elimination of social castes. I venture some thoughts about these alternative foundations.

I also argue that the relevant law should be enacted and implemented by legislatures and administrators, with courts performing a secondary role. Here I suggest a new allocation of authority between the representative branches of government on the one hand and the judiciary on the other. In particular, I argue for a greater role for the representative branches, even or perhaps especially when their actions are inspired by their understanding of what the Constitution requires. I therefore explore the possibility of a more democratic conception of the role of the Constitution in the nation's political life. On that conception, elected representatives and citizens in general ought to be involved in the process of deliberating about the contemporary meaning of constitutional principles. This process of deliberation is not only for the judges.

The Conclusion deals with several conceptions of neutrality that seem to deserve general support. I set out those conceptions and briefly defend them. Here I attempt to find an appropriate place for the ideal of neutrality in constitutional law, and suggest how that ideal might affect legal interpretation in the future. I connect that ideal to constitutional democracy in America.

PART I

IN GENERAL

CHAPTER 1

A Republic of Reasons

In American constitutional law, government must always have a reason for what it does. If it is distributing something to one group rather than to another, or depriving someone of some good or benefit, it must explain itself. The required reason must count as a public-regarding one. Government cannot appeal to private interest alone.

We will encounter several conceptions of neutrality in this book. To distinguish this principle from others, I will describe it as one of impartiality. As I understand it, the principle forbids government from acting on the basis of pure self-interest, or power, or whim. In this light, status quo neutrality is quite different from, even at an opposite pole from, the impartiality principle. From the viewpoint of impartiality, the problem with status quo neutrality is that it takes existing practices as given, and does not require government to bring reasons forward on their behalf. Status quo neutrality refuses to treat the impartiality principle with the seriousness and depth that it demands. It treats existing practices and distributions as a kind of inexorable brute fact. It does not subject them to legal or democratic scrutiny, or to deliberation at all.

For the moment, however, the relationship between the impartiality principle and status quo neutrality must remain a bit obscure. My focus here is on founding aspirations, and on how impartiality is a minimal condition for democratic deliberation.

Monarchy, Self-Interest, Factions

The framers of the American Constitution sought to create a system of government that would simultaneously counteract three related dangers: the legacy of monarchy; self-interested representation by government officials; and the power of faction, or "majority tyranny." The impartiality principle was part of the attempt to respond to all these problems.

Any description of the framing period should note that the period involved a diverse array of influential people and an extraordinarily wide range of sometimes conflicting ideas. In influential writings from the period, we can find, among other things, a belief in a form of aristocratic rule; an enthusiasm for agrarian populism; a willingness to accept interest-group warfare; a belief in the need for radical centralization of politics in the national government; acceptance of slavery in particular and of racial and sexual hierarchy in general; Calvinism; a commitment to natural rights; hostility to commerce; enthusiasm for commerce; and insistence on the need for decentralization as an indispensable part of democratic government. In light of the sheer diversity of influential ideas, any description of the framing commitments will have to be selective. It will inevitably downplay certain elements and emphasize others.

In a short description of the kind that I will be presenting here, the problem of selectivity is compounded. I do not intend to provide anything like an exhaustive historical account. My goal is only to set out certain ideas that did play a prominent role in the founding period and that are especially well suited to those of us now in search of a usable past. Here the impartiality principle is an especially good place to start. It defined many of the framers' central ideas about politics and society. It helped organize their judgments about what was wrong with the institutions and practices against which the American Revolution had been fought. And it speaks powerfully to recurrent dilemmas in America and elsewhere.

The impartiality principle is conspicuously connected with the desire, traceable to the early period of the founding, to limit the potential arbitrariness of the king and indeed of everything entailed by the institutions of monarchy.[1] The Constitution should be understood against the backdrop set by prerevolutionary America, which had been pervaded by monarchical characteristics, including well-entrenched patterns of deference and hierarchy. In the prerevolutionary period, many of these patterns were attributed to nature itself. These included not merely the institution of slavery but also existing family structures, relations between employers and employees, occupational categories, education, the crucial concept of the gentleman, and of course the structures of government. Indeed, those very structures were thought to be modeled on the family and to grow out of the same natural sources.

A large element in the American Revolution consisted of a radical rebellion against the monarchical legacy. The rebellion operated with special force against the traditional belief in a "natural order of things." Thus the Americans insisted, in direct opposition to their English inheritance, that "culture" was "man-made."[2] In America, social outcomes had to be justified not by reference to nature or to traditional practices, but instead on the basis of reasons.

The American framers were alert not only to the legacy of monarchy, but also to the general risk that public officials would act on behalf of their own self-interest rather than the interests of the public as a whole. Actual corruption in government was the most dramatic illustration of this danger. But self-interested representation could be found in many places in which officials seek to aggrandize their own powers and interests at the expense of the people as a whole. The responsibility of the public official was to put personal interest entirely to one side. The impartiality principle, requiring public officials to invoke public-regarding reasons on behalf of their actions, was a check on self-interested representation.

Finally, the framers sought to limit the power of self-interested private groups, or "factions," over governmental processes. For Madison, this was the greatest risk in America: "[I]n our Governments the real power lies in the majority of the Community, and the invasion of private rights is chiefly to be apprehended, not from acts of Government contrary to the sense of its constituents, but from acts in which the Government is the mere instrument of the major number of the constituents."[3] Hence majority rule was, for the framers, a highly ambiguous good. On their view, even an insistent majority should not have its way, if power was the only thing to be invoked on its behalf.

It is relevant here that the framers operated in the light of their experiences under the Articles of Confederation. Under the Articles, powerful private groups appeared to dominate state and local government, obtaining measures that favored them but no one else, and that could be explained only by reference of private self-interest. The new Constitution was intended to limit this risk.

Above all, the American Constitution was designed to create a deliberative democracy. Under that system, public representatives were to be ultimately accountable to the people; but they would also be able to engage in a form of deliberation without domination through the influence of factions.[4] A law based solely on the self-interest of private groups is the core violation of the deliberative ideal.

The minimal condition of deliberative democracy is a requirement of reasons for governmental action. We may thus understand the American Constitution as having established, for the first time, a republic of reasons. A republic of this sort is opposed equally to outcomes grounded on self-interest and to those based solely on "nature" or authority. Where the monarchical system saw government as an outgrowth of a given or natural order, the founding generation regarded it as "merely a legal man-made contrivance having little if any natural relationship to the family or to society."[5]

Founding Institutions

The general commitment to deliberative democracy, and the belief in a republic of reasons, echo throughout the founding period. In *The Federalist* No. 10—James Madison's most outstanding contribution to political thought—the system of national representation is defended as a mechanism with which to "refine and enlarge the public views by passing them through the medium of a chosen body of citizens, whose wisdom may discern the true interest of their country and whose patriotism and love of justice will be least likely to sacrifice it to temporary or partial considerations."[6] On this view, national officials, selected from a broad territory, would be uniquely positioned to operate above the fray of private interests.

In their aspirations for deliberative government, the framers modernized the classical republican belief in civic virtue. The antifederalists, critics of the proposed Constitution, had invoked traditional republican ideas in order to challenge the Madisonian belief that a large territory was compatible with true republicanism. In the antifederalist view, a genuine republic required civic virtue, or commitment to the public good. Civic virtue, they insisted, could flourish only in small communities united by similar interests and by a large degree of homogeneity.

The framers fully accepted the goal; but they firmly rejected the prescription. For the framers, as for those in the classical tradition, virtue was indispensable; and the framers continued to understand virtue as a commitment to the general good rather than to self-interest or the interest of private factions. Thus Hamilton urged that the "aim of every political constitution is, or ought to be, first to obtain for rulers men who possess most wisdom to discern, and most virtue to pursue the common good of the society; and in the next place, to take the most effectual precautions for keeping them virtuous whilst they continue to hold their public trust."[7] But for the framers, a large republic would be more, rather than less, likely to serve republican aspirations. It would do so precisely because in a large republic, national representatives would be in an unusually good position to engage in the deliberative tasks of government. A small republic, as history had shown, would be buffeted about by the play of factions. In a large republic, the various factions would offset each other.

In recent years, there has been an extraordinary revival of interest in republican thought.[8] The revival is directed above all against two groups: people who think that the Constitution is designed only to protect a set of identified "private rights," and people who treat the document as an effort to provide the rules for interest-group struggles among selfish private groups.[9]

The framers' aspirations were far broader. They attempted to carry forward the classical republican belief in virtue—a word that appears throughout the period—but to do so in a way that responded realistically, not romantically, to likely difficulties in the real world of political life. They continued to insist on the possibility of a virtuous politics. They tried to make a government that would create such a politics without indulging unrealistic assumptions about human nature. We might understand the Constitution as a complex set of precommitment strategies, through which the citizenry creates institutional arrangements to protect against political self-interest, factionalism, failures in representation, myopia, and other predictable problems in democratic governance.

The commitment to these ideas explains many of the founding institutions. It helps explain why, in the original system, the Senate and the President were to be chosen by deliberative representatives rather than directly elected by the people. It helps with the mystery of the Electoral College, which was, at the inception, to be a deliberative body, one that would discuss who ought to be President, rather than simply register votes. It helps explain why the framers favored long terms of service and large election districts. All these ideas about government structure were designed to accomplish the same goals, that is, to promote deliberation and to limit the risk that public officials would be mouthpieces for constituent interests. It was in this vein that Madison attacked Congress in 1787 as "advocates for the respective interests of their constituents" and complained of "the County representatives, the members of which are everywhere observed to lose sight of the aggregate interests of the Community, and even to sacrifice them to the interests or prejudices of their respective constituents." [10] The new Constitution was designed to reduce this risk. The framers designed a system in which representatives would have the time and temperament to engage in a form of collective reasoning.

These general aspirations also explain two of the crucial decisions in the early period: the rejection of the "right to instruct" and the closing from public view of the Constitutional Convention. In the first Congress, the representatives rejected a proposal to give citizens, as part of the Bill of Rights, a "right to instruct" their officials. A right to instruct was thought to be inconsistent with the point of meeting, which was deliberation. Roger Sherman's statement was especially clear: "[T]he words are calculated to mislead the people, by conveying an idea that they have a right to control the debates of the Legislature. This cannot be admitted to be just, because it would destroy the object of their meeting. I think, *when the people have chosen a representative, it is his duty to meet others from the different parts of the Union, and consult, and agree with them to such acts as are for the general benefit of the whole community. If they were to be guided by instructions, there would be no use in deliberation. . . ."* [11]

The point casts light as well on the closing of the Constitutional Convention, a decision that Jefferson denounced as an "abominable . . . precedent" based on "ignorance of the value of public discussions." [12] On Madison's view, it was best "to sit with closed doors, because opinions were so various and at first so crude that it was necessary they should be long debated before any uniform system of opinion could be formed. Meantime the minds of the members were changing, and much was to be gained by a yielding and accommodating spirit. . . . [B]y secret discussion no man felt himself obliged to retain his opinions any longer than he was satisfied of their propriety and truth, and was open to the force of argument." [13]

These remarks about the right to instruct and the closing of the convention are extremely revealing. Above all, they show an important feature of political deliberation as it was originally understood. In the process of discussion, there is no effort simply to aggregate existing private preferences, or to treat them as a given. Representatives should not mechanically translate the desires of their constituents into law. Nor should they treat their own beliefs and desires as fixed. The point of the process is not only to protect a given category of rights. Those involved in the process should always maintain "a yielding and accommodating spirit."

Even desires, or current beliefs about what courses of action are best, should not be frozen. The framers insisted that existing views might be a product of partial perspectives, of limited experience, or of incomplete information. People engaged in democratic discussion should thus "meet others from the different parts of the Union, and consult." People should be "open to the force of argument." They should be prepared to give up their initial views when shown "the general benefit of the whole community."

The basic institutions of the resulting Constitution were intended to encourage and to profit from deliberation, thus understood. The system of checks and balances—the cornerstone of the system—was designed to encourage discussion among different governmental entities. So too with the requirement of bicameralism, which would bring different perspectives to bear on lawmaking. The same goals accounted for the notion that laws should be presented to the President for his signature or veto; this mechanism would provide an additional perspective. The federal system would ensure a supplemental form of dialogue, here between states and the national government.[14]

Judicial review was intended to create a further check. Its basic purpose was to protect the considered judgments of the people, as represented in the extraordinary law of the Constitution, against the ill-considered or short-term considerations introduced by the people's mere agents in the course of enacting ordinary law.[15] As we will see, many of the original individual rights can be understood as part of the idea of deliberative democracy. Indeed, the goals of protecting rights and of promoting deliberation were understood to march hand in hand. The special status of property rights was an effort to ensure against precipitous, short-sighted, or ill-considered intrusions into the private sphere. Deliberative government and limited government were, in the framers' view, one and the same.

I have said that the framers' belief in deliberative democracy drew from traditional republican thought, and that it departed from the tradition in the insistence that a large republic would be better than a small one. It departed even more dramatically in its striking and novel rejection of the traditional republican idea that heterogeneity and difference were destructive to the deliberative process. For the framers, heterogeneity was beneficial, indeed indispensable; discussion must take place among people who were different. It was on this score that the framers responded to the antifederalist insistence that homogeneity was necessary to a republic.

Drawing on the classical tradition, the antifederalist "Brutus," complaining of the theory behind the proposed nationalist Constitution, wrote, "In a republic, the manners, sentiments, and interests of the people should be similar. If this be not the case, there will be a constant clashing of opinions; and the representatives of one part will be continually striving against those of the other." [16] Hamilton, by contrast, thought that heterogeneity, as part of the deliberative process, could be a creative and productive force. Thus he suggested that the "differences of opinion, and the jarrings of parties in [the legislative] department . . . often promote deliberation. . . ." [17] As the framers saw it, the exchange of reasons in the public sphere was a condition for this process.

Impartiality, the Republic of Reasons, and Interest-Group Pluralism

Read against this background, the principle of impartiality requires government to provide reasons that can be intelligible to different people operating from different premises. The requirement might be understood in this respect as a check on government by fiat, helping to bar authoritarianism generally. Drawing from our founding aspirations, we might even define authoritarian systems as all those that justify government outcomes by reference to power or will rather than by reference to reasons. At the heart of the liberal tradition and its opposition to authoritarianism lies a requirement of justification by reference to public-regarding explanations that are intelligible to all citizens. [18] The principle of impartiality is the concrete manifestation of this commitment in American constitutional law.

Described in this way, the impartiality requirement might seem trivial and therefore uncontroversial. But the requirement turns out to be in severe tension with one of the most influential approaches to both modern government and American constitutionalism: interest-group pluralism. [19] There are many different forms of pluralism, but the unifying pluralist claim is that laws should be understood not as a product of deliberation, but on the contrary as a kind of commodity, subject to the usual forces of supply and demand. Various groups in society compete for loyalty and support from the citizenry. Once groups are organized and aligned, they exert pressure on political representatives, also self-interested, who respond to the pressures thus imposed. This process of aggregating and trading off interests ultimately produces law, or political equilibrium.

Whether pluralist ideas accurately describe current American politics is a subject of much dispute.[20] There can be little doubt that the American framers were not pluralists.[21] Some people also think that contemporary real-world government outcomes actually reflect reasons and justifications, and that those outcomes diverge from legislative and constituent self-interest (unless the concept of self-interest is understood so broadly as to be trivialized—as in the idea that altruism reflects self-interest, because altruists are interested in altruism). As we will see, interest-group pluralism is not an attractive political ideal. But if interest-group pluralism does describe contemporary politics, a requirement of impartiality, understood as a call for public-regarding justifications for government outcomes, is inconsistent with the very nature of government. It imposes on politics a requirement that simply cannot be met.

In the discussion to follow, I explore the relationship between the principle of impartiality and contemporary constitutional law. I show the extraordinary persistence of the principle across many generations and many constitutional provisions. I do not defend the requirement here; my purpose is descriptive. I claim only that the antiauthoritarian impulse, understood as a requirement of reasons, lies at the heart of American constitutional law.

The Ban on Naked Preferences

Judicial interpretation of many of the most important clauses of the Constitution reveals a remarkably common theme. Although the clauses have different historical roots and were originally directed at different problems, they appear to be united by a concern with a single underlying evil: the distribution of resources or opportunities to one group rather than to another solely on the ground that those favored have exercised the raw political power to obtain what they want. I will call this underlying evil—a violation of the impartiality requirement—a *naked preference*.

The commerce clause, for example, allows one state to discriminate against commerce from another state only if that discrimination is a means of promoting some goal unrelated to helping self-interested insiders. The privileges and immunities clause prohibits a state from preferring its citizens over outsiders, unless the preference is supported by reasons independent of protecting the insiders. The equal protection clause permits laws treating two classes of people differently only if there is a good connection between the distinctions and legitimate public purposes. The due process clause requires all government action to be justified by reference to some public purpose. The contract clause allows government to break or modify a contract only if the action is intended to promote a general public goal and does not reflect mere interest-group power. The eminent domain clause protects private property against self-interested private groups, both by demanding that a "public use" be shown to justify a taking of private property and by distinguishing between permissible exercises of the government power and prohibited takings.

The prohibition of naked preferences therefore underlies a wide range of constitutional provisions. The prohibition is connected with the original idea that government must be responsive to something other than private pressure, and with the associated notion that politics is not the reconciling of given interests but instead the product of some form of deliberation about the public good. As it operates in current constitutional law, the prohibition of naked preferences—like Madison's approach to the problem of factionalism—focuses on the motivations of legislators, not of their constituents. The prohibition therefore embodies a particular conception of representation. Under that conception, the task of legislators is not to respond to private pressure but instead to select values through deliberation and debate.

The notion that governmental action must be grounded in something other than political power is of course at odds with pluralism. Naked preferences are common fare in the pluralist conception; interest-group politics invites them. The prohibition of naked preferences stands as a repudiation of theories claiming that the judicial role is only to police the processes of representation to ensure that all affected interest groups may participate.[22] In this respect, the prohibition of naked preferences reflects a distinctly substantive value and cannot easily be captured in procedural terms. Above all, it presupposes that constitutional courts will serve as critics of the pluralist vision, not as adherents striving only to "clear the channels" for political struggle.[23] And if a judicial role seems odd here, we should recall that the founding generation itself regarded courts as an important repository for representation and preservation of republican virtue, standing above the play of interests.[24]

The Basic Framework

We might distinguish between two bases for treating one group or person differently from another. The first is a naked preference. For example, state A may treat its own citizens better than those of state B—say, by requiring people of state B to pay for the use of the public parks in state A—simply because its own citizens have the political power and want better treatment. Or a city may treat blacks worse than whites—say, by denying them necessary police and fire protection—because whites have the power to restrict government benefits to themselves. In these examples, the political process is a mechanism by which self-interested individuals or groups seek to obtain wealth or opportunities at the expense of others. The task of the legislator is to respond to the pressures imposed by those interests.

Contrast with this a political process in which outcomes are justified by reference not to raw political power, but to some public value that they can be said to serve. For the moment we can define a public value extremely broadly, as any justification for government action that goes beyond the exercise of raw political power. (I describe later how the Constitution limits permissible public values.) For example, a state may relieve a group of people from a contractual obligation because the contract called for an act—say, the sale of heroin—that violated a public policy. Or state A may treat its own citizens better than those of state B—say, by limiting welfare payments to its own citizens—because it wants to restrict social spending to those who in the past have made, or in the future might make, a contribution to state revenues. In these examples, the role of the representative is to deliberate rather than to respond mechanically to constituent pressures. If an individual or group is to be treated differently from others, it must be for a reason that can be stated in public-regarding terms.

These competing portraits of the political process are of course caricatures of a complex reality. It is rare that government action is based purely on raw political power. Losers in the political process may have lost for a very good reason that has little to do with the power of their adversaries. Belief that an action will promote at least some conception of the public good almost always plays at least some role in government decisions. Sometimes people motivated to vote for certain legislation cannot easily disentangle the private and public factors that underlie the decision.

It is also rare for government action to be based on a disembodied effort to discern and implement public values, entirely apart from considerations of private pressure. Representatives are almost always aware of the fact that their vote will have electoral consequences. What emerges is therefore a continuum of government decisions, ranging from those that are motivated primarily by interest-group pressures to those in which such pressures play a very minor role. In any particular case, it may well be difficult to see which of these is dominant. But the occasional or even frequent difficulty should not be taken to obscure the existence of a real distinction. There is all the difference in the world between a system in which representatives try to offer some justification for their decisions, and a system in which political power is the only thing that is at work.

If naked preferences are a legitimate basis for government action, it is sufficient that a particular group has been able to assemble the political power to obtain what it seeks. Might makes right. If naked preferences are forbidden, however, and the state is forced to invoke some public value to justify its conduct, government behavior becomes constrained. The extent of the constraint will depend on two considerations. The first involves the content of the public values that courts will accept as a legitimate basis for government action. The constraint would be strengthened if, for example, the government were barred from relying on disfavored ideas about women or members of minority groups.

The second consideration relates to the devices developed to ensure that public values do in fact account for legislation. If courts are willing to make up a public value as the basis for government action, and if they do not require a close fit between the public value and the measure under review, all or almost all government action will be upheld. By contrast, if courts require a good reason to believe that a naked preference was not at work, many laws will be invalidated.

Let us assume that the content of public values is subject to no limitations and that courts do not carefully scrutinize either the process or the outcome to ensure that a public value was at work. These assumptions generate a "weak version" of the prohibition of naked preferences. The weak version places only a trivial constraint on government action, for it is nearly always possible to justify an action on grounds other than the raw exercise of political power. For example, the Court has upheld a statute prohibiting opticians, but not ophthalmologists, from selling eyeglasses on the ground that the prohibition protected consumers from fraud and deception.[25] In the circumstances of the case, the justification looked specious. The statute was far more plausibly understood as a reflection of the political power of well-organized ophthalmologists.

But because the weak version does require some justification that goes beyond raw political power, it cannot be dismissed as entirely meaningless. It forces those who seek to obtain government assistance to invoke some justification as a basis for assistance. In so doing, even the weak version strikes familiar constitutional chords. By requiring that some reason justify the exercise of governmental power, it acts as a check on the tyranny of factionalism—a core Madisonian evil. The weak version also reflects the idea that the role of government is to engage in a form of deliberation about governing values rather than to implement or trade off preexisting private interests. On this view, the fact that a majority is in favor of a particular measure is not, standing alone, a sufficient reason for it.

The weak version accounts for much of modern constitutional law. So-called rationality review is the prime example. Courts have interpreted the due process and equal protection clauses to impose a requirement that government action be "rational." This requirement simply means that public measures must be a minimally reasonable effort to promote some public value. Modern rationality review is characterized by two principal features. First, the category of legitimate ends is extremely broad. Second, the Supreme Court demands only the weakest link between a public value and the measure in question, and it is sometimes willing to hypothesize legitimate ends not realistically motivating to the legislature. As a result, few statutes fail rationality review.

As described thus far, the weak version is minimal indeed. One might, for example, support preferential treatment of the poor on the ground that they have a special need for assistance; preferential treatment of the rich might be justified as an incentive for more work and investment. Everything, in short, is potentially lawful. To develop a more vigorous set of constraints on government, it is necessary to go beyond the weak version described thus far.

The constitutional text, read in light of its history,[26] unambiguously provides a few—but only a few—of the elements of a more robust set of constraints. Under the privileges and immunities and commerce clauses, a preference for in-staters at the expense of out-of-staters is impermissible. Under the equal protection clause, the same is true for discrimination against blacks. As a constitutional matter, both out-of-staters and blacks are entitled to special protection from discrimination; discrimination against either group cannot be understood as a public value.

Even within this narrow area of protectionism and discrimination against blacks, however, the Constitution is ambiguous. What if a state justifies discrimination against out-of-staters on the ground that they have been the main factor contributing to in-state unemployment, or discrimination against blacks on the ground that, when blacks are jailed with whites, the likelihood of violence is dramatically increased? Outside these areas, the inquiry is even more open-ended. In such cases, how do courts enforce the prohibition of naked preferences? In answering this question, two devices have been of special importance

HEIGHTENED SCRUTINY
The first device involves careful judicial review of governmental claims that a public value is being served by the measure under review. When courts apply "heightened scrutiny," they examine with unusual suspicion a government's argument that a public value motivates its actions. Here we see active judicial policing of politics in the interest of deliberative democracy.

Heightened scrutiny involves two principal elements. The first is a requirement that the government show a close connection between the asserted justification and the means that the legislature has chosen to promote it. If a sufficiently close connection cannot be shown, there is reason for skepticism that the asserted value in fact accounted for the legislation. The second element is a search for less restrictive alternatives—ways in which the government could have promoted the public value without harming the group or interest in question. The availability of such alternatives also suggests that the public value justification is a facade.

Heightened scrutiny is triggered by a concern that in the circumstances it is especially likely that the measure under review reflects a naked preference. The most familiar example is review of racial discrimination under the equal protection clause. Review of statutes that discriminate against noncitizens under the privileges and immunities clause falls into the same category. In both cases, heightened scrutiny is justified by a perception that the groups in question lack the political power to protect themselves against factional tyranny.

By contrast, more lenient scrutiny—typified by rationality review—reflects a strong presumption that a public value is at work. That presumption is conventionally supported by reference to considerations of judicial competence and legitimacy. The underlying idea is, first, that courts lack the capacity to review the factual determinations of other branches of government and, second, that vigorous judicial scrutiny would be inconsistent with the constitutional commitment to representative democracy.

THEORY OF IMPERMISSIBLE ENDS

A second device in a more rigorous version of the prohibition on naked preferences consists of theories designed to distinguish between legitimate and illegitimate bases for government action. The courts attempt to root such theories in the text or history of the Constitution. Such an approach could of course accommodate a wide range of ideas about what government may do. As we will see, status quo neutrality has played a large role here. Modern equal protection doctrine reflects the development of another such theory: courts have come to refuse to recognize government ends that involve the subordination of women, aliens, illegitimates, and members of racial minority groups. In Chapter 5 and in Part II, I will discuss how we might decide what state interests count as illegitimate.

For the moment, I continue with description of the cases. But first a qualification is necessary. Suppose we conclude that the status quo is itself a product of interest-group power. Suppose we think that the status quo embodies a naked preference. In that case, the very failure to enact new measures could reflect a naked preference, or factional power. It would be most troublesome to think that legislation that changes existing states of affairs is constitutional only if it responds to a conception of the public interest, but that the failure to legislate, or existing states of affairs, need not be justified at all. If we thought that, we would be embracing a form of status quo neutrality. This conception of neutrality, in short, would underlie the prohibition on naked preferences if we thought that that prohibition required us (1) to be skeptical about statutory enactments but (2) to take, as a kind of unobjectionable "given," existing practices and the legal structures that underlie them.[27] I will deal with this important point in detail in later chapters.

Illustrations: Naked Preferences and the Clauses

My aim in this section is briefly to survey how the prohibition of naked preferences operates under the different clauses. There have of course been significant changes over time; and there are significant differences among the various clauses. But it is the common theme that is most striking.

DORMANT COMMERCE CLAUSE

The commerce clause, from Article I of the Constitution, confers on Congress the power "to regulate commerce between the states." The clause is both an authorization to Congress and a prohibition on certain state practices burdening interstate commerce. Under the more controversial, so-called dormant commerce clause, the central constitutional evil is protectionism: measures that citizens of one state enact in order to benefit themselves at the expense of out-of-staters. A simple illustration is a California statute that forbids out-of-staters from competing with California liquor sellers. Such a statute would be flatly unconstitutional as a violation of the impartiality principle.

The prohibition of protectionism rests on a familiar idea. When states discriminate against people outside their boundaries, the ordinary avenues of political redress are unavailable to people who are hurt, for they do not vote in the state, and hence do not have access to the state legislature. By contrast, when regulation imposes burdens on in-staters as well as out-of-staters, the political safeguard against partiality is more reliable. If a state imposes regulations on everyone who engages in construction work within its borders, in-staters will be affected in (roughly) the same way as out-of-staters, and should represent the interests of out-of-staters adequately in the political process. Such regulations would raise no serious constitutional question.

PRIVILEGES AND IMMUNITIES CLAUSE

The privileges and immunities clause of Article IV provides that "Citizens of each State shall be entitled to all Privileges and Immunities of Citizens in the several States." The basic themes of the clause are almost identical with those of the dormant commerce clause. Both clauses are aimed at partiality in the form of discrimination against out-of-staters. Both focus on the theme of representation—justifying an active judicial posture when discrimination alerts courts to the like-lihood that unrepresented people have been harmed.

EQUAL PROTECTION CLAUSE

The equal protection clause, part of the Fourteenth Amendment, for-bids a state to deny to any person "the equal protection of the laws." The clause is not concerned solely with the special case of discrimina-tion between in-staters and out-of-staters. Its prohibition is far broader. Indeed, in many respects the clause may be understood as a generalization of the central concerns of the dormant commerce and privileges and immunities clauses, applying to all classifications their prohibition of naked preferences at the behest of in-staters. In this way, the basic requirement of impartiality is applied to everything.

Disadvantaged groups, impermissible ends, and heightened scru-tiny. Discrimination against blacks, the central evil at which the clause was aimed, is the equal protection analogue of discrimination against out-of-staters under the commerce and privileges and immunities clauses. When a statute discriminates on its face against blacks, the Court applies a strong presumption of invalidity.[28] One reason for heightened scrutiny is a belief that when a statute discriminates on its face against members of racial minority groups, a naked preference is almost certainly at work. Here a familiar idea—the relative political powerlessness of members of minority groups—helps to account for that belief. The central notion is that the ordinary avenues of political redress are much less likely to be available to minorities. The danger that such statutes will result from an exercise of (what is seen as) raw political power is correspondingly increased.

Current equal protection law also treats a number of government ends as impermissible. Notably, these prohibited ends involve a wide range of justifications that do not involve the exercise of raw political power in the ordinary sense. The point becomes clearest in cases in-volving classifications drawn on the basis of gender, alienage, and le-gitimacy. For example, when a statute provides that the spouses of male workers automatically qualify for social security benefits, but that spouses of female workers must show dependency, the classifica-tion hardly reflects an exercise of raw political power—narrowly understood—but instead embodies certain conceptions about the na-ture of female participation in the labor market. Invalidation of such statutes cannot be explained only on the basis of the minimal requirement that classifications rest on something other than raw power. Although the Court has not provided a clear rationale for its decisions here, the central ideas seem to be that the relevant groups are politically weak and that the traditional justifications for discrimination both reflect and perpetuate existing injustice.

In an exceptionally controversial set of decisions, the Court has concluded that discriminatory effects—arising from, for example, seemingly neutral tests for employment—on members of disadvantaged groups raise no constitutional problem except insofar as those effects reveal that the state has acted from a discriminatory purpose.[29] This conclusion has dramatically narrowed the antidiscrimination principle. It requires plaintiffs to allege and prove an impermissible motivation—a most difficult burden. It thus insulates from constitutional scrutiny the enormously wide range of enactments that have disproportionate discriminatory effects on blacks and women. I deal with the general question in Chapter 11.

Rationality review. The equal protection clause is also interpreted to call for a general assessment of whether classifications are "rational" even if traditionally disadvantaged groups are not involved. Here, as elsewhere, the exercise of political power, standing alone, is an insufficient basis for classifications. Here, as elsewhere, rationality review is highly deferential and almost always results in the validation of statutory classifications.

DUE PROCESS CLAUSE

The requirement that no person be deprived of life, liberty, or property "without due process of law" is applied to the federal government through the Fifth Amendment, and to the states through the Fourteenth. Because of the substantial identity of the standards under this clause and the equal protection clause, a brief discussion should suffice.

The notion that legislation is unconstitutional if it represents a naked decision to distribute resources to one group rather than to another came through most clearly in the so-called *Lochner* era, in which—as we shall see in Chapter 2—the Court invalidated a number of regulatory statutes. In the *Lochner* period itself, the Court treated many regulatory statutes as naked preferences. It did so because the status quo had a privileged status, and deviations would therefore be treated as "takings" from some for the benefit of others.

Since the New Deal, many justifications count as legitimate. The government is permitted to safeguard the interests of workers, consumers, and victims of discrimination. There has thus been a partial demise of status quo neutrality. One consequence of this development has been to make the line between naked preference and public value quite thin. If protection of the class of statutory beneficiaries is itself seen as a public value, many exercises of raw political power—even if in the service of faction—become automatically justifiable.

Modern due process doctrine contains at least one holdover from the *Lochner* era. An important exception to the usual rule of deference is the Court's protection of certain "fundamental rights," most notably privacy. Here heightened scrutiny is applied.[30] It is under this rationale that the Court has invalidated laws restricting access to and use of contraceptives, interfering with familial intimacy, and prohibiting abortions. The post-1980 Court is quite skeptical of this line of cases, and it seems that they will not be extended and may even be overruled.

CONTRACT CLAUSE

The contract clause prohibits states from passing any "Law impairing the Obligation of Contracts." In the framers' view, contractual obligations frequently had been abrogated because of the acquisition of political power by those who had made agreements that later turned out to disadvantage them. Debtor relief laws were the particular concern. The constitutional concern about the capture of government by faction was thus a prominent theme behind the contract clause.

For a long period, the clause operated as a significant constraint on government action.[31] Eventually it became clear that the nature and extent of the constraint would depend on whether there was a "police power" exception to the general prohibition against contractual impairments—that is, on whether the state could use its normal regulatory authority to interfere with contractual liberty. In early decisions, the Court held that there was such an exception.[32] Surely the clause was not meant to prevent a state from outlawing a contract for murder or for the sale of heroin, even if the impairing law applied retroactively.

Even after the recognition of a police power exception, however, the contract clause remained a significant limitation on state action because the police power was itself highly restricted. There was no general authority to engage in the enormous range of activities of modern government. The key modern case was *Home Building and*

Loan Association v. Blaisdell.[33] The case involved a Minnesota mortgage moratorium statute that allowed courts to postpone the time for redemption from foreclosure sales for a period of thirty days. The consequence of the statute was to relieve debtors of their contractual obligations to lenders—precisely the evil at which the contract clause was originally aimed.

The critical step in the *Blaisdell* Court's reasoning came in the understanding of what the police power allowed, a shift that resulted in a dramatic expansion of the permissible ends of government. According to the Court, the state could intervene to protect, for example, tenants or subgroups thereof. The police power limitation thus threatened to engulf the contract clause—a classic case of an exception's expanding to eliminate the rule. If the police power were broadened to include a wide range of regulatory measures, the prohibition of naked preference would come in its weakest form. As we have seen, such a weak version is almost no prohibition at all.

The contract clause cases are thus another example of an area in which the weak version of the prohibition of naked preferences provides little barrier to government action. Judicial scrutiny is highly deferential—in general, identical with what we have seen under the equal protection and due process clauses.

EMINENT DOMAIN CLAUSE
The eminent domain clause of the Fifth Amendment prohibits the taking of "private property . . . for public use, without just compensation." Two aspects of eminent domain doctrine are centrally concerned with the prohibition of naked preferences: eminent domain law requires that a taking be for a "public use," and it draws a distinction between an impermissible taking and a legitimate exercise of the police power.

A principal theme of the eminent domain cases is that government action cannot be used to serve purely private ends. Taking property from A in order to benefit B is the core example. The text of the clause attests to this idea in the basic requirement that a "public use" be shown before a taking is permitted, even with compensation. The function of this requirement is to prevent purely private wealth transfers—that is, naked preferences in violation of the impartiality requirement.

For a long time, the public use requirement was understood to mean that if government was to take property, it had to be used by the public.[34] Eventually, however, it became clear that this test was unduly mechanical, for a wide range of uses by government served the public at large, even if the public did not actually have access to the property. This change in the public use requirement is the eminent domain analogue of the ubiquitous twentieth-century expansion in permissible government ends. In the modern era, the public use requirement is met by standards that conform to the weak version of the prohibition of naked preferences. Indeed, the test is even more deferential than the rationality requirements of the due process and equal protection clauses, for the legislative judgment on the point is accepted as nearly conclusive.[35]

Similar considerations apply to the distinction, critical to current eminent domain doctrine, between permissible exercises of the police power and impermissible takings. For many years, of course, that distinction has been the key to separating "takings" from "regulation." If government action fell within the police power, there was no need for compensation. The dramatic expansion in the police power has led to a range of current dilemmas. The requirement that a taking be for a public purpose has been eroded by an understanding that almost all government action, even that which transfers property from A to B, can be responsive to some public purpose. It is for this reason that government regulation rarely raises a serious issue under the eminent domain clause.

The Court has not, of course, altogether abandoned the constraint imposed on government action by the eminent domain clause. If the state physically invades a person's property and transfers it to another, compensation is required even if a public use can be shown. In this respect, the eminent domain clause is not merely a prohibition of naked preferences. The Court has required compensation even in cases of unobjectionable government motivation.

The Principle of Constitutional Impartiality

This short survey should suffice to show the wide range of settings in which constitutional doctrines adopt a concept of impartiality that rejects pluralist conceptions of politics. It also reveals some striking variations in the way the prohibition of naked preferences is understood under the various clauses.

Under the due process, contract, and eminent domain clauses, the Court has adopted the prohibition in close to its weakest form. Raw political power is not a legitimate basis for government action, but no other theory limits the ends that the government may pursue. By contrast, the equal protection clause shows a most complex structure of outcomes. Some of the equality cases reflect the weak version of the prohibition. But discrimination against members of racial minority groups triggers a strong presumption of invalidity. Modern equal protection doctrine thus prohibits discrimination against women, aliens, illegitimates, and others, even in cases in which the weak version of the prohibition of naked preferences has not been violated. In part, these results are responsive to the perceived powerlessness of the various groups and to a resulting fear that a naked preference is at work. The cases go further than this, however, by prohibiting measures that are plausibly justified by reference to what might be counted as a public value.

An important question raised by these developments involves the reasons for the New Deal shift from strong neutrality constraint to a weak impartiality principle and—under the equal protection clause—the more recent shift to an aggressive antidiscrimination principle. The due process, eminent domain, and contract clauses in particular reflect an almost identical departure from a pre–New Deal conception of impermissible government ends in favor of modern rationality review. As I discuss in more detail in Chapter 2, a central reason for this shift is the declining centrality of status quo neutrality to modern constitutional law. Legislative efforts to alter an existing distribution in favor of an alternative appear not to be naked preferences, but legitimate efforts to promote the public good.

All this raises a number of questions. We have seen that for the most part, the prohibition of naked preferences is at best weakly enforced. Courts give the legislature the benefit of every doubt, finding justifications in cases in which naked self-interest is quite plausibly at work. Perhaps courts ought to approach such measures more aggressively. Moreover, some of the equal protection cases carry the seeds of a theory that treats some public values as a mask for private power—a development that remains in the most tentative of states.

However these problems are resolved, there can be no question that current legal doctrines reject interest-group pluralism as a constitutional creed. They point instead to a conception of politics that demands a measure of deliberation from government representatives, deliberation that has some autonomy from private pressures. Many provisions of the Constitution are thus aimed at a single evil: the distribution of resources to one person or group rather than to another on the sole ground that those benefited have exercised political power in order to obtain government assistance.

To be sure, the prohibition rarely results in invalidation. But the cases are strikingly unanimous in their vision of the prohibited end. In this way, the impartiality principle lies at the core of American constitutional law.

CHAPTER 2

The Revolution of 1937

A principle of impartiality plays a major role in constitutional law; but as we have seen, that principle does not impose sharp limits on government. In many cases, however, a much more robust principle, also involving neutrality, has turned the general requirement into a real barrier to government action.

We have seen features of this more robust conception—status quo neutrality—in connection with the due process, takings, and contracts clauses. In the late nineteenth and early twentieth centuries, status quo neutrality dominated legal thought. It embodied a pervasive conception of nature and the natural. It organized legal reasoning and legal categories. It made the system of "laissez-faire" into a constitutional requirement.

Spurred by the "free labor" principles that followed the Civil War and the abolition of slavery, courts tried to prevent government from regulating labor-management relations. The resulting conception of neutrality helped give content not only to rights in the labor market, but also to principles of equality on the basis of race and sex. And despite its apparent rejection in the 1930s, the same conception plays an enormous role in current constitutional law.

This more robust conception treats the status quo, and existing distributions of resources and entitlements, as the baseline for deciding what is partisanship and what is neutrality. When government disturbs existing distributions—what people currently have—it is said to be violating its obligation of neutrality, by taking from one group for the benefit of another. When it respects existing distributions, it is treated as if it has remained faithful to that overriding obligation. This view does not see current ownership rights, and other legal rights, as products of law at all. And status quo neutrality makes it possible for people to think that they oppose "government," or believe that government "fails," even though those very people tend to be extremely enthusiastic about the legal rules, created and administered by government, that make markets possible.

All this is fairly abstract. But it can be made quite concrete by exploring three cases decided by the Supreme Court around the turn of the century. These cases rank among the most important cases in the Court's entire history. In *Plessy v. Ferguson,*[1] the Court concluded that segregation on the basis of race did not violate the Constitution. In *Lochner v. New York,*[2] the Court invalidated a maximum-hour law for bakers. In *Muller v. Oregon,*[3] the Court upheld a law providing maximum hours for working women. All three cases were decided under the Fourteenth Amendment, which was ratified in the aftermath of the Civil War and designed, at least in large part, to counteract the social subordination of the newly freed slaves.

Despite their close historical proximity, the three cases are rarely studied together. It is generally agreed that all of them were wrongly decided; none of them represents current law. But the assumptions of the three decisions link them closely together. More important, and more surprising, those same assumptions play a crucial role in current constitutional law and in contemporary political debates. They order our ideas about neutrality. They help define our understandings about when government is even present.

In all three cases, the Court took existing practice as the baseline for deciding issues of neutrality and partisanship. It did so by assuming that existing practice was prepolitical and natural—that is, that it was not itself a function of law, or subject to challenge from the standpoint of justice. This assumption played a critical role in the judicial assessment of the relevant practices: the world of segregation, the distribution of work between men and women, and the conditions of labor markets.

The New Deal, and especially the legal revolution of 1937, should be understood above all as a rejection of these conceptions of neutrality and action. The rejection was self-conscious and explicit. The conceptual break consisted in the insistence that current rights of ownership, and other rights, were a product of law. One need not be a close or subtle student of the period in order to see the point. It is in this sense that the New Deal represented a genuine renovation of the legal culture, a renovation with which we continue to struggle. And the revolution of 1937 should be seen, not principally as an endorsement of "judicial restraint," and much less as an acceptance of particular New Deal programs, but instead as a dramatic shift in the prevailing notions of neutrality and action.

Plessy: Segregation as the State of Nature

Plessy v. Ferguson, upholding racial segregation, counts among the most vilified of all Supreme Court decisions. The vilification has diverted attention from what the Supreme Court actually said. This turns out to be a bit surprising, and more than a bit revealing.

Plessy involved a Louisiana statute, enacted in 1890, requiring railroad companies to provide "equal but separate accommodations for the white and colored races." Claiming to be seven-eighths Caucasian, Plessy attacked the statute on constitutional grounds. Plessy claimed that the provision for separate facilities denied to him "the equal protection of the laws."

The Supreme Court opened its opinion by distinguishing sharply between "civil" and "political" equality on the one hand and "social" equality on the other. "[I]n the nature of things," according to the Court, the Fourteenth Amendment "could not have been intended to abolish distinctions based upon color, or to enforce social, as distinguished from political, equality, or a commingling of the two races upon terms unsatisfactory to either."

It is worthwhile to pause over this distinction and in particular over the category "social rights." For the Court, the Fourteenth Amendment required equality only for civil and political rights. Civil rights were understood to include issues of "legal capacity"; these were most importantly the right to own property, the right to enter into contracts, and the right to sue and to be sued. Political rights covered issues relating to political processes, most prominently the rights to vote and to serve on a jury. By contrast, equality in the "social" sphere—education, public transportation, public accommodations, and so forth—is not guaranteed by the Constitution. Apparently the Court thought that the social sphere does not involve the state at all. In the Court's view, all this followed from "the nature of things."

As the *Plessy* Court understood the Constitution, the state acted properly so long as it was operating under its "police power." The police power in turn permits government "to act with reference to the established usages, customs, and traditions of the people." A system of segregation could be justified precisely by these established usages and customs. In its key passage, the Court said: "If the two races are to meet upon terms of social equality, it must be the result of natural affinities, a mutual appreciation of each other's merits, and a voluntary consent of individuals. . . . Legislation is powerless to eradicate racial instincts, or to abolish distinctions based upon physical differences. . . ."

The Court added that the meaning of segregation was produced by Plessy's reaction to it, and not by anything for which the state could be deemed responsible. "We consider the underlying fallacy of the plaintiff's argument to consist in the assumption that the enforced separation of the two races stamps the colored race with a badge of inferiority. If this be so, it is not by reason of anything found in the act, but solely because the colored race chooses to put that construction upon it."

One of the most striking features of the *Plessy* opinion is that the Court treats the social sphere—and the established usages, customs, and traditions of the people—as if they were free from, independent of, and immune to law. In the Court's view, the social sphere is the arena of voluntary interaction and free choice. "If one race be inferior to the other socially, the constitution of the United States cannot put them upon the same plane." Thus the Court stresses that a segregation law simply reflects the customs of the people. In these ways, the Court treats the social sphere at issue in *Plessy* as one that merely reflects people's desires, and does not involve coercive law, affecting those desires, at all.

This approach is based on a time-honored but highly controversial understanding of law, especially of the judge-made common law. On this understanding, the common law is not an imposition of the judges' will, but instead a reflection of social customs and practices. This view was especially prominent in America in the late nineteenth century. It served to deepen the claim that the common law of tort, contract, and property could be seen as a kind of natural state. The *Plessy* Court took this view one step further. It saw state legislation requiring segregation as a mere reflection of social customs and practices, rather than as something that helped to create those practices.

In some contexts this may be a reasonable way to understand matters. But as applied to segregation, the analysis is extremely puzzling and confused. The *Plessy* Court was dealing with a compulsory seg-regation law. The Court's notion that the law cannot abolish racial instincts or compel integration is surely intelligible, even if far from obvious, if stated as an abstract proposition. It could make sense as a response to a compulsory integration law, or to an effort by a private person to compel integration when the races had segregated them-selves voluntarily.

But *Plessy* did not involve an effort to compel integration. Instead Plessy attacked—and this is the key point—a law requiring segrega-tion. It is not even plausible to invoke "voluntary interactions" as a justification for a law compelling segregation; the whole point of such a law is to forbid voluntary interactions. Indeed, the system of legal segregation can be seen as reflecting "natural affinities" and "volun-tary consent" only if the system of segregation is treated as some nat-ural state, or as prelegal or prepolitical.

This is in fact how the Court viewed the system of segregation. Treating that system as part of a voluntary and law-free "social" sphere, the Court regarded it as a simple means of facilitating private arrangements and private desires—as if the system merely carried out wishes that preceded it. The *Plessy* Court wrote as if segregation was entirely neutral, and indeed as if it did not represent government ac-tion at all. To modern readers, it seems obvious that segregation would constitute or create those arrangements and desires, rather than simply carry them into effect. The system of segregation was a self-conscious effort to use law to create racial separation and subju-gation in the aftermath of slavery. That system affected social arrange-ment and private desires. It helped to shape them. It was not neutral at all. But all this seemed utterly foreign to the Court.

It is most revealing that when the United States Supreme Court up-held segregation against constitutional attack, it was not because of the text or history of the Fourteenth Amendment, but instead because of a conclusion that the system of segregation was purely social, and not a system of law at all. We might consider here the closely related view, also emphasized by the *Plessy* Court, that any feelings of in-feriority generated by legal segregation should be attributed to indi-viduals, and not to the law or the state. On this view, such feelings were a kind of brute social fact, rather than a creation of the legal system that engendered them.

It was not until *Brown v. Board of Education*[4] in 1954 that this set of understandings collapsed. It has collapsed so completely that the notion that the world of segregation should be treated as part of a voluntary and law-free sphere of society seems nearly unintelligible. But we will see that in the contemporary approach to issues of race discrimination, something very close to *Plessy* continues to be at work.

Lochner: Ownership Rights and Common Law Markets as the State of Nature

LOCHNER AND ITS DEMISE

The Supreme Court's decision in *Lochner v. New York*[5] has had the unusual characteristic of giving a name to an entire period of constitutional law. In the so-called *Lochner* period, covering 1905 to 1937, the Supreme Court struck down a large number of state laws attempting to regulate relations between employers and employees.

The period is often thought to symbolize an unjustified form of judicial "activism": judicial intrusions into the democratic process without adequate support from the text and history of the Constitution. Undoubtedly there is much to be said in favor of the conventional wisdom. As we will see, part of what was wrong with the *Lochner* period was indeed the aggressiveness of the Court. But the case should also be understood as rooted in a particular conception of neutrality, one based on existing distributions of wealth and entitlements. The *Lochner* Court treated those distributions as prelegal and just. And in this respect there is an extremely close link between *Lochner* and *Plessy*.

It will be useful to begin with two excerpts from important decisions associated with the *Lochner* period. The first excerpt is from *Adkins v. Childrens Hospital*,[6] a 1923 decision invalidating minimum wage legislation for women and children. The Court said: "To the extent that the sum fixed [by the minimum wage statute] exceeds the fair value of the services rendered, it amounts to a compulsory exaction from the employer for the support of a partially indigent person, for whose condition there rests upon him no peculiar responsibility, and therefore, in effect, arbitrarily shifts to his shoulders a burden which, if it belongs to anybody, belongs to society as a whole."

The next excerpt is from the case generally thought to spell the downfall of *Lochner*. In the 1937 decision of *West Coast Hotel v. Parrish*,[7] the Court upheld a minimum wage law for women. The Court said: "The exploitation of a class of workers who are in an unequal position with respect to bargaining power and are thus relatively defenseless against the denial of a living wage . . . casts a direct burden for their support upon the community. What these workers lose in wages the taxpayers are called upon to pay. . . . The community is not bound to provide what is in effect a subsidy for unconscionable employers."

The notion of subsidy plays a crucial role in both *Adkins* and *West Coast Hotel.* It is hard to make sense of that notion without a baseline from which to make a measurement. We do not say that someone who is forced to return stolen property is being forced to "subsidize" the person from whom the property was taken. Whether someone is being forced to subsidize someone therefore depends on who has a legitimate claim to the item in question. A payment of money counts as a subsidy only if the person paying out the money has a right to it.

A theory of rights, explaining who is entitled to what, is thus necessary to distinguish between subsidies and simple duties. When a person is required to do something that he is justly required to do, he is not being forced to subsidize anyone, but to do what he ought to do. By 1937, the time of *West Coast Hotel,* the concept of subsidy had been turned completely on its head. In *Adkins,* the Court said that minimum wage legislation exacted a subsidy to the public from an innocent employer. Such legislation was thus a kind of taking from the employer for the benefit of the public. According to the Court, if the employee is needy, it is not the employer, but the public at large, that should pay. An understanding of this sort could, and did, draw into question a wide range of regulatory interventions into the marketplace. It was through this understanding that such interventions would be seen to violate the requirement of neutrality, and indeed to qualify as interventions at all.

In *West Coast Hotel,* however, it is the failure of a state to have minimum wage legislation that amounts to a subsidy—this time, from the public to the employer. Free markets and the common law system, for the *West Coast Hotel* Court, turn out to subsidize "unconscionable employers." In the fifteen-year period between *Adkins* and *West Coast Hotel,* the baseline was shifted. What accounts for the shift? In answering that question, we should turn to *Lochner* itself.

Lochner involved a regulation enacted by the state of New York prohibiting employers from permitting or requiring bakers to work for more than sixty hours a week. The Court said that the right of contract—in particular, the right to buy and sell labor—is part of the liberty protected by the due process clause. But as in *Plessy*, the Court recognized that the "police power" could be invoked to justify intrusions on liberty of contract. The scope of the police power was defined largely by reference to the nineteenth-century common law. If the employer had committed a common law wrong, or if an employee had a common law right against the employer, the Constitution would permit the state to correct the situation. Thus, for example, the government could forbid contracts for prostitution or for the sale of heroin. On this framework, some regulation of the labor market could be justified as a "labor law," protecting the vulnerable from exploitation, and other regulation could be justified as a "health law," if health was really at risk.

The *Lochner* Court concluded that the maximum-hour legislation was not permissible as a "labor law," because bakers were of full legal capacity and "in no sense wards of the State." Only wards could be protected through labor legislation. Labor law allowed a measure of paternalism, protecting people against their own judgments, and also a measure of redistribution, that is, efforts to give resources or opportunities to the vulnerable. But insofar as the purpose of labor legislation was indeed paternalistic or redistributive, it was illegitimate except to protect people who were without legal capacity. The state could not protect adult males through law; in a free society, they were supposed to protect themselves. The various pressures of the marketplace were beyond the power of the legislature.

The Court also concluded that the statute could not be defended as a health law. According to the Court, the state could not prove that a maximum-hour law was necessary to protect the health of either bakers or the public; and if the evidence brought forth here were thought sufficient, the state's power would be unlimited. The Court concluded that the statute was "in reality, passed from . . . motives" other than protection of health—motives that were illegitimate but that the Court did not specify. In all likelihood, the Court thought that the illegitimate motive actually at work was the impermissible redistributive one: to transfer resources from employers to employees.

The Court therefore thought that neutrality was what the due process clause commanded, and neutrality was served only by the general or "public" purposes included within the police power. If the statute could be defended as a labor or health law, it would be sufficiently public to qualify as neutral. Since no such justification was available, it was invalidated as impermissibly partisan—what we might now call special-interest legislation. Maximum-hour legislation thus represented a naked preference, a transfer from one group for the benefit of another.

The legislative result was thus, in the Court's view, unprincipled; it depended on partisanship or special pleading. The employer had committed no common law wrong warranting legal remedy. The status of the common law as a part of nature, or as in any case just, helped support the view that the common law should form the baseline from which to measure deviations from neutrality, or self-interested "deals."[8] If the status quo were neither natural nor just, the attempt at redistribution[9] would not seem partisan at all. Thus it is that the *Lochner* Court relied on a conception of neutrality taking existing distributions as the starting point for analysis. And in this sense, *Plessy* and *Lochner* were close indeed.

Lochner was of course an interpretation of the Fourteenth Amendment, and it would be possible to think that the Court had absolutely no justification for transforming a provision designed to protect the newly freed slaves into a prohibition on legal control of the power of employers. Here, in fact, there is a large historical irony: A constitutional provision designed to overcome the legacy of slavery was rapidly turned into a constitutional right to disable government from protecting workers.

In one sense, however, there is real continuity between *Lochner* and the Civil War amendments. The antislavery movement was animated by the general slogan of "free labor!"—a principle embodying a general desire to protect self-ownership and self-direction in the employment market. Plausibly, minimum wage and maximum-hour legislation thus offended the same principle that doomed slavery. If slavery was objectionable partly because it abridged occupational liberty, we can see much regulatory legislation as embodying the same sort of problem: governmental interference with the freedom of human beings to be employed on whatever terms they choose. For this reason, the outcome in *Lochner* need not be so puzzling.

An alternative to this perception of the evil of slavery would point not to the need for free labor markets, but instead to a general principle of nonsubordination, or liberty, that would sometimes find coercion in such markets as well. If coercion and law were seen there, regulation would be a justified corrective. The same principle that doomed slavery could also call for government assistance against the forms of coercion that drive people to take menial jobs at trivial pay, or that force people to work sixty hours per week if they are to work at all. As we will see, the New Deal embodied precisely these ideas.

Justice Holmes's celebrated dissenting opinion in *Lochner* is a rejection of neutrality—and of Madisonianism—altogether. It comes close to modern interest-group pluralism, treating the political process as an unprincipled struggle among self-interested groups. Holmes's opinion treats the political process as a kind of civil war, in which the powerful succeed; if courts interfere, they will be bottling up forces that will express themselves elsewhere in other and more destructive forms.[10] Thus for Holmes, the Constitution does not require a public justification for law. It does not prevent "the natural outgrowth of dominant opinion."[11]

Holmes's opinion is probably best known for its apparent humility: the rejection of Spencer's *Social Statics*,[12] with which Holmes was personally sympathetic; the proposition that the Constitution does not embody any particular social and economic theory; and its author's apparent willingness to disregard his personal views in favor of a dispassionate interpretation of the Constitution. But the opinion is better understood as an outgrowth not of humility, but on the contrary of Holmes's highly personal vision. It is in fact a species of the very constitutional social darwinism that it purports to reject. Holmes's conception of politics—his interest-group theory—was market oriented; it stressed the inevitability of bargains and of victories by the powerful. Holmes was also skeptical that we can discuss values at all, and this skepticism brought him into conflict with the *Lochner* majority, which was acting on the basis of a conception of freedom. These views were the very personal building blocks for Holmes's enthusiasm for judicial deference. That enthusiasm hardly came from the Constitution itself.[13]

The decline of the *Lochner* understanding was slow and wavering. In some cases the Court found a sufficient connection between an end deemed "public" under the *Lochner* framework and the means chosen by the state. Elsewhere, the Court seemed gradually to conclude that redistributive goals could be seen as permissibly public and in some sense neutral; the common law conception of the police power thus broke down.[14] But it was in *West Coast Hotel v. Parrish*—the classic New Deal decision, capturing what I will call the revolution of 1937—that the Court rejected the foundations of the *Lochner* period.

West Coast Hotel involved a statute providing minimum wages for women. Perhaps oddly, at least to modern readers, the emphasis of the opinion was not on the undemocratic character of the Court's previous approach or on the need for judicial deference to legislative determinations. Instead the Court stressed the value of minimum wage regulation, referring to "the exploiting of workers at wages so low as to be insufficient to meet the bare cost of living" and to the fact that "the exploitation of a class of workers who are in an unequal position with respect to bargaining power casts a direct burden for their support upon the community." In perhaps the most striking passage of the opinion, the Court referred to the subsidy issue and added, "The community may direct its law-making power to correct the abuse which springs from [employers'] selfish disregard of the public interest."

In the *Lochner* era itself, of course, the Constitution imposed sharp limits on the use of government power to help those unable to protect themselves in the marketplace. The expansion of that power in *West Coast Hotel* signaled a critical shift, amounting to a wholesale rejection of the *Lochner* Court's conception of the appropriate baseline. The key lies in the notion that the absence of a minimum wage law would amount to "a subsidy for unconscionable employers." The idea that what appears, in the *Lochner* framework, to be government "inaction," or neutrality, could actually amount to a "subsidy" is at first glance quite puzzling. The Court's claim is that the failure to impose a minimum wage is not nonintervention at all but simply another form of action—a decision to rely on a set of common law rules as the basis for regulation.

The downfall of the *Lochner* period thus rests on an understanding that in any case, government—through minimum wage laws or the common law system—is making a choice and is doing so through law. The law created property and contract rights, and the law imposed various limits on those rights. Market wages and market hours were in this sense a creation of law, not of nature, and not of laissez-faire. The common law could not be regarded as a natural or unchosen baseline. Instead its principles amounted to a controversial regulatory system that created and did not simply reflect the social order.

The traditional treatment of both legal rights and the police power was unable to survive this understanding. If the common law helped create the social order, and did not merely facilitate private desires, minimum wage and maximum-hour laws could no longer be seen as the intrusion of government into a system that was private, law-free, or merely given. The status quo had been a legal creation. For the Court in *West Coast Hotel*, the legislature could treat the baseline for analysis as not the common law, but instead a system in which all workers had a living wage.

THE REVOLUTION OF 1937

We should understand the revolution of 1937 as the vindication of the New Deal in the Supreme Court. The vindication was based above all on the understanding that the common law and existing distributions of resources would be entitled to no extraordinary protection from democratic politics. Any revision of existing distributions and of common law rules should be evaluated in terms of its consequences for social efficiency and social justice. Plausible legislative judgments would receive judicial respect. A pivotal point was that ownership rights, and everything that accompanied them, had been created by the legal system.

These ideas had a long legacy. As Bentham wrote, "Property and law are born together and die together. Before the laws there was no property; take away the laws, all property ceases." [15] This basic claim was a prominent part of the legal realist movement. The realists, most notably Robert Hale and Morris Cohen, insisted that common law rules were legal rules, with predictable coercive and distributive effects. [16] What people had was a reflection not of nature or custom, but of governmental choices. This was so always and simply as a matter of fact. Ownership rights were legal creations.

The initial problem with laissez-faire was therefore conceptual. The basic idea was a myth. As Hale wrote, "The dependence of present economic conditions, in part at least, on the government's past policy concerning the distribution of the public domain, must be obvious. Laissez-faire is a utopian dream which never has been and never can be realized." [17]

Common law rules did not merely describe a preexisting set of categories; they were human devices that created the very categories through which judges perceived legal and social realities. Thus Holmes, in some ways the first legal realist, wrote in one of his least noticed but most profound aphorisms: "Property, a creation of law, does not arise from value, although exchangeable—a matter of fact." [18] Holmes too proclaimed that property and value are products of legal rules, not of purely private interactions and much less of nature. Economic value does not predate law; it is created by law. And all this, wrote Holmes, was simply "a matter of fact." The pre–New Deal framework could not survive this insight.

For Hale and Cohen, property, contract, and tort law were social creations that allocated certain rights to some people and denied them to others. They represented government "intervention" into the economy. They were coercive, for they prohibited people from engaging in desired activities. They could not be identified with liberty in an a priori way. Sometimes they disserved liberty.

Hale set forth these ideas with unusual clarity. His special target was the view that governmental restrictions on market prices should be seen as illegitimate regulatory interference with the private sphere. This, said Hale, was a confused way to describe the problem.

> The right of ownership in a manufacturing plant is . . . a privilege to operate the plant, plus a privilege not to operate it, plus a right to keep others from operating, plus a power to acquire all the rights of ownership in the products. . . . This power is a power to release a pressure which the law of property exerts on the liberty of others. If the pressure is great, the owner may be able to compel the others to pay him a big price for their release; if the pressure is slight, he can collect but a small income from his ownership. *In either case, he is paid for releasing a pressure exerted by the government—the law. The law has delegated to him a discretionary power over the rights and duties of others.*[19]

Hale saw property rights as a delegation of public power by government. And a limitation on that delegation—in the form, for example, of a curtailment of "the incomes of property owners"—is "in substance curtailing the salaries of public officials or pensioners." More generally: "Laissez faire is not such, but really gov[ernmen]tal indifference to [the] effects of artificial coercive restr[ain]ts, partly grounded on gov[ernmen]t itself." Thus "the distribution of wealth at any given time is not exclusively the result of individual efforts under a system of government neutrality."[20] And constraints on the freedom of nonowners were an omnipresent result of property law. "To insist that 'a free American has the right to labor without any other's leave'. . . is to insist on a doctrine which involves the dangerously radical consequence of the abolition of private ownership of productive equipment, or else the equally dangerous doctrine that everyone should be guaranteed the ownership of some such equipment."[21]

Or consider these startlingly unambiguous words, from a student essay written in 1935: "Justification for this purported refusal to supervise the ethics of the market place is sought in doctrines of laissez-faire. . . . In general, *the freedom from regulation postulated by laissez-faire adherents is demonstrably nonexistent and virtually inconceiv-*

able. Bargaining power exists only because of government protection of the property rights bargained, and is properly subject to government control." [22] The same point lies behind this suggestion: "[T]hose who denounce state intervention are the ones who most frequently and successfully invoke it. The cry of laissez faire mainly goes up from the ones who, if really 'let alone,' would instantly lose their wealth-absorbing power." [23]

Ideas of this sort were part and parcel of the work of the American pragmatists, and it was through pragmatism that they received their preeminent philosophical exposition. Indeed we might think of the New Deal as the real-world embodiment of the pragmatic tradition. If Franklin Delano Roosevelt was the New Deal's foremost statesman, John Dewey was its foremost philosopher.

For the pragmatists, physical, legal, social, and moral reality were always seen through human filters. We do not have unmediated access to physical, social, or moral facts; these are things that we help to create with our own devices.[24] As Dewey had it, the "spectator theory of knowledge" was a failure; always "mind intervenes." Thus the pragmatists challenged "the notion . . . that the office of knowledge is to uncover the antecedently real." [25] The categories through which reality was perceived were human creations, not natural kinds. For Dewey in particular, writing in 1927, this led to the conclusion that "the doctrine of the individual in possession of antecedent political rights" is "a fiction . . . in politics." [26]

Here, above all, lie the philosophical underpinnings of the New Deal attack on *Lochner*. In law, the pragmatic claim would manifest itself in a recognition that legal categories were not static or given, or merely descriptions of preexisting "kinds." They were instead human creations to be assessed in terms of their consequences for human welfare.

The pragmatists hardly thought that their view implied that there were no criteria by which to evaluate claims of physical, social, legal, or moral truth. Instead the evaluation would come in the form of a practical assessment of how different claims served our needs. In Dewey's words, this would entail a replacement of the search for "the antecedently real" with "the kind of understanding which is necessary to deal with problems as they arise." [27] This kind of understanding would be self-consciously experimental; it would be based on experience. Eschewing dogmatism, it would focus its inquiry on what approaches seemed to work. For pragmatists, the question was: "Grant an idea or belief to be true, what concrete difference will its being true make for anyone's actual life?"[28]

THE NEW DEAL AND THE CONSTITUTION

The New Deal was an outgrowth of many of these ideas.[29] And in *West Coast Hotel*, the Supreme Court ratified the New Deal. But *West Coast Hotel* was only the most conspicuous of a wide range of similar developments. Consider, for example, the law governing property rights, with which *Lochner* must be closely associated. *Miller v. Schoene*[30] involved the constitutionality of a statute requiring the destruction of cedar trees infected with a disease damaging to local apple orchards. The owners of the cedar trees complained that the statute amounted to a taking of their property for which compensation was constitutionally required. That claim depended in turn on the fact that the owners of the cedar trees had committed no common law wrong; there was therefore no basis for government intervention.

In the key passage, the Court responded that "the state was under the necessity of making a choice between the preservation of one class of property and that of the other wherever both existed in dangerous proximity. *It would have been none the less a choice if, instead of enacting the present statute, the state, by doing nothing, had permitted serious injury to the apple orchards within its borders to go unchecked.* When forced to such a choice the state does not exceed its constitutional powers by deciding upon the destruction of one class of property in order to save another."[31] In *Miller*, as in *West Coast Hotel*, adherence to common law or status quo baselines no longer seemed neutral, and departures from those baselines were no longer impermissibly partisan. Both the common law and the statute amounted to legal choices.

Similar ideas account for a dramatic reduction in the limits imposed by the contracts clause. As we have seen, that clause was originally designed to protect contractual freedom from state infringement. The *Blaisdell* decision in 1934,[32] upholding a Minnesota mortgage moratorium law, represented a dramatic broadening in government's "police power," allowing redistributive measures. In this sense, *Blaisdell* and *West Coast Hotel* belong in the same category.

A similar shift accounts for one of the most dramatic legal developments of this century, the decision of the Supreme Court in *Erie R.R. Co. v. Tompkins.*[33] In the great case of *Swift v. Tyson,*[34] the Supreme Court had held that in cases involving citizens of different states, federal courts were not bound by the common law of the states in which they sat; they were instead free to decide what the common law requires. The *Swift* principle—critically important to the growth of American law and perhaps of the American economy as well—was built on a jurisprudential premise and a political aspiration. The two should be understood in concert. They link the regime of *Swift* with the regime of *Lochner*.

The jurisprudential premise was that the common law was to be discovered rather than made. It was a part of nature rather than the will of the sovereign. It was on this premise that state court decisions could be seen as mere evidence of what the common law required, rather than as the common law itself. It was on this premise, too, that the Supreme Court might think that the common law could be discovered through the application of reason by federal judges. The political aspiration was that federal courts would create a uniform body of common law, embodying principles distinctly hospitable to commercial interests and commercial development. Federal courts and federal common law could ultimately displace the parochial state judiciaries, which were hostile to corporate interests and willing to use the common law to deter commercial enterprise.

Along this dimension, *Swift v. Tyson* was a close cousin of *Lochner* itself. In *Swift*, federal courts were to develop common law principles, often with foundations in laissez-faire, so as to avoid state court rulings unfavorable to commerce. In *Lochner*, federal courts were to use common law principles as the basis for something like a constitutional law of commercial relations. In both cases, the common law would serve as a guarantor of principles of economic liberty that were indispensable to the development of a commercial republic.

By 1938, the time of *Erie*, both the jurisprudential premise and the political aspiration of *Swift* had been drawn into sharp question. During the depression, some states undertook to remedy the situation, but others did not; some revised the common law, but others did not. It seemed increasingly difficult to treat the common law as natural rather than as a conspicuous set of social choices. At the same time, the aspiration of *Swift v. Tyson* seemed perverse, at least insofar as it suggested that legal rules reflexively hospitable to commercial interests represented a neutral or necessarily desirable method of social regulation. It is no accident that *Erie* repudiated *Swift* within two years of *West Coast Hotel*. By 1938, the common law was not (in Holmes's famous, revealing, contemptuous phrase) a "brooding omnipresence in the sky," but a creation of human beings to be evaluated as such.

The downfall of *Lochner* also helps to explain one of the most contested decisions of this century, *Shelley v. Kraemer*.[35] In *Shelley*, the Court said that judicial enforcement of a racially restrictive covenant violated the Fourteenth Amendment. The puzzle of the case comes from the fact that judicial enforcement of voluntary agreements is not normally thought to violate the Constitution. The Constitution is aimed at state action, not at private behavior. If judicial enforcement of private agreements were unconstitutional, the exclusion of blacks from private houses or private clubs would itself be unconstitutional—a position that would revolutionize the law.

But *Shelley* merely held that common law rules were "state action," not that the Constitution governs truly private conduct. The *Shelley* Court could so characterize the common law only after such decisions as *West Coast Hotel, Mahon, Blaisdell,* and *Erie,* which involved fundamentally identical issues. In the face of those decisions, common law principles no longer seemed merely to facilitate private desires or to be natural, but instead emerged as a conscious social choice. The revolution of 1937 paved the way for the result in *Shelley*.

We may go even further. In fact *Shelley* is the bridge between *West Coast Hotel* and the most celebrated Supreme Court decision of the twentieth century, *Brown v. Board of Education.* We have seen that in *Plessy,* the Court had treated segregation as prepolitical; it also saw the social meaning of segregation—the insult and degradation that blacks perceived in it—as a creation of blacks, not of segregation law. For the *Plessy* Court, that law merely helped implement social interactions; it did not create or influence them. All this was perfectly consistent with the view of the *Lochner* period, in which the rules that constructed the market were treated as purely facilitative of preexisting individual desires.

After the New Deal, the system of segregation—like the rules of property and contract—was conspicuously a product of law. It helped create social relations; this much seemed obvious. The social meaning of segregation was something for which states were responsible. That meaning could no longer be attributed solely to the individual perceptions of individual blacks. Thus the Supreme Court in *Brown* said precisely this: "To separate [black children] from others of similar age and qualifications solely because of their race generates a feeling of inferiority as to their status in the community that may affect their hearts and minds in a way unlikely ever to be undone."

Shelley is the bridge between *West Coast Hotel* and *Brown* because *Shelley* was made possible only by the New Deal's denaturalization of the common law, and because *Shelley* in turn made possible the *Brown* Court's denaturalization of the world of segregation. In this way there is a direct link between the New Deal reformation and the civil rights movement. In fact, it may not be an overstatement to think that after the New Deal, the civil rights movement was inevitable.

THE NEW DEAL REFORMATION

Lochner failed because it selected, as the baseline for constitutional analysis, a system that was state-created, hardly neutral, and in important respects unjust. This understanding accounts above all for the New Deal reformulation of legal rights.

Of course the New Deal—like the founding period—contained a number of strands, some of them conflicting with one another. Thus there was an interest in saving the capitalist system from radical threats; in cartelizing industry through state-protected monopolies; in radical restructuring of the economy; in protecting special interests, including bankers and agriculture; in promoting greater democratization; in taking advantage of impartial expertise; in aggressively enforcing antitrust laws; and much more. By singling out the claim that ownership rights and the status quo were products of government, I mean to draw attention to the outstanding conceptual break of the period.

It is worthwhile at this point to quote Roosevelt's own description of the New Deal:

> The word "Deal" implied that the Government itself was going to use affirmative action to bring about its avowed objectives rather than stand by and hope that general economic laws would attain them. The word "New" implied that a new order of things designed to benefit the great mass of our farmers, workers and business men would replace the old order of special privilege in a nation which was completely and thoroughly disgusted with the existing dispensation.
>
> The New Deal was fundamentally intended as a modern expression of ideals set forth one hundred and fifty years ago in the Preamble of the Constitution of the United States—"a more perfect union, justice, domestic tranquillity, the common defense, the general welfare and blessings of liberty to ourselves and our posterity."
>
> But we were not to be content with merely hoping for these ideals. We were to use the instrumentalities and powers of Government actively to fight for them.

There would be no effort to circumscribe the scope of private initiative so long as the rules of fair play were observed. There would be no obstacle to the incentive of reasonable and legitimate private profit.

Because the American system from its inception presupposed and sought to maintain a system based on personal liberty, on private ownership of property and on reasonable private profit from each man's labor or capital the New Deal would insist on all three factors. But because the American system visualized protection of the individual against the misuse of private economic power, the New Deal would insist on curbing such power.[36]

The attack on status quo neutrality was made explicit in Roosevelt's suggestion: "We must lay hold of the fact that economic laws are not made by nature. They are made by human beings." Consider as well Roosevelt's emphasis on "this *man-made* world of ours" in arguing for social security legislation.[37] Through this emphasis, Roosevelt proclaimed that poverty was produced by a humanly created system, rather than being an inevitable or natural fact. The basic position was codified in the preamble to the most important New Deal labor legislation, the Norris-LaGuardia Act: "Whereas under prevailing economic conditions, *developed with the aid of governmental authority for owners of property to organize in the corporate and other forms of ownership association,* the individual worker is commonly helpless to exercise actual liberty of contract and to protect his freedom of labor, and thereby to obtain acceptable terms and conditions of employment. . . ."[38]

To the extent, then, that property rights played a role in market arrangements—as they inevitably did—those arrangements were creatures of positive law, including, most notably, property law, which gave some people a right to exclude others from "their" land and resources.[39] Market wages and hours were a result of legal rules conferring rights of ownership. Rather than superimposing regulation on a realm of purely voluntary interactions, minimum wage laws substituted one form of regulation for another.

It is in this sense that the notion of laissez-faire stands revealed as the conspicuous myth that it is. A system of free markets depends for its existence on a set of legal rules establishing who can do what, and enforcing those principles through courts. In this system, a system of free markets is built on government intervention. Recall the assured comment from a student commentator, writing in 1935, that a system of laissez-faire "is demonstrably nonexistent and virtually inconceivable."

The fact that an existing distribution is not natural or prepolitical provides no argument against it. Markets depend on law, but this is not an argument against markets. And when one regulatory system is superimposed on another, it does not follow that all bets are off, or that we cannot evaluate them in constitutional terms or assess their role in diminishing or increasing human liberty. A system of private property is a creation of the state, but it is also an important individual and collective good. The fact of its social creation does not suggest otherwise. At least in general, a market system indeed promotes both liberty and prosperity, and its inevitable origins in law hardly undermine that fact.

To their basic point, however, the New Dealers added a claim that existing distributions were sometimes inefficient or unjust. Different forms of government would be approached pragmatically, democratically, and in terms of their consequences for social efficiency and social justice. As Hale wrote, "the next step is to . . . realize that the question of maintenance or the alteration of our institutions must be discussed on its pragmatic merits, not dismissed on the ground that they are the inevitable outcome of free society." Morris Cohen, writing just before the New Deal, put the point similarly: "[T]he recognition of private property as a form of sovereignty is not itself an argument against it. . . . [I]t is necessary to apply to the law of property all those considerations of social ethics and enlightened public policy which ought to be brought to the discussion of any just form of government." [40]

That evaluation would be self-consciously and unabashedly experimental. It would avoid dogma and precommitments untested by experience. It would look to see what sorts of programs actually worked in the world. Its character is well reflected in Roosevelt's apparently offhand but extremely revealing comment during a press conference: "Obviously a farm bill is in the nature of an experiment. We all recognize that. . . . [I]f the darn thing doesn't work, we can say so quite frankly, but at least try it." [41]

The New Dealers were hardly socialists. They generally appreciated the contributions of markets to prosperity and freedom. But unrestricted markets and existing distributions under the common law protected both too much and too little in the way of rights. The common law protected too much, since it immunized existing holdings of property from democratic control. Not everything that people had was genuinely entitled to legal protection. The preexisting system of rights also protected too little, since it furnished inadequate safeguards against the various hazards of the market economy. It did not include rights to food, shelter, clothing, medical care, education, and assistance in the event of old age or poor health. These rights were explicitly endorsed in President Roosevelt's 1944 State of the Union Address, advocating a "second Bill of Rights." [42]

In general, we may understand the New Deal as carrying forward and deepening the original commitment to deliberative democracy. We have seen that in the early periods of American history, preexisting notions of natural hierarchy came under siege, with a novel and revolutionary insistence that "culture" was "truly man-made." [43] For the American revolutionaries, the problem with the monarchical legacy consisted in its acceptance, as natural, of practices and injustices that could not be justified on the basis of reasons. America's republicanism, in the Revolution and the founding period, consisted largely in the identification of this problem.

The commitment to deliberative democracy is severely compromised by any system that takes the status quo as an unanalyzed given. The New Dealers insisted that any respect for existing distributions would depend on the reasons that could be brought forward on their behalf. The process of deliberation through democratic organs would therefore include an assessment of whether the legal rules already in place served liberty, welfare, or democracy itself. In this way, the New Deal period simply brought forward, and made new, one of the oldest themes in American history.

Enormous changes followed from these understandings. In particular, three of the cornerstones of the American system of public law—federalism, judicial review, and checks and balances—were dramatically revised. The system of federalism had seemed an important guarantor of democracy. It promoted local self-government; it also provided a healthy check on tyrannical law, by enabling oppressed citizens to move elsewhere. But for the New Deal reformers, local government hardly seemed an arena for democratic self-determination. Too often it served as an obstacle to necessary social change; too often it was vulnerable to powerful private groups.

Perhaps even worse, the fact that citizens could move elsewhere was not a guarantor of liberty, but a formidable barrier to necessary social programs. A state that provided generous welfare or employment programs would soon find itself with a large proportion of poor people and a small proportion of wealthy ones. It was no wonder that if such programs were to be forthcoming, the national government had to assume a generative role.

Reliance on the judiciary also seemed unacceptable. Courts were unsympathetic to social reform. They were fatally undemocratic. Moreover, their uncoordinated, decentralized structure made them ill suited to undertaking the necessary initiatives. They could not even begin proceedings on their own. It did not help that they were rarely experts in the matter at hand. As a result, the New Deal period saw a large-scale movement away from the courts as a system of social ordering.

Finally, the system of checks and balances, as it was traditionally understood, appeared to be an obstacle to new social programs. Coordination within government, not competition among public institutions, was now indispensable. None of the three branches had the relevant expertise. Aggressive government initiatives could not easily be generated within a system in which the different branches of government worked against one another. The result of these criticisms was a massive increase in the power of the presidency and the development of new "independent" regulatory commissions. All of these innovations were an outgrowth of the repudiation of status quo neutrality.[44]

WHAT WAS WRONG WITH *LOCHNER*?

The defect of the *Lochner* period can be understood in three different but closely related ways. In its narrowest form, the problem was the decision to take market ordering under common law standards as the baseline from which to decide constitutional cases. More broadly, the *Lochner* Court regarded consideration of the plight of the disadvantaged as impermissible partisanship; it was insufficiently public or general and not neutral at all.

More broadly still, the Court took as natural and inviolate a system that was legally constructed and that did not have a strong claim as a matter of justice. One cannot treat as a taking from A to B a decision to transfer resources to which A had no entitlement in the first place. The whole notion of "taking" depends on a belief in a right to the property in question. Once the common law itself was seen to allocate entitlements and wealth, and the allocation seemed controversial, a decision to generate a new pattern of distribution could not be for that reason impermissible.

These understandings of the *Lochner* era treat judicial activism as only part of the picture. The central problem infected pre–New Deal constitutionalism quite generally. It had to do with the conceptions of neutrality and inaction and the choice of an appropriate baseline.

Muller, Nature, and Gender

In *Muller v. Oregon*,[45] decided in 1908, the Court upheld a maximum-hour law limited to women. The statute was attacked on the ground that it interfered with freedom of contract, an attack that drew strength from the decision in *Lochner* itself. Despite that precedent, the Court held that the statute was permissible.

According to the Court, the law was justified because of "the difference between the sexes." These differences included "woman's physical structure and the performance of maternal functions." The Court emphasized empirical work showing that a reduction of the working day was necessary in light of "(a) the physical organization of women, (b) her maternal functions, (c) the rearing and education of the children, (d) the maintenance of the home." The legally relevant differences therefore included not merely physical ones, but also a set of social roles unique to women. For the Court, a "difference justifies a difference in legislation"; and for the Court there was an "inherent difference" between men and women.[46]

For the modern observer, there are several striking features in the *Muller* opinion. The first is the Court's assumption—supported in the case by an elaborate but highly anecdotal factual brief from Louis Brandeis—that the differences between men and women are sufficiently real and sufficiently large to justify a law targeted at women alone. Perhaps these differences do not exist in sufficient scope to justify differences in law. This is in fact the general answer offered by current constitutional law. The Supreme Court says that measures of the sort upheld in *Muller* reflect "overbroad stereotypes," unacceptable under the equal protection clause.[47]

But the problems in *Muller* go much deeper than this, and those problems have everything to do with status quo neutrality. The Court treated the differences between men and women as "inherent" when in fact some of these differences were a creation of social customs, and indeed of the legal system itself. Of course there are physical differences between the sexes. But consider the rearing and education of children, or "maternal functions," or the maintenance of the home. With respect to these, the Court attributed to "nature" a set of tasks that are socially produced and, as we will see, in part a product of law. Indeed, those tasks are in part a product of laws of the very sort at issue in *Muller*. Such laws help freeze women out of the workforce, by making women employees more costly or less remunerative to employers. This will of course contribute to a sharp division between the social roles of men and women. It will lead women to occupy the domestic sphere and encourage men to leave that sphere.

Thus far the problem with the approach in *Muller* is that the Court saw differences as inherent when in fact they were a product of society and law. Perhaps an even more serious problem is that the Court treated the differences between the sexes as a sufficient justification for laws disadvantaging women. Recall here the Court's claim: "[D]ifference justifies a difference in legislation." But even if men and women are different, the decision to turn any difference into a disadvantage, by helping force women out of the workplace, is a legal and hence social one. That decision must be justified. By itself, the mere fact of difference is insufficient to justify or even to explain disadvantage.

There are many differences among human beings—height, eye color, strength, hormones, gender—and those differences are made meaningful largely through social and legal decisions. Such decisions turn differences into advantages and disadvantages. Sometimes gender differences have social importance only because of social and legal decisions; indeed, gender differences are sometimes even noticed only because of such decisions. The translation of a difference into a disadvantage requires a reason; it is not, standing alone, a reason at all.[48] A law that would impose a minimum wage for people with blue eyes could not plausibly be justified on the ground that such people are "different."

In *Muller*, the Court relied on differences to justify inequality, as if the differences came first and inequality second. In fact the opposite is sometimes true. It is inequality that actually creates many of the relevant differences—the different social roles of men and women, with men being concentrated in the public sphere and women in the private sphere. It is inequality that helps make the differences into something socially and legally relevant.

I do not claim that there are no differences between men and women, either before or after society has acted. Surely there are important biological differences. What those differences *must* mean for society is not likely to be a question that any of us is in a position to answer. Nor have I shown that every social or legal difference between men and women is impermissible. But it should by now be clear that differences, even if real, do not justify laws that treat men and women unequally.

The problem in *Muller*, then, was the conclusion that the existing social roles of women and men were natural and just, and that a law that tended to perpetuate and even helped to create "differences" could be justified by reference to them. Here status quo neutrality played the crucial role.

Status Quo Neutrality and Pre–New Deal Constitutionalism

There are extraordinary similarities among *Plessy, Lochner,* and *Muller*. Most obviously, the reasoning in *Plessy* overlaps a great deal with that in *Muller*. Both courts saw the sphere of sex and race difference as natural and prepolitical, when in fact that sphere is in important respects a creation of law. Both courts saw the laws under attack—producing segregation on the basis of race and a gender-based division in the public and private spheres—as merely facilitating rather than helping create social practice. In both cases, the Court saw "differences" as justifying different treatment through law. The Court treated those differences as a good reason for disadvantage, rather than as what emerges from a system in which disadvantage based on difference has already been put in place.

The system of segregation occupied the same analytic place in *Plessy* as the sphere of different social roles for men and women occupied in *Muller*. Both were used to justify the Court's decision, and treated as prelegal "givens" or as the origin of the practices in question, when more plausibly they were the outcome of those very practices. (A recent illustration, beginning to find its way into the conventional wisdom, is that hunger and poverty themselves—even famines—are largely products of social practices, including law, rather than simple scarcity of food.)[49]

It is probably not controversial to say that on these points, the *Plessy* and *Muller* Courts were both wrong. It is obvious that the system of segregation is a legal creation. Few people would now claim that nature is entirely responsible for the role of women in "the education of children." The Court's claim that legal segregation is a result of voluntary or private interactions is singularly jarring. So too with the notion that women naturally maintain the home. As we will see, however, perceptions of this sort are very much at work in current constitutional law.

For now, however, we should return to the *Lochner* and *Adkins* opinions. There the Court invalidated maximum-hour and minimum wage legislation on the ground that it amounted to a kind of naked wealth transfer—a taking from some for the benefit of others. This framework rested on a belief that market ordering represented a neutral, prepolitical, and just sphere of voluntary interaction. Thus, for the *Adkins* Court, minimum wage laws interfered with the real "value" of labor. If, however, market ordering was seen as pervaded by and indeed as a creation of law, this understanding would be harder to sustain.

Of course market ordering is created in precisely this way. Contract, property, and tort law set out the rules by which workers and employers make arrangements with each other. They allocate rights and entitlements. Wages and hours are determined by bargaining, to be sure, but within the constraints of entitlements that have been created by law. The "value" of labor is a function not purely of voluntary interactions, but also of legal rules telling some people, but not others, that they own certain things and have certain rights.

If this is so, the connections are multiple not only between *Plessy* and *Muller,* but among *Plessy, Muller,* and *Lochner* as well. Just as the *Plessy* Court treated the segregative status quo as prelegal and a product of voluntary arrangements, and just as the *Muller* Court did the same for the world of distributed labor between men and women, so the *Lochner* Court saw the labor market as a freely chosen sphere of private interactions. The "value" of labor, for the *Lochner* Court, occupied precisely the same position as sex "difference" for the *Muller* Court and as race "difference" and segregation for the *Plessy* Court. Properly understood, however, market "value" was the artifact of legal arrangements, rather than (by itself) a good justification or explanation for them; so, too, race and sex difference was an artifact, and in these cases a poor excuse, rather than a good justification for the regimes of segregation and of sexually distributed labor.

For contemporary observers, *Muller* is perhaps a more complex case than *Plessy.* Whether and to what extent the distribution of labor between men and women is a product of law rather than of voluntary choice is at least a controversial question. Indeed, some of the most prominent current approaches to issues of sex equality depend on a perception that the different social roles of men and women are freely chosen and are not a product of coercion. In this sense, the Court's argument in *Muller* is very much a subject of contention today.

On this score, *Lochner* and *Adkins* are more complex still. Whether and how law structures markets, rather than providing a neutral backdrop for voluntary interactions, is something on which there is (to say the least) no current consensus. But on the issue of the presence of law, the three cases are identical. Intriguingly, it was the *Lochner/Adkins* assumption of the prepolitical character of the labor market status quo that was first rejected as a legal matter. Even a preliminary attack on the naturalness of sex and race distinctions would have to wait for many years.

On the conventional view, the defect of the *Lochner* period lay in the Court's readiness to interfere with democracy. This view of course raises something of a puzzle for those who believe (as do most contemporary observers) that *Plessy* and *Muller* were wrong. If courts were supposed to eliminate segregation laws or laws that discriminate on the basis of gender, they would have had to assume an enormous role in American government, invalidating democratic outcomes. The fact that *Plessy* and *Muller* are generally thought to be wrong at least raises a question for those who believe that the *Lochner* decision was flawed because it represented a judicial intrusion into politics.

It is also common, if not exactly conventional, to take the three cases as containing lessons about the risks posed to liberty and equality by "government." On this view, *Plessy* and *Muller* were indeed wrong, but for reasons that actually argue in favor of *Lochner*. In all three cases, the problem was the government's unjustified role in limiting voluntary choices. The solution is to disapprove of all government interference with market arrangements, whether the interference takes the form of segregation or maximum-hour laws.

But if we look more closely at history, and if we explore the understandings that underlay both *Lochner* and the decisions that rejected it, a quite different view emerges. That third view emphasizes not a commitment to free markets or an opposition to "government" but something altogether different: the use, in *Lochner* itself, of the status quo as the baseline from which to distinguish partisanship and neutrality, or government action and inaction.

Rejecting that view, the New Deal period deepened the original constitutional commitment to deliberative democracy, seeing the status quo, like everything else, as subject both to deliberation and to democracy. And if the defect of *Lochner* is understood in this way, we can link the case with *Plessy* and *Muller* as well. In all three cases, the Supreme Court took as natural and prepolitical systems that in fact were created by law and controversial or indefensible from the standpoint of justice.

CHAPTER 3

Status Quo Neutrality
in Contemporary Law

Much of modern constitutional law is based on status quo neutrality, and indeed on the understandings of the pre–New Deal period. Ownership rights are not treated as legally created at all; they appear to be part of nature. Existing distributions often mark out distinctions between action and inaction or between partisanship and neutrality. These distinctions, now as in the early years of the century, prove to be crucial in Supreme Court interpretations of the Constitution.

My purpose in this chapter is to describe constitutional law that relies on status quo neutrality. I will not evaluate the decisions here; I deal with many of them in detail in later chapters. It is important to understand, however, that the fact that a practice or distribution is not natural does not count as an argument against it. A system of racial equality or of private property and freedom of contract requires for its existence a large role for law; but this does not mean that such a system is a bad idea. So, too, practices that are natural or prepolitical do not warrant approval for that reason. For many people, poor hearing is natural, but this is not a reason to refuse hearing aids. The fact that physical violence against others may well be natural does not count as an argument against the criminal law.

John Stuart Mill disposed of the claims of the justificatory force of nature long ago:

> If the artificial is not better than the natural, to what end are all the arts of life? To dig, to plough, to build, to wear clothes, are direct infringements on the injunction to follow nature. . . . All praise of Civilization,

or Art, or Contrivance, is so much dispraise of Nature; an admission of imperfection, which it is man's business, and merit, to be always endeavoring to correct or mitigate. . . . In sober truth, nearly all the things which men are hanged or imprisoned for doing to one another, are nature's every day performances. . . . [I]t remains true that nearly every respectable attribute of humanity is the result not of instinct, but of a victory of instinct; and that there is hardly anything valuable in the natural man except capacities—a whole world of possibilities, all of them dependent upon eminently artificial discipline for being realized. . . . [T]he duty of man is the same in respect to his own nature as in respect to the nature of all other things, namely not to follow but to amend it. . . . Conformity to nature, has no connection whatever with right and wrong. . . . That a thing is unnatural, in any precise meaning which can be attached to the word, is no argument for its being blamable.[1]

Naturalness is, then, not a good reason to approve or disapprove of any system of social ordering. A demonstration that a practice requires a political structure, designed by human beings, is not an argument against that practice. On the other hand, a perception of naturalness sometimes does make a system seem strongly resistant to change. If law is trying to alter nature, it may turn out to be futile or counterproductive. In any case, an effort to reveal the presence of government in practices often taken as prepolitical can help dislodge a belief that those practices must be taken as the baseline for decision. To replace the baseline, however, we must make an argument rather than inquire into nature.

Negative and Positive Rights: Of Welfare and Others

For the last two decades there has been considerable debate about whether the Supreme Court should recognize "positive rights" to government assistance.[2] According to the conventional wisdom, the Constitution is a charter of negative guarantees—rights against government interference—and positive or affirmative rights are exceptional or nonexistent. Government may not intrude on private rights, but there is no claim against the government if it has simply failed to act.[3]

This important conclusion has helped courts to reject claims for various public services, ranging from basic subsistence to education to police protection against domestic violence. One of the most important examples is *Harris v. McRae*,[4] in which the plaintiffs challenged the government's failure to fund abortions that were medically necessary for poor women. The Supreme Court held that while government may not impose barriers on the decision whether to abort, it had no duty to remove barriers "not of its own creation." The idea is that poverty is simply "there"; it is not a product of government action.

It is peculiar, however, to say that the Constitution does not guarantee "affirmative rights." The takings clause protects private property, and in so doing it protects against repeals, partial or total, of the trespass laws. When a state eliminates the law of trespass, it is removing its "affirmative" protection of property rights; but its action is not for that reason constitutionally acceptable. The right to private property is fully positive in the sense that it depends on government for its existence (as people in Eastern Europe are learning all too well). Without the law, there can be no protection against trespass, and in this sense no private property as we understand it.

The protection of private contracts can also be understood as an affirmative right. The contracts clause amounts to a right to state enforcement of contractual agreements. If the state fails to protect by refusing to enforce a contract, it is violating the clause. The original constitutional protection of contracts and property thus created powerful affirmative rights against government—and matters were understood in explicitly these terms at the time of the framing.[5]

Here and elsewhere, it is misleading to understand the Constitution as a guarantor of "negative" rights. The Constitution protects some rights and not others. Whether rights are treated as "negative" or "positive" turns out to depend on assumptions about baselines—the natural or desirable functions of government. We may speculate that state protection of private property and contract often appears to be a "negative" guarantee because it is so usual, indeed built into the very concepts of property and contract. Protection of property and contract are part and parcel of existing distributions, and hardly interfere with those distributions.

By contrast, the provision of welfare, or government protection against private racial discrimination, is thought to involve "positive" rights because these rights interfere with existing distributions and with common law principles. For this reason they seem to involve governmental intrusion into an otherwise well-defined and voluntary private sphere. It is precisely status quo neutrality and the pre–New Deal baseline that account for current constitutional thinking about "affirmative" rights. The line between "negative" and "positive" turns out to be unhelpful.

This point suggests a closely related one. Frequently constitutional claims rejected by courts as a call for positive rights are said to be entirely inconsistent with our legal heritage, which involves only "negative liberty"—claims *against* government rather than claims *to* government assistance. Let us assume, despite what I have just said, that our system is indeed focused on negative liberty alone. Does this mean that we should reject a constitutional claim made (for example) by people who seek to put their political views on the airwaves, or by the homeless?

In fact it does not. Those who claim a right of access to the airwaves are not asserting "positive" liberty. Instead they are claiming that the civil and criminal laws, which would be invoked against them if they attempted to do what they want, violate their negative liberty and thus the First Amendment. They are not seeking governmental assistance. They are complaining about government interference, through the law of property, with a most basic negative freedom.

Similarly, homeless people can be seen to be complaining, not only about the government's failure to provide them shelter, but also about the range of civil and criminal laws that forbid them from using shelter that would be otherwise available.[6] Government restrictions would certainly be called into play if homeless people tried to use a public or private dwelling for their protection. It is partly those restrictions that deprive people of a home. In this way, legal restrictions affect—indeed, constitute—the status of homelessness. No positive liberty need be asserted at all.

The line between positive and negative rights is thus selected, in current law, by reference to existing distributions. Here the crucial factor is the law of property, which is of course built into those distributions, but which, perversely, is not treated as law at all.

State Action

The so-called state action doctrine is a cornerstone of American constitutionalism. The doctrine is a product of an understanding that the Constitution is directed to acts of government rather than to acts of private individuals. Standing by itself, the doctrine should be uncontroversial. With very few exceptions, the text of the Constitution reveals unambiguously that its commands apply only to government, state or federal. Private individuals and organizations are permitted to act freely. They need not be concerned about the Constitution.

The state action principle has extraordinary practical importance.

For example, it exempts private businesses from the constitutional limits on racial discrimination and abridgment of freedom of speech and religion. Private institutions may discriminate, or fire Democrats, or hire only Christians, so far as the Constitution is concerned.

But how do we decide whether government is "acting"? In theory, the legal test could depend on whether government employees are involved in the acts at issue. But that would be too broad. State officials enforce contracts and protect property rights every day, and their willingness to do so is an important backdrop for daily interactions. Does this mean that the Constitution forbids someone from excluding from her house people whose religious views she despises, or from contracting with, or dating, only Republicans? Surely not. If the background involvement of state officials is sufficient to produce "state action," the whole category would be impossibly broad. The actual or potential involvement of state officials in the enforcement of private contract, tort, and property law does not subject all private arrangements to constitutional constraints.

In fact courts do not resolve state action cases by asking whether government officials are involved in the problem at issue—though sometimes they say that they do. Instead, I claim, they resolve such cases by relying on a particular baseline, establishing the normal, natural, or desirable functions of government. These functions are usually not considered state action; other functions are. And in setting forth such a theory, and using it as the basis of inquiry, courts have not merely searched for state action, but instead relied on existing distributions, with which normal governmental functions are not thought to interfere. Normal functions are even defined by reference to existing distributions. Status quo neutrality has thus played the crucial role in the cases. The doctrine is not about "action" at all, but instead rests on that conception of neutrality.[7]

The point may seem puzzling in the abstract. But as the following survey of cases will show, there is simply no other explanation for the fact that governmental repeal of a trespass law or refusal to enforce a contract counts as state action—whereas a repeal of an antidiscrimination law, enforcement of a trespass law, and enforcement of a contract probably does not. The odd pattern of results obviously has nothing to do with state action and, only slightly less obviously, everything to do with status quo neutrality.

Consider first *PruneYard Shopping Center v. Robins*.[8] That case involved a decision by the California Supreme Court, extending rights of free speech under the state constitution, so as to permit people to picket at privately owned shopping centers. In the United States Supreme Court, the shopping center owners argued that the federal takings clause was a bar to the states' abrogation of their property rights. The Supreme Court held that the state's decision did not violate the federal Constitution. But it left absolutely no doubt that the partial abrogation of the state law of trespass was "state action" sufficient to call for constitutional scrutiny. Indeed, a fair reading of the opinion is that some large-scale abrogations of state trespass law would amount to an unconstitutional taking.

This conclusion should not be controversial. Property rights are defined by state law. Elimination of the law of trespass is one of the central meanings of a taking of property. If we say that the trespass law no longer protects someone's property, we are saying that the property is no longer truly his own.

Or consider the fact that enforcement of an antidiscrimination law is clearly state action (though of course lawful on the merits), while, in general, enforcement of a trespass law or invocation of the courts to enforce a contract is not.[9] No constitutional question is raised when private property owners deny the public access to their property. As the Court held in *Hudgens v. NLRB*,[10] the landowners may invoke state trespass law in order to prevent picketers from displaying their messages on private property. An interesting comparison is provided by *Shelley v. Kraemer*,[11] in which the Court invalidated a racially restrictive covenant prohibiting people from selling their property to blacks. As noted in Chapter 2, the Court held that judicial enforcement of the covenant was indeed state action, and unconstitutional as such. But its decision was extremely controversial, and it seems clear that judicial enforcement of contracts is ordinarily insufficient to trigger the Constitution. Thus far, then, the cases show that enforcement of trespass law and of contracts generally does not count as state action, whereas abrogation of trespass law plainly qualifies as such.

Let us now return to the treatment of private racial discrimination. There is general agreement that no constitutional question is raised if a state fails to provide protection from private racial discrimination, or if a state repeals a statute that provided such protection. This understanding is made explicit in one of the most vexing of modern state action cases, *Reitman v. Mulkey*.[12] At issue in *Reitman* was a California constitutional amendment barring the state from enacting any law that interferes with the private right to sell property to whomever the property owner chooses. By a fragile five-to-four vote, the Court invalidated the amendment on the ground that its purpose and effect were to encourage private racial discrimination. But the Court was careful to emphasize that the amendment stood on a very different footing from a "mere" repeal or a "mere" failure to provide protection against private racial discrimination. Such a repeal, or such a failure, would not be state action at all.

For purposes of the Constitution, *PruneYard* appeared an easy case, and the failure to provide protection against trespass was obviously state action. But *Reitman* was quite difficult, and the failure to provide protection against racial discrimination was not obviously state action.

What accounts for this? Why did the abrogation of trespass law in *PruneYard* appear uncontroversially to be state action, while application of the same law was understood to be no such thing in *Hudgens?* We have seen an extraordinarily odd pattern of results: enforcement of trespass laws and agreements is not state action; enforcement of antidiscrimination laws is state action; repeal of trespass laws and refusal to enforce contracts is state action; failure to have antidiscrimination laws or repeal of such laws is not state action. But which cases really involved "action," and which "inaction"? At first glance, the invocation of a trespass law seems much more conspicuously to be "action" than the abrogation of or refusal to enforce the very same law.

The Court's reasoning in these cases confirms that the state action inquiry is not a search for whether the state has "acted," but is instead an examination of whether it has deviated from functions that are perceived as normal and desirable under the relevant constitutional provision. And that examination is powerfully influenced by the common law, which defines the legally relevant status quo. Protection of interests recognized at common law is not state action, whereas protection of other interests does count as such. It is only for this reason that the abrogation rather than the enforcement of a trespass law (familiar at common law) appears to be state action. It is for this reason as well that enforcement of rather than abrogation of, or "mere failure" to enact, an antidiscrimination law qualifies as state action. Antidiscrimination law is unfamiliar to the common law, and thus appears as government "intervention" into the status quo.

Now we have an explanation for a seemingly puzzling pattern of cases. The issues are resolved by the choice of a common law–like, pre–New Deal baseline of government "inaction," one that appears neutral and natural. The results should be attributed not to the requirement of state action, but to a substantive theory that defines (constitutionally troublesome) action and partisanship, and their (constitutionally invulnerable) corollaries inaction and neutrality, by reference to existing practices and distributions. Governmental enforcement of trespass laws and contractual arrangements is thought simply to ratify existing distributions. Rather than interfering with them, legal enforcement of property and contract rights is built into existing distributions. By contrast, antidiscrimination law is thought to disrupt existing distributions—that is one of its principal purposes—and to amount to government "interference" with an otherwise well-defined, regulation-free, and voluntary private sphere.

It is these ideas, and not the requirement of state action, that account for the results in the cases. And of course these ideas are misconceived. Trespass law is no less a governmental intrusion than antidiscrimination law. I do not argue that the state action requirement should be abandoned. Indeed, I have said that it is unexceptionable. I do not even claim that repeal or nonenforcement of a trespass law should be treated the same as repeal or nonenforcement of an antidiscrimination law. All this depends on the governing constitutional principles, which could quite plausibly require trespass law but not antidiscrimination law. Perhaps the Constitution requires government to protect against private invasion of property but not against private discrimination. This is of course a question on the merits, not one of state action.

It is only because of the persistence of pre–New Deal assumptions—and status quo neutrality—that state action was uncontroversially at stake in *PruneYard* but difficult to find in *Reitman*. In *PruneYard*, there was a deviation from the common law baseline. In a case in which the state fails to provide protection against racial discrimination or enforces the law of trespass, there is no such deviation. In contemporary state action doctrine, as before the New Deal period, existing distributions and the common law provide the benchmark from which to measure intervention. Whether the state is even visible to the legal system depends on the answer to that question.

Racial Discrimination

The law of racial discrimination is centrally affected by status quo neutrality and indeed by pre–New Deal premises. Most of the major controversies revisit New Deal disputes. Here, however, the similarity lies not in the use of the common law, but in notions of action and inaction rooted in the status quo.

I will discuss three areas of current discrimination law that reflect these points. But the same issues can be found in an earlier generation, during the discussion of the Supreme Court's decision in *Brown v. Board of Education*,[13] and indeed in the most famous use of the term *neutrality* in all of constitutional scholarship. In "Toward Neutral Principles of Constitutional Law," Herbert Wechsler criticized the opinion in *Brown* on the ground that the Court had not supplied a "neutral" justification for the result.[14] In Wechsler's view, the decision provided a conflict between two sorts of associational preferences: the desire of blacks to attend school with whites, and the desire of whites to attend schools without blacks. So far as Wechsler was concerned, no neutral principle had been brought forward to justify the Court's choice between these two sets of preferences. For Wechsler, the *Brown* decision had not been shown to be neutral. The Court could not simply prefer blacks.

This criticism depends on status quo neutrality. For Wechsler, the existing distribution of opportunities and resources between blacks and whites should be taken by courts as simply "there"; neutrality lies in (what is seen as) inaction. Neutrality is threatened when the Court "takes sides" by preferring those who are disadvantaged. Like the minimum wage legislation in *Lochner,* and for similar reasons, the attack on school segregation appeared impermissibly partisan to some of *Brown*'s critics.

In both cases, moreover, the right response comes from the New Deal period. The existing distribution is not natural and does not provide a neutral baseline; it resulted in part from government decisions, notable among them slavery and segregation itself; efforts to improve the lot of the disadvantaged should not be treated as impermissibly partisan, and may even be constitutionally compelled, especially where there is an equal protection challenge to racial discrimination against blacks.

Indeed, Wechsler's notion that the associational preferences of whites and blacks should be treated "the same" seems to have an otherworldly quality. Those preferences have entirely different origins and consequences. The idea that neutrality demands that the desires be "equally" respected disregards the historical context and the unequal backdrop, that is, the system of racial subordination that reflected and helped create and perpetuate those desires.

Wechsler's principle of neutrality was thus built on a particular conception of the baseline from which partisanship would be measured; and that baseline was the racial status quo. It is for this reason that much of the article seems to be a playing out, on a grand scale, of Wechsler's jarring claim—told in a brief but revealing digression from his criticism of *Brown*—that as a result of the racially based exclusion of the famous black lawyer Charles Houston from the restaurants of the District of Columbia, Houston "did not suffer more than" Wechsler himself.

To some degree, of course, Wechsler's objection was about institutions rather than substance. He was requiring of courts a justification of the sort that the *Lochner* Court required of legislatures. The category of neutral principles, as he understood it, was analogous to the police power as understood by the *Lochner* Court. But these differences should not deflect attention from the same general foundation. In both cases, "taking sides" in favor of the disadvantaged seemed impermissibly partisan.

Similar ideas can be found in modern race discrimination law.

AFFIRMATIVE ACTION

It is now clear that the courts will treat "affirmative action"—discrimination in favor of members of racial minority groups—with nearly the same skepticism as discrimination against members of such groups.[15] The validity of a particular affirmative action scheme will depend on a variety of factors: the nature of the institution that made the decision; the flexible or inflexible character of the scheme; the nature of the harm to members of the majority; and, perhaps most important, the existence of "findings" to the effect that the institution engaging in affirmative action has discriminated in the past.

The final factor has been the most sharply disputed among the justices. The dispute centers on when, if ever, past "societal discrimination" is a sufficient reason for an affirmative action scheme, or whether affirmative action must be justified by a very particularized showing of discriminatory conduct by the institution in question. Current indications are that societal discrimination is almost always insufficient to justify affirmative action.

In many forms, the constitutional attack on affirmative action depends on a perception that the neutral or natural course is to rely on mechanisms—usually the market—thought to be free from distortion by racial discrimination. The Constitution, it is said, requires government to allocate employment and other opportunities on the basis of criteria that have nothing to do with race. On this view, it is not neutral to distinguish discrimination against blacks from discrimination against whites. This approach makes the issue depend on partisanship in a way that violates the constitutional requirement of "equal" protection of the laws. A particularly important point here is that individuals should not be singled out to bear burdens that ought to be placed on the public as a whole. (This suggestion is the same one that played so prominent a role in the period before the New Deal; recall the discussion in Chapter 2.)

But these arguments reflect status quo neutrality. If the current position of blacks is thought not simply to be "there," but instead to be a product of past and present social and legal choices, the argument for permitting affirmative action becomes more powerful. There would be no requirement of "neutrality" understood as mandating measures that are (or seem) indifferent to race. It would not be neutral to use markets, if the predictable consequence was continued second-class citizenship for an identifiable group, a result made possible only through law. Many of the constitutional arguments for and against affirmative action thus track the arguments for and against minimum wage legislation.[16]

Indeed, the very term *affirmative action*—ironically, embraced by defenders of the practice—is based on status quo neutrality. The term suggests that indifference to race (understood here as reliance on markets, understood in turn as inaction) is the natural course, that discriminatory effects deriving from colorblind rules are simply "there," and that something that counters those effects should be labeled "affirmative." By contrast, market mechanisms appear as "negative" and "inaction." The terms *affirmative* and *action* both rely on status quo neutrality. They understand respect for the status quo and for market ordering as the point of departure for constitutional analysis. And in the context at hand, the attack on affirmative action rips the notion of "racial discrimination" out of the very context—of discriminatory purposes and effects connected to the maintenance of a caste system— that gave that notion its meaning and made it into one of opprobrium.[17]

Thus it is that pre–New Deal premises affect the affirmative action controversy. I do not deny that there are good reasons for concern about racial preferences. But with respect to the notion of colorblindness as a constitutional creed, we might consider John Dewey's suggestion: "Even when the words remain the same, they mean something very different when they are uttered by a minority struggling against repressive measures and when expressed by a group that has attained power and then uses ideas that were once weapons of emancipation as instruments for keeping the power and wealth they have obtained. Ideas that at one time are means of producing social change assume another guise when they are used as means of preventing social change." [18]

DISCRIMINATORY EFFECTS

In Chapter 1 we saw that in one of the most important legal developments since World War II, the Supreme Court held that a showing of racially discriminatory intent is necessary in order to establish a violation of the equal protection clause. Discriminatory effects are insufficient. If a seemingly neutral test for police officers happens to exclude a disproportionate number of blacks, or if the deployment of police, fire, and welfare services has a harmful impact on blacks, there is no equal protection problem—even if the test has little relation to capacity to perform the job or if the deployment is hard to justify on race-neutral grounds. The Court has reached this conclusion in part because of a concern that if discriminatory effects were enough, an enormous range of seemingly legitimate government decisions would be called into constitutional doubt. A disproportionate number of blacks are poor, uneducated, unable to perform well on standard examinations, the perpetrators (and victims) of crimes, and so forth.

This understanding also depends on an understanding that discriminatory effects are simply "there," so that the course of neutrality lies in indifference to race (what appears and is treated as inaction). But if discriminatory effects were seen as partly the product of past discrimination by the state, it would be hard to treat them as natural and unobjectionable. If the status quo were perceived as a result of past non-neutrality, discriminatory effects may well be problematic.

DE JURE/DE FACTO

For a long period it was unclear whether de facto segregation—segregation not produced by explicit segregation laws—was a cause for constitutional concern. [19] De facto segregation, largely in the North, is said to arise from the voluntary choices of blacks and whites. By contrast, de jure segregation is racial separation produced by law. As in the case of affirmative action, the terminology rests on artificial premises. The notion of de facto segregation suggests that segregation simply happened; it is just "there." But if the existence of patterns of segregation is always in part an outgrowth of racial discrimination, an attack on de facto segregation might have been more plausible. There are good reasons to immunize some kinds of segregation from constitutional control. But the legal distinction depends on status quo neutrality.

Sex Discrimination

In the last two decades, the Court has invalidated many statutes discriminating against women. Sometimes the Court does so because the statutes are based on inaccurate stereotypes.[20] But the difficult cases arise when the Court faces measures reflecting differences that are real. Consider, for example, *Califano v. Goldfarb*, involving a statute allowing spouses of men automatically to qualify for social security benefits, but requiring spouses of women to establish dependency; *Craig v. Boren*, prohibiting boys from drinking alcoholic beverages until age twenty-one, but allowing girls to drink at age eighteen; *Mississippi Univ. for Women v. Hogan*, involving a nursing school limited to women; and *Rostker v. Goldberg*, upholding a law requiring men but not women to register for the military draft.[21] In all of these cases, the statute under attack responded, even if a bit crudely, to "real differences" between men and women. On what basis did the Court invalidate the first three measures?

A clue can be found in *Craig v. Boren*, in which the Court, responding to statistics showing that boys tended to be cited for drunk driving more often than girls, said that statistical demonstrations are "in tension with the normative philosophy of the Equal Protection Clause." In all of these cases, the differences, even if "real," are at least to some degree creations of society:[22] products of cultural forces, including the legal system, that have given effect to and perpetuated differences between the sexes, or turned these differences into social disadvantages.

Thus in *Goldfarb*, the fact that more men than women are wage earners was not treated as independent of the legal system. Indeed, this fact was reinforced as such, even if in a minimal way, by the very statute in *Goldfarb*, which made the package of work benefits more attractive for men than for women and to this extent made it more desirable for men to work at all. Such a law will ensure that men are more frequently in the workforce and thus will help create "real differences" between the sexes. In the *Hogan* case, the Court said, crucially, that the statute at issue "makes the assumption that nursing is a field for women a self-fulfilling prophecy." A law that restricts nursing schools to women will ensure that with respect to nursing, there will indeed be real differences between men and women.

The cases under discussion thus reject the idea that gender differences are independent variables, and that neutrality lies in reasonable responses to those differences. To this extent, the law of gender discrimination abandons the status quo as a baseline and instead relies on a principle of gender equality operating as a criticism of existing practices.

Many areas of the law of gender discrimination, however, rely on status quo neutrality. The fact that the law has done so little about sex discrimination is a direct result of this very fact. For example, cases involving discrimination on the basis of actual or potential pregnancy, or control of reproductive functions, do not see issues of reproduction as raising problems of equality at all. These decisions depend on the notion that men and women are simply "different." There are indeed differences between men and women; but any such differences have social consequences because of legal (and social) decisions. A law that is targeted at women's reproductive capacities might well be seen as a form of sex discrimination. (I return to this point in Chapters 9 and 11.)

Consider also the well-documented biases in the criminal justice system,[23] which deals inadequately with domestic violence, sexual harassment, and rape. It would not be at all difficult to imagine a constitutional attack, rooted in the principle of equal "protection" of the law, on police practices that fail to protect women against domestic violence and other forms of abuse. Consider, too, current rules of family law, which ensure that after divorce the welfare of most men will increase dramatically, while the welfare of most women will decrease correspondingly. The rules do not reward but rather punish women for their contributions to child care and housework. It takes little imagination to conclude that these problems raise issues of sex discrimination.

Instead it is thought that in all these areas there are "real differences" between men and women, and hence there is no basis for constitutional attack. In this way status quo neutrality affects the law of sex discrimination.

Defining Liberty and Property

The due process clause provides that no state may deprive any person of "liberty" and "property" without due process of law. The Supreme Court has had considerable difficulty in defining the terms *liberty* and *property.*

The hardest problems have arisen in attempts to decide which, if any, benefits provided by statute are entitled to procedural protection, in the sense that government may not remove them without providing some sort of hearing.[24] For many years the Court emphasized that some benefits were "created" by the government—most prominently employment, welfare, and social security—whereas other benefits were not. Only the latter were entitled to constitutional protection.

The dividing line between the two rested largely on whether the interest was protected at common law. Common law rights—in essence, what people currently had, including private property and private liberty—could not be taken without a full hearing. But the statutory benefits of welfare, employment, licenses, and social security had been granted by government as "privileges," and these could be removed at the government's whim. Status quo neutrality, pre–New Deal style, accounts for the difference.

The 1960s saw an assault on this position.[25] Many people warned that the consequence of the traditional view would be to leave citizens dangerously vulnerable to government discretion. Public employees, recipients of social security and welfare benefits, people with public licenses—all of us would be subject to the government's discretion with respect to extremely important things. Subjection of this sort would reintroduce the very dependence and insecurity against which the institution of private property was originally supposed to guard.

In the period from 1968 to the late 1980s, the Court accepted this argument and concluded that statutory benefits will sometimes be considered "liberty" or "property." But they will so qualify only when there is a "statutory entitlement," defined as a legal limitation on the administrator's discretion to provide the benefit in question.[26] There is no right to a hearing if the legislature has not limited the administrator's discretion. For example, a law that allows an employee to be discharged at the government's discretion creates no entitlement and thus no "property." A law that allows an employee to be discharged only after a showing of "cause" does create property, and a hearing is required in the event of an attempted discharge.

To the extent that statutory benefits can sometimes qualify as property, the Court has tried to adapt constitutional safeguards to the activities of modern government. But the adaptation is only partial. For the most part, liberty and property continue to be defined by reference to existing distributions and even to the common law.[27] Interests protected at common law—including most prominently the rights to private property and to bodily integrity—are axiomatically entitled to protection. The difficulties arise with other sorts of rights, including the right to freedom from discrimination, the right to government employment, and the right to welfare. The statutory entitlement approach, allowing some interests foreign to the common law to be treated as "property," is a reformulation of earlier understandings. But the Court's failure to put benefits said to be "created by the government" on the same footing with benefits treated as a pregovernmental "given" is a clear holdover from pre–New Deal thinking. The distinction itself treats things created by the common law as unchosen and statutory benefits as a form of "intervention"—the same understanding as that of the *Lochner* Court. An alternative approach would have been to select liberty and property interests by reference to some criteria independent of the common law, or at least not determined by common law categories.

Thus far I have been discussing procedural due process, or rights to a hearing. Similar issues have arisen in cases involving "substantive" protection under the due process clause, that is, a right to prevent government action at all, whether or not there has been a hearing. In some cases people have argued that "government benefits" should receive substantive constitutional protection. In *Flemming v. Nestor*,[28] the Court concluded that social security benefits were not protected as "property." The government may eliminate such benefits so long as its decision is minimally rational, which is to say whenever it wishes.

The Court's reasoning was that government benefits stand on an altogether different ground from ordinary property, since they are not normally or naturally owned by recipients. Courts have often concluded that government may eliminate benefits of its own creation—where that notion is defined by reference to common law.[29] The failure to grant substantive protection to statutory benefits derives from a sharp distinction between common law interests and other benefits.

The constraints of Article III—which guarantees the availability of a federal court, whose judges enjoy various guarantees of independence—have been interpreted with similar premises. The Court is less likely to require an Article III tribunal when a right created by Congress is at stake, whereas it will if a common law right is involved.[30] The common law thus defines a large amount of the territory captured by Article III requirements.

Campaign Finance Regulation

Many people think that the present system of campaign financing distorts the system of free expression, by allowing people with wealth to drown out people without it. Proponents of campaign finance legislation contend that such legislation is necessary to promote political equality by reducing the effects of private wealth in politics. Indeed, campaign finance laws might be thought to promote the purpose of the system of free expression, which is to ensure a well-functioning deliberative process among political equals. (Of course it is disputed whether such laws in fact serve this purpose or instead operate as incumbent protection bills.)

Buckley v. Valeo[31] involved a first amendment attack on campaign finance regulation. The regulation at issue imposed a ceiling on campaign expenditures by candidates and political parties. In defense of the regulation, the government argued that the law was an effort to diminish inequalities in the abilities of individuals and groups to influence the outcomes of elections. Restrictions on the speech of the wealthy helped disseminate information from diverse and antagonistic sources, and thus promoted a deliberative process among political equals. In *Buckley*, the Court concluded that this justification was illegitimate.

In the striking key passage, the Court said, "the concept that government may restrict the speech of some elements of our society in order to enhance the relative voice of others is wholly foreign to the First Amendment."[32] As far as the First Amendment is concerned, the state may not redress disparities in wealth at all. Indeed, it must take the existence of some with more "voice" than others as a part of nature for which government bears no responsibility. To do otherwise was, for the *Buckley* Court, a kind of First Amendment taking—a silencing of the wealthy for the benefit of people with less money. It was for this reason that the effort at equalization was not within the permissible goals of government.

The Court's reasoning in *Buckley* rests on status quo neutrality. In *Buckley*, as in *Lochner* itself, the existing distribution of wealth is seen as a given, and failure to act—defined as reliance on markets—is treated as no decision at all. Neutrality *is* inaction, reflected in a refusal to intervene in markets or to alter the existing distribution of wealth. This is so despite the fact that markets are conspicuously a regulatory system, and reliance on markets for elections is a regulatory choice. *Buckley,* like *Lochner,* grew out of an understanding that for constitutional purposes, the existing distribution of wealth must be taken as simply "there."

Unconstitutional Conditions

After the creation of the welfare state, questions immediately arose about whether the government could use its new programs in such a way as to influence the exercise of constitutional rights. Might government say that people can receive welfare benefits only if they agree to waive their constitutional right to freedom of speech? Should it matter that such waivers appear voluntary? Could such conditions be coercive?

Questions of this kind have come up in many settings, including the use of secrecy agreements for government employees; requirements that the homes of welfare beneficiaries be opened to state officials; exclusion of abortion from medical programs; unemployment insurance programs that affect religious convictions by requiring people to work on Saturdays; limitations of welfare benefits to people who have been in the state for at least a year.[33]

Initially, the Supreme Court concluded that conditions of this kind raised no constitutional problem.[34] Such conditions were voluntarily accepted by citizens, who therefore had no cause to complain. In the capsule summary of Justice Holmes, responding to the claim that a police officer had been discharged for reasons inconsistent with the First Amendment: "The petitioner may have a right to free speech, but he has no right to be a police officer."[35]

Ideas of this sort were based on a direct use, in the modern state, of *Lochner*-like ideas involving common law and status quo baselines. In these cases, the government had not coerced anyone in the familiar ways. It had not intruded into the sphere of private liberty or private property. It had simply made an offer, which people were free to reject.

Eventually, the Court abandoned this position. In a number of cases—not united by the clearest of rationales—the Court invalidated certain conditions as unconstitutional.[36] Often the Court has appeared to be administering a requirement of government neutrality, policing both the purposes and the effects of any conditions imposed in spending and regulatory programs. To the extent that it has done so, it has indeed adapted constitutional understandings to modern practices. But the hardest cases involving "unconstitutional conditions" arise when the baseline for assessing governmental neutrality is in doubt. In these cases, the continuing legacy of pre–New Deal understandings is unmistakable.

Consider, for example, *Harris v. McRae,*[37] in which the Court upheld the Hyde Amendment, which denied funding for poor women needing abortions for medical reasons. One question in *Harris* was whether the Hyde Amendment operated as a "mere" failure to fund or instead as a "penalty" on the exercise of the constitutional right to have an abortion. To make that distinction work, it is necessary to establish a baseline against which the assessment will be measured. We do not know whether something is a penalty unless we decide about the world that would exist "otherwise"—that is, without the relevant condition. In *Harris,* the Court concluded that the baseline is a world without the Medicaid program; as a result, the denial is a mere failure to fund. But if the post–New Deal baseline is a system in which poor citizens generally are reimbursed for medical services, the denial is really a penalty. In this respect, *Harris* is a close cousin of *Lochner.*

Or consider the Supreme Court's decision in the *Lyng* case,[38] in which the government denied food stamps to workers participating in strikes. The Court upheld the denial, concluding that it was a means of promoting the government's interest in remaining "neutral" in labor disputes. But in a system in which food stamps are generally available to people who need them, a selective denial operates not as a guarantor of neutrality, but instead as a tool of coercion pressuring people not to exercise what the Court assumed to be a constitutional right to strike.

Most recently, in *Rust v. Sullivan,*[39] the Court upheld a regulation forbidding clinics from giving advice about abortion. In response to the claim that the regulations conditioned the receipt of a benefit on the relinquishment of a First Amendment right, the Court said that "here the government is not denying a benefit to anyone, but is instead simply insisting that public funds be spent for the purposes for which they were authorized." This was therefore not a case "in which the government has placed a condition on the *recipient* of the subsidy rather than on a particular program or service, thus effectively prohibiting the recipient from engaging in the protected conduct outside the scope of the federally funded program." If the case had involved "a condition on the recipient," it would be an entirely different matter.

But how does one tell whether there is a "condition on the recipient"? On the Court's approach, the recipient is the person in the preregulatory status quo. Even if that person is pressured by a selective funding decision, she has no basis for complaint unless she is worse off than she was before the program was enacted. This is a conspicuous use of the status quo as the basis for assessing whether government has violated its obligation of neutrality. But would the Court actually conclude that government may grant resources only to those organizations that (say) agree to engage in speech favorable to the party in power?

To make these observations is not to show that *Harris, Lyng,* and *Sullivan* were wrongly decided. What is important is that in these cases the Court treated the preregulatory status quo and the common law as the baseline from which to decide whether there was a "penalty" or instead neutrality.

Judicial Review of Agency Inaction

One of the most important issues in modern public law is whether courts should remedy unlawful inaction by administrative agencies. The issue is of special interest when agencies entrusted with the law are frequently thought to be insufficiently vigorous—in such areas as occupational safety and health, environmental law, civil rights, and labor law. If the Environmental Protection Agency refuses to take action against a dangerous pollutant, might courts require it to do so?

Under the traditional approach, agency *action* is subject to a strong presumption in favor of judicial review. Agency *inaction* faces no such presumption; it is generally unreviewable. Much of administrative law grows out of an understanding that government may interfere with common law rights only if it has been authorized to do so by the legislature.[40] Judicial review is necessary to test the question of authorization. By now it should be clear that the basic idea grows out of status quo neutrality.

Under this framework, there is little room for judicial protection at the behest of "beneficiaries" of regulatory statutes—consumers, those who breathe the air, workers, victims of discrimination, and so forth.

In such suits, no common law right is at stake. This framework accounts for conventional limitations on the class of people entitled to obtain "standing" to review agency action and also for a traditional presumption against review of agency inaction.[41]

In the 1970s, there was a substantial departure from this traditional understanding.[42] Beneficiaries of regulatory programs were allowed to challenge unlawful agency inaction. This trend, rooted in New Deal understandings, represented an effort to put statutory benefits on the same plane as common law interests.

In its exceedingly important decision in *Heckler v. Chaney*,[43] however, the Supreme Court held that agency inaction should be presumed unreviewable. In so holding, the Court emphasized that "when an agency refuses to act it generally does not exercise its *coercive* power over an individual's liberty or property rights, and thus does not infringe upon areas that courts often are called upon to protect."

This understanding is a direct modern analogue to Supreme Court decisions during the *Lochner* period. In both contexts, deviations from the status quo demand special justification. In *Heckler*, as in *Lochner*, it is government interference with common law rights that is subject to legal concern. Government "coercion" is even defined as intrusions on private liberty and property. Governmental "inaction"—fidelity to common law principles—is treated as neutral and legally unobjectionable; indeed, it does not furnish a predicate for judicial intervention.

In the context of administrative law, this phenomenon is especially jarring. As we have seen, the rise of the modern administrative state was based largely on a rejection of common law ordering. For the proponents of the administrative agency, the common law system was hardly unchosen or neutral, but was instead highly partisan. Coercion consisted in the individual's vulnerability to poverty, environmental degradation, intolerable working conditions, and so forth. Administrative law doctrines, based on traditional private law, thus continue to reflect premises apparently repudiated during the rise of the administrative state.

Standing

Similar ideas apply to the problem of standing—the question of who may obtain judicial review of administrative decisions. Originally, only people whose common law interests were at stake had standing to challenge administrative action. A "legal interest" was required, and a legal interest meant, at its inception, that an interest protected by the common law must be at risk.[44] This test was built on an analogy to private law, where people harmed by illegality could not always challenge it. A bystander, C, could not enforce a contractual obligation owed by A to B; it was necessary to show not merely illegality or even injury to C, but also that someone had violated some legal duty owed to C. The result was a system of public law that owed its origin and shape to common law understandings and to status quo neutrality.

Eventually the Supreme Court decided that an interest protected by statute could also be a basis for standing.[45] This was a crucial development, especially insofar as it gave beneficiaries the same rights as objects of regulations. Finally, in *Association of Data Processing Service Organization v. Camp*,[46] the Supreme Court rejected the "legal interest" test altogether, requiring only an injury "in fact" and "arguably within the zone" of statutory protection in order to test administrative action. Since *Data Processing*, many beneficiaries of regulatory programs have been permitted to bring suit to protect their interests against discrimination, poverty, pollution, and other legal harms.

But modern standing doctrine still contains principles drawn from the common law. The Court has often relied on notions of judicial restraint to justify limitations on standing; and as it has administered those limitations, it has sharply distinguished between the interests of regulatory beneficiaries and those of regulated industries. The former, it is sometimes said, are for the political process rather than the courts: the distinctive judicial role is claimed to be the protection of traditional private rights.[47] This reasoning is not, in fact, based on a general belief in judicial restraint; instead it distinguishes between two categories of interests in a way that reflects status quo neutrality. The interests of regulated industries are uncontroversially a basis for judicial review, whereas the interests of regulatory beneficiaries are not. The notion of judicial restraint is largely camouflage; status quo neutrality is what is really at work.

Private law notions also turn up in the application of the Court's requirements of "nexus" as a basis for standing.[48] With those requirements, the plaintiff must show that his injury is attributable to the defendant's conduct and that the injury is likely to be remedied by a decree in his favor. In such cases, the Court has generally required plaintiffs to show injuries of the sort required by traditional private law. New regulatory interests—those that Congress intends to protect—are sometimes found insufficient.

In the key cases,[49] the plaintiffs attempted to describe their injuries as systemic or probabilistic. These were not common law–like harms at all. As I discuss in more detail in Chapter 11, the Court's refusal to allow such suits is ironic in light of the usual purposes of regulatory statutes. Such statutes are quite typically designed to reduce risks, to restructure incentives, or increase opportunities. They do not involve discrete injuries of the sort characteristic of common law. In requiring such injuries, standing doctrine continues to be based on status quo neutrality.

Preferences and the Law

Both public and private law generally take private preferences as the appropriate basis for social choice. In private law, paternalism is disfavored, and the best-known conceptions of public law understand the purpose of legislation to be the aggregation of private preferences.[50] To this degree, preferences are treated as independent and fixed variables; and legal interferences with those preferences are thought to be partisan and illegitimate. The processes of preference formation, and the possibility of distorting factors, are not subjects for legal inquiry.

Sometimes, however, courts do conclude that preferences are a product of law and indeed of some kind of distortion. Consider, for example, the fact that freedom of choice plans are constitutionally inadequate as a remedy for school segregation.[51] At first glance it is hard to see why this is so, for such plans allow blacks and whites to send their children to whatever schools they prefer. If the result of such plans is continuing segregation, the problem might be thought to lie in free private choices rather than in the legal system.

The Court's hostility to freedom of choice plans depends in part on a conclusion that the preferences of whites and blacks are produced by the history of discrimination.[52] Blacks may prefer not to send their children to predominantly white schools because of a fear of racial hostility and antagonism. Whites may be reluctant to send their children to black schools because of racial prejudice brought about in part through law. In these circumstances, the preferences are not simply "there" and to be taken as natural; they are partly a result of legal rules. Genuinely remedial measures should take that into account.

A similar issue is raised by *Palmore v. Sidoti*,[53] in which the Supreme Court invalidated a child custody system favoring parents of the same race as the child. The Court reasoned that the state may not sanction racial prejudice through law. But it is unclear why the Constitution should forbid government from taking into account the reality of private racism. Here too the answer depends on a perception that racism is partly a product of legal choices and is properly subject to legal remedy. (The same considerations apply in the area of gender.) What emerges is therefore a system that generally treats preferences as fixed, independent of law, and a proper basis for social choice, but that in certain limited contexts concludes that preferences are produced by distortions brought about by, among other things, the legal system itself.

Takings and Contractual Impairments

Some constitutional provisions seem to take existing distributions as the baseline for decision. The takings clause, protecting private property, provides the analytical foundations for *Lochner* itself. And it is hard to read the provision without accepting, at least to some degree, status quo neutrality. The takings clause bans redistribution of property, and redistribution is most plausibly understood from the standpoint of existing rights.

The contracts clause comes from the same framework as the takings clause. But in the last fifty years, the constraints of the contracts and takings clauses have been significantly curtailed by the dramatic expansion of the police power (see Chapter 1). The expansion is a product of a partial abandonment of status quo neutrality. It would be difficult, however, to abandon those baselines altogether without reading the contracts and takings clauses out of the Constitution. Those provisions should hardly be ignored. Nothing in the New Deal would justify so radical a step. But it is interesting to see that the narrowing of the contracts clause has almost converted it into a constitutional redundancy; the takings clause is still important, but mostly in the context of physical invasions.

Status quo neutrality plays a prominent role in modern public law. But I conclude this chapter with an important distinction. Sometimes status quo neutrality is used as a basis for judicial invalidation of government measures. Sometimes courts use this conception of neutrality in order to uphold such measures. As we will see, the courts' use of the status quo tends to be most objectionable when invalidation is the result.

CHAPTER 4

Interpreting the Constitution: Method

I have said that constitutional law is pervaded by status quo neutrality; but this is merely a description. It offers no reason for change. To explore that issue, we must examine the question of method in constitutional law. My argument in this chapter can be summarized very briefly. Constitutional interpretation inevitably requires us to use principles external to the Constitution. There is no such thing as interpretation without interpretive principles, and these cannot be found in the Constitution. But this does not mean that we are in chaos, or an abyss, or that law is simply politics. Instead it means only that the external principles must be identified and defended. In Chapter 5, I begin to identify and defend these principles.

Although the problem of constitutional interpretation has produced an avalanche of complex and sometimes barely digestible theorizing, in one sense the issue is very simple. Everyone agrees that the Constitution is law. If the Constitution is law, then it stands above politics. All public officials—whether Democratic, Republican, or something else—must obey. The Constitution does not mean what particular people want it to mean; otherwise it would not be law at all.

On the other hand, the text of the Constitution is often extremely vague. Reasonable people disagree about what it means. Some people think that a Constitution that guarantees "the equal protection of the laws" requires affirmative action policies, in order to remove the effects of past and present discrimination. Other people think that a state that engages in affirmative action is violating this very guarantee.

Some people think that a Constitution that protects "the freedom of speech" prohibits campaign finance regulation. Others think that such regulation is consistent with and even promotes the constitutional guarantee. Both groups are perfectly capable of reading English, and both believe that their views are compelled by the Constitution. On so many of the central constitutional questions, the words of the Constitution tell us much less than we need to know.

If the words of the Constitution do not resolve hard constitutional cases, it seems undeniable that people who interpret the document have to look to something other than those words in order to do their jobs. This idea seems to many both unavoidable and intolerable, the latter because it endangers the status of the Constitution as law. It means that interpretation of the Constitution must be based on principles external to the words of the Constitution. Those principles have to be created rather than found; the Constitution does not contain the instructions for its own interpretation (and if it did, we would need principles to make sense of the instructions). If interpretive principles must be created by the judges, it seems, to many, that the Constitution could mean almost anything at all, and is not law after all.

In the history of constitutional law, many people have tried to respond to this problem. Here too a conception of neutrality has played a large role. On that conception, judgments about constitutional law are quite different from political judgments in the sense that the former do not require us to resort to views on principle or policy. Much of what is popularly understood as "law" consists of neutral or deductive, even mechanical, applications of judgments made by others.

This idea receives shorthand form in the idea that we have a government by laws rather than by men. In recent years, this view of interpretation—typically in the form of an assault on the methods and reasoning of the Warren Court—has helped transform the performance and self-conception of the federal judiciary. In some respects, moreover, the distinction between legal and political judgments is highly salutary.

I have two purposes in this chapter. The first is to challenge three ideas about interpretation in the law. The first approach, to which I will devote most of the discussion, is *formalism*. The formalist creed, as I understand it here, insists that the meaning of texts is usually or always a simple matter of fact. The task of interpretation is to uncover that fact.[1] Mistaken interpretation consists of mistakes in this endeavor.

On one especially influential version of this view, constitutional law should be undertaken on the basis of a sharp distinction between the neutral, apolitical invocation of the original understanding of the founders on the one hand, and the subjective, value-laden use of the judge's own preferences on the other. This view is set out in Judge Robert Bork's *The Tempting of America: The Political Seduction of the Law*.[2] I focus on Judge Bork's book not because it is eccentric, but on the contrary because it states a certain widely held view of constitutional neutrality in such stark form.

Both formalism and Judge Bork's approach to interpretation have encountered a variety of sharp criticisms in recent years. My particular concern is what seems to me the most interesting defect of formalism in constitutional law, that is, the failure to acknowledge the need for *interpretive principles* in construing any legal (or other) text, including the Constitution. It is impossible to interpret any written text without resort to principles external to that text. There is no "fact" of constitutional meaning until such principles have been brought to bear. Disagreement in constitutional law is often disagreement about the appropriate interpretive principles, and this is what needs to be discussed. In insisting on the need for interpretive principles, I will make some critical remarks about positivism in law and also about Ronald Dworkin's alternative conception of law.

I will argue as well that an inadequate understanding of interpretive principles is the failing of some enthusiastically antiformalist approaches to constitutional law. On the influential *conventionalist* view, the meaning of a legal text is simply a function of the interpretive views of people with power in the legal community. Since meaning is a function of conventions, which are a product of power, and since there is nothing outside conventions, the Constitution means simply what it means, and there is not much more to be said than that. For those who stress *indeterminacy,* the meaning of the Constitution is open-ended. There are no rational criteria by which to resolve interpretive disputes, but instead exercises of will, or subjective opinions, or even power and whim. Those who hold these various views have, I suggest, a great deal in common with their formalist adversaries.

My second purpose is to make some general claims about the nature of reason in constitutional law. I claim that the process is not one of deduction or pure logic; but it is nonetheless a form of reasoning. So understood, it is not something to be disparaged, but on the contrary a valuable and even inevitable method for evaluating human affairs. I offer some general remarks about reason in law, in a world in which existing distributions are sometimes seen as unjust, and in which interpretive principles are understood to be a part of the process of giving meaning to legal texts. The creation of interpretive principles should not, however, be freestanding. I conclude with a discussion of the role of text, history, and structure in constitutional interpretation.

"Originalism" and Its Consequences

In *The Tempting of America,* Robert Bork sets out a distinctive approach to constitutional interpretation. The argument is straightforward. Some judges are "neutral"; they follow the law. Other judges are political; they participate in "a major heresy"; that is, they deny "that judges are bound by law." The line between the two depends on whether a judge "is bound by the only thing that can be called law, the principles of the text, whether Constitution or statute, as generally understood at the enactment." No one who disagrees with this view "should be nominated or confirmed." [3]

According to Bork, judges who reject this view "not only share the legislative power of Congress and the state legislatures, in violation both of the separation of powers and of federalism but assume a legislative power that is actually superior to that of any legislature." The heresy is particularly indulged by "people [who] see the Constitution as a weapon in a class struggle about social and political values," are "egalitarian and socially permissive," "hold only contempt for the limits of respectable politics," or invoke "a kind of restless and unprogrammatic radicalism that does not share but attacks traditional values and assumptions." The "philosophy of original understanding" has the large contrasting value of "political neutrality in judging." [4]

One might think that the "fall" from neutrality is a recent phenomenon, but Bork describes it as something that immediately followed the ratification of the Constitution. Not merely Justice Brennan, and not merely the "liberals" on the Warren Court, but also Chief Justice Marshall and Justices Holmes, Brandeis, Frankfurter, Jackson, and Harlan were seduced by the temptation to substitute politics for law. They too were tempted to abandon the Constitution.

Bork thus begins with the proposition that the Constitution is law and that those who ignore the Constitution are acting lawlessly. He adds to this uncontroversial claim a thesis about interpretation, that is, an identification of "the Constitution" with the understanding about its meaning held by those who ratified it. On this view, a judge who rejects the original understanding rejects the Constitution itself, or is, in effect, in a free-fall, or abyss, in which meaning is supplied by his own predilections or value judgments. For such a judge, the Constitution becomes irrelevant. Only his own views count. It is here that neutrality, and hence legitimacy, is wanting on the judge's part. For Bork, avoidance of value judgments is a crucial part of the task of law. Reliance on the original understanding alone serves that function.

The consequences of this view are not obscure. There is no right of privacy. Indeed, liberty receives no substantive protection under the Fourteenth Amendment. Rational basis review—effectively ensuring validation—would apply to all forms of discrimination other than those based on race and ethnicity. So too, discrimination on the basis of gender, or on almost any other basis, is likely to be upheld (though Bork is not entirely clear here). Poll taxes are permissible, as are violations of the principle of one person–one vote. The federal government can discriminate on the basis of race or indeed on any other ground. If it chose, it could segregate on the basis of race or exclude blacks from federal employment. Compulsory sterilization of some criminals would be acceptable. Many federal programs of the New Deal period and after would be unconstitutional. Congress would be barred from invalidating state literacy requirements. Affirmative action would be banned.

Perhaps most dramatically, the Bill of Rights would probably not apply to the states at all, though on this point Bork is somewhat cautious. One need not disagree with all of these conclusions in order to recognize that the resulting understanding of the Constitution would be dramatically different from the understanding that prevails today.

Before looking at the merits of Judge Bork's argument, it is worthwhile to pause over this matter of consequences. It is surprising but true that many of the principles of constitutional liberty most prized by Americans were created, not by the founders, but by the Supreme Court during this century. At the very least, the understandings that have given those principles their current life are very recent creations. Indeed, for most of the country's history the liberties chartered in our Bill of Rights were sharply circumscribed. The overriding reason for their expansion has been the interpretive practices of the modern Supreme Court.

If contemporary Americans looked at the view of constitutional freedom in America as it existed in 1940, or if they could imagine an emerging democracy (say, in Eastern Europe) committing itself to that view, they would see a system falling far short of their ideals. It is because of the Warren Court that constitutional liberty includes a general right to freedom from discrimination on the basis of race; to broad protection of political speech, subject to a sharply limited "clear and present danger" exception; to political participation, including equal rights in voting; to rights to a hearing for those receiving government benefits, including employment, licenses, and social security; to freedom from sex discrimination; and to general protection of religious conscience.

A return to a narrowly described "original understanding" would result in the elimination, in one bold stroke, of many constitutional safeguards. All this may not count by itself as a sufficient argument in favor of the role set by the twentieth-century Court. But it is at least a useful prelude. More than that, the question of consequences is relevant to the selection of interpretive principles—not because we should be "result-oriented," but because we cannot choose among interpretive principles except in terms of results in some general sense.

Why (and How) External Justifications Are Inevitable

It might be right to think that the meaning of the Constitution is settled by the original understanding held by its ratifiers. But surely an argument is necessary before one should accept that position. This is so especially, perhaps, in view of its repudiation by so many leading members of the Court, and of the extent to which the position would undermine principles of constitutional liberty that have and deserve widespread support.

Actually those who believe that the original understanding is not decisive do not reject the Constitution. They do not believe that the Constitution is not binding. They do not put to one side "the actual Constitution." Instead they think that the proper interpretation of the Constitution requires resort to considerations not contained in the original understanding (narrowly understood). Often they claim that their preferred conception of interpretation is itself historically required. In any case they propose, not to abandon the Constitution, but instead to discern its meaning by reference to something other than the original understanding (again, narrowly understood).[5]

What argument does Judge Bork offer on behalf of his view? In an especially revealing passage he squarely addresses the question: "It has been argued . . . that the claim of proponents of original understanding to political neutrality is a pretense since the choice of that philosophy is itself a political decision. It certainly is, but the political content of that choice is not made by the judge; it was made long ago by those who designed and enacted the Constitution."[6]

On this view, the original understanding is binding because the original understanding was that the original understanding is binding. The historical claim is itself debatable.[7] The breadth of the words of the Constitution invites the view that its meaning is capable of change over time. There is evidence that the framers did not believe that their original understanding would control the future. But we should put that point to one side. Bork's claim is that the binding character of the original understanding is settled by the original understanding. This is not an argument at all; it is circular, or a rallying cry. To those who believe that it is necessary to defend the view that the original understanding is binding, it cannot be persuasive.

Bork does offer several different strategies for justifying the belief in reliance on the original understanding. On some occasions he argues by shifting the burden of argumentation: "Why should the Court, a committee of nine lawyers, be the sole agent for overriding democratic outcomes? The man who prefers results to processes has no reason to say that the Court is more legitimate than any other institution capable of wielding power. If the Court will not agree with him, why not argue his case to some other group, say the Joint Chiefs of Staff, a body with rather better means for enforcing its decisions? No answer exists."[8] Bork seems to be arguing here that a decision deserves respect if it can be connected to a judgment by "the people." It does not if it cannot.

This brief argument has been given greater attention in recent work by Frank Easterbrook.[9] Easterbrook starts from the proposition that any view about judicial interpretation must be focused on the particular context for which it is developed, that is, definition of the role of a judiciary in democratic government. According to Easterbrook, a view on interpretation must be attentive to the need to justify judicial review itself. There will be little to be said on behalf of a system of constitutional interpretation that is not matched to the particular reasons that *courts* are allowed to give final interpretations to the document. Thus far, Easterbrook seems entirely right. Ideas about constitutional interpretation cannot simply borrow from other interpretive systems as these have developed in, say, literature or theology.

Easterbrook proceeds from here to argue that judicial review is justified, if at all, only because "the people" specifically authorized it. Easterbrook claims that any defensible system of interpretation must follow from this insight. The conclusion is that any such system that does not rely on what "the people" specifically authorized goes beyond the reasons that justify judicial review in the first instance. It follows that nonoriginalist review is illegitimate. On this crucial point, Bork and Easterbrook are at one.

But this is an inadequate approach to the question of legitimacy. Obedience to the Court is not justified simply because its decisions follow from a judgment made by the people—especially when the relevant people died long ago, and indeed excluded large segments of the polity (including all blacks and all women). A prior agreement of that sort does not provide a moral justification for obedience. Ultimately obedience is justified, if it is, for some amalgam of substantive political reasons: our Constitution is on balance a good one; it has a democratic pedigree, both in its original adoption and in the possibility of amendment; the consequence of a decision to abandon the Constitution would be intolerable chaos; unlimited judicial discretion would be unacceptable. When taken together, these factors do indeed justify adherence to our Constitution. By itself, however, the fact that there was agreement on the document many generations ago is insufficient for legitimacy. A decision by the Supreme Court does not warrant obedience for that reason alone.

If this is true, Supreme Court decisions do not lose their claim to allegiance merely because they are not compelled by a particular decision of the Constitution's ratifiers. Any judicial decision deserves allegiance, if it does, for a complex set of reasons, roughly analogous to those that support a decision to be bound by the Constitution itself. A tight connection with a specific previous decision of the polity is neither a necessary nor a sufficient condition for legitimacy.

So much for the matter of legitimacy. Bork also argues for the original understanding on the ground that abandonment of that understanding will lead judges to make "moral choices." Bork says that such choices cannot be made in the face of obvious disagreements within the populace. On this view, which seems to be widely held, the avoidance of moral choices is a central task of any neutral theory of constitutional interpretation. A key point, for Bork, is that all "revisionist" theorists require judges "to make a major moral decision." Legitimate judges, by contrast, are simply agents of the people.

A key point here is that people cannot "all agree to a single moral system." For this reason judges cannot properly invoke morality at all: "Why is sexual gratification more worthy than moral gratification? Why is the gratification of low-cost electricity or higher income more worthy than the pleasure of clean air?" [10]

On Bork's account, the fact that these questions cannot be answered in a neutral way means that judges must not even ask them; moral or political questions are not subject to rational defense. Precisely because they involve questions of value on which reasonable people differ, they cannot be resolved in any way other than the assertion of a preference.

There is, however, no way for those interpreting the Constitution to avoid moral decisions, even major ones. The view that the original understanding is binding requires a moral or political theory—in terms of, say, a theory of democracy. Acceptance of that view itself rests on a controversial moral foundation. Bork's own approach thus relies on political and moral decisions. These decisions are necessarily external to the Constitution. They need to be defended. This is not a decisive argument against originalism; perhaps a defense is indeed available. But the point suggests that the argument for originalism would have to take a quite different form. It would have to be based on something other than history.

The most general point here is that no text has meaning apart from the principles held by those who interpret it, and those principles cannot be found in the text itself. Without such principles, reading cannot occur. We must distinguish here between two categories of interpretive principles: the *semantic* and the *substantive*.

Semantic principles are those whose acceptance counts as part of what it means to speak the relevant language in a simple, dictionary sense. People who reject semantic principles reveal that they just do not understand what certain words mean. To say, for example, that a German Shepherd is not a dog is to show that one does not know what a dog or a German Shepherd is. So too, the constitutional provisions requiring that constitutional amendments be ratified by three-quarters of the states, and that the President be at least thirty-five years of age, have clear meanings simply because the governing semantic principles are well-known to those who read English. Here a dispute over meaning reveals that some of the disputants do not speak the language. They need instruction from people who do.

Substantive principles are different. Such principles require not a language lesson or a dictionary, but a substantive political justification. The idea that the original understanding is (or is not) binding falls within the category of substantive principles. So too with the idea that constitutional provisions should always be read to promote the functioning of democratic processes. These ideas are contested not because one side does not understand English, but because there is disagreement over the best way to make sense of the Constitution. The language of the Constitution does not say whether the original understanding controls its meaning. Similarly, the constitutional words *equal protection* do not by themselves decide among the competing conceptions of equality that underlie different views about affirmative action programs. In these instances, there is no preinterpretive brute fact of the matter, to be uncovered without resort to controversial substantive ideas.

The central characteristic of substantive principles is that their selection must be justified in moral and political terms; we cannot defend a system of interpretation in law without mounting a substantive defense. None of this means that constitutional language imposes no constraints, that history is irrelevant, or that meaning lies solely with the interpreter. But interpretive principles are inevitable, and they go well beyond semantics.[11]

In any case, a commitment to the original understanding is a substantive principle. That commitment must be defended. It is impossible even to decide how to characterize the original understanding without relying on moral considerations. The history itself is inadequate. To reiterate some familiar points:[12] We need to decide whether a clause embodies a general concept capable of change over time, or instead the particular understandings once held by those who ratified it. We need to know whether to select the framers' hopes, expectations, or convictions; these may well vary. We need to distinguish between what they wanted in the short run and what they wanted in the long term. Perhaps history can help us on some of these matters; perhaps we can find out, for example, whether the ratifiers sought a general concept or a particular understanding. But then we need to decide whether we are bound by their views on that question, and for this a substantive argument, rather than history, is again necessary.

We need also to apply the original understanding in conditions that the ratifiers could not have anticipated. How, for example, does the Fourth Amendment prohibition on "unreasonable searches and seizures" apply to the practice of wiretapping? How do we apply the guarantee of "the freedom of speech" to electronic broadcasting? Here it is necessary to translate a constitutional proscription into new conditions. To carry out these tasks, interpreters must invoke something other than the historical record. No final answers can be found there.

Bork sometimes defends his position through references to democracy, and here he is on firm ground. Any plausible theory of constitutional interpretation must pay a great deal of attention to the democratic aspirations of the American constitutional tradition. But by itself, the general principle of democracy is too vague to justify any particular conception of the judicial role. Democracy and majority rule are not identical concepts. If we are true democrats, we might sometimes urge an exceptionally aggressive judicial effort, if this is necessary to protect the right of political participation.[13] The goal of democracy might well require courts to go beyond the original understanding in order to ensure that very goal. To answer these questions, we need a specification of what is entailed by the notion of democracy.

It is no accident that the position set out in *The Tempting of America* is not so much defended as proclaimed. If the position were actually to be defended, the book's central claims would take on entirely new dimensions. The rhetoric of heresy and seduction would have to be abandoned; the line between neutrality and moral judgments would be unsettled; the defense would have to be rooted in moral and political judgments. An argument for originalism or for (what is not the same thing) a modest judicial role will have to speak of political theory, and not only of the framers.

It will be useful to conclude this section with a summary that slightly generalizes the point. Every legal text requires interpreters to draw on background principles that they must supply. It is often true that a text has a plain meaning, or that there is no room for interpretive doubt. But when this is so, it is because there is no disagreement about the appropriate background principles. It is not because there is a preinterpretive "fact" that people can uncover without resort to substantive principles.

Those who deny the existence of such principles are without self-consciousness. They believe that their own views are so self-evident that they do not amount to interpretive principles at all, but instead are just "part" of the text. But interpretive principles are always at work. That is no embarrassment to constitutional law, or indeed to law itself, but instead an inevitable part of the exercise of reason in human affairs. The question is not whether interpretive principles exist, but whether they can be defended in substantive terms.

Originalism is merely the most prominent version of formalism in the law.[14] Formalism is captured in the pretense that one can decide hard cases entirely by reference to value judgments made by someone else. Those who indulge that pretense usually end up not by abandoning value judgments, but by making them covertly. They treat the meaning of words as requiring a language lesson rather than a reason. The real fault of Judge Bork's version of originalism is that it attempts to mask its own foundations.

Interpretation without Substantive Arguments?

Judge Bork's conception of interpretive neutrality is an extreme version of a general tendency in constitutional law: the derivation of interpretive principles without acknowledging the substantive arguments that have to be made on their behalf. The same problem can be found in John Hart Ely's *Democracy and Distrust*,[15] an especially distinguished contribution to the subject. Ely argues that judicial review should attempt to reinforce rather than displace democratic process—so far, so good (see Chapter 5). But his argument to that effect rests on the insistence that judges should not impose their "own values." A procedural, democracy-reinforcing approach is "significantly different from the value-oriented approach" because it builds on the democracy-reinforcing text and "is not inconsistent with, but on the contrary . . . entirely supportive of, the underlying premises of the American system of representative democracy." Thus Ely thinks that his approach is an outgrowth of "the nature of the United States Constitution."[16]

Here we run into some serious difficulties.[17] The Constitution specifies many substantive values. It is not limited to the identification of fair procedures. More fundamentally, the general idea of representative democracy requires a defense in terms of substance. That idea is not merely procedural. Even its procedural features—rights to a hearing, rights to political participation—depend on substantive beliefs.

Even more fundamentally, any particular conception of representative democracy must be selected from a universe of possibilities. That particular conception must be argued for rather than identified with the general idea itself. Ely's own conception is a most attractive one. But it is not "in" the Constitution in any simple sense; the document does not, without supplemental ideas of Ely's own, call for that particular conception. If the Constitution is to be interpreted as imposing Ely's particular conception, it must be on the basis of good arguments—a "value-oriented approach," which is what Ely seeks to avoid.

For those who think that this is a decisive objection to Ely—why should *we* accept *his* conception?—it is important to remember that any approach to judicial review must be defended on the basis of substantive reasons. No view fails because it depends on them. But Ely has not provided the defense that is required; instead he resorts to a claim of mere procedure and thus, in a crucial and altogether unnecessary sense, to a claim of neutrality.

Similar problems can be found in a recent book by Laurence Tribe and Michael Dorf, *On Reading the Constitution*.[18] Tribe and Dorf rightly insist that any approach to the Constitution should pay attention to text and structure. They also show how both of these help to organize and channel interpretation. In the end Tribe and Dorf are particularly concerned to challenge the Supreme Court's decision in *Bowers v. Hardwick*,[19] which upheld a law forbidding sodomy among consenting adults.

Attempting an inquiry into the Constitution's structure, Tribe and Dorf generalize from the First (protecting speech), Third (preventing against the quartering of troops), and Fourth (protecting against unreasonable searches and seizures) amendments a broad right to be protected from government intrusion into intimate consensual relations within the home. It is certainly plausible to say that if the Court is to protect liberty, it should discipline its inquiry by looking at what has been given specific constitutional protection. Tribe and Dorf so argue, and they claim that if we do discipline our inquiry in this way, we will come to recognize a constitutional right to intimate sexual activity among consenting adults.

But this is really a version of formalism. It might be equally plausible to construct instead from those very amendments—especially when combined with the Fifth (protecting against the taking of property without just compensation)—a general right against redistributive regulation by government, including, for example, minimum wage and maximum-hour laws. We might say, for example, that the First Amendment shows an aversion to government interference with private behavior; that the Third is rooted in an effort to immunize property from public incursion; that the Fourth reflects the same idea; that the Fifth attempts to ensure that property can be taken only with compensation. In light of all this, perhaps "liberty" should include the right to freedom from any governmental effort to take resources from one person for the benefit of another. Minimum wage and maximum-hour laws would of course run afoul of this principle. Indeed, such a right would endanger much of what the federal government has done since the New Deal.[20] But Tribe and Dorf are hardly in favor of that.

Inferences from constitutional text and structure sometimes involve a large measure of discretion. In using these sources of law, we must often resort to ideas external to text and structure. A decision to infer a right to homosexual conduct within the home, and not to freedom from redistributive regulation, has to depend in large measure on substantive views about homosexuality and redistributive regulation—not only on what the Constitution specifically protects.[21] What is necessary, then, is a full-scale defense of those substantive views, combined with an explanation of why those views should be implemented by the federal judiciary in the name of the Constitution.

The point sheds light on many disputes about the meaning of the Constitution. Consider, for example, the important debate about whether free speech belongs in a "preferred position" as compared to other constitutional rights, such as the protection of private property and freedom of contract. Some people think that all rights should be treated "the same," and that judges should not be allowed to give some rights more protection than others. All constitutional rights, in this view, deserve equal respect.[22] Other people think that certain rights, most notably free speech, do indeed deserve a preferred position, because (for example) they are so uniquely central to democratic processes. But both camps talk as if constitutional provisions have a plain, preinterpretive meaning, so that the question is whether to treat all of them "the same" or instead to "prefer some to others." It is this view that cannot be sustained.

If meaning is inevitably a function of interpretive principles, it is not at all clear that the current approach—general lenience toward most legislative interference with property rights, more careful review of most legislative interferences with free speech—treats some provisions "differently" from others or prefers some rights to others. Instead, the Supreme Court uses a set of interpretive principles, which are always necessary to ascertain meaning, that produce the current set of outcomes. It may be that these principles are wrong for substantive reasons. But it is simple confusion to say that they are wrong because they prefer some rights to others.

That form of criticism, purporting to invoke the plain text of the Constitution, is actually based on a (controversial and unarticulated) theory of how the provisions should be interpreted. The criticism depends on interpretive principles that it does not identify but instead ascribes to the Constitution "itself." The claim that, under current conditions, some provisions are taken more seriously than others turns out to trade on formalist conceptions of meaning. It assumes that there is a preinterpretive understanding of the relevant provisions that the Supreme Court has ignored. That assumption cannot be defended.

Reasons and Power

The Tempting of America is an especially dramatic illustration of what might be called "legal authoritarianism," a somewhat tendentious term that I mean to use in a special sense. I intend the term to refer to all approaches to law that are not defended by reference to reasons. Such approaches ultimately trace legal legitimacy to an exercise of power, to the view that might makes right, or to some prior settlement among those with political authority. On this view, legal legitimacy need not and indeed must not be justified by reference to substantive claims about the right or the good. The ultimate and the only real justification is force or bargaining. A deep foundation of the authoritarian view may be a belief that law, to qualify as such, must have sources external to human purposes and human agency.[23]

Thus understood, the category of authoritarianism is a broad one. I use it here because of its close connection with the original constitutional hostility to the arbitrary exercise of monarchical power. Part of that hostility stemmed from the fact that the king was not required to offer reasons for his action. He was not called to account; he could appeal to his authority alone. Nowadays we might well describe as authoritarian a system of law in which the judges thought it unnecessary to offer reasons or to write opinions on behalf of their conclusions.

Authoritarian approaches might, on this view, be highly democratic. A democrat would believe, as Judge Bork obviously does, that it is best to repose legal authority in majorities rather than in kings or tyrants. The label "authoritarianism," as I use it, refers to the fact, on which Judge Bork joins many others in insisting, that majorities are entitled to prevail not because there is anything to be said in favor of what they do, but "for no better reason than that they are majorities." [24] It follows from this that the constitutional prohibition on naked preferences seems unacceptably undemocratic. It should be unsurprising that those who are hostile to the prohibition find it nearly unintelligible, as we saw in Chapter 1.

Authoritarianism in law has no political program; it is not necessarily allied with liberalism, conservatism, or anything else. Democratic authoritarianism finds prominent expression in the writings of Oliver Wendell Holmes and Hugo Black, both of whom emphasized, as a centerpiece of their approaches to law, the need for judges to give effect to prior agreements reached by those with political power. For Holmes, "the ultimate rationale of sovereignty is force." [25] For Black, interpretive principles seemed unnecessary and indeed hubristic, since they introduced a large measure of discretion and nonneutrality into law. For Black, the constitutional text was usually self-interpreting. Thus Black—the most celebrated guardian of the principle of free expression in the nation's history—proclaimed that his views could be traced directly to the text of the Constitution. The First Amendment says that "Congress shall make no law abridging the freedom of speech"; and Justice Black emphasized, time and again, that he read "no law abridging" to mean "no law abridging"—as if those words resolved hard constitutional cases by themselves. [26] The terms are not, however, without ambiguity; many people disagree over what falls within "the freedom of speech." Those who wrote them surely rejected the meaning that Justice Black ascribed to them.

The literal meaning of the words of the First Amendment thus cannot do the work that Black claimed for them. This is a hallmark of authoritarianism in law: the attribution of a definitive resolution to some external source of law, and the denial of the covert, unarticulated judgment actually made by the attributer.

Legal authoritarianism has a number of characteristic features. It sees laws, constitutional or otherwise, as deals among self-interested actors. It is usually skeptical of all efforts to reason about social and economic problems. It disparages such efforts as a mere mask for self-interest or as incapable of resolving social and political disputes, which it treats as based on premises too fixed and incommensurable to be a subject of deliberation. (It should therefore be unsurprising to see a sharp rise in this view in the wake of the 1960s, when fundamental premises came under assault, and when many doubted that reason was sufficient to mediate among the resulting disagreements. A characteristic reaction to the 1960s is a return to formalism—an insistence on the unadorned legal "text," because of the apparent absence of other methods for resolving conflicts.) Resolution is possible only by warfare or compromise among self-interested bargainers.

Disagreements about ethical and political problems are not an occasion for shared reasoning but instead proof of its impossibility. "Value judgments," understood as prejudices, are the consequence. If we depart from the enterprise of tracing legal outcomes directly to a legitimating decision, usually an exercise of force, we will fall into the chaos of evaluation, something on which there are deep cleavages in society. This is a crucial aspect of formalism as I understand it here. No judge can claim the ability or the warrant to say anything about those cleavages.

There is a distinctive authoritarian style in constitutional law as well. Authoritarianism provides the foundation for one conception of judicial restraint. Because ordinary legislative outcomes reflect the play of social forces, they should not be disturbed unless the interference is the result of some other, superior decision by such forces. Authoritarianism is also drawn to firm linguistic anchors—to "the text"—and for two quite independent reasons. First, the text reflects the authoritative allocation of power, and it is that allocation that legitimates the exercise of legal authority. Second, departures from the text leave interpreters in the world of unfettered value judgments and prejudices. Without the text, there is nothing else on which to base legal decisions. The law is left to the free play of personal prejudices. It falls into the abyss of value judgments or of whim and whimsy.

Finally, and perhaps most fundamentally, the authoritarian position treats most of its claims as axioms, in need of no real defense. The very call for a defense is often said to mark people as heretics, or as requiring their exclusion from the relevant community. When defended in substantive terms, the authoritarian claim takes on altogether new dimensions and ceases to be authoritarian at all. Thus, for example, the view that the original understanding is binding because we ought, for reasons, to treat it as binding, is a position entitled to serious consideration and respect. It is altogether different from the kind of view that I am identifying here.

Notes on Legal Positivism

The ideas that I have been describing are connected with legal positivism, an extraordinarily influential and appealing conception of law. Legal positivism has been defended and elaborated in different forms by J. L. Austin and H. L. A. Hart.[27] What I have said here obviously bears on the important debate between positivism and its opponents, and it will therefore be useful to offer a few notes on that debate here. I offer a highly compressed description of both the positivist view and the traditional critique of positivism. In the process I offer a brief but perhaps distinctive challenge to legal positivism.

The central positivist claim is that there is a difference between a statement about what the law is and a statement about what the law should be. To say that the Constitution forbids affirmative action is not to say that the Constitution should do so; to say that the speed limit is fifty-five miles per hour is not to say that vehicles should be banned from going over that speed. So far so good. A major puzzle for the positivist is to explain how something becomes "law." Austin saw law as the commands of the sovereign. Despite its simplicity and general plausibility, this conception seems unable to help us in identifying who "the sovereign" is. This is a crucial gap, for modern societies have multiple institutions claiming to be sources of law. The failure to identify "the sovereign" is especially important in light of the fact that Austin, seeing law as a command backed by force, made it hard to distinguish between some very different sorts of commands. Consider, for example, the difference between a law setting a speed limit of fifty-five miles per hour and an order by someone having a gun telling you to get him to the church on time.

Hart has attempted to respond to these and other difficulties in Austin's account of law. Hart draws a distinction between "primary rules," which impose duties directly on citizens, and "secondary rules," which explain how primary rules may be enacted, modified, or eliminated. A law including a primary rule may be binding either because it conforms to a secondary rule or because the people that the rule governs are willing to accept the rule as a justified constraint on their behavior. An especially fundamental secondary rule is a "rule of recognition," which stands above all other rules, explaining when something counts as law. A rule of recognition counts as law only because it is accepted.

Hart's approach remedies many of the puzzles of positivism. It allows us to distinguish between different sorts of commands backed by force, showing why only some of these count as law. And the distinction between primary and secondary rules, accompanied by an understanding of the rule of social acceptance, makes it unnecessary to inquire into the identity of "the sovereign." Of course Hart acknowledges that in some cases the legal rules are indeterminate, or of "open texture." In such cases, Hart writes, the judges exercise their discretion.

Formalist accounts of constitutional meaning attempt to build on some version of positivism, especially the positivist insistence on a distinction between law and morality. Hart's approach helps to explain how that distinction makes sense. The most influential attack on Hart's formulation has come from Ronald Dworkin. In his early writing, Dworkin offered the following response.[28] Any legal system contains principles and standards that play a large role in judicial decisions. These include, for example, the ideas that no one may profit from his own wrong and that people who do not read a contract before signing it cannot later relieve themselves of its burdens. These ideas are not really rules—they do not operate in "all-or-nothing" fashion—but they must nonetheless be counted as part of law.

In hard cases, judges resort to these principles. Dworkin claims that it is therefore incorrect to say, as Hart does, that when rules do not cover cases, judges simply have discretion. Moreover, the use of principles creates grave difficulties for the system of primary and secondary rules. It is hard to show how the principles that operate in the courts derive from some secondary rule or from social acceptance.

More recently, Dworkin has made a related but slightly different argument. His target here is the "plain fact" view of law, in accordance with which a statement that "the law is X" amounts to a notion that if we look in the right places, we will find some statement "X." Dworkin argues that when there is a disagreement about what the law is, there is actually a disagreement not about a plain fact, but about "the best constructive interpretation" of some past legal event. In other words, Dworkin claims that a disagreement about whether (for example) the equal protection clause forbids affirmative action is a disagreement about what interpretation of that clause makes the clause "the best it can be." On this view, a statement that "the law is X" is in part description and in part evaluation. It is reducible to neither.

The evaluative dimension comes in trying to make the law *the best* it can be. The descriptive part comes in trying to make *the law* the best it can be. The positivist view is thus incorrect because it claims that there is a plain fact to be discovered in authoritative places. In truth, Dworkin says, the law is not a fact, but a product of various efforts to put the existing legal materials in their best or most favorable light. A statement about what "the law is" therefore cannot be rigidly separated from a statement about what "the law should be." "What the law is" turns out to be a product, in part, of what people think it should be. This much follows from abandoning the "plain fact" view of law.

In this space, I cannot do justice either to the positivist view or to Dworkin's responses. But this much seems clear. The positivists are correct to insist that a statement about what the law is cannot be reduced to a statement about what the law should be. Often there is a sharp difference between these statements, as no one seems to deny. Moreover, there are important pragmatic advantages in separating the descriptive and evaluative inquiries, a separation that in most settings eliminates unnecessary confusion. But from what has been said thus far, it seems that a key problem with the positivist view is that it disregards the need for interpretive principles with which to give meaning to a legal text. Those principles are inevitably external to the text. They cannot be found in any authoritative place. Even if they could be, we would need interpretive principles to understand the principles themselves.

In easy cases, which is to say most cases, the positivist project seems and is extremely plausible. But this is only because the governing interpretive principles are uncontested (and therefore invisible). Everyone agrees on them. In hard cases, the principles are in dispute, and here law involves substantive arguments over which principles to adopt. These arguments cannot be adequately described as an effort to uncover some command, to "exercise discretion," or to find something that has been socially accepted.

Thus far my criticism of positivism is close to that offered by Dworkin. But there are important differences. I have said that meaning is a function of interpretive principles and that it is necessary to have good principles rather than bad ones. But this is quite different from saying that judges do and should make the law "the best it can be." This view assumes too sharp a distinction between the inquiry into what is "best" and the inquiry into the relevant "it." With respect to law, there is no freefloating, acontextual "it"; the existing law is not a brute fact, but always and inevitably a product of interpretive principles. Dworkin's depiction of the "it" seems to repeat the positivist mistake of seeing law as something to be found. Nor do lawyers try, in some very abstract way, to make law "the best it can be." Their inquiry into what is "best" is indeed evaluative, but it is also quite disciplined, in the sense that it draws from principles already internal to the legal culture. Dworkin sometimes writes as if the inquiry into what is "best" were a matter of political philosophy. For lawyers, it is something quite different, that is, a more internal, though value-laden, inquiry into what positions now within the legal culture can be supported by good arguments.

We can make the point more clearly with reference to the equal protection clause. Does an affirmative action program deny people "the equal protection of the laws"? It would not be entirely right to think that lawyers and judges work from an "it," the equal protection clause, and then try to turn that clause into "the best it can be." Instead they decide on the meaning of the clause by using interpretive principles of various kinds. Sometimes these principles are uncontested, and then we have an easy case; the constitutional text is said to be unambiguous or plain. Sometimes the relevant principles are in dispute, and then we have to decide which ones are best justified. The search for the best justification, as it operates in law, is largely internal in the sense that it works from the (usually ample) resources of existing legal culture. Of course in unusual cases, those resources are found inadequate, because of some external assault; and in such cases something like political philosophy does play an explicit role in law.

This picture departs in some major ways from Dworkin's two-step inquiry, asking what makes some textual "it," apparently to be found without the aid of interpretation, into some normative "best," to be decided as a matter of political philosophy. But the two descriptions are allied in their rejection of positivism in law, and perhaps the differences between them are matters of emphasis and detail.

Disappointed Formalists: Conventionalism and Indeterminacy

I now turn to two approaches that have been highly influential and that seem, at least at first glance, to be sharply opposed to formalism.

Both approaches are, I think, direct outgrowths of the social movements of the 1960s. Whereas those movements led many to return to formalism—because of the apparent failure of reason to resolve disputes—they persuaded many others to reject all methods of interpretation, on the theory that every method was "political," and therefore based on values that could not be thought through but instead merely asserted.

Conventionalism is one species of antiformalism in law.[29] Conventionalists see the meaning of words as a function of the interpretive principles held by those in positions of authority. The reason words mean what they do is simply that meaning is settled by people with power to do the settling. The conventions that determine meaning inevitably grip and constrain interpretation. They are not subject to anything like substantive or reasoned defense.

According to the second position, sometimes labeled "deconstruction" and in any case borrowing from certain forms of contemporary literary theory, the meaning of texts is indeterminate, undecidable, or irreducibly "political" and "subjective."[30] Members of this group stress the open-endedness of language and what they see as the intractability of interpretive disputes. On this view, meaning is created rather than found, and hence a function of one's perspective. Perspectives and creations differ along ideological lines. In the face of conflicting perspectives, often operating across such divides as race, class, and gender, the imposition of one meaning rather than another is a product of arbitrariness, or power, or whim.

Conventionalists differ from those who stress indeterminacy and perspective. For conventionalists, meaning is always constrained. But the two agree on an important matter. Both groups reject the idea that interpretive disputes can be settled through reason or argument. Both believe that the existence of competing and value-laden principles provides a basis for rejecting the call for reasons altogether. In this sense, both of these positions share with formalism the view that the meaning of legal texts, including the Constitution, is decided on the basis of something other than the reasons that can be offered on behalf of one or another position. Something like an exercise of power, or perhaps an existential commitment, is the ultimate justification—which is another way of saying that justifications are unavailable.

It is for this reason that those who belong to both camps tend to believe that there is no distinction between rhetoric and any other form of argument, between propaganda and reasoned argument, between persuasion and force, between manipulation and claims based on evidence.[31] For those who interpret legal texts, truth and objectivity are false, even naive aspirations, coming from people who cling to the anachronistic and unfounded belief that there is a method for vindicating or grounding arguments that is wholly external to the world.

We can now see an important agreement between the formalists and those who invoke conventions or stress indeterminacy.[32] All three have a similar understanding of what objectivity in interpretation would have to mean in order to be objectivity; all three have similar views about what reason has to be to count as such. All of them stress the incapacity of interpreters to mediate, through discussion and argument, the different views about which principles ought to be invoked in considering the meaning of the Constitution.

We might think of these most recent and influential approaches to interpretation as taking the inevitably situated and value-laden character of interpretation as reasons to give up on notions of truth and objectivity altogether. The distinction between rhetoric and reasoned argument—like all those distinctions that set apart justification from force—collapses because we cannot find external foundations with which to ground reason itself. In this sense, members of both camps can be understood as disappointed formalists, that is, as people who share the same (transcendental) conception of what truth and objectivity must mean, and who, seeing no conditions for that conception—we all live in the world—give up on truth and objectivity altogether.

Indeed, conventionalists and those who stress indeterminacy seem especially wedded to the old, formalist idea of reason. For reason to qualify as such, we need entirely external or transcendental grounds for judgment. Without these, we are left simply with play, conventions, or power.

But here there are non sequiturs. It is right to say that there is no external perspective, that interpretive principles are inevitable, and that legal meaning cannot be grounded without language or culture. But this does not mean that all argument is manipulation or that good reasons cannot be offered on behalf of one view rather than another. Human beings do not have unmediated access to reality, scientific or moral; we always apply interpretive prisms to our perceptions.[33] But from this it does not follow that the process of reason-giving is a charade or that we are left simply with whatever people now happen to think. This choice—between transcendental foundations on the one hand and chaos or arbitrariness on the other—is unnecessary, indeed unfaithful to the ways in which reason works in law and elsewhere.[34]

Consider, for example, how a debate might go over the role of original meaning in constitutional law. Let us suppose, plausibly, that the outcome in *Brown v. Board of Education* was not contemplated by the framers of the Constitution and that those who ratified the Fourteenth Amendment did not want to abolish segregation. If this is so, then everyone who believes that *Brown* was right must reject a prominent view of what adherence to the original meaning actually requires. Since the commitment to *Brown* seems nearly inevitable for all participants in the American constitutional tradition, such participants must claim that the original meaning of the Fourteenth Amendment is actually not decisive, that one must characterize the original meaning in a broad rather than narrow way, or that interpreters of the Constitution should have the license to translate the original meaning into new circumstances in order to be faithful to that very meaning. Those who reject all such routes and insist that adherence to the original meaning entails a fairly mechanical task of examining whether the ratifiers contemplated invalidation of the specific practice at hand must reject *Brown* itself (and much of constitutional law that everyone takes to lie at the foundation of our constitutional heritage). If they do that, they must explain how their conception of interpretation will lead to a superior system of constitutional law. Some justification of this kind is indispensable to make sense of their position or to explain why anyone should agree with it.

Perhaps they would emphasize the dangers of judicial discretion that come from abandoning the original understanding; and then we would enter into a discussion of what sorts of interpretive strategies will create a better constitutional system for the human beings who live within it. This is not a question of physics or mathematics, but it is hardly something on which reason has nothing to offer.

Indeed we now have a wealth of questions, involving facts and values, with which to grapple. What would our society look like if the original understanding were followed? What other constraints are there on the judges? Does democracy entail plain majority rule? If not, under what circumstances should judges be licensed to use a broad text to invalidate democratic outcomes? How effective is the Court in producing social reform, assuming it seeks to do so?

We might generalize the *Brown* example by suggesting that any dispute about interpretive principles must be resolved through an exploration of what sort of constitutional system will be produced by one set of principles rather than another. A theory of interpretation must therefore also be a theory of constitutional democracy. Such a theory is created in large part by seeing what sort of system is produced, by the alternative approaches, for people in the world. The notions of truth and objectivity in the law might well be understood to entail an honest and straightforward engagement with questions of this sort.

In this chapter I have challenged a conception of neutrality that sees the method of legal interpretation as essentially mechanical; in earlier chapters I discussed a conception of neutrality that finds partisanship in disruption of existing distributions. At first glance the two conceptions seem to have little to do with each other. The first conception—formalism—is a theory of meaning; it is about language rather than about justice. It calls for a principle of interpretive neutrality. The second conception—status quo neutrality—is at least implicitly a theory of substantive justice, put in the form of constitutional law; it is about what government ought to be allowed to do, and apparently not about meaning or language at all. This is a principle of substantive neutrality.

The principle of substantive neutrality has identifiable sources. When it operates, it usually does so because of reflex or some kind of commitment to existing distributions. The belief in interpretive neutrality does not have such sources, for it can come from those who accept and those who reject existing distributions in various contexts. The two positions do, however, have common social and psychological roots.

Status quo neutrality is often rooted in a fear that it is necessary to ensure that decisions will not be chaotic and unordered, that everything will not be "up for grabs." To abandon the baseline of the status quo is to enter the abyss of no baselines at all or to require people to create baselines in a way that gives free rein to the prejudices of those in authority. Reliance on the status quo seems to anchor decisions. So too, the appeal of formalism is that it promises to ensure that personal prejudices are cast to one side and to allow people in authority to connect their decisions to something firm and above all external.

The appeal of both conceptions of neutrality, then, is that they appear to offer a high degree of determinacy and a refuge from open-ended judgments of value. Indeed, the avoidance of such judgments is a principal goal of both versions of neutrality in law. In both cases, the notion that judgments of value might be mediated—through reasons, conversation, or otherwise—seems fanciful.

But the connection is, I think, even tighter than this. The failing of both conceptions of neutrality is not merely an analogy; in one sense it is close to an identity. The formalist approach disregards the inevitable use of interpretive principles—value-laden, potentially unjust, and created by human beings—in giving meaning to legal texts. Status quo neutrality similarly disregards the ways in which existing distributions are a product of law, humanly constructed, value-laden, and potentially unjust. Both of these conceptions bury what is controversial, that is, the existence of contestable substantive grounds in creating any theory of meaning or justice.

Moreover, the theory of meaning works best when the relevant interpretive principles can assume such prominence, or be insisted upon with such vehemence, that they disappear as choices or principles at all, and instead are treated as part of the necessary meaning of "the text" and thus as inseparable from it.[35] To say that the words *equal protection of the laws* necessarily forbid affirmative action or that the words *no law abridging* necessarily protect obscene speech is to avoid relying on controversial political principles and thus to rule such principles out of bounds.

The theory of neutrality works best when existing distributions are treated as brute social facts and indeed removed from the agenda for inquiry, so that our notions of what constitutes action and partisanship seem not to flow from any theory, or indeed from any viewpoint at all, but instead to be an unmediated way of understanding how things simply *are* in the legal system. Thus it is that an attack on status quo neutrality can be (and often is) met with the response that the attack politicizes what had been objective, or introduces controversial ideas where none had existed before. An attack on formalism often meets precisely the same response.

The problem is that both the formalist conception of meaning and the substantive theory of neutrality deny their own ultimate dependence on a controversial point of view, and then generate theories of meaning and legal justice that hide that point of view from sight. In this sense, the two conceptions of neutrality are very much the same. The theory of meaning, like the theory of justice, obscures its dependence on substantive commitments. Its ultimate goal is to escape responsibility. We should not, however, equate that goal with the rule of law.

Text, Structure, History

It will be useful to conclude this discussion with an outline of the appropriate role of the basic foundations of constitutional decisions: text, structure, and history. Nothing said so far suggests that these sources are unhelpful or irrelevant. On the contrary, each of them is crucial to interpretation. This is so even if we acknowledge, as we should, that the meaning of these sources of law is a function of interpretive principles.

Any system of interpretation that disregards the constitutional text cannot deserve support. This is not merely an axiom. It depends on some substantive political arguments: requiring adherence to the text is a central way of disciplining judges and of preventing the arbitrary exercise of judicial power. To be sure, the case for adherence to the text would be far weaker if the text in question were tyrannical or oppressive. Part of the argument for textualism in American constitutional law is that our constitutional text, generally speaking and properly interpreted, does indeed promote human liberty. A text that guaranteed general slavery or allowed frequent torture need not be taken as binding. Its tyrannical character would be an occasion for exercising the right of revolution, which amounts to (among other things) a rejection of otherwise authoritative written texts. A decision to follow the text of the American Constitution furnishes no such occasion. That text is properly treated as binding.

The constitutional text, read in light of semantic principles and substantive principles on which there is general agreement, will indeed impose constraints on interpretation. But we have also seen that often the text is open-ended, failing to provide complete guidance. Sometimes its meaning depends not on semantics or on universal interpretive principles, but on principles that conspicuously require a substantive defense. It would be fortunate if some such principles could be built up with the aid of the Constitution itself. Is this possible?

Constitutional structure does provide a degree of assistance. For example, it seems correct to infer, from the federal structure of the Constitution, a general right to travel from one state to another. A denial of that right would be inconsistent with the Constitution's structural commitments to national supremacy and national citizenship. If there were no right to travel, these commitments would unravel; states could restrict citizens to state borders. Through reasoning of this general form, a good deal of constitutional interpretation can take place.[36]

It also seems right to insist on reading constitutional provisions not as isolated dots, but in light of one another. Interpretations that make sense out of the document as a whole have the advantage of promoting coherence and rationality in constitutional law. Where coherence and rationality are possible, surely they should be obtained. It follows, for example, that one ought not to read the equal protection clause in a way that would do fundamental damage to the explicit protection of private property and freedom of contract. A socialist system would indeed be unconstitutional.

Any view of the equal protection clause that compels socialism is foreclosed by the document (as well as by good independent arguments). Through interpretive strategies of this kind, much progress might be made. Constitutional commitments are best understood in light of other values in the document.

There are, however, limits to structural analysis. As we have seen, competing inferences or no inferences at all are sometimes the lesson of constitutional structure. By itself, the structure does not really provide much help to those who seek to decide how the Constitution speaks on the issues raised by regulation of scientific speech, government funding of the arts and public education, affirmative action, abortion, campaign finance regulation, or pornography. On such questions, both text and structure leave conspicuous gaps.

In the face of gaps, it seems reasonable to look to history. Indeed, any conception of constitutional meaning should make our history relevant. Here too the justification is, as it must be, self-consciously political; we make the history count because there are good reasons for doing so. If the text is binding because it imposes constraints on the judges and limits the arbitrary exercise of judicial power, it appears to follow that where the document is unclear, interpreters should also give weight to the historical understanding of the meaning of that text.

This device is a means of disciplining judicial judgments and of giving deference to the considered judgments of the past citizenry. It reflects an appropriate degree of humility and a respect for (somewhat) democratic processes involving a large number of people in the past. In this sense, those who insist on the "original understanding" are appealing to a lasting and incontrovertible truth—not because the founders saw things this way, but because there are good political arguments for so seeing things.

But there are major limits to the usefulness of history in constitutional law. For one thing, the particular history behind a constitutional provision becomes less helpful with the passage of time. As the decades elapse, the ratifiers' original understanding, if described at a level of great specificity, is likely to be decreasingly pertinent to constitutional meaning.[37] At that level of specificity, the original understanding will often speak to problems that are no longer even relevant. The particular threats to free speech foremost in the minds of the framers—licensing schemes and other prepublication clearance—are almost nonexistent today. Should the First Amendment therefore be treated as an anachronism?

Moreover, the answers given by originalism to our own dilemmas may turn out to be wrong, in the sense that they are based on thinking that is inadequate to the particular matters at hand. And if we are to be faithful to those very answers, we must translate them into different circumstances that could not have been foreseen. Consider the likely possibility that the ratifiers of the Fourteenth Amendment intended to permit segregation, and the certainty that they intended to permit sex segregation. Must we be limited to these intentions?

Here as elsewhere, history should be taken as binding only to the extent that an interpretive principle to this effect would improve the operation of a constitutional democracy. When a good deal of time has passed, the history, narrowly conceived, is unlikely to do this.

This does not mean that judges should do whatever they want, or that the history becomes irrelevant. It continues to inform the meaning of the text, especially if the pertinent constitutional goals can be described at a relatively high level of generality. We might do well, for example, to take the equal protection clause as an effort to eliminate caste systems in America (see Chapter 11), to see the takings clause as a commitment to existing holdings of property (see Chapter 5), or to understand the First Amendment as centered on democratic self-government (see Chapter 8). All these positions are strengthened precisely because there is historical support for them. People who adopt these positions are restricted in their discretion and are able to draw from considered judgments of past polities. Courts should play a limited role in a constitutional democracy. One way to limit that role is to create a system in which the judges try to draw on history.

In enterprises of this sort, however, the best characterization of the history—like the best characterization of the text—will have evaluative dimensions and be a function of substantive interpretive principles. The search for justifications will not be entirely untethered or open-ended; it should not be merely "what the judge thinks." Always there is (for good reasons) an overriding commitment of fidelity to text, structure, and history, and these will discipline the inquiry. But the discipline is not a straitjacket. Reasonable people will differ. And in solving those differences that remain, interpretive principles must have some other source.

CHAPTER 5

Interpreting the Constitution: Substance

How should constitutional law proceed if it is not always to take existing distributions as the baseline for analysis? If ownership rights are a creation of law, which, if any, of current constitutional understandings should be abandoned? What is the basis for the relevant interpretive principles?

My most general response is that such principles should be derived from the general commitment to deliberative democracy. This commitment provides a clue to the original constitutional structure. It was deepened and strengthened by the Civil War amendments and the New Deal itself. The commitment helps to explain when an aggressive role for the Constitution is most appropriate. It also explains why courts should usually be reluctant to intrude into politics. In this chapter I explain how the commitment to deliberative democracy might help resolve concrete controversies, including those raised by affirmative action, welfare rights, education, rationality review, and the state action doctrine.

In the abstract, status quo neutrality is hard to defend. Existing distributions are partly a product of law, and they are frequently unjust. In this light there are three principal alternatives to the courts' reflexive resort to the status quo: to abandon all baselines altogether, to defend the use of existing distributions in terms other than those offered thus far, or to develop baselines for use in constitutional law through an approach not necessarily wedded to or based on existing distributions.

Law without Baselines? Holmes and Others

It is tempting to think that the Supreme Court should play no role in deciding whether existing distributions should be changed. This view has a distinguished pedigree. It is associated with prominent strands in the New Deal and the legal realist movement, and it was clearly presaged by Holmes's *Lochner* opinion. It also appears prominently in Learned Hand's celebrated lectures on the Bill of Rights, James Landis' influential work on administrative law, and the opinions of Justice Felix Frankfurter.[1] This view has enjoyed a renaissance in the 1990s.

Under what we might call the Holmesian view, it does not matter, for constitutional purposes, whether the state is reaffirming or rejecting the common law, or whether it is dramatically changing, or instead protecting, the current set of legal entitlements. The abandonment of common law baselines means an abandonment of baselines altogether, at least for constitutional law. Neutrality is not required, because it cannot be achieved. Legal rules are for political rather than judicial determination.

Sometimes this view is founded on interest-group pluralism. Neutrality, understood as a requirement of public-regarding legislation, is inconsistent with the very nature of politics, which consists of self-interested deals. Judicial intrusions are fundamentally undemocratic; democracy itself entails "deals" unsupported by any real justifications. We have seen that Holmes himself was committed to this understanding of politics.

More recently, and more dramatically, the abandonment of baselines has been urged by people skeptical about the notion of objectivity and about distinctions of any kind between reason and power.[2] For those skeptical about objectivity, neutrality and related ideas inevitably represent failed efforts to stake out a position that is itself political and likely to reflect some kind of social interest. In its most extreme form, this latter position is reflected in a wide range of work questioning the legacy of the Enlightenment, work that has been especially influential in literary criticism.

Let us take Holmesianism and the more extreme view in sequence. Approaches that follow Holmes certainly have the advantage of ease of administration, because they tell courts to abandon the field to politics. Such approaches are even reflected in some current law under the contracts, due process, and takings clauses, which, as we have seen, show enormous deference to the legislature. Because they counsel respect for politics, they can claim as well a proper appreciation of democratic values. The Holmesian position is of course reflected in traditional understandings of the lesson of the *Lochner* period and of the New Deal itself, which is often taken as a confirmation of the need for courts to yield to democratic consensus.

In so broad a form, however, this position is unacceptable precisely because it is based on crude understandings of American constitutionalism and of the workings of majoritarian government. At its inception, the Madisonian structure was far from an endorsement of interest-group conceptions of politics. On the contrary, its purpose was to ensure against a system of government as interest-group deals. The Holmesian position has a weak historical pedigree.

Nor is majoritarianism, in its Holmesian formulation, easy to defend on grounds of principle. Suppose, for example, that the purpose of politics is indeed to aggregate private preferences, and that this is what we want our political system ultimately to accomplish. There are severe difficulties in obtaining such an aggregation through majority rule—certainly as it operates in practice, and even in its ideal form. Collective action problems—the fact that some groups are very well organized and others are not organized at all—will make it hard to ensure that politics accurately aggregates private preferences.[3] There is significant slippage between constituent pressures and legislative outcomes. What happens in Congress does not always track "what the people want."

The field of social choice theory, given birth by work for which Kenneth Arrow won the Nobel Prize, has shown another problem. In a multimember body, no single outcome will represent the desires of the people. Cycling problems, the order in which issues arise, strategic behavior, and sheer chance will prevent the process of aggregation from having any unitary solution.[4]

Even worse, for the Holmesian view, is the difficulty of defending the view that politics should attempt to aggregate preferences. Some preferences, for example, ought not to be counted; consider sadism or racial bigotry. One of the functions of both democracy and judicial review is to minimize the effect of such preferences, or to ensure that they are "laundered" through processes of deliberation, including political discussion and debate. A central task of politics is to identify preferences that are distorted by various factors or that have objectionable effects if translated into law.[5]

The Holmesian approach would of course result in a failure to enforce constitutional provisions that are intended as limits on the ability of government to restructure or to fail to restructure the existing order. The resulting position would amount to an abandonment of constitutionalism altogether. Its emphasis on democracy is important; but its crude and conclusory references to the primacy of electoral outcomes are insufficient to support that abandonment.

So much for Holmesianism. What about the more extreme modern attack on baselines? We might loosely describe this attack as a version of postmodernism—recognizing that the postmodern position has many different incarnations, and that it is not always easy to understand exactly what is being asserted. In law, the postmodern position overlaps with the contemporary emphasis on "indeterminacy," discussed in Chapter 4. I make a few brief additional observations here.[6]

First, any position about law and politics, to be worth holding, must be justified by reference to reasons. We should not consider the category of "reasons" to be a narrow one, or to be strictly Cartesian; but a view unsupported by reasons is unlikely to be a view deserving consideration. In many forms, however, the postmodern position appears largely to reject the process of reason-giving altogether, and to put in its place play, power, or conventions.[7] The substitution is likely to be unproductive for law and politics. It ensures that postmodernists "can give no account of the normative foundations of [their] own rhetoric."[8]

Second, the fact that there is no wholly external point of view—no place outside the world from which to view the world—does not mean that we are left in an abyss, with the free play of conflicting perspectives, or with the Tower of Babel. Instead the absence of a wholly external perspective means simply that participants in law and politics must discuss what they always have: the effects of different systems on the lives of human beings who are affected by law and politics. For purposes of constitutional law, baselines should be generated from this inquiry.

Third, stability is not an intrinsic social evil, and fluidity is not an intrinsic social good. Everything depends on the particular thing that is being stabilized (sex equality?) or made fluid (rights of free speech?). Sometimes postmodernism prizes fluidity and transformation in themselves, and offers these as foundations for constitutional practice.[9] To the extent that it does so, it seems to point in the wrong directions.

Most generally, the valuable postmodern claims tend to be not postmodern at all, but instead part of the philosophical heritage of pragmatism. The pragmatic heritage consists in the critique of metaphysical realism, that is, the view that human beings have unmediated access to the world without the aid of their own interpretive filters.[10] Pragmatism hardly calls for a general attack on the efforts of human beings to develop baselines by which to distinguish between partisanship and neutrality. On the contrary, it helps to orient that effort. It insists that human categories, in law and elsewhere, are humanly constructed. But it understands this point as the beginning of the effort to construct our categories well, by reference to our goals and needs, and not as a reason to abandon the whole enterprise.

Status Quo Neutrality: Defenses

Thus far I have treated the courts' use of the status quo as if it were reflexive or unreasoned, or a product of patterns of thinking that have been internalized before there is an opportunity even to think about them. This is often a correct description of the situation. But it would be wrong to think that this conception of neutrality is never defended. Four defenses seem especially plausible. None of them, however, establishes as much as it claims.

PRAGMATIC CONSIDERATIONS

Sometimes it is urged that changes in the status quo will be futile or more likely counterproductive. This concern does not rest on a belief in a natural or just private sphere. The fear is that any changes will have unanticipated bad consequences—perhaps hurting the very people one wants to help, perhaps harming some group not before the court, or perhaps having other harmful effects.[11]

This concern is reflected in many different ideas. The minimum wage may increase unemployment, and thus harm the least advantaged in society. Aggressive desegregation remedies may increase racial antagonism. The creation of hearing rights for government employees may reduce salaries for government employees. Judicial protection against sex discrimination may demobilize the women's movement and spur its opponents.

It is surely right to warn that any change from the status quo may have unanticipated consequences. This fact does offer an important reason for caution. But the possibility that the change will be counterproductive is far too abstract and contingent to provide a general reason for status quo neutrality. Of course interference with any status quo, whether by judges or others, may fail to do what one hopes. Of course this is a reason to pause and think. It is no more than that.

Some constitutional provisions are best interpreted as using the status quo as the baseline for deciding cases. It is true that existing distributions are not prepolitical and are sometimes unjust; but this does not undermine the claim that the Constitution protects them—whether or not prepolitical, and even whether or not just.

Return, for example, to the takings clause of the Fifth Amendment. We should insist that to say that no state shall "take private property for public use, without just compensation" is not, without the aid of at least some extratextual considerations, to say much at all—and even less to proclaim that existing distributions must be used as the baseline for analysis. Whether there is a taking depends on a theory of who owns what. The words of the takings clause do not contain a theory of ownership rights.

Indeed, a state might be thought to "take private property" if it does not ensure that everyone has property and if it uses law to disable the unpropertied from obtaining things. Imagine a society in which the prevailing theory posited a general right to subsistence. In such a world, the takings clause might even provide the basis for a constitutional right to welfare. The words of the clause, construed apart from their context and culture, might in this way support a large-scale, constitutionally mandated plan of redistribution of existing entitlements.

Most people would find this view implausible. They would be right to do so—not because of the bare words of the takings clause, but because of the wild inconsistency of this view with the understanding of those words as they have existed within the legal culture since they were written. The clause was originally understood as a means of protecting against government disruption of whatever holdings people currently had. It has been so understood ever since. To remove the clause from its moorings in existing distributions would therefore repudiate a huge amount of long-standing law. Judges should hesitate before doing that.

Of course the hesitation could be overcome if the long-standing interpretation were conspicuously implausible or unjust. But the notion that a constitutional provision should protect existing holdings of property from governmental disruption seems not merely plausible, but on the contrary fully justified. That notion protects an important form of stability for individuals and for the system at large. It also creates and safeguards expectations that in turn help promote economic planning, investment, and prosperity. Perhaps most fundamentally, it is a way of ensuring a degree of independence from the whim of the state, which is a precondition for the practice of citizenship. A system in which private property is open to freewheeling public readjustment may well subject all citizens to open-ended state power. This form of insecurity introduces a kind of serfdom that is debilitating to democracy itself.

In this light, an interpretation of the takings clause that fits with its historical understanding hardly makes for absurdity or injustice. The clause is therefore best read to take the status quo as the baseline for decision. Other provisions, most notably the contracts clause, should be interpreted along similar lines. Nothing that I have said suggests that such interpretations are wrong.

STABILITY AND EXPECTATIONS

A decision to take existing distributions as the starting point might be justified very generally, on the ground that a system that respects current distributions will create far more stability than a system that does not. That kind of stability is important for individuals and for society as a whole. As the framers were well aware, a system in which existing distributions of property are continually reexamined is likely to break down along factional lines and also to undermine both individual security and planning for the future.[12] Insecure citizens are not likely to be able to plan at all. Not incidentally, they are not likely to invest, and investment of various sorts is indispensable to prosperity, which is of course a human good. Most generally, coherent reform requires selectivity. Most things (at any single time) must be left unreformed in order for reform movements to be successful.

The status quo, whether or not natural, may well be a basis for legitimate expectations. The rule of law—carving out a realm of security from government—is itself associated with ideas of this sort.[13] And as noted, protection of existing distributions promotes citizenship precisely because it serves the goals of security and independence.

All of this suggests that no state should subject existing distributions to frequent or constant revision. The takings clause is a concrete reflection of the basic point. But this does not support the far more extreme claim that existing distributions should be taken as the baseline from which to decide whether there has been partisanship and neutrality. Security is merely one goal among many. The fact that security is threatened by governmental decisions cannot by itself be decisive. Protection of expectations is surely a good idea, but often the question is whether the relevant expectations are legitimate. Did the expectations of the slaveowners, who relied after all on legal guarantees, argue against abolition? It is hardly clear that employers and the able-bodied have a legitimate expectation to continue workforce requirements that effectively exclude the disabled.

The legal question frequently involves the weight, in the particular case, of the interests in stability and protection of expectations. It is hard to see why the Constitution ought generally to stand in the way of that assessment.

BURKEANISM

The final and most complex defense of status quo baselines has its origins in Edmund Burke; it is also elaborated in the work of Friedrich Hayek.[14] Justice Antonin Scalia appears to speak most clearly for this view today.[15] The central point is that the status quo and existing practice have a kind of rich complexity and wisdom that no critic is in a position to appreciate. Current practices have developed through the work of millions of people over (at least) hundreds of years. They therefore profit from a collective intelligence that will transcend what any single mind, or particular set of minds, can hope to produce.

The tradition operates as a sort of market, capturing simultaneously the seemingly uncoordinated desires and beliefs of many people who have thought long and hard about different problems. Just as a single government attempting to decide the correct price for a good is much inferior to the uncoordinated efforts of people in the marketplace, so a single court or government, attempting to evaluate existing practices, will make terrible mistakes.

This view also provides a valuable cautionary note. It correctly suggests that reformers might overlook something of value in existing practices. We should be humble about reform proposals developed by few people or over short periods; current practices may have more to offer than at first appears. But Burkeanism is far too broad and general to generate a useful approach to constitutional law. Sometimes existing practices are the result not of a rich rationality, but instead of such things as sheer chance; economic, physical, and social power; injustice; and the arbitrary sequence of events.

To take only the most obvious example, the system of segregation could not readily be justified on Burkean grounds, however long it may have persisted. Far from representing a wise social response to the complexities of race relations, it was a mechanism for perpetuating the system of white supremacy. To say this is not to say that Burkean arguments were not offered in this setting; indeed, they were all too common. Their very commonness in that context suggests that Burkean arguments are often offered on behalf of practices that do not really have a good defense. This is especially true for systems of sex discrimination, for which these arguments have often been made in the last generation. Whether such systems should be reformed depends not merely on whether they are long-standing, but instead on the arguments that might be made in their support.

Nor would it be right to take the limitations of human reason as a justification for the status quo, or for thinking that current practice embodies a kind of wisdom inaccessible to people who claim to evaluate them. To be sure, reform efforts are inevitably situated within the world, but this does not mean that reformers are unable to think about what it would be like to live in a world different from our own. To say that everyone in a position of evaluation lives within a culture is hardly to say that no one can assess what it means to operate within that culture.

At least in law, modern Burkeans are simultaneously far too optimistic about current practices and far too pessimistic about the capacities of reason. And while some constitutional provisions might well be read as protective of tradition, others are self-conscious restrictions on tradition; and the tradition-rejecting aspirations should be respected. I return to this point below.

ROLE DIFFERENTIATION
It might be argued that status quo neutrality follows from an appropriate allocation of authority between judges and legislators. We might begin with the proposition that law is different from politics in the following, simple way: Some issues are, for good reasons, ruled off limits to judges, even though these issues are properly taken up by other government officials. A judge in a contract case usually pays no attention to the wealth of the parties, even though wealth might well be relevant for other officials deciding other questions. This is a basic idea of role differentiation; it may well have consequences for status quo neutrality. We might conclude, for example, that the question

whether to alter the status quo is to be answered by politically accountable officials. Judges, at least, should respect existing practice, whether or not it is ultimately justified. Status quo neutrality is correct, not because the status quo is good, but because it is to be evaluated by the democratic process rather than by the judiciary.

There is much truth to this general view. It is indeed right to think that the distinction between law and politics consists of a judgment to put certain considerations off limits to judges (though this judgment must always be defended). It is also right to think that in many cases, courts should not deem themselves authorized to engage in a wholesale evaluation of the status quo, or of existing social practices. Many things should indeed be held constant. But these points, important as they are, do not justify status quo neutrality.

The first problem is that some constitutional provisions should be taken in whole or in part as self-conscious revisions of the status quo. It is therefore perverse to use existing practice as the basis for giving meaning to those provisions. The equal protection clause is the best example. As we have seen, this provision was designed to revise existing allocations of authority as between blacks and whites; it should not be defined by reference to those allocations. The second problem goes deeper. Even when the Constitution should not be used to revise existing practice, courts should allow legislatures to do so—and often courts do indeed invoke the Constitution, read by reference to status quo neutrality, as a barrier. Consider, for example, the view that the First Amendment forbids Congress from regulating broadcasters in order to increase diversity of view and attention to public affairs (see Chapter 7). The notion of role differentiation hardly justifies a judicial decision to prohibit this form of experimentation. That notion is far too general to amount to a defense of status quo neutrality.

If Holmesianism is rejected, there is only one real alternative. That alternative would call for an attempt to generate baselines through some theory of the meaning of the Constitution not necessarily rooted in the status quo. Approaches of this sort might understand the Constitution as a unit, to be treated as reflecting a single overarching theory. It would be far more sensible, however, to proceed provision by provision, acknowledging that different provisions are aimed at different problems. It would then be necessary to develop theories for each constitutional clause. The constitutional text would be the basis for an approach that might be independent of the status quo and could serve as a basis for evaluating it.

Such an approach would force us to ask how the issue of natural-ness is relevant to a legal question. It is important here to understand some of the complexities in the use of "nature" or "the natural" as the basis for evaluating social practices. In classical philosophy, nature was a normative notion; it connoted human flourishing in connection with a certain kind of activity, and with lack of obstacles to that flourishing.[16] Nature did not mean an absence of social or legal intervention. In modern political and legal theory, the classical notion of nature as flourishing is sometimes conflated with an altogether different conception of the natural, one that is indeed based on an inquiry into what would happen without social or legal action.

The conflation—an important untold story in the history of juris-prudence and philosophy—creates serious confusion. It would be hard indeed to defend the idea that human beings flourish without social or legal action, or that things are best when law and society do not intervene. Eyeglasses are not natural, but they are not for that reason objectionable. Laws forbidding violence may run against nat-ural impulses, but this does not count as an argument for their repeal. The fact that a practice is artificial hardly means that it should be changed; and the fact that it is in some sense natural is not necessarily a reason to respect it. Naturalness is irrelevant from the moral or legal point of view.

It is sometimes thought that interferences with practices that are an outgrowth of nature are doomed to futility and failure. Sometimes this is true. The law cannot turn men into women, or vice versa. But when existing practices are simply a particular system of social order-ing—or a system of law—they are not themselves nature, and the ob-jection will be irrelevant. If, for example, a preference is revealed simply to be an adaptation to the legal status quo, new legal rules may not be futile; with the new rule, new preferences may emerge. The fact that a practice is a creature of government thus removes some ar-guments for retaining it, though by itself, it is hardly a reason to change it.

Deliberative Democracy

We should develop interpretive principles from the goal of assuring the successful operation of a deliberative democracy. This goal can be traced to the earliest days of the American republic. It has been broad-ened and deepened by important developments since the founding. The governing ideal of deliberative democracy has a close connection with constitutional aspirations as they have been understood at the important periods in our history. An effort to build interpretive principles from this ideal therefore has the advantage of continuity with the Constitution's structure and history. The ideal also has considerable independent appeal.

I will not be attempting to offer a full elaboration and defense of deliberative democracy or to measure it against the many alternative sources of interpretive principles. To undertake such tasks, it would be necessary to set out a complete theory of what government should do. It is unfortunate but true that a fully adequate theory of constitutional interpretation would probably have to do exactly this. My goal here is much more modest. I hope only to set out the commitments of deliberative democracy; to suggest its plausibility, its historical roots, and its general appeal; and to see how it might bear on the development of interpretive principles in various areas of law.

In the United States, the notion of deliberative democracy should be understood with reference to three conspicuous sources.[17] The first is the liberal republicanism that has characterized American public law since the founding period (see Chapter 1).[18] The second is the Civil War and its aftermath. The third is the New Deal reformation of the constitutional system. Through emphasizing these periods, constitutional interpreters can maintain fidelity with the basic document and with its fundamental principles as these have been understood over time.

POLITICAL DELIBERATION

From its inception, liberal republicanism, as embodied in American constitutionalism, has been founded on several commitments. The most important is a belief in political deliberation. We saw in Chapter 1 that in American public law, political outcomes should not be a reflection of the self-interest of well-organized private groups. Nor are they to consist merely in the protection of given or prepolitical private rights. Instead they are to be produced by an extended process of deliberation and discussion, in which new information and new perspectives are brought to bear.

On this view, majority rule should not be understood as the simple translation of existing desires into law. As Dewey wrote, "what is more significant is that counting of heads compels prior recourse to methods of discussion, consultation and persuasion." These methods include "antecedent debate, modification of views to meet the opinions of minorities, the relative satisfaction given the latter by the fact that it has had a chance and that next time it may be successful in becoming a majority."[19] A goal of politics is thus to reflect on and sometimes to change existing preferences, not simply to implement them. Preferences are not static; they are a subject of conversation and debate. People must justify social outcomes by reference to reasons.

As we saw also in Chapter 1, the principle of political deliberation, thus understood, is part and parcel of the original Madisonian conception of politics. It resonates in our governmental institutions, including national representation, checks and balances, federalism, and judicial review. It is connected with the American belief that disagreement and heterogeneity are creative forces, indispensable to a well-functioning republic.

We have also seen that the New Deal extended the commitment to political deliberation through its insistence that the status quo and existing ownership rights could no longer be reflexively accepted or be thought to be part of nature. The status quo, too, may be accepted only on the basis of the reasons that can be brought forward on its behalf. In this respect, the New Dealers subjected the status quo to a version of the impartiality principle, on the antiauthoritarian ground that the distribution of social benefits and social burdens must always be defended by reference to reasons. There is a strong continuity between the republican attack on monarchy and the New Deal challenge to status quo neutrality.

There is nothing in this framework hostile to rights, which are indeed central to American constitutionalism. Rights will often be preconditions for the deliberative process, and therefore not vulnerable to it. Free speech is only the most obvious example. Rights will sometimes be the outcomes of deliberation. But reasons must always be invoked on their behalf.

CITIZENSHIP

From the belief in political deliberation follow three additional commitments. Liberal republicanism prizes citizenship. Of course it does not require that all decisions be made by town meeting; but it refuses to treat political participation as simply another "taste" that some people have, or as dispensable in a well-functioning democracy. For this reason it seeks to ensure that political outcomes benefit from widespread participation by the citizenry. A system in which such participation is lacking is to that extent a failure.

The commitment to citizenship requires that people have a large degree of security and independence from the state. The original constitutional protection of private property was justified in large part on this ground. As we have seen, immunity from the state, in one's basic holdings, is a precondition for the independence that is necessary for the role of citizen. If the state can take property at its whim, the citizenry is likely to be beholden and therefore subject to it. Spurred by this insight, the American "Revolution became a full-scale assault on dependency."[20]

Ideas of this sort do not imply a prohibition on redistribution of wealth. For a society to have the requisite security, it is not necessary for existing holdings to be entirely immune from democratic revision. To take just one example, a progressive income tax hardly endangers citizenship (even if it might be objectionable on other grounds). Indeed, the assault on dependency implies both property rights and social programs designed to ensure that no one is dependent. Poverty brings about very much the same sort of dependency, for the poor, as occurs for people whose holdings are freely subject to government adjustment. Thus a sustained attack on poverty might well grow out of the same concerns that justify the creation of property rights. As discussed below, both Madison and Jefferson insisted on both private property and redistribution.

The commitment to citizenship also helps explain the Fourth Amendment's prohibition on unreasonable searches and seizures. Like the right to private property, this prohibition immunizes the citizen from governmental discretion and control. It creates a sphere of autonomy into which the state may not enter. This sphere helps in turn to guarantee the security on which citizenship depends. Of course the First Amendment protection of freedom of speech is a conspicuous safeguard of the right of citizenship.

The Civil War amendments, with their broad inclusionary features, fortified this original commitment. They can be taken to cast into constitutional doubt all efforts at political exclusion of identifiable groups on the basis of morally irrelevant characteristics. The Fifteenth Amendment prohibition on racial discrimination in voting is the most conspicuous example of this goal. But the Fourteenth Amendment made all persons born or naturalized in the United States into "citizens." And the Thirteenth Amendment abolished involuntary servitude, thus amplifying, in a crucial place, the constitutional effort to create the independence from the will of others that is a precondition for citizenship.

AGREEMENT AS A REGULATIVE IDEAL

Liberal republicanism is also committed to the view that agreement is a regulative ideal for politics. Liberal republicans reject the view that political differences are merely matters of perspective, situation, or taste. They believe that there are frequently correct answers to political controversy. Answers are understood to be correct through the only possible criterion, that is, agreement among equal citizens.[21] The original notion of political deliberation becomes intelligible only in light of this commitment. If all we have are differences or similarities in perspective, deliberation is pointless.

POLITICAL EQUALITY

The final commitment is to political equality, and here things become a bit more complex. At a minimum, the commitment to political equality, viewed through the lens of deliberative democracy, bans large disparities in the political influence held by different social groups. Madison thus defined a republic as "a government which derives all its powers directly or indirectly from the great body of the people; and is administered by persons holding their offices during pleasure, for a limited period, or during good behavior. It is *essential* to such a government that it be derived from the great body of the society, not from an inconsiderable proportion, or a favored class of it. . . . It is *sufficient* for such a government that the persons administering it be appointed, either directly or indirectly, by the people. . . ."[22]

On Madison's view, disenfranchisement is therefore banned. This was also a central lesson of the Civil War amendments, which gave new and more concrete meaning to the Madisonian claim. The commitment to political equality has implications for many issues. Above all, it bears on freedom of speech. As we will see in Chapter 7, our current conception of freedom of speech often disserves the ideal of political equality. A far more sustained commitment to equality in the distribution of political influence is therefore consistent with the legacy of the founding document.

That commitment also bears on the question of access to a good education. It suggests that such access is indeed connected with constitutional aspirations, even if courts should play a limited role. As we will see below, there is room for government initiatives designed to provide freedom in the formation of preferences and values, and precisely in the interest of the constitutional principle of political equality.

A guarantee of political equality does not, however, translate into a guarantee of economic equality. Egalitarianism, as a political creed, is foreign to liberal republicanism as it has been understood in American public law. The rejection of egalitarianism—defined as an effort to ensure against large disparities in wealth and resources—is based on three principal goals: to promote liberty,[23] to provide incentives for productive work, and to reward and recognize achievement and excellence. Insofar as constitutional proposals have egalitarianism as their foundations—and they hardly ever do—they are indeed inconsistent with the liberal republicanism that undergirds American public law. Nothing in the Civil War or New Deal periods compromised this basic understanding.

On the other hand, the insistence on political equality does have connections to what can happen in the economic sphere. These connections help to identify and make intelligible three narrower conceptions of equality that do play an important role in American law.

The first principle is a belief in *freedom from desperate conditions*. No one should be deprived of adequate police protection, food, shelter, or medical care. These are universal human needs, to be met in any just society.[24] This principle is hardly egalitarian, since it allows large variations in living standards. But it does protect people from falling below a specified floor. This commitment is closely connected to the belief in deliberative democracy and indeed the commitment to citizenship. A modest minimum of food, medical care, and shelter is necessary for people who hope to obtain the status of citizens. People without these advantages cannot attain that role at all. And on this view, the very ideas that support a right to private property also call for governmental protection against desperation.

The belief in this form of freedom is not a twentieth-century creation. It was enthusiastically endorsed by both Jefferson and Madison—a point worth emphasizing in a period in which the welfare state is often said to be inconsistent with our founding aspirations. Jefferson wrote, "I am conscious that an equal division of property is impracticable. But the consequences of this enormous inequality producing so much misery to the bulk of mankind, legislatures cannot invest too many devices for subdividing property, only taking care to let their subdivisions go hand in hand with the natural affections of the human mind. . . . *Another means of silently lessening the inequality of property is to exempt all from taxation below a certain point, and to tax the higher portions of property in geometrical progression as they rise.* Whenever there is in any country, uncultivated lands and unemployed poor, it is clear that the laws of property have been so far extended as to violate natural right. The earth is given as a common stock for man to labor and live on."[25]

Consider also Madison's list of the means of combatting the "evil of parties": "1. By establishing a political equality among all. 2. By withholding unnecessary opportunities from a few, to increase the in-equality of property, by an immoderate, and especially an unmerited, accumulation of riches. 3. By the *silent* operation of laws, which, without violating the rights of property, reduce extreme wealth towards a state of mediocrity, and raise extreme indigence towards a state of comfort."[26]

It was Roosevelt's second Bill of Rights, outlined in Chapter 2, that embodied this freedom in its canonical form. Notably, the second Bill of Rights was designed for legislative rather than judicial enforcement. Here the role of the judiciary is necessarily limited, for courts lack the electoral legitimacy and the basic tools to introduce and manage a social welfare state on their own. But the Constitution is not entirely an irrelevance.

Even if courts are not to guarantee this form of liberty, Congress and the President may well take heed of it as part of their own consti-tutional obligations. And judicial interpretation of statutes often op-erates in the shadow of the Constitution. The Constitution sets out the background principles in whose light ambiguous statutory terms will be read. Courts should therefore interpret hospitably, rather than grudgingly, those measures that reflect a legislative effort to implement the second Bill of Rights.

The second equality principle is an *opposition to caste systems*. In the American tradition, caste systems are traditionally disfavored. The Fourteenth Amendment expresses this aspiration most straight-forwardly. Indeed, the opposition to caste is the defining feature of the Civil War Amendments. But the general idea is traceable to the earliest days of the American republic.[27] Here, too, the idea is closely con-nected with the broader commitment to deliberative democracy. A caste system is inconsistent with that commitment. It denies the prin-ciples of citizenship and political equality (see Chapter 11).

The final principle involves *rough equality of opportunity*. Having rejected the egalitarian principle, we might nonetheless insist that the life prospects of a child born to one family in one part of the country should not be radically different from those of another child born to another family elsewhere. In America, this was a central theme in the framing period itself. The attack on the monarchical legacy was founded on a belief that human differences were often a product of differences in opportunities. It followed that differences in opportunities should be equalized.[28]

Of course it is inevitable that in a liberal society, different families will have different resources and education, and these differences will impose a sharp constraint on the basic principle. Nonetheless, there is much that government can do to help. It can ensure that good education is available to all. It can promote awareness and understanding of public issues and a capacity, on the part of all citizens, actually to affect outcomes. It can create training programs so as to give solid prospects to people born in average or below-average conditions. It can minimize rather than increase the risk that economic differences will translate into large disparities in the life prospects of different citizens.

The role of courts in this process will be limited. But some cases raise relevant issues. Consider in this connection one of the most important decisions of the post–World War II era, *San Antonio Independent School District v. Rodriguez.*[29] In that case, the Court was confronted with a system of school financing based on property taxes imposed by local school districts. The result was substantial interdistrict disparities in per-pupil expenditures—with variations ranging from $558 to $248 per pupil. The Court rejected the equal protection challenge to the system. In the process, it suggested that rough equality of educational opportunity was not a constitutional imperative. But there is a close connection between education and constitutionally specified rights, and equality in basic life prospects is a clear theme of the Civil War amendments. In this light, the Court erred in failing to require at least a solid justification for the Texas funding system.

More important, the meaning of the Constitution outside the courtroom bears on the obligations of government to provide roughly equal educational opportunity. The President, Congress, and state government should be encouraged to adhere to that principle, which is systematically violated in modern America. Perhaps courts, for institutional reasons, ought to play a minor role; this idea supplies the best argument for *Rodriguez* itself. But only a bizarre fixation on judges could make *Rodriguez* decisive on the question of the constitutional duties of nonjudicial institutions. The Constitution thus bears importantly on efforts to improve and equalize public education.

The commitments of liberal republicanism—to deliberation, citizenship, agreement as a regulative ideal, and political equality—embody the principles of deliberative democracy. These commitments can draw on diverse starting points; this is no sectarian creed. The liberalism of Mill and Rawls is entirely compatible with the account that I have offered. Certain forms of utilitarianism[30] place a high premium on political deliberation, prize political equality, and do not take existing preferences and distributions as the basis for social choice. Thus understood, utilitarianism is fully compatible with liberal republicanism.

John Dewey emphasized the need to develop a conception of liberty dedicated to establishing the social preconditions for political deliberation.[31] This form of pragmatism has close links to the constitutional tradition I am describing. The contemporary revival of Aristotelianism[32] is rooted in the perceived need to create social institutions to allow development of the capabilities of all citizens. This approach to political life will lead to the four commitments I have described. The fact that the commitments can draw from so wide a variety of traditions surely adds to their general appeal. It is even more important that these commitments have been given shape and direction through the defining moments of American constitutionalism.

We can see too that one of the basic points of deliberative democracy is to develop salutary human characters and characteristics. Sometimes liberal constitutionalism is praised because it responds accurately to "human nature" and does not try to tinker with it. On this view, it is neutral as among different possible human natures. There is something to this idea. Efforts fundamentally to revise human character are usually doomed to failure, and often they end up in tyranny. But liberal constitutionalism is best understood and defended, not on the ground that it is neutral among types, but on the quite different ground that it has healthy effects on human character. Democracy itself tends to inculcate valuable characteristics in human beings. John Stuart Mill was insistent on the point. And John Rawls has emphasized that liberal institutions influence "people's deepest aspirations" and "can have decisive long-term social effects and importantly shape the character and aims of the members of society, the kinds of persons that they are and want to be."[33]

Deliberative Democracy and Interpretive Principles

Might it be possible to derive interpretive principles from these ideas? An enterprise of this sort would benefit from close attention to history. It would also have considerable support as a matter of principle. A system that actually realized the commitments of liberal republicanism would simultaneously promote those aspects of our great traditions, liberalism and republicanism, that have the strongest claim to contemporary support. Such a system would promote an appealing conception of liberty. It would also embody some powerful conceptions of equality. A particular virtue is that constitutional liberty and constitutional equality would be understood in such as way as to be in no tension at all.

Of course an enormous amount of work would remain to defend and give content to these ideas. I will attempt to carry out this task, at least in a preliminary way, in Part II of this book. And of course any role for the judiciary would have to take account not simply of substantive principles, but also of the properly limited place of the courts in any system of American government. But at least we have a place to begin.

It appears as well that the much-vaunted opposition between constitutionalism and democracy, or between rights and democracy,[34] tends on this account to dissolve entirely. Many rights are indispensable to democracy and to democratic deliberation. If we protect such rights through the Constitution, we do not compromise self-government at all. On the contrary, self-government depends for its existence on firmly protected democratic rights. Constitutionalism can thus guarantee the preconditions for democracy by limiting the power of majorities to eliminate those preconditions.[35]

Moreover, rights-based constraints on the political process are necessary for a well-functioning democracy; they are not antithetical to it. Unchecked majoritarianism should not be identified with democracy. A system in which majorities are allowed to repress the views of those who disagree could hardly be described as democratic.

From the commitment to deliberative democracy, it follows that the case for an aggressive role for courts is especially strong in two classes of cases. The first involves rights that are central to the democratic process and whose abridgment is therefore unlikely to call up a political remedy. Governmental interference with the right to vote or the right to speak calls for active judicial protection of the background conditions for political deliberation, political equality, and citizenship. The point suggests that our interpretive principles ought to be especially attuned to harmful effects on the system of free expression and on political participation and representation. In these cases, courts should not adopt the normal attitude of deference to legislative processes.

At least a supplemental judicial role in the provision of roughly equal educational opportunity also follows from the commitment to deliberative democracy. Because protection of private property is a precondition for security from the state and thus for citizenship, firm protection of property rights would be similarly justified in a system emerging from (say) Communism. But in the Anglo-American culture, the institutions of private property and civil society are firmly in place. A democratic justification for aggressive protection of property rights seems implausible under current conditions.[36]

The second category involves groups or interests that are unlikely to receive a fair hearing in the legislative process. If a group faces obstacles to organization or pervasive prejudice or hostility—for example, homosexuals—it would be wrong to indulge the ordinary presumption in favor of democratic outcomes. Courts should give close scrutiny to governmental decisions that became possible only because certain groups face excessive barriers to exercising political influence. Such scrutiny is justified in the interest of democracy itself. The anticaste principle will play a critical role in this assessment.

In *Democracy and Distrust*,[37] John Hart Ely set out suggestions very much like these, and I have drawn on his treatment here. Ely's theory has been criticized on a number of grounds. It seems correct to say, as against that theory, that the choice of democracy as the source of interpretive principles is itself a substantive value. This is a point that Ely, apparently following the familiar conception of interpretive neutrality, tended to obscure, in part because his treatment reflects a kind of skepticism about value judgments that, if taken seriously, would in the end prove fatal to his own enterprise. We must therefore try to justify the substantive values of democracy, in order to support the view that democracy should be the foundation for interpretive principles.

It also seems correct to say, against Ely, that democracy is far from a self-defining idea. Any particular conception of democracy has to be defended as the right one, rather than simply identified with the general idea itself. A pervasive problem with Ely's account is that his own conception of democracy is never defended, but simply understood to be an inevitable reading of the general ideal. Courts need a quite particular conception of democracy in order to decide cases. There is always a risk that their conception will be parochial or misconceived.

It is right, too, to insist that any theory of the role of constitutionalism cannot simply point to the existence of politically disadvantaged groups, or of prejudice, as if these were simply brute facts. Any claim of disadvantage, of prejudice, or of insufficient influence is a value-laden one requiring defense. We need a self-consciously substantive theory to identify the features of a system without disadvantage, prejudice, or sufficient influence. The notion of "excessive barriers to political influence" has a misleadingly procedural character. When we say that someone is "prejudiced," we are often making a moral judgment about their view. The word *prejudice* should not obscure the fact that our moral judgment needs to be defended. Sometimes Ely uses that word as a placeholder for a moral theory that is not fully identified or justified.

Finally, it seems correct to emphasize, as against Ely, that the American system should not be considered one of interest-group pluralism, with the courts assuming what Ely describes as an "antitrust" role of assuring the conditions for political competition. The deliberative aspirations of the system require the courts to do something other than provide a fair system of horse-trading. A careful judicial role is appropriate not when there is exclusion from competition, but instead when deliberation is impaired.

None of these claims, however, fundamentally damages the view that interpretive principles should be based first and foremost on considerations of democracy. We should agree that this is a substantive choice requiring a defense; this is to open the discussion, not to close it. To say that one's conception of democracy needs to be defended is to ask for further exploration about how to implement any system of constitutional interpretion that takes democracy as its starting point. To say that deliberation is required is only to ask how courts and other institutions might promote that aspiration.

I take up many of these issues in Part II. At this point, I suggest only that an insistence on the democratic character of American constitutionalism provides the right source of interpretive principles. In most cases that view would lead to judicial caution. In others it would lead to a more aggressive role. In all cases it would provide a helpful orientation.

If interpretive principles are generally to grow out of democratic commitments, it follows that a judicial role in social reform will frequently be unjustified. We might even be able to generate a set of criticisms of an aggressive role for the judiciary in the name of the Constitution. These criticisms will help in the development of interpretive principles.

Institutional Limits of Courts

Courts have serious institutional limits, and these argue against a major judicial role in social reform. Three problems are of special interest.

DEMOCRACY, CITIZENSHIP, COMPROMISE

Reliance on the courts may impair democratic channels for seeking changes, and in two ways. It might divert energy and resources from politics, and the eventual judicial decision may foreclose a political outcome.

On both counts, the impairment of democracy can be very serious. The resort to politics tends to mobilize citizens on public matters, and the mobilization is good for individuals and society as a whole. It can inculcate political commitments, broader understandings, feelings of citizenship, and dedication to the community. An emphasis on the judiciary often compromises these values. Judicial foreclosure of political outcomes might well have corrosive effects on democratic processes. In this connection it is important to recall that Martin Luther King was quite possibly a far more important source of constitutional change than any or even all of the Warren Court's race decisions.[38]

In any case, political channels are often far better for sensible and effective reform. Individual values can more easily be reflected in outcomes that are beneficial to diverse groups and interests. And if questions of morality tend to become questions of constitutional law, their resolution before nine judges can be harmful to the practice of citizenship. Some of this effect is already visible in the context of the abortion controversy. The Supreme Court's partial retreat from *Roe v. Wade* has spurred the women's movement in extremely important ways. There is increasing evidence that the same is true in the context of race discrimination. The inhospitality of the current federal judiciary has led civil rights advocates to think about more creative, imaginative, and long-term solutions. These will involve ideas and tools ill suited to the judiciary.

In an influential book, Ronald Dworkin defended an active role for the judiciary on the theory that the Supreme Court is the "forum of principle," countering the horse-trading characteristic of interest-group politics.[39] But the Court was never intended to be the only principled institution in American government. Nor has it been the only such institution in our history. On the contrary, the major reflections of principled deliberation in the American history have come from Congress and the President, not the courts. In the twentieth century the labor movement, the New Deal, the environmental movement, the deregulation movement, and the women's movement are simply a few examples.

In the 1960s and 1970s it became commonplace for constitutional lawyers to oppose a principled, deliberative judiciary to a reflexive, interest-ridden political process. Some such view developed into a staple of academic commentary on the Court.[40] One problem with this position is that it amounts to a counsel of despair; it gives up too quickly and with too little evidence on the possibilities of democratic politics. It also disregards the phenomenon, frequently observed in practice, of deliberative government. We have seen that the belief in deliberative politics has been central to American constitutionalism since its inception. There is no sufficient reason to abandon that belief now.

I do not deny that judicial review can make up for systemic inequalities in majoritarian processes or introduce principles that come to such processes only with difficulty. But an aggressive Court is the furthest thing from an unambiguous good; and this is so even if the Court's goals are sound.

EFFICACY

Judicial decisions are often surprisingly ineffective in bringing about social change. Study after study has documented this conclusion.[41] *Brown v. Board of Education* is usually taken as a counterexample. The Court's decision in *Brown* is often said to have shown the remarkable ability of the federal judiciary to reform large social institutions, and indeed to have abolished apartheid in America.

In fact, however, *Brown* confirms the weak institutional position of the judiciary.[42] Ten years after the decision, no more than about 1.2 percent of black children in the South attended desegregated schools. It was not until 1964, after the involvement of Congress and the executive branch, that there was widespread desegregation.

Of course it is possible that the legislative and executive actions would not have occurred without the spur of *Brown*. But even this is highly uncertain. There is little evidence, direct or indirect, that *Brown* provided an impetus for political action. The example shows that at least ordinarily, the Court is far more effective in vetoing a decision than in attempting to bring about social change on its own.

The decision in *Roe v. Wade* may be another illustration of the Court's limits, though the picture here is mixed. It is undoubtedly true that the decision increased women's access to safe abortions.[43] Surprisingly, however, it did not dramatically increase the actual number and rate of abortions. It is thus inaccurate to say that there have been significantly more abortions as a result of the Supreme Court's decision.

In fact most states were moving in the direction of liberal abortion laws well before *Roe,* resulting in 600,000 lawful abortions per year. Astonishingly, the rate of increase in *legal* abortions was higher in the three years before that decision than in the three years after. It may well have been the case that states would generally have legalized abortion without *Roe.* Perhaps more fundamentally, the decision probably contributed to the creation of the "moral majority"; helped defeat the Equal Rights Amendment; prevented the eventual achievement of consensual solutions to the abortion problem; and severely undermined the women's movement, by defining that movement in terms of the single issue of abortion, by spurring and organizing opposition, and by demobilizing potential adherents.

There is much evidence for these propositions. Consider the extraordinary public reaction to the Supreme Court's *Webster* decision, in which the Court retreated from *Roe.*[44] The Court's partial retreat may well have galvanized the women's movement in a way that will have more favorable and fundamental long-term consequences for sexual equality than anything that could have come from the Supreme Court. To say this is not to say that *Roe* was necessarily wrong, either as a matter of constitutional interpretation or as a matter of principle; in fact I defend the decision, though on grounds of equal protection rather than privacy, in Chapter 9. But its effectiveness has been limited, largely because of its judicial source. Effectiveness bears in turn on the development of appropriate interpretive principles.

THE NARROWING FOCUS OF ADJUDICATION
Adjudication is an exceptionally poor system for achieving large-scale social reform. Courts are rarely experts in the area at hand. Moreover,

the focus on the litigated case makes it hard for judges to understand the complex, often unpredictable effects of legal intervention. Knowledge of these effects is crucial but sometimes inaccessible. A decision to require expenditures on school busing might, for example, divert resources from an area with an equal or greater claim to public resources—including medical and welfare programs for the poor. Creation of a legal right against pollution may have a variety of harmful and unintended effects, including greater unemployment, more poverty, and higher prices.

Ideas of this sort provide some support for the Court's aversion to the recognition of so-called positive rights. Judicial enforcement of such rights would have harmful effects on other programs, many of them quite important. Such effects can be taken into account by legislators and administrators, but rarely by judges.

Moreover, legal thinking and legal procedures are most comfortable with ideas, growing out of the tradition of compensatory justice, that are poorly adapted to the achievement of serious social reform. On the compensatory model, A injures B; B must restore the status quo ante by making payment. As discussed in more detail in Chapter 11, this way of thinking cannot achieve much in the way of social reform. For example, the problem of discrimination is usually not the commission of particular acts of discrimination by identifiable actors at identifiable times to identifiable victims. It is instead the existence of castelike systems. Constitutional adjudication is ill adapted to undertaking the necessary changes.

These considerations bear on the development of interpretive principles with which to give meaning to ambiguous constitutional provisions. They suggest that courts should be cautious in giving broad meaning to open-ended phrases whenever such a meaning would require courts to undertake large-scale social reform on their own. It is obvious that interpretive principles should attempt to reduce judicial discretion. These points suggest that a constitutional democracy ought not to place heavy reliance on the judiciary for tasks of reform.

It will be helpful to draw some distinctions here. Firm protection of the right of free speech draws large support from the aspirations of deliberative democracy. Moreover, it will rarely run afoul of the institutional limits of courts. The narrowing focus of adjudication is not a major obstacle to protection of speech. And if courts interfere with democratic infringements on expression, there will be no important harmful effects on the practice of citizenship.

On the other hand, the creation of a legal right to subsistence would create a range of problems. It is unclear if judicial implementation of that right would actually be successful. The political process must respond, and it may refuse to do so. Courts do not have the tools to choose among the various possible ways of satisfying a subsistence right. They are in a poor position to assess the relationship between that right and other desirable social goals, including the provision of training and employment programs, not to mention incentives for productive work. Judicial recognition of a right to subsistence might also have harmful effects on democratic deliberation about various methods for helping poor people out of poverty; it might even preempt such democratic efforts. A similar analysis applies to a constitutional right to protection against environmental degradation.

The Continuing Importance of Judicial Restraint

I have argued against the Holmesian approach to the Constitution. Courts should not abandon the field. But a less extreme view might take the foregoing points to suggest that in all constitutional cases, it is highly relevant whether the Court is permitting government to act or prohibiting it from doing so. In general, courts should be inclined to uphold legal measures that do not affect existing distributions— just as they should be inclined to validate legislation attempting to disrupt them. A healthy deference to representative government argues in favor of this approach. The parallel of modern decisions to *Lochner* is closest when the Court is invoking status quo baselines to invalidate democratically enacted legislation.

In short: The status quo should generally be subject to democracy. It should not be insulated from democratic deliberation. It is only in rare cases that courts should, on their own, strike down existing distributions when these have been approved by democratic politics. So too, courts should usually allow democratic politics to alter existing distributions.

The argument for upholding the campaign finance law in *Buckley v. Valeo* was therefore quite strong. The case was very close to cases decided during the *Lochner* era, in the sense that the legislature was disrupting existing distributions, and doing so for plausible reasons. Moreover, there was a powerful claim that campaign finance legislation actually promoted democratic goals (see Chapter 7).

Measures calling for "affirmative action" should generally not be thought to raise a serious constitutional issue. When a legislature enacts an affirmative action program, it does not operate against a baseline that is in any sense neutral or just. The current distribution of benefits and burdens along racial lines is partly a product of discrimination, even of a system with castelike features. The text and history of the Fourteenth Amendment do not argue for invalidation of affirmative action programs. On the contrary, the history strongly suggests that such programs are permissible.[45] Efforts to eliminate the second-class citizenship of blacks should hardly be regarded in the same way as efforts to perpetuate it. There is nothing partisan or non-neutral in this claim.

To be sure, many reasonable people think that affirmative action is a bad idea. Such programs can stigmatize their purported beneficiaries, produce unfairness, and bring about a range of other social harms.[46] Often or even usually, it may be best to have a race-neutral policy benefiting the disadvantaged, rather than reserving benefits to members of identified racial groups. But these are questions for the political process, not for courts. The courts should let this difficult issue be decided through democratic means.

Indeed, there are real ironies in the use of the equal protection clause to invalidate affirmative action programs. Most of the constitutional critics of affirmative action urge that constitutional interpretation pay attention to history; but the history of the Fourteenth Amendment strongly suggests that the framers did not intend to prevent affirmative action. Indeed, the federal government that proposed that amendment itself engaged in affirmative action. If we look closely at history, we will be inclined to permit such programs.

Moreover, the constitutional critics of affirmative action generally favor a modest judicial role. But centralized judicial invalidation of programs developed by the President, the Congress, and hundreds of state and local governments hardly promotes the goal of judicial restraint. Democratic considerations strongly argue against an aggressive judicial role in this setting. In general, courts ought not to intrude into state and federal legislative processes where the text and history are ambiguous and where the arguments from basic principle are so unclear.

Similar considerations apply to redistributive measures enacted under the contracts and takings clauses. Notwithstanding recent criticism,[47] current law under both clauses is generally sound. It permits a wide realm of action for legislatures. This is the right conclusion in the face of textual ambiguity, the evident desires of the citizenry, changed circumstances, and the genuine difficulty of the issue as a matter of principle. In all these contexts, an understanding like that in *West*

Coast Hotel (overruling *Lochner;* recall the discussion in Chapter 2) should continue to operate as a "shield" against constitutional attacks on legislation, just as it has in the aftermath of the New Deal.

Thus far I have argued that courts should usually respect legislative efforts to alter the status quo. More difficult questions arise when courts are asked to attack status quo neutrality on their own. In this category can be put all efforts to require the courts to disrupt current distributions on the ground that they are constitutionally unjust. Prominent here is the view that discriminatory effects, without discriminatory intent, are invalid under the equal protection clause. Many arguments in the racial and gender area attempt to use the attack on status quo neutrality as a basis for requesting courts to commandeer government in certain directions.

An especially powerful argument can be made that the criminal law, as currently administered, does indeed deny equal protection of the laws to both blacks and women. It does so because blacks do not have the same protection as whites against criminal violence, and women do not have the same protection as men. It is tempting to say that this is really a problem of private violence, and the Constitution has nothing to say about that. In fact, however, it is the government's deployment of resources that fails to provide the required equal protection. The current situation does indeed violate the constitutional principle.

Especially severe problems are posed by the absence of solid protection against sexual assault, including domestic violence. Here women are deprived of equal protection of the laws. A response from Congress and state legislatures would be necessary to bring about compliance with the Fourteenth Amendment guarantee. But there may be reason for courts to hesitate. Judicial involvement in the situation would raise all the problems of citizenship and efficacy that are introduced by an aggressive judicial role in social reform. I do not argue that courts should necessarily stay out of this difficult area; but there are certainly plausible grounds for them to do so.

In the same category can be placed the claims for welfare rights and the view that some form of "fairness doctrine," offering a private right of access to the media, is constitutionally compelled. In such cases, the fact that the plaintiff is attacking democratic outcomes counts against recognition of the claim. Courts should be far readier to uphold campaign financing, fairness doctrines, affirmative action, or legislation against pornography than to suggest that all of these are constitutionally compelled.

I do not claim that these concerns should control the constitutional question. They are not decisive; they are merely relevant. Constitutional law, as it operates in the courts, is an uneasy mixture of substantive theory and institutional constraint. Constitutional results are not simply a matter of the right general principles; the distinctive position of the judiciary must always be considered. Institutional limits force the courts to limit the scope of substantive constraints on government action.

Understandings of this sort help to account for some otherwise confusing and potentially important decisions of the Supreme Court in its interpretation of section 5 of the Fourteenth Amendment. That section, the great underused provision of the Constitution, allows Congress to "enforce" that amendment "by appropriate legislation." In *Lassiter v. Northampton Election Board*[48] the Supreme Court held that literacy tests did not violate the Fourteenth Amendment. The discriminatory effects of such tests were not impermissible. In *Katzenbach v. Morgan*,[49] however, the Court upheld a congressional ban on literacy tests.

In the most controversial part of the decision, the Court said that Congress has power to interpret the Fourteenth Amendment differently from the Court. The Court was willing to defer to Congress' interpretation. This conclusion appeared to threaten the basic principle, associated with *Marbury v. Madison,* that it is the Court rather than Congress whose interpretation of the Constitution is authoritative and final.

The reasoning of *Katzenbach* can be understood as a recognition that for institutional reasons, the Court will sometimes uphold certain practices even if those practices could justifiably be found unconstitutional by an institution not facing the limits that the judiciary does. If this is right, it should be entirely unsurprising to find that literacy tests are unconstitutional even if the Court would not invalidate them. The notion that discriminatory effects are constitutionally unproblematic *from the Court's point of view* cannot be understood apart from the fact that it would be difficult, even hubristic, for courts to enforce such a prohibition on their own. But other institutions of government do not face those difficulties. Such an institution may well have the constitutional right, even the constitutional duty to understand the equal protection clause more broadly than does the Court.

The framers of the Fourteenth Amendment were entirely correct in thinking that Congress, rather than the courts, should be the principal vehicle for enforcement of the Fourteenth Amendment. In a period in which the Supreme Court approaches that amendment cautiously, it becomes all the more crucial for Congress to take its responsibilities very seriously. In the future, we should see far more legislative attention to the Fourteenth Amendment. Courts should be hospitable to the resulting initiatives.

The Lawyer's Response: The Nature of the Right

We cannot come to terms with status quo neutrality without reading each constitutional provision on its own. Some provisions are best taken to embody status quo neutrality; others are not.

PROVISIONS (BEST TAKEN AS) ROOTED IN EXISTING DISTRIBUTIONS
The takings clause was built on a belief in the importance of protecting private property. We can have many disputes about the clause; but whatever it means, it requires government to pay for whatever property it "takes." For reasons discussed in Chapter 4, we would be hard pressed to read that clause to be rooted in anything other than existing distributions. The same conclusion is appropriate under the contracts clause. That clause forbids impairment of whatever contractual obligations people have created; to this extent, it takes existing distributions as the baseline. At a minimum, then, the takings and contracts clauses cannot easily be read to create a constitutional baseline other than that of the status quo.

The eminent domain and contracts clause, then, are most naturally read to embody status quo neutrality. In their origins and in their judicial development, they have defined property by reference to status quo baselines, not to holdings under an independently defined conception of appropriate rights.

I do not claim that it would be linguistically impossible to remove both provisions from their foundations in status quo neutrality. In particular, courts might recognize the social construction of property and understand the term *takings* against the backdrop set by independent theories of rights and by an appreciation of the particular social functions of private ownership. All of this would be quite complex, but in the end whether there was a taking would depend not solely on the simple fact of previous ownership, but on whether there was a legitimate claim of right to the property in question. It might even be a taking, under the independently defined theory of right, not to furnish a basic level of subsistence.

Changes of this sort would of course call for radical shifts in current law; and they would not be easy to defend. So sharp a departure from previous practices requires very good justification. A principle of this sort disciplines judicial discretion, and it makes perfect sense in a system in which previous practices are not conspicuously unjust. Moreover, we have seen that there are indeed good reasons to protect existing ownership rights from governmental takings.

PROVISIONS REJECTING EXISTING DISTRIBUTIONS

In sharp contrast to the takings and contracts clauses, the equal protection clause is most easily read as a self-conscious rejection of status quo neutrality. The original point of the clause was to break up the system of subordination of blacks. The best interpretation of the clause sees it as a recognition that the existing distribution of authority among the races is both artifactual and illegitimate. The clause is an attack on castelike features of current systems. It is an attack on the status quo.

It should not be surprising that insofar as the challenge to status quo neutrality has played a role in constitutional law, the equal protection clause has almost always been the source of decision. In fact much of equal protection law grows directly out of attacks on existing distributions. Consider not only the challenge to racial discrimination, but also antidiscrimination law involving poverty, illegitimacy, alienage, and perhaps above all gender. The equal protection clause is most obviously a rejection of status quo neutrality, just as the takings and contracts clauses are most obviously its constitutional embodiments.

INTERMEDIATE CASES

Some clauses fall in an intermediate category. The First Amendment is the most important example here. As we will see in more detail, the Court has usually interpreted the clause to embody status quo neutrality. Hence campaign finance laws and efforts to redress the effects of unequal access to the media are generally invalid.

Why has the Court rejected status quo neutrality under the due process clause at the same time that it has vigorously reaffirmed them under the First Amendment? It is too facile to point to the text of the Constitution. To be sure, the First Amendment protects "freedom of speech," but whether regulation of powerful private speakers might sometimes promote freedom of speech is the question to be decided. On the other hand, a wholesale abandonment of status quo neutrality might wreak havoc with existing First Amendment doctrine—as it did earlier in the century with property rights under the due process clause. But there is much room for improvement in our current understandings of freedom of speech. I deal with this issue in detail in Chapters 7 and 8.

The Consequences

Thus far I have suggested that in deciding whether to reject status quo neutrality, it is important to inquire into considerations of democracy, into the judicial role that would result from a decision either way, and into the nature of the particular provision at issue. But the relevant decisions should be affected as well by a broad look at the social consequences.

Consider, for example, recognition of a constitutional right to welfare. We should agree that poverty is in some sense a creation of the state. In any case, the poverty that now exists certainly cannot be blamed on "nature" or described as just. Perhaps the failure to provide basic subsistence should count as a denial of equal protection of the laws. But if it were to follow that welfare was constitutionally guaranteed, the result may be to burden other programs with a good claim to public assistance, to produce unemployment and inflation, and to undermine incentives for labor.

Of course these issues are sharply disputed; but there is a real risk that a right would harm the very people whom courts are trying to protect. We have already seen that a right to welfare would impose on the courts large problems of definition and implementation. These considerations suggest that the right to welfare, if it exists at all, is a good candidate for membership in the class of judicially underenforced constitutional principles.

Another example is discriminatory effects. If the existence of such effects was sufficient to produce invalidity, the social consequences would be enormous. Opportunities and income generally correlate with race. As a result, tests, taxes, medical benefits, and many other programs would be placed under a constitutional cloud. Affirmative action would be constitutionally mandated. The decision about which discriminatory effects were permissible and why would be enormously complex. As with a right to welfare, serious strains would be imposed on the judiciary, particularly in the remedial process. And invalidation of measures with discriminatory effects might well produce a range of additional social and economic burdens, including, for example, less effective police forces, higher prices, and inferior social programs.

The social consequences—including the enforcement problems—of abandoning status quo neutrality are thus relevant to the constitutional inquiry. They will tend to be largest in cases in which other branches of government support the practice under attack. When, for example, Congress has enacted a statute abandoning status quo neutrality—for example, a welfare statute, an affirmative action program, a statute protecting the handicapped, a parental leave measure—these considerations are secondary. In such cases the elected branches have made a decision about the consequences. Any problems of judicial enforcement will be minimized. Where the elected branches are on the other side, however, any such problems are properly taken into account.

Toward Post–New Deal Constitutionalism

From what I have said thus far, it should be clear that we cannot say in the abstract whether and how status quo neutrality should be abandoned. That issue depends on a mixture of considerations. No broad rules will be adequate; principles of interpretation do not operate like algorithms. Law is not mathematics.

But we are not entirely at sea. Some generalizations and examples may be helpful. In *Lochner* itself, the decision was hardly compelled by the text; and the outcome reached by the Court ran in the face of a powerful and mounting national consensus in the other direction. Crucially, that consensus was supported by good reasons. Courts should therefore defer, under the due process clause, to regulatory legislation that benefits people who have at least a plausible claim to help.

Similar considerations justify, at least in broad outline, the Court's current approach to the takings and contracts clauses. These provisions are best understood as based on status quo neutrality; they cannot and should not be read out of the Constitution. But a generous approach to government power is appropriate under both provisions.

As a matter of law, affirmative action for both race and gender is relatively easy. The measures in question have been adopted by democratic bodies. The equal protection clause is best taken as an attack on the status quo as between blacks and whites. It is designed to overcome the castelike status of blacks, rather than to eliminate all legal differentiation between blacks and whites (see Chapter 11). Taken in context, the text and history of the clause do not provide solid arguments against affirmative action. The word *equal* cannot resolve the question, for there are plausible but different conceptions of equality, arguing for or against affirmative action. The history argues powerfully in favor of permitting affirmative action. Moreover, consequentialist concerns cannot be said to count powerfully against affirmative action and may even argue in favor of validation. In the face of uncertainty, courts should defer to the legislature.

At least in the absence of extremely unusual circumstances—involving, for example, quota systems having no realistic connection to the numbers of plausibly qualified applicants—affirmative action should not raise a serious constitutional question. This is so even though such programs do raise difficult questions of morality and politics. Those questions should be debated by the democratic process. They should not be foreclosed by the judges.

Judicial review of agency inaction and standing for beneficiaries of regulatory programs (see Chapter 3) are also relatively easy. Here Congress has created and endorsed a broad presumption in favor of the availability of courts, and, most important, review would serve only to vindicate constitutional and statutory provisions as against the executive branch. There is no longer a good reason for a sharp distinction between common law interests and benefits that are the creation of statute. The emergence of hearing rights for beneficiaries of spending and regulatory programs is therefore appropriate.

More difficult questions are raised by cases involving discriminatory effects under the equal protection clause and welfare rights. Viewed through the lens of the attack on status quo neutrality, these decisions seem incorrect in their reasoning and questionable in their outcomes. All of them depend on premises about the appropriate baseline that were properly rejected during the New Deal period.

As we have seen, however, there are powerful reasons for judicial caution here. For the foreseeable future, claims of a constitutional right to welfare and of a right to freedom from discriminatory effects should be rejected. At the same time, legislation that recognizes such rights should be hospitably interpreted in light of the constitutional backdrop. Congressional efforts on these scores might well be regarded as the fulfillment of constitutional responsibilities owed by the national government, but not subject to judicial enforcement.

A similar analysis should be applied to education. In contemporary

America, the current educational system systematically violates a constitutional principle rooted in the equal protection clause. Perhaps the Supreme Court should have redressed some of the existing inequalities. But whether or not it is willing to do so, the Constitution imposes a continuing duty on other branches.

A still harder question is posed by allegations that the criminal justice system violates the equal protection of the laws because it fails to protect blacks equally with whites, or women equally with men. We have seen that these allegations seem right; but there are also good reasons for courts to hesitate in the face of such broad-gauged claims. If it can be shown that the police fail to respond to domestic violence or refuse to treat sexual assault as a serious crime, the hesitation should be overcome. If the deployment of police protects whites from serious crime, but leaves blacks vulnerable, the Constitution has been violated. If the courts refuse to act, other government officials should live up to their constitutional responsibilities.

THE CONTINUING LEGITIMACY OF RATIONALITY REVIEW

We have seen that before the New Deal, courts administered the constraints of the due process clause through a test for "rationality." The modern legal framework retains the pre–New Deal conception of the role of national representatives—that they must deliberate rather than respond to constituent pressures—but substantially abandons the idea that existing distributions are entitled to special protection from majoritarian processes. Decisions to redistribute resources or opportunities, or to adapt the preexisting structure of entitlements and preferences, may well be based on an effort to promote the public good. If representatives choose to restructure the existing distribution of wealth, entitlements, or preferences, their choice is usually not, for that reason, unconstitutional.

Since the end of the *Lochner* period, the Court has not been engaged in a serious or sustained effort to police the operation of interest-group politics. It has continued to assert that decisions based on raw power are prohibited, to accept redistribution as a permissible social goal, and to be highly deferential to Congress in examining whether a statute is in fact solely a response to interest-group pressures. The prohibition of naked preferences should be regarded as a member of the extremely important class of judicially underenforced constitutional norms.

A truly Madisonian approach to judicial review would, however, cause courts to enforce the rationality requirement somewhat more stringently. It is not difficult to argue for such a change in the law. Moderately more aggressive review would be designed to ensure that legislative outcomes are justified by reference to something other than an exercise of political power by those benefited—or, to state the matter positively, to ensure that representatives have exercised some form of judgment instead of responding mechanically to interest-group pressures.

As an example, consider *United States Retirement Board v. Fritz*.[50] At issue there was a statute designed to improve the financial condition of the railroad retirement system—an analogue of social security—by eliminating certain benefits. Most of those whose rights had vested were unaffected by the statute. The principal disadvantaged group consisted of a narrow set of people that had not been able to participate in the legislative negotiations. The Court upheld the classification on the ground that "equitable considerations" justified the discrimination.

As it turned out, the legislative history suggested a very different story. All the available evidence indicated that members of Congress believed that no group of beneficiaries would be harmed by the statute. Indeed, Congress intended to protect the reliance interests of all employees. The statute in fact had been drafted by private groups—representatives of labor and management—none of whom had an interest in protecting the plaintiffs, former railroad employees, from loss of their benefits. *Fritz* is thus a striking example of a kind of Madisonian nightmare: national legislators abdicating their obligations because of pressure applied by powerful private groups.[51] In vindicating the Madisonian understanding, cases like *Fritz* provide an opportunity for some modestly helpful steps.

THE STATE ACTION QUESTION RECONCEIVED

The discussion thus far suggests a way to handle the vexing state action cases.[52] Under our Constitution, it is entirely correct to say that only government behavior, and not private action, is subject to constitutional constraints. By its very terms, the Constitution (with the exception of the Thirteenth Amendment, barring involuntary servitude) is directed against government. The lesson of the attack on status quo neutrality is emphatically not that there is no line between public and private action, or that private action is constitutionally restricted. The lesson is that the law of contract, tort, and property is just that—law. It should be assessed in the same way in which other law is assessed.

If this is correct, the state action doctrine calls for an inquiry into whether the state action *at issue in the relevant case* violates the pertinent provision of the Constitution. It is always necessary to identify what the state has done, and to evaluate it under the constitutional provision that the plaintiff has invoked. To repeat: The Constitution does not govern private conduct. But when a state enforces a racially restrictive covenant, of course it is acting. When the trespass law is used to evict someone from private property, the state is involved.

The real issue is whether the decision to enforce such a covenant or to bring about the eviction violates the equal protection clause or any other constitutional provision. That question is not always an easy one, but it is the right one. It is a question about the meaning of the Constitution, not about state action. When a state repeals a law forbidding private racial discrimination, the question is whether anything in the Constitution requires such a law—not whether the state has acted. When a state enforces or repeals a trespass law, there is unquestionably state action of some sort. The issue is whether that action offends the Constitution.

For this reason, *Shelley v. Kraemer* (discussed in Chapter 2) was a remarkably easy state action case. How could the government's enforcement of a racially restrictive covenant, through its courts, be anything but state action? The case was difficult only because it is unclear whether the Constitution forbids the state's apparently neutral use of its courts to enforce contracts, including racially restrictive property agreements. That is a hard question about the meaning of the equal protection clause. It is not a hard question about state action.

So, too, the use of trespass law to exclude political protesters from a shopping center is unquestionably state action. The same is true for the use of federal law allocating broadcasting licenses to prevent people from speaking on the networks. The decisions of the shopping center owners and of the broadcasters do not themselves implicate the Constitution; they are indeed purely private. But the use of law does raise a First Amendment question. To answer that question, we need to know something about the First Amendment (see Chapter 7). The state action issue is unhelpful.

I emphasize that this view does not suggest that "everything is state action" or that the decisions of ordinary people are subject to constitutional constraints. When one person excludes another from his own home, there is no state action; the state action consists only in the availability or actual use of the trespass laws. It would be impossible to argue that the availability or use of those laws offends any constitutional provision. So, too, the enforcement of a contract and the availability of contract law are state action; but usually contract law does not offend the Constitution. The decisions of private people to reach agreements are not state action at all. It is only state action that is state action; and that is how I propose to shift the analysis.

This reformation would not by itself resolve cases. But it would focus our attention on the right questions. Rather than using a state action doctrine that reflexively treats the status quo as the baseline for distinguishing between "action" and "inaction," we would have to support, with reasons, the view that a particular provision of the Constitution permits or bars what the government has done. A large-scale generalization of this proposition accounts for a good deal of what I have suggested in this chapter.

CHAPTER 6

Democracy, Aspirations, Preferences

We have seen that constitutional interpretion must rely on principles external to the constitutional text, and that the commitment to deliberative democracy is a promising source of those principles. We have also seen that the commitment calls not for egalitarianism, but for a principle of political equality; for a certain category of specified rights, many of them deriving from the notion of citizenship; and, most generally, for a form of "government by discussion."

But the commitment to deliberative democracy has only been sketched. In this chapter, I explore some of the foundations of that commitment. I do so by asking three related questions. Should private preferences be the basis for government action? Should political and legal decisions always be based on an inquiry into what people "want"? How are we to ascertain what people "want," and what is the appropriate role of their desires in governmental outcomes?

Both the temptation to rely on existing preferences and the frequent objection to governmental interference with them embody an influential conception of neutrality. On that view, government takes citizens' desires as they are and does not seek to evaluate or to change them. It is impartial among them. Both government action and government partisanship are often defined as rejection, by the state, of existing preferences. Inaction and neutrality are often defined as respect for those preferences. Here we find a special illustration of status quo neutrality. The illustration is particularly important, because it helps to provide the foundations for that conception of neutrality in many areas of the law.

In a good deal of contemporary thought, respect for existing preferences is a major theme. In politics and law, current preferences occupy a central place. Thus "paternalism"—understood as the substitution of governmental for individual choices—is strongly disfavored in both the public and the private realms.[1] The political process is often understood, within the legal community, as a system for aggregating and trading off people's preferences.[2] Much of current thinking about the constitutional system is founded on the idea that ours is a system of "majority rule." Majority rule, it is often thought, entails respect for existing preferences as measured through voting.

Modern economics is dominated by a conception of welfare based on the satisfaction of existing preferences—as measured by how much people are "willing to pay" for the goods in question. Even social choice theory, which amounts in many respects to a critique of economic models of democracy, sees the political process as an effort to aggregate preferences.[3]

In this chapter, I argue that social outcomes should not be based on existing preferences, and that the use of such preferences is unsupportable by principles of neutrality, autonomy, or welfare—the very ideas that are said to justify it. Existing preferences should be the basis of government decisions only to the extent that this approach will serve human freedom and welfare. To a considerable extent, the approach will not serve these ends at all. In so arguing, I emphasize two points: the existence of democratic aspirations that depart from private preferences, and the possibility that current preferences represent an adaptation to an unjust status quo.

Ideas of this general sort took a particular shape during the founding period, with the recognition of the "man-made" quality of culture and the emphasis on the role of education and the state in forming wants, beliefs, and achievements.[4] Such ideas played a role after the Civil War as well, with the understanding that the institution of racial subjugation had affected the development of desires and beliefs of both blacks and whites. They were particularly influential during the New Deal period. Thus John Dewey wrote, "the serious defect in the current empirical theory of values, the one which identifies them with things actually enjoyed irrespective of the conditions upon which they depend, is that it formulates and in so far consecrates the conditions of our present social experience." And "[t]o those who appreciate this fact, it is evident that the desires, aims and standards of satisfaction which the dogma of 'natural' economic processes and laws assumes are themselves socially conditioned phenomena. They are reflections into the singular human being of customs and institutions; they are not natural, that is, 'native,' organic propensities. They mirror a state of civilization."[5]

A large part of my focus is on the phenomenon of endogenous preferences. By this term, I mean simply to indicate that preferences frequently are not fixed and stable, but instead adapt to a wide range of factors—including the context in which the preference is expressed, the existing legal rules, current information, past consumption choices, and culture in general. The phenomenon of endogenous preferences casts severe doubt on the notion that a democratic government ought to respect private desires and beliefs in all contexts. It throws status quo neutrality into particular question. It opens up the territory for a large amount of explanatory work in economics, psychology, and elsewhere.

Perhaps most important for present purposes, it helps deepen the case for deliberative democracy. There is a crucial difference between the economic principle of "consumer sovereignty"—by which consumers, in markets, decide on the allocation of goods and services through registering their "preferences"—and the Madisonian principle that vests ultimate sovereignty in the people. On the Madisonian principle, citizens and representatives are supposed not to seek and pay for "what they want," but to deliberate about social outcomes. They are required to offer reasons on behalf of one view rather than another. They are required to listen and talk to one another. The goal, in Madison's own words, is a system of "discussion" in which "minds [are] changing," in which "much [is] gained by a yielding and accommodating spirit," and in which no man is "obliged to retain his opinions any longer than he [is] satisfied of their propriety and truth, and . . . open to the force of argument."[6]

In the Madisonian understanding, I suggest, lie the roots of the American commitment to political deliberation. On this view, democratic outcomes reflect the considered judgments of the citizenry rather than an aggregation of consumption choices.

A Conceptual Problem

The idea that government ought to take preferences as the basis for law and government is a quite modern one. Despite its relative novelty, the idea has been extraordinarily influential. It has set the basic agenda in much of economics and rational choice theory, ensuring that existing preferences are taken as a constant for purposes of understanding both private and public action. And many people think that the government, even or perhaps especially in a democracy, should base its decisions exclusively on the subjective preferences held by its citizens. This idea embodies a conception of political justification that might be described as "subjective welfarism."

Many approaches to law and to politics turn out to be versions of subjective welfarism. These include, for example, certain forms of utilitarianism; the view that economic efficiency ought to be treated as the foundational norm for political life; approaches to politics modeled on bargaining theory, rational or otherwise; and conceptions of politics that see the democratic process as an effort to aggregate individual preferences.

It is important to understand that subjective welfarism, thus defined, may or may not be accompanied by a broader notion that all ethical and moral questions should be treated in the same terms. People who subscribe to subjective welfarism might freely acknowledge that individuals are entitled to criticize the choices made by other individuals, and that the criticism can be based on good reasons. It is as a political conception—that is, as a guide to what government should do—that subjective welfarism underlies a wide range of approaches to public life.

Moreover, efforts to take existing preferences as a given have much to be said in their favor. In part the idea is a function of the perceived (if overstated) difficulty of making interpersonal comparisons of utility. Perhaps we are unable to compare a gain in welfare for one person with an apparently similar gain for another. If so, our incapacity argues against basing social judgments on anything other than private preferences as subjectively perceived.[7] In part subjective welfarism is a product of the difficulties in assessing someone's preferences in terms of their true connection with individual welfare. Person A prefers option X or good Y. Some bystander thinks that A is not promoting her welfare. How would we even begin to untangle that problem, which is only partly empirical?

Above all, perhaps, the attraction of subjective welfarism comes from the genuine political dangers of allowing government to base its decisions on something other than the actual wishes of the citizenry. Respect for those wishes seems to reflect governmental neutrality. It also seems to limit the risk of tyranny. Indeed, many of the most objectionable forms of government involve self-conscious and continuous indifference or hostility to the desires of the citizenry. Totalitarian governments are often totalitarian for this very reason. For all these reasons, a theory of law and politics could do much worse than to take existing preferences as the basis for governmental action.

Moreover, many of the most important gains in positive social science have come from the valuable simplifying device of taking preferences as given. We are able, for example, to predict and explain many legislative outcomes by assuming that representatives attempt to maximize their chance of reelection.[8] In these circumstances, the decision to work from existing preferences seems quite defensible. Indeed it appears to embody plausible ideas about neutrality, freedom, and welfare.

THE ENDOWMENT EFFECT

There is, however, an initial objection to the view that government should take preferences "as they are": one of impossibility.

The basic problem is that full governmental neutrality among preferences really cannot be achieved. Whether people have a preference for a good, a right, or anything else is often in part a function of whether the government or the law has allocated it to them in the first instance. There is simply no way to avoid the task of initially allocating a legal entitlement, at least short of anarchy—the only system without initial allocations. What people "have" is partly a product of what the law protects as "theirs." And everything people "have" is, simply as a matter of fact, a creation of legally conferred rights. (Recall here the discussions in the Introduction and in Chapter 2.)

The decision to grant an entitlement to one person frequently makes that person value that entitlement more than he or she would if the right had been allocated to someone else. (It also makes other people, not given that entitlement, value it less than they otherwise would.) The initial allocation—the legal rule saying who owns what, before people begin to contract with one another—serves to create, to legitimate, and to reinforce social understandings about presumptive rights of ownership. That allocation often helps produce individual perceptions about the entitlement—the good or the right—in question. Here lies a major problem for status quo neutrality with respect to preferences.

I do not claim that private preferences are always an artifact of law. In some cases, people order their affairs on the basis of social norms that operate independently of law, and the preferences that undergird those norms are not legally constructed.[9] Often, however, preferences are indeed a function of legal rules. The point is simply a factual one, and it has received considerable empirical confirmation.

The effect on preferences of the initial allocation of a commodity or an entitlement is commonly described as the "endowment effect."[10] The endowment effect seems like a technical point, but it has immense importance. It is fatal to status quo neutrality. It suggests that any initial allocation of an entitlement—and government cannot refuse to make an initial allocation—may well have effects on preferences.

Economists and psychologists have found this effect in many places, including both surveys and real exchange experiments. For example, a recent study showed that people who were given certain objects— pens, coffee mugs, and binoculars—placed a much higher value on those objects than did those who were required to purchase them. People initially given such things required a relatively high price from would-be purchasers; people not initially given such things offered a relatively low price to would-be sellers.[11] No such effects were observed for money tokens in otherwise identical experiments.

A similar study gave some participants a mug and others a chocolate bar, and told members of both groups they could exchange one for the other. Participants in a third group, not given either, were told that they could select one or the other; 56 percent of these selected the candy bar. By contrast, 89 percent of those initially given the mug refused to trade it for the candy bar, and only 10 percent of those initially given the candy were willing to trade it for the mug.[12] The different evaluations could not be explained by reference to anything other than the initial endowment.

Studies based on survey research have made identical findings. One such study found that people would demand about five times as much to allow destruction of trees in a park as they would pay to prevent the destruction of those same trees. When hunters were questioned about the potential destruction of a duck habitat, they said that they would be willing to pay an average of $247 to prevent the loss—but would demand no less than $1,044 to accept it. To accept degradation of visibility, participants in another study required payments ranging from five to more than sixteen times as high as their valuations of how much they were willing to pay to prevent the same degradation. According to yet another study, the compensation demanded for accepting a new risk of immediate death of 0.001 percent was one or two orders of magnitude higher than the amount of willingness to pay to eliminate an existing risk of the same magnitude.[13]

In short: A powerful status quo bias affects reactions to risks or losses.[14] Inevitably the status quo and existing entitlements are a function of legal rules. It is for this reason that status quo neutrality is not neutrality at all. If preferences are sometimes created by legal rules and are not independent of them, legal rules cannot be justified as neutral reflections of preferences.

In many settings, then, it has been shown that people place a higher value on rights or goods that they currently hold than they place on the same goods in the hands of others. There are multiple possible explanations for endowment effects.[15] Some studies suggest that the initial assignment creates the basic "reference state" from which judgments of fairness are subsequently made, and that those judgments affect preferences and private willingness to pay.[16] On this account, people perceive things as fair if they stay close to the status quo. An especially influential approach to the endowment effect stresses "loss aversion," which refers to the fact that a negative change from the status quo is usually seen as more harmful than a positive change is seen as beneficial. Here too there is a status quo bias.[17]

Perhaps people prefer what they have to what they might have because of psychological attachments. Endowment effects may reflect an effort to reduce cognitive dissonance: High valuation of what one owns and low valuation or what one does not are means of reducing dissonance and in some respects are highly adaptive.[18] Perhaps, too, the initial allocation has an important legitimating effect—suggesting that the entitlement "naturally" belongs where it has been placed, and putting a social burden on even voluntary changes. In some cases the divergence between willingness to pay and willingness to accept is probably a product of the change in social attitudes brought about by the change in the allocation of the entitlement.

For present purposes, it is enough to say that the initial allocation shapes preferences, and that no legal system can operate without initial allocation. If this is so, there is no acontextual "preference" with which to do legal or political work. Government cannot be neutral among preferences because—and this is the key point—it does not know what preferences are until it has acted, and because there is no sense in which it can refuse to act (again, short of anarchy).

It is tempting to respond that government might indeed refuse to act—for example, by failing to create liability at all. Railroads might be freely permitted to emit air pollutants; employers might be allowed to discharge people at their discretion, or to engage in race and sex discrimination. Are these not cases of inaction? Might not a system of this sort turn out to be neutral, in the sense that it refuses to take a position and simply allows people to do what they want in light of their (prelegal) preferences?

The answer is that such a system would not be neutral, that it would not involve inaction, that it would indeed take a position, and that it would not simply allow people "to do what they want." A decision to permit railroads to emit pollutants is a grant, by law, of a legal entitlement; it allocates the relevant right to the railroads. A decision to allow discharge at the employers' discretion on the basis of race and sex discrimination is a similar allocation. It will not do to point to what would happen in anarchy or in the state of nature. In anarchy or nature, the state does not enforce entitlements at all. In anarchy or nature, the state does not prohibit people from taking corrective action (of whatever sort) when they are victimized. In our world, however, a right to pollute or to discriminate is indeed backed by the force of law. It is accompanied by state-enforced prohibitions on certain sorts of corrective action by victims, including physical violence, or the attempted taking, by victims, of relevant property interests. It is in this sense that the state, so long as it exists, inevitably allocates entitlements.

When it exists, the endowment effect creates a large problem for the extremely influential Coase theorem, for which Ronald Coase received the Nobel Prize in economics.[19] According to the Coase theorem, the initial assignment of a legal entitlement will be irrelevant to the ultimate use of property or the level of activity, at least in the absence of transaction costs (that is, costs of contracting and bargaining). The Coase theorem suggests, for example, that when transaction costs are zero, it does not matter whether an entitlement is given to breathers or to polluters, to railroads or to farmers—since the two will in any case bargain to a result that is both efficient and the same. The point has had an extraordinarily large effect on legal analysis of both public and private law, and it is also beginning to affect legal outcomes.[20]

I cannot discuss the Coase theorem in detail here; there can be no doubt that it has produced large advances in thinking about legal problems. But in light of the endowment effect, the Coase theorem appears at least sometimes to be false, since it overlooks the effects of the initial allocation on preferences. The endowment effect shows that contrary to the Coase theorem, the entitlement will tend to stay where it has been initially allocated.

IMPLICATIONS

If all this is correct, large consequences follow. One would expect that a decision to give employees a right to organize, farmers a right to be free from water pollution, or women a right not to be subject to sexual harassment would have an impact on social attitudes toward labor organization, clean water, and sexual harassment. (There can be no doubt that something like this has happened with sexual harassment, where the creation of the entitlement has had a large influence on the preferences of many men and women.) The allocation will affect the valuation of the rights by both current owners and would-be purchasers. In this sense, neutrality as among preferences cannot be achieved through legal rules, because the preferences will sometimes be a function or a creation of legal rules. To repeat: For this reason, status quo neutrality is not neutrality at all.

More generally, much of governmental behavior will be a product of endowment effects. For example, private and public reactions to risks reflect a status quo bias. Government regulation of new risks will probably be more stringent than government regulation of (equivalent) old risks—precisely because the public demand for regulation will be a product of the endowment effect. This is in fact what we observe. New risks are regulated far more stringently than old ones, even though this strategy sometimes creates extremely perverse results, by perpetuating the life of the especially severe old risks and thus damaging public health and safety.[21]

There are other implications as well. Political participants should be able to exploit endowment effects by attempting to describe the status quo in a way that takes advantage of the phenomenon of loss aversion. Politicians are frequently successful when they are able to identify and control the perception of the status quo. One example is provided by constant political efforts to lower expectations by describing the status quo as systemically worse than in fact it is—so that the citizenry will rarely perceive deviations as losses but instead only as gains. The phenomenon occurs during elections, during wars, and during debate over the economy. The fact that it is so difficult to bring about even rational regulation through tax increases—on, for example, commodities that produce harm, such as polluting vehicles or gasoline—might be understood in terms of the endowment effect.

Another example is the constant effort to describe a proposal as a "restoration" of the status quo ante rather than as a new departure. Thus the various civil rights proposals of the late 1980s and the early 1990s were characterized as "restoration" acts, when in fact they were no such thing. The attack on the nomination of Robert Bork to the United States Supreme Court emphasized above all that Bork would "turn back the clock" on civil rights. When officials can describe things in these terms, there are important political benefits.

The dramatic public outcry over the Supreme Court's partial repudiation of *Roe v. Wade* may well have been fueled by the fact that the right to an abortion had come to be seen as part of existing endowments. We might doubt whether a similar reaction would be produced by the Court's failure to recognize an otherwise analogous but not yet established right. The inability of the political process to restrict social security benefits is undoubtedly in part a product of the endowment effect brought about by the social security system itself.

More generally, the constitutional protection provided to existing distributions of property can be better understood in this light. We have seen that the Constitution does not protect rights to property that people do not currently own, even if their need is very great. An existing endowment is a prerequisite for a constitutional claim under the Fifth Amendment. This idea might well be attributable to the psychological effects of existing endowments, which, other things being equal, make the loss of what one now owns far worse than the failure to obtain an (equivalent) gain. All of this tends to buttress the point, made in Chapter 5, that status quo neutrality finds a partial defense in the effort to protect expectations.

The distinction between acts and omissions might be understood in similar terms. We have seen that this distinction often turns on a baseline, that is, current practice, or the existing distribution of entitlements. A sharp distinction between acts and omissions might seem controversial to those who believe that existing distributions are not sacrosanct. But the distinction might be an outgrowth of, and partly justifiable by reference to, the endowment effect, which suggests that it is far worse to lose what one has than not to obtain an equivalent gain. Legal hostility to "acts" (understood as questionable conduct that disrupts existing ownership rights) might therefore be more intense than legal hostility to "omissions" (understood as questionable conduct that retains such rights). Here too we might find the beginnings of a substantive argument for status quo neutrality.

Yet another illustration is provided by fiscal policy. People sometimes perceive a tax credit or deduction as a restoration of the status quo, in which money resides with the individual taxpayer, whereas they see a government expenditure as a departure from the status quo. In this light it should be unsurprising that there is constant pressure in the direction of having government subsidies take the form of tax deductions rather than ordinary expenditures.[22]

If, then, legal rules have inevitable effects on preferences, it is hard to see how a government might even attempt to take preferences as "given" in any global sense. And when preferences are a function of legal rules, the rules cannot be justified by reference to the preferences. Social rules and practices cannot be justified by practices that they have produced. Often there is no such thing as a prelegal or prepolitical "preference" that can be used as the basis for decision. And the endowment effect might also be used to create a range of predictions about the nature and consequences of different legal regimes, and about the processes of preference formation in various areas of law.

I will briefly note an important related point. Sometimes people who defend respect for preferences act as if these are internal psychological drives, actual "things" inside people's heads. On this view, the task for law and government is to identify, in some neutral way, these "things," and then to respect them. But this is a crude and inaccurate picture. People have preferences, values, fears, cares, and commitments; sometimes these conflict. People have preferences, but also preferences about their preferences, and perhaps preferences about these as well. As Jean Hampton has shown, it is therefore wrong to think that we can identify and work with some "thing" called a preference.[23] And if this is true, it is much too simple to object to seemingly paternalistic laws on the ground that they are disrespectful of preferences.

Suppose, for example, that someone buys a pound of candy at a store. Did he really "prefer" the candy? To other things in the store? To other things in the world? To the money he spent on the candy? What if he immediately regrets the purchase, or told his friend to make sure to stop him from buying candy on that day? Government respect for the purchase of the candy is almost certainly appropriate; but this is not because such respect reflects a neutral decision to respect some real preference inside the purchaser's head. We can and usually should respect choices, to be sure; but the connection between choices and preferences is quite ambiguous.

When we identify something as a "preference" or as someone's real concern, we are not simply describing a "thing," but instead taking some value-laden stand about what really counts. This is so even when we respect ordinary consumption choices. To take such a stand, we must say something about what sorts of desires are truly connected with human well-being. And to do this, we must abandon the notion that there is some "thing," called a preference, that can be identified and used. Instead there are various different human motivations, which are expressed in diverse external choices in different contexts. A government inevitably respects some such motivations and not others. Inevitably it takes a stand. It cannot put evaluation to one side or try to find a "preference" and then use it.

On Liberty and Welfare

To some degree, perhaps, these considerations can be disregarded. Surely there is a difference between a government that concerns itself self-consciously and continuously with private preferences and a government that sets up the basic rules of property, contract, and tort and then lets things turn out however they may. To say that no legal system can avoid some preference-shaping effects is not to deny that in making particular decisions, a system can respect preferences once they have been formed by existing institutions (including legal ones). Often a state can indeed respect preferences after they are in place. Perhaps we can simply call preferences "choices," and avoid many of the difficulties in this way. And sometimes the particular decision at issue will have no effects on preferences.

In this sense, there is a fully workable distinction between a system that respects preferences as expressed through choices—at least in individual cases—and one that does not. The frustration, resentment, and economic misallocations that are bred by governmental rejection of existing desires are quite familiar. These can be minimized and perhaps even avoided.

Moreover, a legal system that provides an initial allocation of entitlements—that is, any system—should not be confused with one that attempts to ensure that citizens adhere to a particular or unitary conception of the good. Any just system will allow large diversity in the available conceptions. That diversity promotes individual liberty and freedom of choice. American constitutionalism respects such diversity and such freedom, in part because of their salutary effects on public deliberation. And perhaps endowment effects are in many cases small or nonexistent. Perhaps across a fairly large territory, preferences and desires, within a culture, are constant and impervious to dramatic change through different legal rules. Perhaps preferences are creations far more of culture than of law. Perhaps law and culture can be separated fairly cleanly. Nothing in the empirical literature yet proves that this hypothesis is false.

If we put endowment effects to one side in this way, disagreements about the relationship between politics and preferences turn on competing notions about autonomy or freedom on the one hand and welfare on the other. Subjective welfarism is founded on the claim that an approach that treats preferences as the basis for social decisions is most likely to promote both individual freedom, rightly conceived, and individual or social welfare. An evaluation of this view will help not only in coming to terms with subjective welfarism, but also in responding to the tempting suggestion that if preferences are endogenous, it follows that any valuation of preferences is also endogenous, and hence that any view about these matters puts us in a hopeless abyss or a vicious circle. To this suggestion, we should respond that any system of social ordering should be evaluated in terms of its consequences for the people in that system. Any such evaluation will of course come from human beings in the world, equipped with their cultural influences. But surely this fact cannot by itself impeach their evaluation—or immunize it from criticism, or approval, on the basis of the reasons brought forward on its behalf.

It will be useful to begin with welfare. Even if we accepted a purely utilitarian view, we might think that the process of promoting utility should not take place by satisfying current preferences. Instead it might promote whatever preferences fit with the best or highest conception of human happiness. This view is connected with older (and some current) forms of utilitarianism, most famously Mill's. It also has roots in Aristotle.[24] Here one does not take existing preferences as given, and one does not put all preferences on the same plane. A criterion of welfare remains the ultimate one, but the system is not focused solely on preference satisfaction. It insists that welfare and preference-satisfaction are entirely different things.[25]

A central point here is that preferences are often shifting and endogenous rather than fixed and exogenous—endogenous to, or a function of, current information, consumption patterns, legal rules, and social pressures most generally. An effort to identify welfare with preference-satisfaction would be easier to understand if preferences were rigidly fixed at some early age or if learning were impossible. If this were so, legal efforts to reflect on, change, or select preferences would breed only frustration. But when preferences are shifting and endogenous, and when the satisfaction of existing preferences might lead to unhappy or deprived lives, a democracy that treats all preferences as fixed will lose important opportunities for welfare gains.

With respect to welfare, then, the key point is that efforts to alter existing desires may produce social improvements. The problem is not with the origin of desires but with their malleability. At least if the relevant cases can be confidently identified in advance, and if collective action can be justified by reference to particular good reasons, the argument for democratic interference will be quite powerful. Respect for preferences that have resulted from unjust background conditions and that will lead to human deprivation or misery appears hardly the proper course for a constitutional democracy.

For example, legal rules discouraging addictive behavior may have significant advantages in terms of welfare. Regulation of heroin or cigarettes—at least if the regulation can be made effective—might well increase social welfare, by decreasing individually harmful behavior, removing the secondary effects of the harms, and producing more healthful and satisfying lives. Or government action relating to the environment, broadcasting, or culture may in the end generate (or, better, prevent obstacles to generation of) new preferences, providing increased satisfaction and in the end producing welfare gains. The same may well be true of antidiscrimination measures, which can affect the desires and attitudes of discriminators and victims alike. A system that takes private preferences for granted will sacrifice large opportunities for social improvement on welfarist criteria.

This point was a crucial one in the early stages of utilitarian thought; it has been lost more recently. In a deliberative democracy, it is important to stress the continuing importance of this point. Indeed, we might defend constitutional democracy itself not on the ground that it respects existing preferences, but on the quite different theory that it helps to inculcate the best or highest kinds of desires and beliefs. The great theorists of constitutional democracy, John Stuart Mill and John Rawls, insist on the point.[26] Rawls, for example, suggests that liberal institutions influence "people's basic aspirations" and "can have decisive long-term effects and importantly shape the character and aims of the members of society, the kinds of persons they are and want to be."[27]

So much for welfare. It might be thought that government should respect private preferences in the interest of freedom. But the satisfaction of private preferences, whatever their content and origins, does not respond to a persuasive conception of liberty or autonomy. The notion of autonomy should refer instead to decisions reached with a full and vivid awareness of available opportunities, with all relevant information, and without illegitimate or excessive constraints on the process of preference formation.

For those who think this idea foreign to the liberal tradition in America, it might be worthwhile to recall John Dewey's words: "Liberalism knows that social conditions may restrict, distort, and almost prevent the development of individuality. It therefore takes an active interest in the working of social institutions that have a bearing, positive or negative, upon the growth of individuals. . . . It is as much interested in the positive construction of favorable institutions, legal, political, and economic, as it is in the work of removing abuses and overt oppressions." And elsewhere, in an essay on freedom, Dewey wrote: "We may say that a stone has its preferential selections set by a relatively fixed, a rigidly set, structure. . . . The reverse is true of human action. In so far as a variable life history and intelligent insight and foresight enter into it, choice signifies a capacity for deliberately changing preferences." [28]

When there is inadequate information or opportunities, decisions and even preferences should be described as unfree or nonautonomous. For this reason it is most difficult to identify autonomy or freedom with preference-satisfaction. If preferences are products of available information, existing consumption patterns, social pressures, and governmental rules, it seems odd to suggest that individual freedom lies by definition in preference-satisfaction or that current preferences should, on grounds of autonomy, be treated as the basis for settling political issues. It seems even odder to suggest that all preferences should be treated the same, independently of their origins and consequences or of the reasons offered in their support.

Consider, for example, a decision to purchase dangerous foods, consumer products, or cigarettes by someone unaware of the health risks; an employer's decision not to deal with blacks because of racial hostility in his community; a person who disparages or has no interest in art and literature because the culture in which he has been reared consists mostly of television; a decision of a woman to adopt a traditional gender role because of the social stigma of refusing to do so; a decision not to purchase a car equipped with seatbelts or to wear a motorcycle helmet because of the social pressures imposed by one's peer group; a lack of interest in environmental diversity resulting from personal experiences that are limited to industrialized urban areas.

An especially vivid real-world example comes from India. In 1944, the All-India Institute of Hygiene and Public Health surveyed widows and widowers about their health. About 48.5 percent of the widowers said that they were "ill" or in "indifferent" health, compared with 2.5 percent of widows so describing their condition. In fact the widows were in worse condition than the widowers.[29] In these circumstances it would seem odd to base health policy on subjectively held views about health conditions. Such an approach would ensure that existing discrimination would be severely aggravated.

A recent study of social attitudes in America before the Revolution makes a similar point. In that period, American society was extremely hierarchical, and "common people" were "made to recognize and feel their inferiority and subordination to gentlemen. . . . But since their ignorance, inferiority, and subordination seemed part of the natural order of things, many common folk . . . dutifully made their bows and doffed their caps before ladies and gentlemen; they knew their place and willingly walked while gentlefolk rode; and as yet they seldom expressed any burning desire to change place with their betters."[30]

The source of the problem varies with each of these examples. But in all of them, the interest in liberty or autonomy does not call for governmental inaction, even if that were an intelligible category. Indeed, in many or perhaps all of these cases regulation removes a kind of coercion.

One goal of a democracy, in short, is to ensure autonomy not merely by allowing satisfaction of preferences, but also and more fundamentally by protecting free processes of preference formation. There are strong traces of this view in the period of the American founding. Thus William Byrd wrote that "the principal difference between one people and another proceeds only from the differing opportunities of improvement," and Benjamin Rush contended that differences in character were a result of "climate, country, degrees of civilization, forms of government, or accidental causes." In fact a large theme in colonial America was that differences in human personality—information, beliefs, desires—were a product of social forces, not of nature.[31] Mill himself was emphatic on this point, going so far as to suggest that government itself should be evaluated in large measure by its effects on the character of the citizenry.[32] The view that freedom requires an opportunity to choose among alternatives finds a natural supplement in the view that people should not face unjustifiable constraints on the free development of their preferences and beliefs.

Government action might also be justified on grounds of autonomy when the public seeks to implement, through democratic processes culminating in law, widely held social aspirations or collective desires. People may seek, through law, to implement a democratic decision about what courses to pursue. If so, it is ordinarily no violation of autonomy to allow these considered judgments to be vindicated by governmental action. Collective aspirations, produced by a process of deliberation in which competing perspectives are brought to bear, reflect a conception of political freedom having deep roots in the American constitutional tradition. Indeed, the central idea of deliberative democracy is founded on this conception.

On this view, political autonomy can be found in collective self-determination, as citizens decide, not what they "want," but instead who they are—what their values are and what those values require. What they seek through law must be supported by reasons. The point has roots in the Madisonian conception of sovereignty. And here again we may refer to Dewey: "The fact that something is desired only raises the *question* of its desirability; it does not settle it. Only a child in the degree of his immaturity thinks to settle the question of desirability by reiterated proclamation: 'I want it, I want it, I want it.' What is objected to in the current empirical theory of values is not connection of them with desire and enjoyment but failure to distinguish between enjoyments of radically different sorts." [33]

To summarize: The mere fact that preferences are what they are is an insufficient justification for political action—the principle of impartiality described in Chapter 1. More broadly, a democratic government should sometimes take existing preferences as an object of debate, discussion, and control—this last an inevitability in light of the need to provide initial allocations of entitlements—and precisely in the interest of welfare and autonomy.

Of course there are serious risks of overreaching here, and there must be some constraints—usually described as "rights"—on this process. As we have seen, checks laid down in advance are an indispensable part of constitutional government. Those checks will include, at a minimum, basic guarantees of political liberty and personal security, and such guarantees may not be compromised by processes of collective self-determination. I return to this point below.

Democratic Rejection of Preferences: A Catalogue

In this section I specify the claims made thus far, by describing cases in which considerations of autonomy and welfare justify government action that subjective welfarism would condemn. In all of these cases, I claim that participants in a deliberative democracy ought to be concerned with whether its citizens are living good lives, and that the salutary liberal commitment to divergent conceptions of the good ought not to be taken to disable government from expressing that concern through law. I also note some implications of the discussion for positive or predictive work, especially in economics and psychology. The cases fall in three basic categories.

COLLECTIVE JUDGMENTS AND SOCIAL ASPIRATIONS
Citizens in a democratic polity might use law to embody not the preferences that they hold as private consumers, but instead what might be described as collective considered judgments, including social aspirations. Measures of this sort are a product of deliberative processes on the part of citizens and representatives. In this sense they call up the original constitutional commitment to deliberative democracy.

The dependence of preferences on context. Frequently, political choices cannot easily be understood as a process of aggregating private desires. Some people want nonentertainment broadcasting on television even though their own consumption patterns favor situation comedies; they seek stringent laws protecting the environment or endangered species even though they do not use the public parks or derive benefits from protection of species; they approve of laws calling for social security and welfare even though they do not save or give to the poor; they support antidiscrimination laws even though their own behavior is hardly race-neutral. The choices people make as political participants are different from those they make as consumers. In part for this reason, democratic outcomes are distinct from those that emerge from markets.

The widespread disjunction between political and consumption choices presents something of a puzzle. Indeed, it sometimes leads to the view that market ordering is undemocratic and that choices made through the political process are a preferable basis for social ordering.

A generalization of this sort would be far too broad in light of the multiple breakdowns of the political process and the advantages of market ordering in many arenas. Respect for private markets is an important way of respecting divergent conceptions of the good, and it is properly associated with individual liberty. Respect for markets is also an engine of economic productivity, an important goal. But it would be a mistake to suggest, as some people do, that markets always reflect individual choice more reliably than does politics; that democratic choices differ from consumption outcomes only because of confusion, as voters fail to realize that they must ultimately bear the costs of the programs they favor; or that voting patterns merely reflect a willingness to support governmental provision of certain goods so long as other people are footing the bill.

Undoubtedly there is something true about each of these claims. Consumer behavior is sometimes a better or more realistic reflection of actual preferences than is political behavior. But in light of the fact that preferences depend on context, the very notion of a "better reflection" of "actual" preferences is a confusing one. There is no such thing as an "actual" (in the sense of unitary or context-free) preference in these settings. Moreover, the difference might be explained by the fact that political behavior reflects a variety of influences that are present only in the context of political deliberation, and that justify giving special weight to what emerges through the political setting. These include four closely related phenomena.

First, citizens may seek to implement their aspirations in political behavior but not in private consumption. As citizens, people may seek the aid of the law to bring about a system that they consider to be in some sense higher than what emerges from market ordering.

Second, people may, in their capacity as political actors, attempt to satisfy altruistic, justice-related, or other-regarding desires. These can diverge from the self-interested preferences sometimes characteristic of markets.[34] The deliberative features of politics can have salutary consequences here.

Third, political decisions might vindicate what might be called meta-preferences or second-order preferences. People have wishes about their wishes. Sometimes they try to vindicate those second-order wishes, including considered judgments about what is best, through law.

Fourth, people may precommit themselves, in democratic processes, to a course of action that they consider to be in the general interest. They may do so in order to protect themselves against what they know to be their own selfishness, myopia, or impulsiveness. The story of Ulysses and the Sirens is the model. The adoption of a Constitution is itself an example of a precommitment strategy.

Several qualifications are necessary here. First, these claims might be proved false in any particular case. It might well be that a law justified as reflecting altruistic desires in fact results from the pressures of well-organized private groups and has nothing to do with altruism at all. This phenomenon is of course a common one. A detailed study of the forces that produce particular legislation, and of divergences between public and private choices, is necessary to evaluate the claims made here. There is thus a rich source for empirical work.

Second, some of these objections might be translated into the terms of subjective welfarism. Some preferences, after all, are most effectively expressed through democratic processes. We might support that expression precisely on the ground that these preferences are subjectively held and connected to a certain form of welfare. My broader point, however, is that political choices will be based on a kind of reflection and reasoning that, too often, is inadequately captured in the marketplace.

Third, to point to these various possibilities is not at all to deny that market and private behavior frequently reflects considered judgments, altruism, aspirations, or far more complex attitudes toward diverse social goods than are captured in conventional economic accounts about self-interested preferences. There are numerous counterexamples to any such claim. All I mean to suggest is that divergences between market and political behavior will sometimes be attributable to phenomena of this sort.

Fourth, a democratic system must be built on various safeguards to ensure that its results are in fact a reflection of deliberative processes of the sort described here. Often such processes are distorted by the fact that some groups are more organized than others, by disparities in wealth and influence, and by public and private coercion of various kinds.

Explanations. Thus far I have suggested that people may seek, through law, to implement collective desires that diverge from market choices. Is it possible to come up with concrete explanations for the differences? There are a number of possibilities.

First, the collective character of politics, permitting a response to collective action problems, is critical here. People may not want to implement their considered judgments or to be altruistic unless there is assurance that others will do so as well. More simply, people may prefer not to contribute to a collective benefit if donations are made individually, with no guarantee that others will participate; but their favored system, obtainable only or best through democratic forms, might be one in which they contribute if (but only if) there is assurance that others will do so. Perhaps people feel ashamed if others are contributing and they are not. Perhaps they feel victimized if they are contributing and others are not.

In any case, and most fundamentally, the satisfaction of aspirations or altruistic goals will sometimes have the characteristics of the provision of public goods or the solution of prisoners' dilemmas.[35] Indeed, one can think of both altruism and aspirations as having the features of a public good, that is, something that cannot be provided to one person without simultaneously being provided to many or all people. (National defense is a classic example.) Aspirations are not conventional public goods, because the market does not fail according to ordinary understandings of "market failure." But if the most preferred option is to reflect and carry out aspirational or altruistic goals, political action may be the best alternative. Market behavior, even when working well, may fail to do the job.

Second, the collective character of politics might overcome the problem, discussed below, of preferences and beliefs that have adapted, or to some extent adapted, to an unjust status quo or to limits on available opportunities. Without the possibility of collective action, the status quo may seem intractable, and private behavior and even beliefs will adapt accordingly. But if people can act in concert, preferences might take on a quite different form. Consider social movements involving the environment, labor, and race and sex discrimination.

Third, social and cultural norms might incline people to express aspirational or altruistic goals more often in political behavior than in markets. Such norms may press people, in their capacity as citizens, in the direction of a concern for others, for justice, or for the public interest.

Fourth, the deliberative aspects of politics, bringing additional information and perspectives to bear, may affect preferences as expressed through governmental processes. A principal function of a democratic system is to ensure that through representative processes, new or submerged voices, or novel depictions of where interests lie and what they in fact are, can be heard and understood. It should hardly be surprising if preferences, values, and perceptions of both individual and collective welfare are changed as a result of that process.

Fifth, and finally, consumption decisions are a product of the criterion of private willingness to pay. Willingness to pay is a function of ability to pay, and it is an extremely crude proxy for utility or welfare. Poor people may be unwilling to pay much for something that they very much want; rich people may be willing to pay a good deal for things toward which they feel relatively indifferent. Political behavior removes this distortion (which is not to say that it does not introduce distortions of its own).

Qualifications. The argument for respecting collective desires seems irresistible if the measure at issue is adopted unanimously. But more serious difficulties are produced if (as is usual) the law imposes on a minority what it regards as a burden rather than a benefit. Suppose, for example, that a majority wants to require high-quality television and to ban violent and even dehumanizing shows, but that a significant minority wants to see the latter. It might be thought that those who perceive a need to express an aspiration should not be permitted to do so if the consequence is to deprive others of an opportunity to satisfy their preferences.

The foreclosure of the preferences of the minority is unfortunate, but in general it is hard to see what argument there might be for an across-the-board rule against collective action of this sort. If the majority is prohibited from vindicating its considered judgments through legislation, an important arena for democratic self-government will be eliminated. The choice is between the considered judgments of the majority and the preferences (and perhaps considered judgments as well) of the minority. On the other hand, the foreclosure of the minority should probably be permitted only when less restrictive alternatives, including private arrangements, are unavailable to serve the same end. Often such alternatives are indeed available.

Of course the argument for democratic outcomes embodying collective judgments is not always decisive. It is easy to imagine some cases in which that argument is weak. Consider a law forbidding atheism or agnosticism, or barring unpatriotic political displays. And although I cannot provide a full discussion here, it might be useful to describe, in a preliminary way, three categories of cases in which constraints on collective judgments seem especially appropriate.

First, if the particular choice foreclosed has some special character, and especially if it is a precondition for deliberative democracy itself, it is appropriately considered a right, and the majority has no authority to intervene. Political expression and political participation are prime examples. The equal citizenship rights of members of the minority should always be respected, even in the face of a general aspiration held by the majority. So, too, other rights fundamental to individual autonomy or welfare—such as consensual intimate sexual activity—ought generally to be off-limits to government.

Second, some collective desires might be objectionable or a product of unjust background conditions. A collective judgment that racial intermarriage is intolerable could not be enforced through law even if it were said to reflect a collective aspiration. To explain why, it is of course necessary to offer an argument challenging that judgment. Such an argument might itself invoke notions of autonomy or welfare. However that may be, the example suggests that the collective judgment must not be objectionable on moral grounds.

Third, some collective desires might reflect a special weakness on the part of the majority; consider a curfew law, or perhaps the prohibition era. In such circumstances, a legal remedy might remove desirable incentives for private self-control, have unintended side effects resulting from "bottling up" desires, or prove unnecessary in light of the existence of alternative, less coercive remedies.

When any of these concerns arise, the case for protection of collective judgments is implausible. But in many contexts these concerns are absent, and legal controls initiated on these grounds are justified.

A note on commensurability. People who take preferences as the basis for social choice often assume that preferences are commensurable. On this view, private and public desires should be ordered along a single metric and assessed accordingly. But diverse social goods should not be assessed according to such a single metric. Consider the view that we should see all of the following as simple "costs": unemployment, higher prices, the adaptation of workplaces to accommodate people in wheelchairs, environmental degradation, sexual assault, and chilling effects on speech. If we understand all these things as "costs," to be assessed via the same metric, we will disable ourselves from making important qualitative distinctions.

To make diverse goods commensurable in this way is to do violence to our considered judgments about how all these should be characterized.[36] Those considered judgments are far from embarrassing; they are part of what it means to think well. Some otherwise unintelligible political outcomes might well be understood as responsive to a public conviction that social goods are not commensurable or fungible, and that they should be assessed in a way that is responsive to this fact. To say that they are not commensurable is not to say that they are infinitely valuable; but it is to say that they are qualitatively different from other things. Measures reflecting social aspirations might well embody a conviction of this kind.

EXCESSIVE LIMITATIONS ON OPPORTUNITIES OR UNJUST BACKGROUND CONDITIONS

Citizens in a constitutional democracy might override existing preferences in order to foster better and more diverse experiences. Their ultimate goal might be to provide broad opportunities for the formation of preferences and beliefs, and for distance on and critical scrutiny of current desires. The previous rationale for rejecting preference-satisfaction is rooted in democracy; this rationale is not. Here the argument is that if we are seeking to promote either welfare or liberty, we do this poorly by satisfying whatever preferences people happen to have.

Instead of satisfying preferences, democratic systems would do better to begin with an account of human interests and human needs. That theory need not be rooted in anything transcendental or external to actual human life; it should grow out of ideas about what human beings, in order to live good lives, should be entitled to be and to have. Any such theory would not stifle people with uniform prescriptions about the particular shape of a good life. It might well be a "thin" theory of the good, in the sense that it is not a comprehensive theory of what belongs in a good human life, but is instead restricted to the "bare essentials" about what such a life should contain.[37] If it is not a thin theory in this sense, it might specify in a more or less comprehensive way what a good human life contains, including, for example, food, friendship, love, recreation, education, and shelter. But this more comprehensive theory might well be vague, in the sense that its requirements can be satisfied in multiple different ways through multiple different forms of life.[38]

Whether thin or vague, the theory would allow people large room for individual choice. It would do so because individual choice is itself an important part of a good human life. For this reason, no democracy should impose on citizens a particular or unitary conception of what their lives ought to be like. But whether thin or vague, the theory would not depend on whatever "preferences" people happen to have.

In all likelihood, an approach of this sort will ultimately support both private ordering and freedom of contract. These tend to promote social diversity, freedom of choice, and self-reliance, and all of these are likely to be important human goods. But legal safeguards extending beyond the creation of markets are sometimes necessary. Here the argument for governmental controls, with an origin in John Stuart Mill, stresses the need to cultivate divergent conceptions of the good and to ensure a degree of reflection on those conceptions. Consider in this regard the many examples, set out earlier in this chapter, of preferences that have adapted to limited opportunities or unjust background conditions.

A system that took this goal seriously could start from a range of different foundations. It might find its roots in the principles that underlie a deliberative democracy itself.[39] Here the notions of autonomy and welfare would be defined by reference to the ideal of free and equal persons acting as citizens in setting up the terms of democratic life. That ideal will impose constraints on the sorts of preferences and beliefs that a political system would be permitted to inculcate; it is opposed, for example, to passivity, to servility, and to a refusal to be exposed to and to reflect on different ideas about the good life. Indeed, the system of constitutional democracy might be justified on the ground that it creates a kind of energy and independence of mind that are important human goods. As noted, the best defense of that system, rooted in Mill and Rawls, points not toward neutrality toward preference formation, but on the contrary toward beneficial consequences on precisely that score.

Perhaps more controversially, the system could be regarded as embodying a mild form of liberal perfectionism. Such a system would require government to ensure access to critical and disparate attitudes toward prevailing conceptions of the good. Liberal education is of course the principal place where government discharges this task. But the principles embodied in liberal education need not be confined to the school system. The point has clear echoes in the framers' preoccupation with the possibilities of education and with the educative role of the state in general.[40] Dewey wrote in similar terms: "Schooling is a part of the work of education, but education in its full meaning includes all the influences that go to form the attitudes and dispositions (of desire as well as of belief), which constitute dominant habits of mind and character." The point has echoes as well in Mill, who understood education to include not merely "whatever we do not ourselves and whatever is done for us by others for the express purpose of bringing us somewhat nearer to the perfection of our nature; it does more; in its largest acceptation it comprehends even the indirect effects produced on character and on the human faculties by things of which the direct purposes are quite different; by laws, by forms of government. . . . Whatever helps to shape the human being, to make the individual what he is or hinder him from being what he is not, is part of his education." [41]

Still another foundation for such a system would be Aristotelian. Here the governing goal would be to ensure that individual capabilities and functionings are promoted and not thwarted by governmental arrangements. [42] And this set of ideas, a different kind of perfectionism, is not so dramatically different from versions of utilitarianism that can be found in Mill and many others.

If government can properly respond to preferences that grow out of limitations on available opportunities, it might well undertake aggressive initiatives with respect to the arts and broadcasting—subsidizing public broadcasting, ensuring a range of disparate programming, or calling for high-quality programming provided only a little or not at all by the marketplace. Indeed, the need to provide diverse opportunities for preference formation suggests that there are reasons to be quite skeptical of unrestricted markets in communication and broadcasting. There is a firm theoretical justification for government regulation here, including the much-criticized, and now largely abandoned, "fairness doctrine," which required broadcasters to cover controversial issues and to ensure access for competing views. I return to this subject in Chapter 7.

Moreover, private preferences sometimes adjust to undue or unjust limitations in current practices and opportunities. People may well adapt their conduct and even their desires to what is now available. Consider here the story of the fox and the grapes. The fox does not want the grapes, because he considers them to be sour; but his belief to this effect is based on the fact that the grapes are unavailable. It is therefore hard to justify their unavailability by reference to his preferences. [43] Mary Wollstonecraft's *A Vindication of the Rights of Women* is in the same vein; it can be seen as an extended discussion of the social formation of preferences and the phenomenon of the adaptation of preferences, beliefs, and desires to an unjust status quo. Thus

Wollstonecraft writes, "I will venture to affirm, that a girl, whose spirits have not been damped by inactivity, or innocence tainted by false shame, will always be a romp, and the doll will never excite attention unless confinement allows her no alternative."[44]

When an adaptation of this sort is at work, respect for preferences seems unjustified on grounds of autonomy and perhaps welfare as well. A legal system that has produced preferences by limiting opportunities unjustly can hardly justify itself by reference to existing preferences. Preferences might be regarded as nonautonomous insofar as they are reflexively adaptive to unjust background conditions; and legal responses to such preferences might yield welfare gains as well.

Similar ideas help account for antidiscrimination principles. Most generally, the beliefs of both beneficiaries and victims of existing injustice are affected by efforts to reduce the cognitive dissonance produced by such injustice.[45] The strategy of blaming the victim, or assuming that an injury or an inequality was deserved or inevitable, tends to permit nonvictims or members of advantaged groups to reduce dissonance by assuming that the world is just—a pervasive, insistent, and sometimes irrationally held belief.[46] The reduction of cognitive dissonance, a powerful motivational force, has been shown to operate as a significant obstacle to the recognition of social injustice or irrationality.

Victims also participate in dissonance-reducing strategies, including the lowering of self-esteem to accommodate both the fact of victimization and the belief that the world is essentially just. Sometimes it appears easier to assume that one's suffering is warranted than that it has been imposed cruelly or by mere chance. Consider here the astonishing fact that after a draft lottery, those with both favorable and unfavorable results decided that the outcomes of the purely random process were deserved.[47] The phenomenon of blaming the victim also reflects the "hindsight effect," through which people unjustifiably perceive events as more predictable than they in fact were, and therefore suggest that victims or disadvantaged groups should have been able to prevent the negative outcome. All this can make reliance on existing preferences highly problematic.

There is suggestive evidence in the psychological literature to this effect. Some work here reveals that people who engage in cruel behavior change their attitudes toward the objects of their cruelty and thus devalue them; observers tend to do the same.[48] Such evidence bears on antidiscrimination law in general. Aspects of American labor and race discrimination law can be understood as responses to the basic problem of beliefs and preferences that have adjusted to insufficient opportunities or to an unjust status quo. For example, the Supreme Court has emphatically rejected freedom-of-choice plans as a remedy for school desegregation.[49] Such plans would simply permit whites and blacks to send their children wherever they wish. The Court's rejection of such plans might well be puzzling to people who believe in respect for existing preferences. But the outcome becomes more plausible if it is linked to the idea that preferences and beliefs have conspicuously grown up around and adapted to the world of segregation. In these circumstances, freedom of choice is no solution at all; indeed the term seems to be an oxymoron in view of the background and context.

The collective action problem faced by individual parents complements this difficulty. Individual black parents might rationally send their children to all-black schools, because it would be difficult to have one's children be among the only blacks at a white school. But if (and only if) government requires real desegregation, it will be possible to satisfy the probably widespread desire to prevent the continuation of all-black and all-white schools.

In the labor area as well, American law rejects freedom of contract and freedom of choice in order to protect collective bargaining. Some of this legislation must have stood on a belief that private preferences might have adapted to a system that is skewed against unionization. Special steps are therefore necessary in order to encourage collective bargaining. The same argument might be made in favor of occupational safety and health laws. Workers may be unwilling to confront the real magnitude of risks faced in the workplace because it is too distressing to do so. In these circumstances, a regulatory solution may well be necessary.[50]

Of course poverty itself is the most severe obstacle to the free development of preferences and beliefs. In this light, programs that attempt to respond to the multiple deprivations faced by poor people are fully justified. Such programs work most obviously by eliminating poverty, but also through broad public education and regulatory efforts designed to make cultural resources generally available regardless of wealth. These should hardly be seen as objectionable paternalism or as unsupportable redistribution. Consider in this regard John Dewey's suggestion: "Much of the alleged unchangeableness of human nature signifies only that as long as social conditions are static and distribute opportunity unevenly, it is absurd to expect changes in men's desires and aspirations."[51]

Indeed, poverty and similar forms of intense social disability can

impair the formation of goals themselves, breeding instead a combi-
nation of frustration and resignation.[52] Severe deprivation influences
and even closes off the development of desires. An important reason
to respond to the deprivation is to promote freer and better processes
of desire formation. To generalize the point only slightly, we might
take the argument for liberal education to call for a broad social effort
to ensure that desires and beliefs are formed under conditions that
inform people of a range of information and opportunities.

Sometimes, of course, preferences are only imperfectly adapted. At
some level there is a perception of an injury, but a fear of social punishment of some kind, or a belief that the cause is intractable, prevents
people from seeking redress. Here the collective character of politics,
permitting the organization of numerous people, can be exceedingly
helpful.

Standing by itself, the fact that preferences are shifting and endogenous is hardly a sufficient reason for democratic controls. Many preferences are to some degree dependent on existing law and current opportunities, and that fact cannot be a reason for government action
without creating a license for tyranny. Moreover, a preference is not
impeached merely by virtue of being a social product; recall from
Chapter 2 that the mere fact of social influences is irrelevant to moral
assessment. The argument for democratic controls in the face of endogenous preferences must rely on a belief that human welfare or autonomy will thereby be promoted. Usually governmental interference
with existing preferences should be avoided, and precisely because it
produces frustration and resentment without accomplishing much
good. But too often, our healthy belief in respect for divergent conceptions of the good is transformed into an unwillingness to protect
people from unjust background conditions or a sheer lack of options.

The actual content of democratic controls here will of course be
controversial, and it probably should begin and usually end with efforts to provide information and to increase opportunities. Flexible
solutions, promoting individual choice rather than displacing it,
should ordinarily be sought. Restructured incentives are usually better
than governmental commands. Thus, for example, governmentally required disclosure of risks in the workplace is a highly plausible approach. In a few cases, however, these milder strategies are inadequate. A moderately intrusive possibility is financial incentives; these
might take the form of tax advantages or cash payments. For example,
government might give economic inducements to day-care centers as

a way of relieving childcare burdens. Such a system might well be preferable to direct transfers to families—a policy that will predictably lead many more women to stay at home. In view of the sources and consequences of the differential distribution of childcare burdens—a system of sex discrimination—it is fully legitimate for government to take steps in the direction of equalization. The most intrusive option, usually to be avoided, is direct coercion, as in the case of governmentally mandated use of safety equipment.

The category of democratic responses to endogenous preferences of this sort overlaps with that of measures that attempt to protect collective aspirations. Frequently aspirations form the basis for laws that attempt to influence and improve processes of preference formation.

INTRAPERSONAL COLLECTIVE ACTION PROBLEMS
There is also an argument for legal interference with existing preferences when such preferences are a function of past acts of consumption and when such acts alter people's desires or beliefs in such a way as to cause long-term harm to them. Here the purpose of collective controls is to affect the development of certain preferences. In such cases, the two key facts are that preferences are endogenous to past consumption decisions and that the effect of those decisions on current preferences is pernicious. The effect is pernicious when the aggregate costs of consumption, over time, exceed the aggregate benefits. For government to act in this context, it is important that it be confident of its conclusions. In the face of uncertainty, freedom of choice is appropriate here. An absence of information is usually a necessary condition for legal controls.

Regulation of addictive substances, myopic behavior, and bad habits are familiar examples. In the case of an addiction, the problem is that the costs of not consuming the addictive substance increase dramatically over time, while the benefits of consumption remain constant or fall sharply. The result is that the aggregate costs, over time or over a life, of consumption exceed the aggregate benefits, even though the initial consumption choice provides benefits that exceed costs. As a result, people are made much worse off, even by their own lights. In such cases, people, if fully informed, would in all likelihood not want to become involved with the good in the first place. Because of the effect of consumption, over time, on preferences, someone who is addicted to heroin is much worse off even though the original decision to consume is not irrational if one looks only at immediate costs and benefits.[53] Laws that regulate addictive substances respond to a social belief that the relevant preferences should not be formed in the first place.

We might describe this situation as involving an "intrapersonal collective action problem,"[54] in which the costs and benefits, within a particular person, of engaging in the relevant activity change dramatically over time. The key point is that consumption patterns bring about a significant change in preferences, and in a way that makes people miserable in the long run.[55] With addictions, there is a connection between intrapersonal collective action problems and preferences that are adaptive to unjust background conditions, at least as a general rule. The problem of drug addiction is hardly distributed evenly throughout the population, and the process of addiction is partly a product of social institutions that severely limit the available options.

While addiction is the most obvious case, it is part of a broad category. Consider, for example, myopic behavior, defined as a refusal—because the short-term costs exceed the short-term benefits—to engage in activity having long-term benefits that dwarf long-term costs. Another kind of intrapersonal collective action problem is produced by habits, in which people engage in behavior because of the subjectively high short-term costs of changing their behavior notwithstanding the fact that the long-term benefits exceed the short-term benefits. Akrasia, or weakness of the will, has a related structure. Some laws respond to individual akrasia; consider measures calling for a "cooling-off period" before purchase of certain goods. Other laws respond to collective akrasia; the Constitution itself is the best example.

For the most part, problems of this sort are best addressed at the individual level or through private associations, which minimize coercion. But legal solutions are possible. Statutes that subsidize the arts or public broadcasting, require disclosure of information, or discourage the formation of some habits and encourage the formation of others are illustrations. There is a similar argument for compulsory recycling programs (the costs of participation in which decrease substantially over time, and often turn into benefits) and for democratic restrictions on smoking cigarettes.[56] Here deliberative democracy can work to overcome weakness of will or myopia.

Neutrality, Partiality, and Preferences

Respect for existing preferences is often thought to signal governmental neutrality. In an important respect, however, such neutrality is impossible. Preferences are often a product of legal rules. They are endogenous to the initial legal allocation of rights. When this is so, one cannot decide on the content of legal rules by resort to preferences. There are no prelegal preferences that can be used as the baseline for analysis.

This claim has important implications. It suggests the outlines of a large agenda for research on preference formation and preference change—with applications to, for example, environmental controls, the market for regulation in general, the problem of paternalism, and constitutional democracy in general. It helps to explain why status quo neutrality is, with respect to preferences, not neutrality at all. It even helps to explain why constitutional democracy is an affirmative good.

Even when preferences are in place, it is by no means clear that politics and law should be based on existing preferences. The most important point is that sometimes citizens in a polity will have collective aspirations that depart from consumption choices. At least in general, those aspirations deserve respect in a Madisonian system.

Sometimes, moreover, interference with preferences can be justified on grounds of freedom or autonomy. This is so when such interference protects against excessive or illegitimate constraints on processes of preference formation. Sometimes protection of existing preferences will have harmful effects on both freedom and welfare. Legal regimes that depart from current preferences can have beneficial consequences. Consider requirements of high-quality broadcasting, controls on addictive or myopic behavior, or protection of pristine areas.

It would be foolish to suggest that one might obtain from ideas of this sort a clean and crisp program for research, much less a sure basis for legal or political reform. It would be equally foolish to deny that there are grave risks of abuse in any case in which government self-consciously takes preferences as an object of regulation and control. To use preferences as an important part of the process of democratic governance is surely a good idea.

But two clear lessons emerge from the discussion. We should not deny the preference-shaping effects of different legal rules, but instead explore and if possible predict the nature of those effects in different settings. And for those trying to decide what a constitutional democracy should do, the better course is not to proclaim reliance on context-free preferences—there is no such thing—but instead to examine the settings in which reliance on existing preferences, or legal interference with those preferences, will promote autonomy or welfare, rightly conceived.

It is now time for details. In Part II, I examine a variety of areas of law. I hope to show the omnipresence of status quo baselines and to argue for new understandings of constitutional freedoms once those baselines have been repudiated. The focus throughout will be on the system of deliberative democracy and its implications for constitutional theory and practice. The area of free speech is the place to begin.

PART II

APPLICATIONS

CHAPTER 7

Speech in the Welfare State: A New Deal for Speech

Many people think that the Supreme Court should play a very limited role in American government or that the Constitution's meaning is fixed by the original understanding of its ratifiers. Here the First Amendment poses a special embarrassment. The current state of free speech in America owes a great deal to extremely broad interpretations by the Court, which has invalidated legislative outcomes on many occasions. These decisions could not be justified by reference to the original understanding.[1] They also involve a highly intrusive judicial role in politics.

In one sense, however, there is real continuity between current practice and the original understanding, and between current practice and principles of democratic government. The continuity lies in the distinctive American contribution to the theory of sovereignty. In England, sovereignty lay with the king. "In the United States," as James Madison explained, "the case is altogether different. The People, not the Government, possess the absolute sovereignty." The location of sovereignty in the people rather than in the government had important implications for freedom of speech. As Madison understood it, the new conception of sovereignty entailed a judgment that any "Sedition Act," punishing speech critical of government, would be unconstitutional. Indeed, Madison thought that the power represented by such an act ought, "more than any other, to produce universal alarm; because it is levelled against that right of freely examining public characters and measures, which has ever been justly deemed the only effectual guardian of every other right."[2]

With Madison's pronouncements in mind, we might think of the American tradition of free expression as a series of struggles to understand the relationship between this novel conception of sovereignty and a system of free expression. Indeed, we might understand the extraordinary protection now accorded to political speech to be an elaboration of the American understanding of sovereignty.

My goal in this chapter and the next is to defend this basic proposition and to evaluate the current system of free expression in light of it. As we will see, an effort to root freedom of speech in popular sovereignty suggests that our current understandings are off the mark—protecting speech that ought not to be protected, misdirecting the basic inquiry, and, worst of all, invalidating democratic efforts to promote the principle of popular sovereignty under current conditions. Many of the failures are a product of status quo neutrality, and a rejection of that conception of neutrality has surprising implications for free speech.

The New First Amendment

American children watch a good deal of television—about twenty-seven hours per week[3]—and American television contains a good deal of advertising. For adults, every hour of television contains nearly eight minutes of commercials. For most of its history, the Federal Communications Commission (FCC) imposed limits on the amount of advertising that could be shown on shows aimed at children. In 1984 the FCC eliminated the limits. In the wake of deregulation, some stations show from eleven to twelve minutes per hour of commercials during children's programming on weekends, and up to fourteen minutes per hour on weekdays. Some shows are actually full-length commercials, because the lead characters are products.

In 1990 Congress enacted a law imposing, for children's programming, a limit of ten and a half minutes of television commercials per hour on weekends, and twelve minutes per hour on weekdays. President Bush withheld his approval, invoking the First Amendment. According to the President, the Constitution "does not contemplate that government will dictate the quality or quantity of what Americans should hear—rather, it leaves this to be decided by free media responding to the free choices of individual consumers." The President did "not believe that quantitative restrictions on advertising should be considered permissible."[4]

The Children's Television Act of 1990 has nonetheless become law.

It is likely that it will be challenged on constitutional grounds. Perhaps the constitutional attack will be successful. Certainly the plausibility of the constitutional argument has played a role in the debate over controls on children's advertising, and indeed deterred stronger efforts to encourage high-quality broadcasting for children.

The episode reveals that something important and perhaps even strange is happening to the First Amendment. In the 1940s, 1950s, and 1960s, the principal First Amendment suits were brought by political protesters and dissidents. But many of the current debates involve complaints by commercial advertisers, companies objecting to the securities laws, pornographers, businesses selling prerecorded statements of celebrities via "900" numbers, people seeking to spend huge amounts on elections, industries attempting to export technology to unfriendly nations, newspapers disclosing names of rape victims, and large broadcasters resisting government efforts to promote diversity in the media. How has this happened?

To attempt an answer, we must step back a bit. From about 1940 to 1970, American constitutional debate over freedom of expression was divided along clear lines. On the one side were those accepting what came to be the dominant position, a form of First Amendment "absolutism." On the other side were the advocates of "reasonable regulation." The two sides could be identified by their views about four central ideas.

The first idea is that the government is the enemy of freedom of speech. Any effort by the nation or the states to "regulate" speech is threatening to the principle of free expression. Somewhat more subtly, an effort to regulate speech is defined as an attempt, by government to interfere with communicative processes, taking the status quo—the common law, property rights, wealth, and so on—as a given. I will explain this point in more detail below.

Second, the First Amendment should be understood as embodying a commitment to a certain form of neutrality. Government may not draw lines between speech that it likes and speech that it hates. All speech stands on the same footing. Thus speech protection extends equally to Communists and Nazis, the Ku Klux Klan and the Black Panthers, Martin Luther King and George Wallace. Government should ensure that broadcasters, newspapers, and others can say what they wish, constrained only by the impersonal pressures of the marketplace. Neutrality among different points of view ("viewpoint neutrality"), thus understood, is the government's first commitment.

Third, the principle of free expression is not limited to political speech. It is extremely difficult to distinguish between political and nonpolitical speech; indeed, any such distinction is likely itself to reflect politics, and in an illegitimate way. Thus the free speech principle extends not simply to efforts to contribute to politics, but also and equally to sexually explicit speech, music, art, and commercial speech. Speech, simply, is speech.

Finally, any restrictions on speech, once permitted, have a sinister and nearly inevitable tendency to expand. Principled limits on government are hard to come by; to allow one kind of restriction is, in practice, to allow many other kinds as well. "Slippery slope" arguments therefore deserve a prominent place in the theory of free expression. For the same reason, "balancing" ought so far as possible to play no role in free speech law. Judges should not uphold restrictions on speech simply because government seems to have good reasons for the restriction in the particular case.

Since 1965 or so, these principles have commanded enormous respect. They were advocated with special enthusiasm by the press itself, but also by many teachers in law schools and political science departments, and of course by numerous litigators, most notably the American Civil Liberties Union.

In the same period, the components of the opposing position are also easy to identify.[5] On this view, balancing is an inevitable part of a sensible system of free expression, and "reasonable regulation" should be upheld. The meaning of the First Amendment should be settled by reference to history, including the relatively limited aims of the framers and the complexities of the Supreme Court's own precedents. Certain categories of speech fall outside the First Amendment altogether. These excluded categories include advocacy of crime, dangerous speech, commercial speech, hate speech, sexually explicit speech, and libel. Government has an appropriate role in maintaining a civilized society, and this principle means that it may guard against both the degradation produced by (for example) obscenity and the risks posed by speech advocating overthrow of the government. Large-scale neutrality makes no sense.

From the perspective of the present, it is hard to remember the vigor and tenacity with which the opposing camps struggled over their respective positions. The basic commitments of the first view are now clichés, even dogma. Despite its novelty and the absence of much historical support on its behalf, it has won a dramatic number of victories in the Supreme Court. This is so at least with respect to govern-

ment efforts to restrict speech on the basis of its content. Here special
judicial scrutiny is routine, except for quite narrow categories of excluded speech.[6] Thus constitutional protection has been accorded to
commercial speech; to most sexually explicit speech; to many kinds of
libel; to publication of the names of rape victims; to the advocacy of
crime, even of violent overthrow of the government; to large expenditures on electoral campaigns; to corporate speech; and of course to
flag burning.[7]

It is not an overstatement to say that taken all together, these developments have revolutionized the law of free expression. For many, the
new law is an occasion for a sense of triumph and, perhaps, a belief
that the principal difficulties with First Amendment law have been
solved. The remaining problems might be thought ones of applying
the hard-won doctrinal wisdom to ever-present threats of censorship.

In recent times, however, the commitments that emerged from the
last generation of free speech law have come under extremely severe
strain. Those commitments have been tested by emerging controversies over such issues as campaign finance regulation, hate speech,
"dial-a-porn," the securities laws, scientific speech, nude dancing,
commercial advertising, pornography, and regulation designed to produce quality and diversity in broadcasting. With these developments,
previous alliances have come apart. Sometimes the belief in "reasonable regulation" seems to have been resurrected for the new disputes.
Often one or more of the four basic commitments has been drawn into
sharp question.

The ironies in all this are abundant. The new coalitions have
spurred plausible arguments of hypocrisy: free speech advocates claim
that the liberal commitment to free speech is abandoned as soon as it
turns out that the commitment is inconvenient or requires protection
for unpopular causes. Indeed, it has been charged that for many, the
commitment to free speech stands revealed as merely contingent and
convenient, and not principled at all.

On the other hand, the broad enthusiasm for application of free
speech principles to the new settings seems ironic as well. The constitutional protection accorded to commercial speech, for example, is
extremely new, and it was once rejected by (among many others) Justices Douglas and Black,[8] probably the most vigorous advocates of
free expression in the history of the Supreme Court. The notion that
the First Amendment protects libel of ethnic groups, or hate speech, is
itself a quite modern development (if it is a development at all). The

First Amendment has not until recently been thought to cast any doubt on the securities laws. Until the last few decades, the states had very broad authority to regulate sexually explicit material. How the free speech principle interacts with campaign spending and broadcasting surely raises complex and novel issues.

In these circumstances it seems peculiar to insist that any regulatory efforts in these areas will inevitably pave the way toward quite general government incursions on speech. Insistence on the protection of all words seems especially odd when it is urged by those who otherwise proclaim the need for judicial restraint, for freeing up democratic processes from constitutional compulsion, and for a firm attention to history—ideas that would, in these contexts, argue most powerfully against invocation of the First Amendment.

Current constitutional law, then, faces a new set of constitutional problems. The contemporary issues have shattered old alliances and promise to generate new understandings of the problem of freedom of expression. I want to set out and evaluate two possible responses to the current state of affairs. Both responses draw on the distinctive American contribution to the theory of sovereignty.

The first proposal, described in this chapter, calls for a New Deal for speech. It would apply much of the reasoning of the New Deal attack on the common law to current questions of First Amendment law. Such an approach would produce significant changes in existing understandings of the nature of the free speech guarantee. At a minimum, it would insist that many imaginable democratic interferences with the autonomy of broadcasters or newspapers are not "abridgments" of free speech at all. It would also argue that such autonomy, created and guaranteed as it is by law, may sometimes be an abridgment.

The second approach, set out in Chapter 8, is less dramatic. It would proclaim that the overriding goal of the First Amendment, rightly perceived, is to protect democratic politics from government. This view would clarify a number of current controversies without fundamentally changing existing law.

Ultimately, I suggest that an insistence that the First Amendment is fundamentally concerned with democratic self-government, combined with modest steps in favor of a New Deal for speech, would resolve most of the current problems in free speech law without seriously compromising the First Amendment or any other important social values. But in order to reach this conclusion, it will be necessary to abandon or at least to qualify the basic principles that have dominated judicial and academic thinking about speech in the last generation.

Free Speech and Laissez-Faire?

A New Deal is necessary for speech, one that would parallel the New Deal provided to property rights during the 1930s, and that would be rooted in similar concerns.[9] We have seen that before the New Deal, the Constitution was often understood as a constraint on government "regulation." In practice, this meant that the Constitution often prohibited governmental interference with existing distributions of rights. On the pre–New Deal view, existing distributions marked the boundary not only between neutrality and partisanship but also between inaction and action. The rallying cry "laissez-faire" of course captured such ideas. The fear and (more important) the very conception of "government intervention" did the same. Status quo neutrality was the defining principle.

We have also seen that the New Deal reformers argued that this entire framework was built on fictions. Ownership rights were a creation of law. The government did not "act" only when it disturbed existing distributions. It was responsible for those distributions in the first instance. What people had, in markets, was partly a function of the entitlements that the law conferred on them. The notion of "laissez-faire" thus stood revealed as a conspicuous fiction. Different forms of governmental ordering had to be evaluated pragmatically and in terms of their consequences for social efficiency and social justice. Markets would not be identified with liberty in any a priori way; they would have to be evaluated through an examination of whether they served liberty or not.

These ideas have played little role in the law of free speech. For purposes of speech, contemporary understandings of neutrality and partisanship, or action and inaction, are identical with those that predate the New Deal. The category of government "intervention" is defined accordingly. Status quo neutrality dominates the law of free expression.

The recent First Amendment controversies confirm the wisdom of the New Deal on this score, and they show that American constitutionalism, with respect to freedom of expression, has failed precisely to the extent that it has not taken that reformation seriously enough. I do not mean at all to suggest that speech rights should be freely subject to political determination, as are (say) current issues of occupational safety and health. I do not mean to suggest that markets in speech are generally abridgments of speech or that they usually disserve the First Amendment. I do mean to say that at a minimum, what seems to be government regulation of speech might, in some circumstances, promote free speech, and should not be treated as an abridgment at all. I mean also to argue, though more hesitantly, that what seems to be free speech in markets might, on reflection, amount to an abridgment of free speech. Consider here Robert Hale's suggestion, capturing much of my argument, to the effect that "the power to set judicial machinery in motion for the enforcement of legal duties" should "be recognized as a delegation of state power." [10] This recognition is precisely what is missing from current free speech law.

A general clarification is necessary at the outset. It will be tempting to think that my argument amounts to a broad and perhaps bizarre plea for "more regulation" of speech. Many of the practices and conditions that I will challenge are commonly taken to involve private action, and hence not to involve the Constitution at all. (Recall the state action doctrine, which means that private behavior is not subject to the Constitution.) The outcome of the "market" for expenditures on campaigns, and the practices of broadcasters and managers of newspapers, raise no constitutional question. It is "regulation" of "the market" that is problematic.

In fact there should be enthusiastic agreement that the First Amendment is aimed only at governmental action, and that private conduct raises no constitutional question. On this point the Constitution is clear. It seems clear, too, that to find a constitutional violation, one needs to show that governmental action has abridged the freedom of speech. That action must usually take the form of a law or regulation.

But if the New Deal is taken at all seriously, it follows, not that the requirement of state action is unintelligible or incoherent, but that governmental rules lie behind the exercise of rights of property, contract, and tort. This is so especially when common law rules grant people rights of exclusive ownership and use of property. From this it does not follow that private acts are subject to constitutional constraint, or even that legally conferred rights of ownership violate any constitutional provision. To find a constitutional question, it is always necessary to point to some exercise of public power. And to find a constitutional violation, it is necessary to show that public power has compromised some constitutional principle. But a claim on behalf of, say, new efforts to promote greater quality and diversity in broadcasting is a claim for a new regulatory system, not for "government intervention" where none existed before.

Another clarification is in order. I have suggested that legal rules lie behind private behavior, and it will be tempting to think that this suggestion does dissolve the state action requirement. If private exclusion of speech is made possible by law, does not it turn out that the First Amendment invalidates private behavior after all? Is not all private action therefore state action? The answer is that it is not. A private university, expelling students for (say) racist speech, is not a state actor. The trespass law, which helps the expulsion to be effective, is indeed state action. The distinction matters a great deal. The trespass law, invoked in this context, is a content-neutral regulation of speech; the state allows use of the trespass law quite independently of the content of the speech. This form of regulation does not violate the First Amendment. It operates without regard to content, and it is supported by sufficient justifications to survive the moderate scrutiny applied to content-neutral restrictions.

By contrast, the behavior of the university is content-based, and if engaged in by a public official, it would indeed violate the First Amendment. We always need to identify the exercise of public power. Without it, there is no free speech issue, even on the New Deal view. And such power, when identified, often raises no serious constitutional issue when it takes the content-neutral form of protecting ownership rights.

What I want to suggest here is, first and foremost, that legal rules that are designed to promote freedom of speech and that interfere with other legal rules—those of the common law—should not be invalidated if their purposes and effects are constitutionally valid. It may also follow that common law rules are themselves subject to constitutional objection, and in some surprising places, if and when such rules "abridge the freedom of speech" by preventing people from speaking at certain times and in certain places.

Thus far these remarks are uncomfortably abstract; I will give them much more specific content below. Whether general or particular, they might seem unconventional. In fact, however, they have a clear foundation in no lesser place than *New York Times v. Sullivan*,[11] one of the defining cases of modern free speech law. There the Court concluded that a public official could not bring an action for libel unless he could show "actual malice," that is, knowledge of or reckless indifference to the falsity of the statements at issue. The *Sullivan* case is usually taken as the symbol of broad press immunity for criticism of public officials. Even more, *Sullivan* is often understood to reflect the conception of freedom of expression advocated by Alexander Meiklejohn[12]—a conception of self-government, connected to the American principle of sovereignty.

It is striking that in *Sullivan*, the lower court held that the common law of tort, and more particularly of libel, was not state action at all, and was therefore entirely immune from constitutional constraint.[13] A civil action, on this view, involved a purely private dispute. The Supreme Court quickly disposed of this objection, as seems obviously right. The use of public tribunals to punish speech is conspicuously state action. What is interesting is not the Supreme Court's rejection of the argument, but the fact that the argument could be made by a state supreme court as late as the 1960s. How could reasonable judges perceive the rules of tort law as purely private?

The answer lies in the persistence of status quo neutrality and pre– New Deal understandings—to the effect that the common law simply implements existing rights or private desires and does not amount to "intervention" or "action" at all. The view that the common law of property should be taken as prepolitical and just, and as a refusal to use government power—the view that the New Deal repudiated— was the same as the view of the state supreme court in *Sullivan*. Reputation is of course a property interest, and just as in the pre–New Deal era, the protection of that interest did not appear to involve government action at all.

The Supreme Court's rejection of that claim seemed inevitable in *Sullivan* itself, and indeed this aspect of the case is largely forgotten. But many aspects of current law are based on precisely the same understandings as underlie the forgotten view of that obscure court. In fact we might generalize from *Sullivan* the broad idea that protection of property rights, through the common law, must always be assessed pragmatically in terms of its effects on speech. This idea has major implications. In a regime of property rights, there is no such thing as no regulation of speech; the question is what forms of regulation best serve the purposes of the free speech guarantee.

Consider, for example, the issues raised when people claim a right of access to the media or seek controls on broadcasting in general. Suppose that most broadcasters deal little or not at all with issues of public importance, restricting themselves to stories about movie stars or sex scandals. Suppose too that there is no diversity of view on the airwaves, but instead a bland, watered-down version of conventional morality. A large part of the problem, for the system of free expression, is the governmental grant of legal protection—rights of exclusive use—to enormous institutions having huge resources with which to dominate communication.

That grant of power—sometimes through the common law, sometimes through statute—is usually taken not to be a grant of power at all, but instead to be purely "private." Thus the exclusion of people and views from the airwaves is immunized from constitutional constraint, on the theory that the act of exclusion is purely private; thus rights of access to the media are thought to involve governmental intervention into the private sphere; so too with attempted limits on campaign expenditures.

In *Sullivan* the Supreme Court said, as against a similar claim, that common law rules should be inspected for their conformity with the overriding principle that government may not restrict freedoms of speech and press. "The test is not the form in which state power has been applied but, whatever the form, whether such power has in fact been exercised." [14]

We might apply this understanding to current problems. If the First Amendment is regarded as an effort to ensure that people are not prevented from speaking, especially on issues of public importance, then the commitments that currently dominate free speech law seem ill adapted to current conditions. Above all, the conception of government regulation turns out to misstate important issues and sometimes to disserve the goal of free expression itself. With broadcasting, the "form" of the exclusion is rights of exclusive ownership that prevent certain people from speaking, and do so through law.

Some regulatory efforts, superimposed on current regulation through current property rules, may promote free speech, whereas the property rules may undermine it. Such efforts might not be "abridgments" of freedom of speech; they might increase free speech. To know whether this is so, it is necessary to understand their purposes and consequences. Less frequently, the use of property rules to foreclose efforts to speak might represent impermissible restrictions on speech. To know whether this is so, it is necessary to assess the effects of such rules in terms of their consequences for speech. In any case both reform efforts and the status quo must be judged by their consequences, not by question-begging characterizations of "threats from government."

It is tempting to understand this argument as a suggestion that the New Dealers were concerned about private power over working conditions, and that modern constitutional courts should be more interested in the existence of private power over expression or over democratic processes.[15] But this formulation misses the real point, and does so in a way that suggests its own dependence on status quo neutrality and pre–New Deal understandings. The major problem is not that private power is an obstacle to free speech; even if it is, private power is not regulated by the First Amendment. Nor would it be accurate to say that employer power was the central concern for the New Dealers. The real problems are that public authority creates legal rules that restrict speech; that new exercises of public authority can counter the existing restrictions; and that any restrictions, even those of the common law of property, must be assessed under constitutional principles precisely because they are restrictions.

Consider, for example, a case in which the owners of a large shopping center exclude from their property war protesters who believe that the center is the best place to draw attention to their cause. The Supreme Court has said that the First Amendment is not implicated, since no government regulation of speech is involved. All that has happened is that private property owners have barred people from their land.[16]

In fact this is a poor way to understand the situation. It is actually the state court's view in *Sullivan*. The owners of the shopping center are able to exclude the protesters only because government has conferred on them a legal right to do so. The conferral of that right is an exercise of state power. It is this action that restricts the speech of the protesters. Surely it is a real question whether the grant of exclusionary power violates the First Amendment, at least in circumstances in which it eliminates the only real way of making a political protest visible to members of the community.

Or consider a case in which a network decides not to sell advertising time to a group that wants to discuss some public issue or to express some dissident view. Under current law, the refusal raises no First Amendment question, in part because a number of the justices—perhaps now a majority—believe that there is no state action.[17] But broadcasters are given property rights in their licenses by government, and the grant of such rights is unambiguously state action. To be sure, it is generally good to have a system in which government creates ownership rights or markets in speech, just as it is usually good to create rights of ownership, and markets, in property. But it remains true that a right of exclusive ownership in a television network is governmentally conferred; the exclusion of the would-be speakers is backed up, or made possible, by the law of (among other things) civil and criminal trespass. It is thus a product of a governmental decision.

A system in which only certain views are expressed or made available to most of the public is a creation of law. The constitutional question is whether reforms eliminating exclusive ownership rights—or, more precisely, eliminating an element of such rights by conditioning the original grant—are consistent with the First Amendment, or whether the government grant of exclusive ownership rights violates the First Amendment. We cannot answer such questions merely by saying that ownership rights are governmental. We need to know the purposes and effects of the grant. That question cannot be answered a priori or in the abstract. We need to know a lot of details.

It might be tempting to respond that the Constitution creates "negative" rights rather than "positive" ones, or at least that the First Amendment is "negative" in character—a right to protection against the government, not to help from the government. So stated, the claim certainly captures the conventional wisdom. Any argument for a New Deal for speech must therefore come to terms with the view that the Constitution does not create positive rights and should not be understood to do so.

There are two responses to this view. The first and most fundamental is that no one is asserting a positive right in these cases. Instead the claim is that government sometimes cannot adopt a legal rule that imposes a (negative) constraint on who can speak and where they can do so. When someone with view X is unable to state that view on the networks, the incapacity exists because the civil and criminal law prohibits him from doing so. Negative liberty is indeed involved.

This is the same problem that underlies a wide range of familiar constitutional claims; consider a ban on door-to-door soliciting. An attack on content-neutral restrictions of this kind is not an argument for positive government protection. It is merely a claim that legal rules that prevent certain people from speaking in certain places must be reviewed under First Amendment principles. In fact the response that a New Deal for speech would create a "positive right" trades on untenable, pre–New Deal distinctions between positive and negative rights.[18]

The second point is that the distinction between negative and positive rights fails even to explain current First Amendment law. There are two obvious counterexamples. The Supreme Court has come very close to saying that when an audience becomes hostile and threatening, the government is obligated to protect the speaker. Under current law, reasonable crowd control measures are probably constitutionally compelled, even if the result is to require a number of police officers to come to the scene.[19] The right to speak thus includes a positive right to governmental protection against a hostile private audience.

Or let us return to the area of libel. By imposing constitutional restraints on the common law of libel, the Court has held, in effect, that those who are defamed must subsidize speakers, by allowing their reputation to be sacrificed to the end of broad diversity of speech. Even more than this, the Court has held that government is under (what might be seen as) an affirmative duty to "take" the reputation of people who are defamed in order to promote the interest in free speech. The First Amendment requires a governmentally produced subsidy of personal reputation for the benefit of speech.[20]

Cases of this sort reveal that the First Amendment, even as currently conceived, is no mere negative right. It has positive dimensions as well. Those positive dimensions consist in a command to government to take steps to ensure that the system of free expression is not violated by legal rules giving too much authority to private persons. In the hostile audience case, government is obliged to protect the speaker against private silencing; in the libel cases, government is obliged to do the same thing, that is, to provide an extra breathing space for speech even though one of the consequences is to infringe on the common law interest in reputation.

In any case, a constitutional question might well be raised by a broadcasting system in which government confers on networks the right to exclude certain points of view. In principle, the creation of that right is parallel to the grant of a right to a hostile audience to silence controversial speakers, subject only to the speakers' power of self-help through the marketplace (including the hiring of private police forces). In the hostile audience setting, it is insufficient to say that any intrusion on the speaker is private rather than governmental. It is necessary instead to evaluate the consequences of the system by reference to the purposes of the First Amendment—just as it is necessary to evaluate the consequences of any system in which property rights operate to hurt some and benefit others.

None of this demonstrates that the creation of property rights in broadcasting fails to produce broad diversity of views and an opportunity to speak for opposing sides. If it does, the market system created by law is constitutionally unobjectionable. But it is surely conceivable that a market system will have less fortunate consequences.

We might look in this connection at the Court's remarkable opinion in the *Red Lion* case.[21] There the Court upheld the fairness doctrine, which required attention to public issues and a chance to speak for opposing views. (At least the doctrine required these in theory; it was rarely enforced in practice.)[22] In the *Red Lion* opinion, the Court actually seemed to suggest that the doctrine was constitutionally compelled. According to the Court, the fairness doctrine would "enhance rather than abridge the freedoms of speech and press," for free expression would be disserved "by unlimited private censorship operating in a medium not open to all." The Court suggested that

> as far as the First Amendment is concerned those who are licensed stand no better than those to whom licenses are refused. A license permits broadcasting, but the licensee has no constitutional right to be the one who holds the license or to monopolize a radio frequency to the exclusion of his fellow citizens. There is nothing in the First Amendment which prevents the Government from requiring a licensee to share his frequency with others and to conduct himself as a proxy or fiduciary with obligations to present those views and voices which are representative of his community and which would otherwise, by necessity, be barred from the airwaves.

Thus the Court emphasized that

> the people as a whole retain their interest in free speech by radio and their collective right to have the medium function consistently with the ends and purposes of the First Amendment. It is the right of the viewers and listeners, not the right of the broadcasters, which is paramount. It is the purpose of the First Amendment to preserve an uninhibited marketplace of ideas in which truth will ultimately prevail, rather than to countenance monopolization of that market, whether it be by the Government itself or a private licensee. It is the right of the public to receive suitable access to social, political, esthetic, moral, and other ideas and experiences which is crucial here. That right may not constitutionally be abridged either by Congress or by the FCC.[23]

Compare this suggestion from the head of the FCC in the 1960s: "It was time to move away from thinking about broadcasters as trustees. It was time to treat them the way almost everyone else in society does—that is, as businesses. . . . [T]elevision is just another appliance. It's a toaster with pictures."[24]

The *Red Lion* vision of the First Amendment stresses not the autonomy of broadcasters (made possible only by current ownership rights), but instead the need to promote democratic self-government by ensuring that people are presented with a broad range of views about public issues. In a market system, this goal may be compromised. It is hardly clear that "the freedom of speech" is promoted by a regime in which people are permitted to speak only if other people are willing to pay enough to allow them to be heard.

This argument applies most conspicuously to broadcasters, since the role of the government in allocating licenses is obvious. It applies most clearly in a system of scarce licenses, as the Court emphasized. But it has force elsewhere as well. It applies, for example, to newspapers, whose property rights also amount to a legally conferred power to exclude others. Simply as a matter of fact, that power is a creation of the state. It is a function of the law of property. The resulting system must be assessed in terms of its consequences for speech. And it is not clear that the problems disappear even when licenses are plentiful. Even in such a system, markets may disserve free speech goals—a point taken up in detail below.

If all this is correct, the first two commitments of current First Amendment law come under severe strain. The idea that threats to speech come from government is undoubtedly correct, but as usually understood it is far too simple. Sometimes threats come from what seems to be the private sphere, and, much more fundamentally, the threats are made possible only by legal entitlements that enable some people but not others to speak and to be heard. And when this is so, a large risk to a system of free expression, not readily visible to current law, is the existence of legal rights that diminish opportunities to exercise rights of free expression.

Second, the idea that government should be neutral among all forms of speech seems right in the abstract, but as frequently applied it is no more plausible than the idea that it should be neutral between the associational interests of blacks and those of whites under conditions of segregation, or between the freedom of employers and workers under conditions in which market pressures drive hours dramatically up and wages dramatically down. The difficulty with this conception of neutrality is that it takes existing distributions of resources and opportunities as the baseline for decision.

The most general problem is that neutrality is frequently thought to be exemplified in the use of economic markets to determine access to the media and thus an opportunity to be heard. This form of neutrality actually embodies a collective choice, captured in the use of the market and the creation of particular legal standards for its operation, that ensures that some will be unable to speak or to be heard at all, and at the same time that others will be permitted to dominate public communication. Markets usually promote both liberty and prosperity. But when the legal creation of a market has harmful consequences for free expression—and it sometimes does—it must be reevaluated in light of free speech principles.

Practice

A core insight of the *Red Lion* case is that the interest in private autonomy from government is not always the same as the interest in free speech through democratic self-governance. To immunize broadcasters from legal control may not promote quality and diversity in broadcasting. It may be inconsistent with the First Amendment's own commitments. The question then becomes what sorts of regulatory strategies have the most beneficial effects for the system of free expression.

We might be able to generate a First Amendment New Deal, with many proposals for constitutional reform. I describe those proposals in summary fashion here. Of course a more detailed discussion would be necessary in order fully to come to terms with any one of them.

BROADCASTING

For much of its history, the FCC has imposed on broadcast licensees the so-called fairness doctrine, which requires licensees to allocate some time to issues of public importance and creates an obligation to allow access by people of diverse views.

The last decade has witnessed a mounting constitutional assault on the fairness doctrine. Licenses are no longer technologically scarce; indeed, there are far more radio and television stations than there are major newspapers. The FCC recently concluded that the fairness doctrine violates the First Amendment, because it involves an effort by government to tell broadcasters what they may say. On this view, the fairness doctrine represents a form of impermissible government intervention into voluntary market interactions. For this reason it is a violation of the government's obligation of neutrality, reflected in respect for market outcomes.[25] Influential judges and scholars have reached the same conclusion. The analysis is an especially important illustration of status quo neutrality in current law.

The Constitution does forbid any "law abridging the freedom of speech." But is the fairness doctrine such a law? To its defenders, the fairness doctrine promotes "the freedom of speech" by ensuring diversity of views on the airwaves, diversity that the market may fail to bring about. Actually the FCC's attack asserts, without a full look at the real-world consequences of different regulatory strategies, that the doctrine involves governmental interference with an otherwise purely law-free and voluntary private sphere.

Instead those entrusted with interpreting the Constitution should deal with the fairness doctrine by exploring the relationships among a market in broadcasting, alternative systems, and the goals, properly characterized, of a system of free expression. On the one hand, it seems clear that a market will provide diversity in available offerings, especially in a period when there are numerous outlets. So long as the particular view is supported by market demand, it should find a supplier. The broadcasting status quo is far preferable to a system of centralized government regulation, at least if such a system sharply constrains choice. Markets do offer a range of opinions and options. A government command-and-control system, if it restricted diversity of view and attention to public affairs, would indeed abridge "the freedom of speech." Nothing I have said argues in favor of governmental foreclosure of political speech.

We should therefore distinguish among three possible scenarios. First, the market might itself be unconstitutional if it produces little political discussion or little diversity of view. For reasons suggested below, courts should be cautious in so concluding, in part because the issue turns on complex factual matters not within the competence of judges. Second, government regulation of the market might well be upheld, as against a First Amendment challenge, if the legislature has made a considered judgment, based on a record, that the particular regulation will indeed promote free speech goals. Third, regulation of the market should be invalidated if it discriminates against certain viewpoints, or if regulation actually diminishes attention to public affairs or diminishes diversity of view. On this latter, highly factual question, the legislature is entitled to a presumption of constitutionality.

Importantly, the existence of a market will make it unnecessary for government officials to oversee the content of speech in order to assess its value. The fact that a market removes official oversight surely counts strongly in its favor. The restrictions of the market are content-neutral, in the sense that the content of the speech is not directly relevant to the application of property law. But the restrictions of the fairness doctrine, or of any similar alternative, are content-based, in the sense that any such doctrine would have to be applied with government attention to the content of the speech.

On the other hand, a market in communications will create many problems. Imagine, for example, if someone proposed that the right to speak should be given to those people to whom other people were willing to pay enough to qualify them to be heard. Suppose, in other words, that the allocation of speech rights was decided through a pricing system, like the allocation of soap, cars, or candy. It would follow that people would be prevented from speaking if other people were not willing to pay enough to entitle them to talk.

Surely this would be a strange parody of democratic aspirations—the stuff of science fiction, rather than self-government. It would be especially perverse insofar as it would ensure that dissident speech—expression for which people are often unwilling to pay—would be foreclosed. But in many respects, this is precisely the system we have. Broadcasting licenses and speech opportunities are allocated very much on the basis of private willingness to pay.

In one respect our system is even worse, for programming content is produced not merely by consumer demand, but also by the desires of advertisers. Viewers are in this way the product as well as its users. This phenomenon introduces some large additional distortions. In any case, the First Amendment issues must depend in part on the details.

Some facts. Much information has now been compiled on local news, which began, incidentally, as a direct response to the FCC's fairness doctrine. In fact very little of local news is devoted to genuine news. Instead it deals largely with stories about movies and television and with sensationalized disasters of little substantive interest. "The search for emotion-packed reports with mass appeal has led local television news to give extensive coverage to tragedies like murders, deaths in fires, or plane crashes, in which they often interview survivors of victims about 'how they feel.' "[26]

During a half hour of news, no more than eight to twelve minutes involves news at all. Each story that does involve news typically ranges from twenty to thirty seconds. Even the news stories tend not to involve issues of government and policy, but instead focus on fires, accidents, and crimes. Government stories are further deemphasized during the more popular evening show. And even coverage of government tends to describe not the content of relevant policies, but instead sensational and often misleading "human impact" anecdotes. In addition, there has been greater emphasis on "features"—dealing with popular actors, or entertainment shows, or even the movie immediately preceding the news. Economic pressures seem to be pushing local news in this direction even when reporters would prefer to deal with public issues in a more serious way.

With respect to network news, the pattern is similar. In 1988 almost 60 percent of the national campaign coverage involved "horse race" issues—who was winning, who had momentum—while only about 30 percent involved issues and qualifications. In the crucial period from January to June 1988, there were about 450 minutes of campaign coverage, of which no less than 308 minutes dealt with the "horse race" issues.[27]

It is notable in this regard that for presidential candidates, the average block of uninterrupted speech fell from 42.3 seconds in 1968 to only 9.8 seconds in 1988. A statement of more than 10 seconds is therefore unlikely to find its way onto the major networks. There is little sustained coverage of the substance of candidate speeches.

There has been an increase as well in stories about television and movies, and a decrease in attention to public questions. In 1988, coverage of arts and entertainment news averaged thirty-eight minutes per month; in the first half of 1990, the average was sixty-eight minutes per month. According to one person involved in the industry, "By the necessity of shrinking ratings, the network news departments have had to, if not formally then informally, redefine what is news." According to the executive producer of NBC's nightly news, "A lot of what we used to do is report on the back and forth of where we stood against the Russians. But there is no back and forth anymore. I mean nobody is talking about the bomb, so you have to fill the time with the things people *are* talking about."[28] Note the problem of circularity: What people are talking about is in part a function of what sorts of things are presented on the popular media.

There is evidence as well, though so far largely anecdotal, of advertiser influence over programming content. No conspiracy theory will have plausibility. But some recent events are disturbing. There are reports, for example, that advertisers are having a large impact on local news programs, especially with respect to consumer reports. In Minneapolis, a local car dealer responded to a story involving consumer problems with his company by pulling almost $1 million dollars in advertisements. He said: "We vote with our dollars. If I'm out trying to tell a good story and paying $3,000 for 30 seconds, and someone's calling me names, I'm not going to be happy." Consumer reporters have increasingly pointed to a need for self-censorship. According to one, "We don't even bother with most auto-related stories anymore"; according to another, "I won't do the car repair story, or the lemon story . . . It's not worth the hassle." [29] In a revealing recent episode, Turner Broadcasting Systems (TBS) and the Audubon Society produced a program dealing with the spotted owl controversy between loggers and environmentalists in the Pacific Northwest. Believing that the program was biased, members of the logging industry did not want it to be aired; all eight advertisers (including Ford, Citicorp, Exxon, and Sears) pulled their sponsorship of the program. TBS aired the program anyway, but was forced to lose the $100,000 spent on production.[30] Similarly, NBC had severe difficulties in finding sponsors for its television movie "Roe v. Wade." Fearful of boycotts by religious groups, hundreds of sponsors solicited by NBC refused to participate.[31] It seems highly unlikely that advertisers could be found for any program adopting a "pro-life" or "pro-choice" perspective.

Educational programming for children on television simply cannot acquire sponsors. On ordinary commercial networks, high-quality fare has been practically unavailable, and programming has been designed largely to capture attention and to sell products. In the 1960s, the FCC issued recommendations and policy statements calling for "programming in the interest of the public" rather than "programming in the interest of salability." In 1974 it concluded that "broadcasters have a special obligation to serve children," and thus pressured the industry to adopt codes calling for educational and informational programs. In 1981, the new FCC Chair, Mark Fowler, rejected this approach, and educational television for children tends to be limited to the Public Broadcasting System.[32] Since 1981, good network programming for children has dramatically decreased, and programs based on products have taken its place. Thus children's television has become "a listless by-product of an extraordinary explosion of entrepreneurial life forces taking place elsewhere—in the business of creating and marketing toys." [33] In 1983 cartoons based on licensed characters accounted for fourteen programs; by 1985 the number had risen to more than forty. It has increased since.

Most of the resulting shows are quite violent, and the violence has increased since deregulation. Statistical measures are of course inadequate, but it is at least revealing that before 1980 there were 18.6 violent acts per hour for children's programs, whereas since 1980 the number has increased to 26.4 acts per hour. Children's daytime weekend programs have been consistently more violent than prime-time shows. Few of these shows have educational content.

More generally, there is a high level of violence on television.[34] Seven of ten prime-time programs depict violence; during prime time in 1980 there were on average 5 to 6 violent acts per hour. By 1989 the number had increased to 9.5 acts per hour. In 1980 ten shows depicted an average of more than 10 acts of violence per hour; by 1989 the number was sixteen; the high mark was in 1985, with twenty-nine such shows. Violence on children's television has been found to increase children's fear and also to contribute to their own aggression.[35]

Empirical studies also show that news and entertainment programming sometimes discriminates on the basis of gender. In the news, women are most frequently depicted as "family members, that is, they [are] the mothers or other relatives of hostages, gunmen, spies, afflicted children and the like."[36] Next most frequent is the appearance of women as victims, including battered women, stabbing victims, and residents of areas affected by earthquakes and toxic waste sites. When women appear as speaking subjects on some public issue, they often do so against some position traditionally associated with women; thus Christie Hefner was used as a prominent critic of an antipornography report, and a female doctor was seen to defend a company policy of transferring women out of jobs dealing with hazardous chemicals. Television programming in general has been found to show women in subordinate positions.[37]

Children's programming frequently consists exclusively of male characters, and when a female character is added, "a group of male buddies will be accented by a lone female, stereotypically defined."[38] On this pattern, "the female is usually a little-sister type" or functions as "a girl Friday to . . . male superheroes." Thus "[g]irls exist only in relation to boys." Of dramatic characters in one survey, women made up only 16 percent, and "females were portrayed as younger than males, more likely to be married, less active and with lower self esteem."[39]

Potential correctives. Regulatory strategies cannot solve all these problems. But they could help with some. Some such strategies should not be treated as abridgments of the freedom of speech.

In an era of cable television, the relevant problems might be supposed to disappear. People can always change the channel. Some stations even provide public affairs broadcasting around the clock. Both quality and diversity can be found in the dazzling array of options made available by modern technology. In this light, a concern about the broadcasting market might seem to be a puzzling, even bizarre rejection of freedom of choice. Ought not government foreclosure of expressive options to be considered an infringement on freedom of speech?

There are several answers. First, information about public affairs has many of the characteristics of a "public good," like national defense or clean air.[40] It is well known that if we rely entirely on markets, we will have insufficient national defense and excessively dirty air. The reason is that both defense and clean air cannot be feasibly provided to one person without simultaneously being provided to many or all. In these circumstances, each person has inadequate incentives to seek or to pay for the right level of national defense or clean air. Acting individually, each person will "free ride" on the efforts of others. No producer will have the right incentives. The result will be unacceptably low levels of the relevant goods.

Much the same is true of information, especially with respect to public affairs. The benefits of a broad public debate, yielding large quantities of information, accrue simultaneously to many or all people. Once information is provided to one person or to several, it is also provided to many others, or it can be so provided at minimal cost. The production of information for one or some persons thus yields large additional benefits for other people as well. But—and this is the key point—the market provides no mechanism to ensure that these benefits will be adequately taken into account by those who produce the information, in this case the newspaper and broadcasting industries.

At the same time, the benefits of informing one person—of making someone an effective citizen—are likely to accrue to many other people as well, through that person's contribution to multiple conversations and to political processes in general. But these additional benefits for each person will not be taken into account in individual consumption choices.

Because of the "public good" features of information, no single person has sufficient incentive to pay for the benefits received. The result will be that the market will produce too little information. Reliance on free markets in information will therefore have some of the same problems as reliance on markets for national defense or environmental protection. For this reason a regulatory solution, solving the public good problem, is justified.[41]

So much for the public good issue. The second problem with reliance on the large number of outlets is that sheer numbers do not explain why there is a constitutional objection to democratic efforts to increase quality and diversity by ensuring better programming on individual stations. Even with a large number of stations, there is far less quality and diversity than there might be. Of course people can change the channel. But why should the Constitution bar a democratic decision to experiment with new methods for achieving their Madisonian goals?

Third, it is important to be extremely cautious about the use, for constitutional and political purposes, of the notion of "consumer sovereignty." Consumer sovereignty is the conventional economic term for the virtues of a free market, in which goods are allocated through consumer choices, as these are measured by how much people are willing to pay for things. Those who invoke the notion of free choice in markets are really insisting on consumer sovereignty. But Madison's conception of sovereignty is the relevant one, and that conception has an altogether different character.

On the Madisonian view, sovereignty entails respect not for private consumption choices, but for the considered judgments of a democratic polity. We saw in Chapter 6 that in a democracy, laws frequently reflect those judgments, or what might be described as the aspirations of the public as a whole. Those aspirations can and often do call for markets themselves. But they might also call for intrusions on markets—a familiar phenomenon in such areas as environmental law, protection of endangered species, social security, and antidiscrimination law. Democratic liberty should not be identified with "consumer sovereignty." And in the context at hand, the people, acting through their elected representatives, might well decide that democratic liberty is more valuable than consumer sovereignty.

Finally, private broadcasting selections are a product of preferences that are a result of the broadcasting status quo, and not independent of it—a particular application of the argument also set out in Chapter 6. In a world that provides the existing fare, it is scarcely surprising that people generally prefer to see what they are accustomed to seeing. They have not been provided with the opportunities of a better system. When this situation prevails, the broadcasting status quo cannot, without circularity, be justified by reference to the preferences. Preferences that have adapted to an objectionable system cannot justify that system. If better options are put more regularly in view, it might well be expected that at least some people would be educated as a result. They might be more favorably disposed toward programming dealing with public issues in a serious way.

It is tempting but inadequate to object that this view embodies a form of "paternalism" unjustifiably overriding private choices. If private choice is a product of existing options, and in that sense a product of law, the inclusion of better options, through new law, does not displace a freely produced desire. At least this is so if the new law has a democratic pedigree. In that case, the people, in their capacity as citizens, are attempting to implement aspirations that diverge from their consumption choices.

For those skeptical about such arguments, it may be useful to note that many familiar democratic initiatives are justified on precisely these grounds. As against the two-term rule for the president, it is hardly decisive that voters can reject the two-term president in individual cases if they choose. The whole point of the rule is to reflect a precommitment strategy. And to those who continue to be skeptical, it is worthwhile to emphasize that a Constitution is itself a precommitment strategy, and that this includes the First Amendment itself.

What approaches might emerge from considerations of this sort? Here we should be frankly experimental. Flexible solutions supplementing market arrangements should be presumed preferable to government command-and-control.[42] There is a strong case for public provision of high-quality programming for children or for incentives, imposed by government on broadcasters, to provide such programming. The provision of free media time to candidates would be especially helpful, simultaneously providing attention to public affairs and diversity of view, while overcoming the distorting effects of "sound bites" and financial pressures.

More generally, government might award "points" to license applicants who promise to deal with serious questions or to provide public-affairs broadcasting even if unsupported by market demand. Or government might require purely commercial stations to provide financial subsidies to public television or to commercial stations that agree to provide less profitable but high-quality programming. It is worthwhile to consider more dramatic approaches as well—such as compulsory public-affairs programming, rights of reply, reductions in advertising on children's television, content review of such television by nonpartisan experts, or guidelines to encourage attention to public issues and diversity of view.

Of course there will be room for both discretion and abuse in making decisions about quality and public affairs. There is thus a legitimate concern that any governmental supervision of the sort I have outlined would pose risks more severe than those of the status quo. The market, surrounded by existing property rights, will indeed restrict speech. But at least it does not entail the sort of substantive approval or disapproval, or overview of speech content, that would be involved in the suggested "New Deal." Surely it is plausible to say that the relative neutrality of the market minimizes the role of public officials in a way that makes it the best of the various alternatives.

There are two responses. The first is that the current system is worse than imperfect; it creates extremely serious obstacles to a well-functioning system of free expression. The absence of continuous government supervision should not obscure the point. With respect to attention to public issues and diversity of view, the status quo badly disserves Madisonian goals.

The second point is that it does indeed seem plausible to think that the key decisions can be made in a nonpartisan way, as is generally the case for public television. Regulatory policies have helped greatly in the past. They are responsible for the very creation of local news. They have helped increase the quality of children's television. Public television, which has a wide range of high-quality fare, needs government help. We have no basis for doubting that much larger improvements could be brought about in the future.

How might all this bear on the constitutional question? It seems quite possible that a law that contained regulatory remedies would promote rather than undermine "the freedom of speech," at least if we understand that phrase in light of the distinctive American contribution to the theory of sovereignty. The current system does not plausibly promote that understanding, but instead disserves and even stifles citizenship.

I have not argued that government should be free to regulate broadcasting however it chooses. Regulation designed to eliminate a particular viewpoint would of course be out of bounds. All viewpoint discrimination would be banned. More draconian controls than those I have described—for example, a requirement of public affairs broadcasting around the clock—would raise quite serious questions. But at the very least, legislative "fairness doctrines" would raise no real doubts.[43]

Legislative efforts to restructure the marketplace might even be seen as the discharge of the legislature's constitutional duty, a duty that courts are reluctant, for (good) institutional reasons, fully to enforce. We might understand the courts' unwillingness to require something like a fairness doctrine to be a result of the judiciary's lack of a democratic pedigree, lack of fact-finding powers, and limited remedial authority. A legislature faces no such institutional limits. Its actions can therefore be treated as a response to genuine, though unenforced, constitutional obligations.

CAMPAIGN FINANCING
In Chapter 3 we saw that laws that restrict expenditures on campaigns have been justified as an effort to promote political deliberation and political equality by reducing the distorting effects of disparities in wealth. We also saw that the Supreme Court invalidated such laws as a kind of First Amendment "taking" from rich speakers for the benefit of poor ones. Thus it was that the Supreme Court pronounced, in *Buckley v. Valeo*, that "the concept that government may restrict the speech of some elements of our society in order to enhance the relative voice of others is wholly foreign to the First Amendment."

We also saw that *Buckley* reflects status quo neutrality, indeed that it should be seen as the modern-day analogue of *Lochner v. New York*:[44] a decision to take the market status quo as prepolitical, and use of that decision to invalidate democratic efforts at reform. Reliance on markets is governmental neutrality; use of existing distributions for political expenditures marks out government inaction. But from what I have said thus far, it should be clear that elections based on those distributions are actually subject to a regulatory system, made possible and constituted through law. That law consists, first, in legal rules protecting the present distribution of wealth, and more fundamentally, in legal rules allowing candidates to buy speech through markets.

Because it involves speech, *Buckley* is in one sense even more striking than *Lochner*. Efforts to redress economic inequalities or to ensure that they are not translated into political inequalities should not be

seen as impermissible redistribution or as the introduction of government regulation into a place where it did not exist before. Instead
campaign finance laws should be evaluated pragmatically in terms of
their consequences for the system of free expression.[45]

There are some hard questions here. The case for controls on campaign expenditures is plausible but hardly clear-cut; such controls
might well turn out to be incumbent protection measures. But an inquiry into these considerations would raise issues quite different from
those invoked by the *Buckley* Court.

RIGHT OF ACCESS

If it were necessary to bring about diversity and attention to public
matters, a private right of access to the media might even be constitutionally compelled. The notion that access will be a product of the
marketplace might well be constitutionally troublesome.[46] I have suggested that we would make a mockery of the democratic ideal if we
adopted a system allowing people to speak in accordance with the
amount of resources that other people were willing to pay to hear
them. In practice, our current system of free expression has many of
these features.

Suppose, for example, that a group objecting to a war or to the
practice of abortion seeks to buy advertising time to set out its view.
Suppose too that the networks refuse the deal because they object to
the message. It is fully plausibly that the refusal, backed up by the law,
violates the First Amendment, at least if other outlets are unavailable
or far less effective.

If a right of access is to be denied, it should be done because of the
Court's appropriate institutional modesty. The creation of such a right
would call for an unusually intrusive judicial role. It might also strain
judicial competence in light of the courts' limited fact-finding and pol-
icymaking capacities. As Robert Hale wrote in an analogous setting:
"It is perhaps fortunate, in some respects, that the courts have been
blind to the fact that much of the private power over others is in fact
delegated by the state, and that all of it is 'sanctioned' in the sense of
being permitted. This power permeates the entire economic system,
and attempts to alter it may have repercussions that require more
comprehensive treatment than a court is capable of doing; they may
also involve conflicts of interest that can be resolved better by legislative means."[47]

PROPERTY AND SPEECH

The creation of rights of exclusive use of property would raise constitutional problems whenever the consequence was to deprive people of a chance to present their views to significant parts of the public. We should review the creation of such rights under the standards applied to content-neutral classifications. This would mean that some form of balancing would be applied to the use of property law to exclude people from places plausibly indispensable for free and open discussion. Government would have to show that the harmful consequences on the exercise of rights of free speech were justified by important interests.

Ideas of this sort would entail a new look at the "shopping center" cases.[48] In these cases, people sought to use the grounds of the shopping center in order to engage in political protest. They claimed that access to those grounds was necessary if the public was to be presented with a certain point of view. In form, their claim is the same as underlies the notion (accepted by the Court) that the state may not ban leafletting or door-to-door solicitation.[49] In view of the role of the shopping center in many areas of the country, a right of access might well be justified. At a minimum, state legislatures and state courts should be encouraged to create such a right.

It would follow that insofar as newspapers invoke the law to prevent people from reaching the public, they too might be regulable without abridgment of the freedom of speech.[50] If the government seeks to promote quality and diversity in the newspapers, some mild regulatory efforts should be upheld, especially in view of the fact that many newspapers operate as de facto monopolies. Of course the regulation could not be based on point of view, and any regulation of content would have to be neutral, so as to remove concerns with viewpoint discrimination.

PUBLIC FORUMS

The "public forum" doctrine would have to be rethought. Current law appears to take the following form.[51] The state may not close off streets, parks, and other areas held open to the public "from time immemorial." Here the public has earned a kind of First Amendment "easement." Reasonable regulations will be upheld, but they cannot eliminate the basic right of access. The same rules apply to other areas if they have been "dedicated" to the public, that is, if the state has generally opened them for expressive activities. But still other areas—and this is a very large category—need not be open at all. Any restrictions will be upheld so long as they are minimally rational.

This system in fact turns on common law rules. It gives access only if the area has been "dedicated" by tradition for public access. This determination is based on whether, at common law, the area in question was held open. In a period when streets and parks were principal places for communicative activity, this historical test nicely served the basic free speech goal, which was the creation of access rights to places where such rights were most effective and most crucial.

But the streets and parks no longer carry out their common law roles. Other areas—certainly airports and train stations, perhaps mailboxes, probably broadcasting stations—are the modern equivalents of streets and parks. It is here that current doctrine is especially ill suited to current needs. To keep the streets and parks open is surely important. But it is far from enough, if we want to allow broadly diverse views to reach the public. For this reason the Court should abandon the common law test and look instead to whether the government has sufficiently strong and neutral reasons for foreclosing access to the property. Certainly Congress, state legislatures, and state courts should undertake this assessment. At least airports and train stations should be open to communicative efforts.

The Supreme Court was therefore incorrect when it ruled, by a five-to-four vote, that airports are not public forums for First Amendment purposes. As Justices Kennedy and Souter emphasized in dissent, it is absurd to say that only "traditional" public forums will qualify as such. For contemporary Americans, new arenas, unknown to the framers or to the common law, have assumed the role of those traditional forums. If the government has broad discretion to close off the areas where most people meet and congregate, it has broad discretion to undermine the system of free expression. In Justice Kennedy's words, "public forum doctrine ought not to . . . convert what was once an analysis protective of expression into one which grants the government authority to restrict speech by fiat." [52]

CONTENT DISCRIMINATION

It would become necessary to reassess the distinction between content-based and content-neutral restrictions on speech—the most central distinction in contemporary free speech law.

Under current law, the Court is very skeptical about any law that makes the content of speech relevant to restriction. If, for example, Congress tries to prevent speech dealing with a war from appearing on billboards, it is probably acting unconstitutionally. But content-neutral restrictions are treated more leniently. If Congress bars all speech on billboards, the measure will be subject to a balancing test. The reason is that the latter approach is neutral. On the conventional view, content-neutral restrictions do not skew the thinking process of the community and are unlikely to reflect an impermissible governmental motivation.

There is much to be said in favor of this conception of neutrality. In certain respects, however, it reproduces the framework of the *Lochner* era. It takes the market status quo as natural and just insofar as it bears on speech. It sees partisanship in alteration of that status quo, and neutrality in government decisions that respect it. But there may be no neutrality in use of the market status quo when the available opportunities are heavily dependent on wealth, on the common law framework of entitlements, and on what sorts of outlets for speech are made available, and to whom. In other words, the very notions "content-neutral" and "content-based" seem to depend on taking the speech status quo as if it were unobjectionable.

At least two things follow. The first and most important point is that many content-neutral laws have constitutionally troublesome content-differential effects. They do so precisely because they operate against a backdrop that should not be treated as prepolitical or just. The government's refusal to allow Lafayette Park in Washington, D.C., to be used as a place for dramatizing the plight of the homeless[53] is a prominent example. So too with a refusal to allow political speech on telephone poles, or to permit protesters to place material without stamps in mailboxes.[54]

These decisions have powerful harmful consequences for poorly financed causes. Rules that are content-neutral can, in view of an unjust status quo, have severe adverse effects on some forms of speech. Serious judicial scrutiny of content-neutral restrictions, with careful attention to this risk, is therefore appropriate.

The second point is to draw into question a familiar justification for skepticism about content-based regulation of speech. That justification is that such regulation "skews" the marketplace of ideas.[55] This idea has two problems. First, we do not have a full idea of what a well-functioning marketplace of ideas would look like. The preconditions of an economic marketplace can be specified by neoclassical economics. The same is not true for the preconditions of a system of free expression. What, for example, would be the appropriate distribution of basic rights and economic wealth in such a system? That question cannot be answered in the abstract, at least without a quite contestable theory of what ideas deserve representation.[56]

Second, the idea of skewing depends on taking the marketplace as unobjectionable in its current form. If it is already skewed, content-based regulation may be a corrective. It would be exceptionally surprising, moreover, if there were no such skewing. The marketplace of ideas is of course a function of existing law, including property law, which is responsible for the allocation of rights that can be turned into speech.

Thus far, then, I have suggested that some content-neutral restrictions should be carefully scrutinized, and that some content-based restrictions might plausibly be seen as a corrective to a content-based status quo. In general, however, the existence of an unjust status quo should probably not be a reason to allow regulation of the content of speech. The first reason is that the inquiry, for First Amendment purposes, is probably beyond governmental capacity. There is a serious risk that judicial or legislative decisions about the relative power of various groups, and about to whom redistribution is owed, will be biased or unreliable. Judgments about who is powerful and who is not must refer to some baseline. In making such judgments, government will inevitably be operating with its own biases, and those biases will thus affect any regulatory strategy. This risk seems unacceptable when speech is at stake.

What is distinctive about regulation of speech is that such regulation forecloses the channels of change; it prevents other views from being presented at all. Nothing like this can be said for the social and economic New Deal. Instead of allowing restrictions, we should encourage efforts to promote a better status quo. I have discussed some such efforts above in connection with the broadcasting market.

SPEECH AND DOLLARS
It would be necessary to reemphasize that there are limits on government's power to affect processes of speech through the use of government funds.

On this point, the Court's cases are exceptionally hard to unpack. It seems clear that in general, government may not use its power over funds or other government benefits so as to pressure people to relinquish rights that they "otherwise have." Thus, for example, the government may not say that in order to receive social security benefits, you must agree to vote for a Republican; or that if you want a driver's license, you must speak out in favor of your current senator. The idea here is that the government may not use funding as a lever to force people to speak in ways that they would otherwise refuse to do.

What if the government does not do this, but simply decides to allocate money to projects containing viewpoints that it prefers? What if government selectively funds certain projects, without saying that people who receive such funds must use "their own" time and resources in a certain way? The Court's most recent decision suggests that so long as the government is using its own money, and not affecting "private" expression, it can channel its funds however it wishes.

The problem in *Rust v. Sullivan*[57] arose when the Department of Health and Human Services issued regulations banning federally funded family planning services from engaging in counseling concerning, referrals for, and activities advocating abortion as a method of family planning. The plaintiffs claimed, among other things, that these regulations violated the First Amendment. In particular, they said that the regulations discriminated on the basis of point of view.

The Court disagreed. In the key passage it said: "The Government can, without violating the Constitution, selectively fund a program to encourage certain activities it believes to be in the public interest, without at the same time funding an alternate program which seeks to deal with the problem in another way. In so doing, the Government has not discriminated on the basis of viewpoint; it has merely chosen to fund one activity to the exclusion of the other." In response to the claim that the regulations conditioned the receipt of a benefit on the relinquishment of a right, the Court said that "here the government is not denying a benefit to anyone, but is instead simply insisting that public funds be spent for the purposes for which they were authorized."[58]

Taken very broadly, *Rust* seems to establish the important principle that government can allocate funds to private people to establish "a program" that accords with the government's preferred point of view. In fact the Court seems to make a sharp distinction between government coercion—entry into the private realm of markets and private interactions—on the one hand and funding decisions on the other.

So made, this distinction replicates pre–New Deal understandings.

It sees funding decisions as unproblematic because they do not interfere with the voluntary sphere. But this is merely a form of status quo neutrality. In fact there are no such fundamental distinctions among the law that underlies markets, the law that represents disruption of markets, and the law that calls for funding decisions. All of these are law. All of them must be assessed in terms of their purposes and effects.

To say this is not to say that funding decisions should be treated in the same way as other sorts of decisions. As we will see in Chapter 10, the development of constitutional limits on funding that affects speech raises exceedingly complex issues. But we now have reason to doubt whether *Rust* would be taken to its logical extreme. Can it be seriously argued that the government could fund the Democratic convention and refuse to fund the Republican convention? Is it possible that government could give grants only to people speaking in ways government likes? Affirmative answers would pose a serious threat to free speech under modern conditions.

Conclusion

A New Deal for speech has much to be said in its favor. Above all, such a reformation would reinvigorate processes of democratic deliberation, by ensuring greater attention to public issues and greater diversity of views on those issues.

Some qualifications are necessary here. A system of free markets in speech—surrounded by the law of property, contract, and tort—has major advantages over other forms of regulation. Such systems are content-neutral, at least on their face. This is an important point, above all because in markets no government official is authorized to decide who will be allowed to speak. There is no need to emphasize the risk of bias when government decides that issue. Markets have the enormous advantage of eliminating that risk. This is so even though markets have biases of their own.

In addition, markets are highly decentralized. For both the print and the electronic media, there are now many outlets. Someone unable to find space in the *New York Times* or on CBS may well be able to find space elsewhere. A great advantage of a market system is that other outlets remain available. At least some other forms of regulation do not have this salutary characteristic. In any case it is always important to ensure that any regulation does not foreclose certain points of view.

But our current system of free expression does not serve the Madisonian ideal. Free markets in expression are ill adapted to the American understanding of the principle of sovereignty. If we are to realize that principle, a New Deal for speech would be highly desirable.

CHAPTER 8

Speech in the Welfare State: The Primacy of Political Deliberation

A New Deal for speech would renovate the free speech tradition. Whether or not we attempt such a New Deal, the Madisonian conception insists that the First Amendment is principally about political deliberation. A renewal of this view, asserted most vigorously in the work of the philosopher Alexander Meiklejohn,[1] would help to resolve many current controversies. It would do so while maintaining the focus on deliberative democracy, and without sacrificing the basic features of free speech law as it now stands. It would be compatible with the New Deal for speech; but it could be accepted even if the New Deal were rejected.

On the Madisonian view, ours is a two-tier First Amendment.[2] Political speech lies at the core of the amendment, and it may be regulated only on the basis of the strongest showing of harm. But the presence of words or pictures is not, standing by itself, a sufficient reason for full constitutional protection. Bribery, criminal solicitation, threats, unlicensed medical advice, conspiracies, perjury—all these are words, to be sure, but they are not by virtue of that fact entitled to the highest level of constitutional protection. They may be regulated on the basis of a lesser showing of harm than is required for political speech. They are not entirely without constitutional protection; they count as "speech." But they do not lie within the core of the free speech guarantee.

Theory

THE TWO-TIER FIRST AMENDMENT

In order to defend this proposal, I begin by exploring whether there should indeed be a two-tier First Amendment, for the view that some forms of speech are less protected than others is frequently met with alarm. Notwithstanding the controversy, a view of this sort receives strong support from existing law. Indeed every justice has expressed some such view within the last generation. For example, the Supreme Court gives less than complete protection to commercial speech. It excludes obscenity from the First Amendment altogether. It treats libel of private persons quite differently from libel of people who are public figures.[3] The absence of protection for conspiracies, purely verbal workplace harassment of individuals on the basis of race and sex, unlicensed medical and legal advice, bribery, and threats appears to owe something to a distinction between the political and nonpolitical use of speech.

The Court has yet to offer a clear principle to unify the categories of speech that it treats as "low value." The apparent absence of a unifying principle is a source of continuing frustration to people who try to make sense of free speech law. It is tempting to think that some speech is unprotected because it is "really" not speech at all, but merely "action." But this notion is unhelpful. Conspiracies, unlicensed medical advice, and bribes are speech, not action; literally, they consist only of words, not of nonverbal behavior. If they are to be treated as action—that is, if they are not to be protected—it is because of their distinctive features. This is what we must discuss. The word *action* is simply a placeholder for that unprovided discussion.

Thus far, then, we see that the Supreme Court understands the First Amendment to have two tiers, and that the speech/action distinction is inadequate. But is a two-tier First Amendment either inevitable or desirable? It does seem that any well-functioning system of free expression must ultimately distinguish among different kinds of speech by reference to their centrality to the First Amendment guarantee.[4] It would not be plausible to say that all speech stands on the same footing, and that regulation of (for example) campaign speeches must be tested under the same standards applied to misleading commercial speech, child pornography, conspiracies, libel of private persons, and threats. If the same standards were applied, one of two results would follow; and both are unacceptable.

The first would be that the burden of justification imposed on government would have to be lowered as a whole, so as to allow for regulation of misleading commercial speech, private libel, and so forth. The effect would be an unacceptably high threat to political expression. A system in which political speech received the same (partial) protection given to commercial speech would produce serious risks to democratic self-governance. Government can regulate misleading or false commercial speech. If the standards were the same, government would also be allowed to regulate political speech when it is misleading or false, and this would provide too little breathing space for crucial speech. A system in which libel of government officials received no less protection than libel of ordinary citizens would produce the same risks. Such a system would deter criticism of government.

The second possibility would be that the properly stringent standards applied to efforts to regulate political speech would also be applied to commercial speech, private libel, and child pornography. The central problem with this approach is that it would ensure that government controls could not be applied to speech that in all probability should be regulated. We would make it difficult or impossible for government to regulate (among other things) criminal solicitation, child pornography, unlicensed medical advice, private libel, and false or misleading commercial speech. The harms that justify such regulation are of course real, but they are simply not grave enough to permit government controls under the extremely high standards applied to regulation of political speech. Under those high standards, the Constitution would require child pornography to be regulated not through controls on speech, but through controls on the production itself; criminal solicitation would be constitutionally permitted (it is often harmless because ineffectual), and only criminal conduct restricted.

These would in fact be the right conclusions if we impose, in these cases, the severe burden applied to government restrictions of "core" speech. If courts are to be honest about the matter, an insistence that "all speech is speech" would require the elimination of many currently unobjectionable and even necessary controls; or, more likely, judgments about value, because unavoidable, would continue to be made, but covertly.

If a distinction must be drawn between low- and high-value expression, the many efforts to understand the First Amendment only as a protection of "autonomy" may well be doomed to failure.[5] It has been suggested, for example, that the free speech principle protects the autonomy of speakers or of listeners, first by safeguarding their speech, and second by forbidding government to regulate speech because listeners might be influenced by it.

These suggestions are extremely valuable. They help explain why government interference with speech is especially troublesome. They also help account for the Court's protection of speech that is wholly nonpolitical. Government should not intrude on the individual's decision about what to believe; at least as a general rule, it should respect each person's capacity to make that choice for himself. This principle rules out certain commonly offered reasons for regulation of speech. It also helps explain why art, literature, and even commercial speech are entitled to constitutional protection.

But an autonomy principle is unlikely to provide a complete basis for understanding the free speech guarantee. I must be tentative about the point here, but it seems likely that any autonomy-based approach will make it difficult or impossible to make the necessary distinctions between different categories of speech. If we protect speech because and when people want to talk or listen, it is not easy to come up with standards by which to distinguish among different kinds of speech. Perhaps we will be able to say that the interest in autonomy calls for protection of art and literature but allows restrictions on bribery, threats, and even false commercial speech. Perhaps we can elaborate an autonomy principle in such a way as to make the appropriate distinctions. Perhaps we can even use such a principle to generate a two-tier First Amendment. I cannot fully discuss this possibility here. But it seems plausible that the adjustments of the autonomy principle will have a disturbingly ad hoc quality, and that something other than autonomy will really be at work. It seems hard, for example, to think that an autonomy principle can entirely explain the division between specially protected speech on the one hand and purely verbal sexual harassment, unlicensed medical or legal advice, child pornography, and misleading commercial speech on the other.

Moreover, an approach rooted only in a norm of autonomy may make it difficult to understand what is special about speech at all. Almost all voluntary acts, like almost all speech, seem to serve the goal of autonomy as this idea is usually understood by advocates of an autonomy-based conception of the First Amendment.[6] If autonomy in the abstract is the principle, there may be nothing distinctive about speech to explain why it has been singled out for constitutional protection. An approach to the First Amendment that does not account for the distinctiveness of speech would be untrue to constitutional text and structure. And if we do not account for the distinctiveness of speech, it will be very hard to decide hard free speech cases.

It is surely plausible to say that autonomy is a free speech value, and the interest in autonomy helps explain why all words are entitled to at least a degree of constitutional protection. But unless it can account for a two-tier system, autonomy is inadequate as a full account of the First Amendment.

THE CASE FOR THE PRIMACY OF POLITICS

It remains, however, to explain by what standard courts might accomplish the task of distinguishing between low-value and high-value speech. Of all the possible standards for distinguishing between forms of speech, an emphasis on democracy and politics seems likely to be best. To support this argument, it is of course necessary to define the category of political speech.

For present purposes I mean to treat speech as political *when it is both intended and received as a contribution to public deliberation about some issue.* It seems implausible to think that words warrant the highest form of protection if the speaker does not even intend to communicate a message. The First Amendment does not put jibberish at the core even if it is taken, by some in the audience, to mean something. An act of arson does not belong at the core simply because some people think that the act is a political protest; it is necessary that the speaker be trying to contribute to political deliberation.[7] By requiring intent, however, I do not mean to require a trial on the question of subjective motivation, and certainly I do not suggest that juries should make ad hoc decisions on that matter. Generally this issue can be resolved by making reasonable inferences from the speech at issue. We can think of some borderline cases, but it is probably not worth worrying much over them. In the real world, almost all cases will be easy on this score.

By requiring that the speech be received as political, I do not mean that all listeners or readers must see the political content. It is sufficient if some people do. Many people of course miss the political message in some forms of speech that should unquestionably qualify as political—especially art or literature. But if no one at all can see the political content, it is hard to understand why the speech should so qualify.

Finally, both requirements must be met, although in almost all cases speech that is intended as political will be seen by some people as such.

The requirements do belong in the conjunctive: The mere fact that some speech is seen by some as political is insufficient if we assume that it is not so intended. Consider, for example, an act of arson, commercial speech, obscenity, or private libel. If some people understand the speech in question to be political, it cannot follow that the speech qualifies as such for constitutional purposes, without treating almost all speech as political and therefore destroying the whole point of the two-tier model. Of course the definition I have offered leaves many questions unanswered, and there will be hard intermediate cases. I offer it as a starting point for analysis.

An approach that affords special protection to political speech, thus defined, is justified on numerous grounds. Such an approach receives firm support from history—not only from the framers' own theory of free expression, but also from the development of that principle through the long history of American law. There can be little doubt that suppression by the government of political ideas that it disapproved of or found threatening was the central motivation for the clause.[8] There can be little doubt that the main examples of unacceptable censorship in America and elsewhere involve efforts by government to insulate itself from criticism. A political conception of the First Amendment is also supported by the bulk of judicial interpretations over time.

Such an approach has the further advantage of corresponding to our initial or considered judgments about particular free speech problems. Any approach to the First Amendment will have to take substantial account of those particular judgments and adjust itself accordingly.[9] It seems clear that political protests cannot be regulated without a powerful demonstration of harm. It also seems clear, on reflection, that such forms of speech as perjury, bribery, unlicensed medical advice, threats, misleading or false commercial advertising, criminal solicitation, and libel of private persons—or at least most of these—are not entitled to the highest degree of constitutional protection. The political approach accounts well for our considered judgments about all or most of these cases. It may not do so perfectly, and some people will differ about some cases; but no other general approach seems nearly as well suited to this task.

In addition, an insistence that government's burden is greatest when political speech is at issue responds well to the fact that it is in the political setting that government is most likely to be biased or to be acting on the basis of illegitimate considerations.[10] Government is rightly distrusted when it is regulating speech that might harm its own interests. The premise of distrust is strongest when politics is at issue. It is far weaker when government is regulating (say) commercial speech, bribery, private libel, unlicensed medical advice, or obscenity. In such cases there is less reason to suppose that it is likely to be biased or to be insulating itself from criticism.

Finally, a political approach protects speech not only when regulation is most likely to be biased, but also when it is most likely to be harmful. Restrictions on political speech have the distinctive feature of impairing the ordinary channels for political change. Because they make democratic corrections less effective, such restrictions are especially dangerous.[11] If there are controls on commercial advertising, for example, it always remains possible to argue that such controls should be lifted. Any damage to democratic processes is minimal; democracy can correct the situation. If the government bans violent pornography, citizens can continue to argue against the ban. But if some political argument is foreclosed, the democratic corrective is severely impaired. A ban on speech critical of a war, or a prohibition on libel of public officials, will undermine an ordinary political response to possible government failure. Controls on speech that is not political do not have this uniquely damaging feature.

Taken in concert, these considerations suggest that government should be under a special burden of justification when it seeks to control speech that is intended and received as a contribution to democratic deliberation. To be sure, there are some powerful alternative approaches. Perhaps we should hold speech to be entitled to special protection whenever it involves rational thought. An idea of this sort would extend well beyond the political to include not merely literary and artistic work, but commercial and scientific expression as well. Perhaps such an approach can ultimately be defended. But the "rational thought" approach will produce major anomalies. It seems unlikely that (for example) technological data with potential military applications should be given the same protection as political speech, or that misleading commercial speech deserves the same protection as misleading political speech. A conclusion of this sort would make it difficult or impossible to justify the regulation of misleading advertising or of the export of such data to unfriendly foreign countries. These results, apparently required by the "rational thought" idea, seem to be jarring.

Alternatively, it might be thought that the core of the free speech principle includes any representation through words or pictures that reflects deliberation or imagination in a way that is relevant to the development of individual human capacities.[12] An approach of this sort has yet to be elaborated fully, and it might carry considerable promise. But at first glance such an approach would also produce anomalies. It would, for example, make it hard to distinguish between scientific and political speech, and it might also include within the top tier such materials as child pornography.

Much work remains to be done to elaborate and evaluate alternatives of this sort. But a conception of free speech that is centered on democratic governance appears, at the present time, to hold out the best promise for organizing our considered judgments about the range of cases likely to raise hard First Amendment questions.

If the First Amendment offers special protection to political speech, it would of course be necessary to reject the proposition that all forms of speech stand on the same ground—that distinctions cannot be drawn between obscenity and political protest, between misleading commercial speech and misleading campaign statements, or between proxy statements and party platforms. It would also be necessary to resort far less readily to the view that a restriction on one form of speech will necessarily lead to another.

COUNTERARGUMENTS

The problems with a political conception of the First Amendment are not unfamiliar; they raise all the questions that produced the current First Amendment preoccupation with line-drawing. How, for example, are we to treat the work of Robert Mapplethorpe, the music of a rock group, or nude dancing? Both commercial speech and pornography are political in the crucial sense that they reflect and promote a point of view, broadly speaking ideological in character, about how important things in the world should be structured. The recent attack on pornography has drawn close attention to its political character, and in this sense might be thought to invalidate efforts to regulate it. (See Chapter 9.)

Or, more generally: Is it so clear that speech that has nothing to do with politics is not entitled to First Amendment protection? Must we exclude music or art or science?[13] Surely it is philistine or worse to say that the First Amendment protects only political platforms. Often the deepest political challenges to the existing order can be found in art, literature, music, or (perhaps especially) sexual expression; sex is familiarly a metaphor for social rebellion. Sometimes government attempts to regulate these things for precisely this reason. And even when politics are not involved, art and literature involve matters central to human life and individual development. Is the First Amendment indifferent to this fact?

These are hard questions without simple solutions. I can venture only some brief remarks in response. The first is that the existence of real line-drawing problems should not be taken, by itself, to foreclose an attempt to distinguish between political and nonpolitical speech. Surely the problem counts against the attempt, but it cannot be decisive in light of the enormous problems produced by refusing to make that distinction. If the distinction is otherwise plausible, and if systems that fail to make it have severe problems, the difficulty of drawing lines is acceptable.

Even more fundamental, there is no way to operate a system of free expression without drawing lines. Not everything that counts as words or pictures is entitled to full constitutional protection. No one really believes that the First Amendment is an absolute, that all words and pictures belong on the same tier. The question is not whether to draw lines, but how to draw the right ones. For this we need some kind of theory.

The second point is that the category of the political should be broadly understood. The definition I have offered would encompass not simply political tracts, but all art and literature that have the characteristics of social commentary, which is to say most art and literature. Such a broad conception seems right, first, because much of this speech is in fact political in the relevant sense despite initial appearances, and, second, because it is important to create a large breathing space for political speech by protecting expression even if it does not explicitly fall within that category. This second point is crucial, since our institutions are inevitably both fallible and biased, and we should therefore build into free speech law protective principles to counteract problems of application. Both Joyce's *Ulysses* and Dickens' *Bleak House* are therefore political for First Amendment purposes. The same is true of Robert Mapplethorpe's work, which attempts to draw into question current sexual norms and practices. We might even conclude that art and literature generally belong in the top tier because often these are indeed relevantly political, and because courts are not capable of drawing in an unbiased way the line between political and nonpolitical art and literature.

But to say this is emphatically not to say that all speech that has political consequences is by virtue of that fact "political" in the constitutional sense. Obscenity is surely political in the sense that it has political wellsprings and effects; the same is true of commercial speech, which affects the world in important ways, and even of bribery—certainly bribery of public officials. An employer's purely verbal sexual or racial harassment of an employee surely has political consequences, including the creation of a deterrent for women and blacks to go to that workplace at all; this is unquestionably a political effect.

All these forms of speech are not by virtue of this fact entitled to the highest form of constitutional protection. If we concluded that speech is political because it has political causes and effects, we would be saying that nearly everything that counts as words or pictures is immunized from legal regulation. For reasons suggested above, that cannot be right. For purposes of the Constitution, the question is whether the speech is intended and received as a contribution to political deliberation, not whether it has political effects or sources. Thus, for example, there is a distinction between a misogynist tract, which is entitled to full protection, and many pornographic movies, which are not, but which are in essence masturbatory aids. There is a difference between face-to-face racial harassment by an employer of an employee, which is not entitled to full protection, and a racist speech to a crowd, which is so entitled. There is a difference between a racial epithet and a tract in favor of white supremacy. And there is a difference between an essay about the value of unregulated markets in oil production and an advertisement for Texaco—even if both are written and published by an oil company.

The definition I have offered would exclude much speech from the high-value category, and for this reason it might pose an unacceptable danger of censorship. A more general response is that the definition would offer exceptionally fragile safeguards for art, music, literature, and perhaps much of commercial entertainment. A First Amendment offering so little protection to so much might be embarrassingly weak and thin. If the exclusion of such materials results from a theory that is not compelled by the Constitution's text, surely that theory should be repudiated.

A possible elaboration of this view would build on a point made above. Free speech law should be devised to "overprotect" speech, and for good institutional reasons. That is, we might include materials that would not, in a world with perfect prosecutors and judges, receive protection—simply because without such protection, people in positions of authority will, in our world, draw lines in a way too threatening to the system of free expression.

In fact, however, the framework I propose would allow much room for powerful First Amendment challenges to most government regulation of speech. No speech can be regulated on the basis of whim or caprice. Something stronger than rationality review, though weaker than "strict scrutiny," should be applied to low-value expression. Even under a two-tier First Amendment, speech that falls within the second tier cannot be censored without a substantial showing of harm. This is in fact current law. Thus, for example, commercial speech receives a good deal of protection. It is regulable when government can show both a solid reason and a solid connection between the means of regulation and the reason in question. This system ensures that commercial speech is generally allowed if truthful and not misleading.[14]

In addition, the government may not regulate speech on the basis of constitutionally disfavored justifications. The Constitution generally disfavors regulation of speech if the government fears that people will be persuaded or influenced by what is said, or if it seeks to protect against ideas that offend people. Frequently the real reason for regulating speech will be disfavored in this sense, even if the speech is low value. For example, regulation of pornography could not be permitted if the purpose of regulation is to repress a message rather than to redress genuine harms. The First Amendment makes certain reasons for regulation illegitimate even if those reasons are invoked against low-value speech. The most important principle here is that government may not regulate speech of any kind if the reason is that it disapproves of the message or disagrees with the idea that the speech expresses. An effort to regulate music because it is "offensive" or because it stirs up passionate feeling would run afoul of the free speech clause. The approach I suggest will therefore give a good deal of protection to non-political speech.

Of course there will be hard cases, in which it has to be decided whether a legitimate justification is at work. The resolution of these cases will require judgment, and cannot be purely mechanical. But even if the First Amendment is especially concerned with political speech, there is little reason to fear a large increase in official censorship.

Practice

An approach of this sort would not require major substantial changes in the law. Its advantage is that it would help us deal with new controversies, not that it would unsettle resolution of the old ones. The Court has already created categories of speech that are less protected or not protected at all. What the Court has not done is to give a clear sense of the unifying factors that justify the creation of these categories. But it is highly revealing that political speech never falls within them, and that all speech that does so is not political in the sense that I understand the term here. The principal difference between the approach I suggest and current law is the explicit statement that nonpolitical speech occupies a lower tier—a statement that the Court has yet to make. For reasons suggested below, however, it is unclear that even this distinction would make much of a difference.

There would, however, be several new developments in current law. My suggested approach would mean that so-called public figures not involved in governmental affairs—famous movie stars and other celebrities, for example—could bring libel suits more easily. Under contemporary law, celebrities are constrained in libel actions in the same way as public officials. They must show "actual malice"—knowledge of falsehood or reckless indifference to the matter of truth or falsehood.[15] But there is no special constitutional reason to protect the breathing space of the press insofar as it is discussing athletes or movie stars. On what possible principle must a legal system provide special breathing space to libelous falsehoods about famous people?[16] The test for special protection should be whether the matter bears on democratic governance, not whether the plaintiff is famous.

Another possible change relates to sexually explicit speech. Under current law, such speech usually receives protection, certainly if it has significant social value, even when that value is scientific or literary rather than political. An emphasis on the political foundations of the First Amendment appears to threaten this basic idea. But under the approach I suggest, regulation of sexually explicit speech would also be invalid in most cases. Such regulation would usually be unsupportable by reference to a legitimate justification. A narrow category of materials combining sex with violence would, however, be regulable (see Chapter 9).

The securities laws would, however, raise no serious question. Indeed, many of the controversies with which I began would be resolved fairly automatically. Disclosure of the names of rape victims could certainly be prevented. In most cases, the disclosure has no real political content. The government can easily justify a ban on the ground that disclosure of such names is both a deterrent and a penalty to those who attempt to redress rape, an especially underenforced crime.

The hardest case here is hate speech. Such speech quite plausibly has political content in the sense that it is a self-conscious statement about how current political controversies should be resolved. The analysis here would depend on the extent to which something labeled as hate speech is actually intended and received as a contribution to thought about some public matter. Most of the regulations of "hate speech," on the campus and elsewhere, do in fact apply to political speech in this sense. Those regulations are unconstitutional.

By contrast, speech that amounts to simple epithets, showing visceral contempt, would be deprived of protection. By analogy with the obscene telephone call, a university can prevent students and teachers from using words in a way that is not plausibly part of democratic deliberation about an issue. But racist, homophobic, or sexist speech, even if offensive and harmful, would not be regulable so long as it was plausibly part of the exchange of ideas. The general conclusion is that the "speech codes" of public universities are generally unconstitutional, except insofar as they are limited to the narrow category of epithets.

The approach suggested here would also mean that some forms of scientific speech should be regulable. This conclusion bears on an important current issue: It would allow the government to regulate the export of technology with military applications. This is so even though the showing of harm is too speculative to suffice under the stringent standards properly applied to regulation of political speech. Technological information is not entitled to the same high level of protection. The possibly serious risks posed by improvements in the military capability of other nations do provide an adequate justification for such restrictions.

What of art and literature? In the many instances in which these are highly political, they belong in the core of constitutional protection. Indeed, the fact that they are frequently political—combined with the severe difficulty of deciding on their political quality on an ad hoc basis—argues powerfully in favor of the view that art and literature should generally be taken as core speech. When government seeks to censor art or literature, it almost always does so because of the political content. Any such efforts are impermissible. And even when art or literature stands outside the core, government can never regulate speech because it disagrees with the message. A legitimate justification is always required, and a legitimate justification is what is almost always lacking. "Offensiveness" or fear of persuasion and influence is per se illegitimate.

An approach of this general sort would solve most of the current First Amendment problems without making it necessary to enter into complex debates about power and powerlessness, or about neutrality in constitutional law. Such an approach would also have the considerable advantage of drawing on history, on the best theories about the function of the free speech guarantee, and on a sensible understanding about when government is least likely to be trustworthy. There is much to be said in favor of a movement in this direction.

AN EXAMPLE: CROSS-BURNING

It will be useful to explore an issue of great current controversy, that raised by community efforts to regulate cross-burning and similar forms of "hate speech." I build the example from the important recent Supreme Court decision of *R.A.V. v. St. Paul*,[17] involving a ban on cross-burning that produced certain audience reactions. We can use this as a case study. It tests and helps give content to many of the principles discussed above.

We might be tempted to begin with the suggestion that cross-burning is action, not speech, and therefore outside the First Amendment altogether. We might suggest a proposition:

I. *Action is unprotected by the First Amendment. To claim constitutional protection, a person must be saying or writing words.*

Is proposition I true? As a matter of basic principle, it seems hard to disqualify "expressive conduct" from constitutional protection. If speech is entitled to special protection because and when it expresses a point of view about some public issue, the line between "words" and "expressive conduct" seems extremely artificial. Some forms of conduct, such as flag-burning, are clearly expressive in character; in this way they qualify as "speech." If the flag-burning example seems controversial, we might think about sign language, or wearing black armbands, or demonstrating. All of these are in a way "action," but they nonetheless deserve constitutional protection. In any case we know that flag-burning qualifies as speech.[18] Given this fact, it seems hard to claim that cross-burning does not.

Thus far, then, we know that cross-burning counts as speech. Suppose that a criminal prosecutor invokes the law of criminal trespass to proceed against someone who has burned a cross on a private lawn. (I put to one side possible issues of selective prosecution.) Here we have a content-neutral law—the law of trespass—invoked to suppress an expressive act. Hence it might be suggested:

II. *Content-neutral restrictions on acts that qualify as speech are generally permissible.*

How shall we evaluate proposition II? At least in general, the use of the trespass law does seem constitutionally acceptable, even after the analysis in Chapter 7. Surely the law of criminal trespass could be used to prevent someone from drawing pictures on my house or from using my property as a place for a pro- or antiwar demonstration. At least in general, the law of property can be invoked to protect, in a content-neutral way, private lands and dwellings from invasion, whether through expression or otherwise. The Court has so held on several occasions, and this conclusion is the clear implication of the *R.A.V.* case.[19] The law of trespass might well be unconstitutional if it forecloses a crucial arena for expression—an arena to which there are no good alternatives—and if the state has no good reason to protect property rights in this way. But the state has extremely good reasons to protect ordinary homes from expressive invasion, and the grant of such protection does not seriously compromise the system of free expression.

Suppose, however, that a locality believes that the law of trespass is inadequate. Suppose it believes that it is important to enact a special statute explicitly forbidding expressive conduct of a certain sort. The resulting law might make it a crime to "place on public or private property a symbol, including but not limited to a burning cross or a Nazi swastika, which one knows or has reason to know arouses anger or resentment in others on the basis of race, color, or creed." (This is a minor variation on the law at issue in the *R.A.V.* case.) Such a law might be invoked to forbid a public demonstration of cross-burning. This leads to another proposition, quite different from II:

III. *Acts that qualify as speech can be regulated if they produce anger or resentment.*

From basic principle, as from the flag-burning cases, we know that III is false. The mere fact that an expressive act produces anger or resentment cannot be a sufficient reason for regulation. An expressive act cannot, consistently with the First Amendment, be prohibited simply because it upsets the audience.[20] To defend the law, it would therefore be necessary to show the particular properties of a burning cross (and other banned symbolic speech) that take it out of the realm of constitutional protection. That is, it would be necessary to show that there is a relevant difference between the ordinary anger or resentment produced by many expressive acts and "anger or resentment on the basis of race, color, or creed." That is, we have a new proposition:

IIIa. *Acts that qualify as speech can be regulated if they produce anger or resentment on the basis of race, color, or creed.*

On one view, IIIa is really just a subcategory of III. The anger or resentment produced by this kind of speech may be more intense than other forms; but there is at most a quantitative difference between the two. On another view, the anger or resentment produced by symbolic acts such as cross-burning and based on race, color, or creed is qualitatively different from other forms. It is properly treated differently.

If we were starting fresh, there might be room for some disagreement here. But the legal analogies seem to foreclose the claim that there is such a qualitative difference, at least in the context of an attempt to ban otherwise protected racist speech that produces anger or resentment. Speech that causes racial hatred has not been treated differently from other speech that causes ordinary offense or anger.

Suppose that there is no such difference, as the cases conclude. Defenders of the ban on cross-burning must therefore concede that the hypothetical law is unconstitutional. It is just like any other law that regulates speech that upsets people. We might, then, imagine that the locality proceeds to narrow the reach of its ordinance, as did the state supreme court in the *R.A.V.* case. Suppose that the locality prohibits cross-burning that produces anger or resentment if and only if the speech in question is regulable under existing standards as "incitement" or "fighting words." That is, the prohibition will not be triggered unless the circumstances of the expressive conduct fit within an already-established exception to First Amendment protection.

How does this affect the analysis? At first glance it seems to dispose of the issue.[21] The law now covers only speech unprotected by the First Amendment. Surely such a law is acceptable. This appears to be the conclusion of Justices White, Blackmun, and O'Connor in the *R.A.V.* case.[22] Thus we have a new, highly attractive proposition:

IV. *Unprotected acts of expression may be regulated by the state as and however it wishes.*

But the first glance is misleading. We can prove that IV is wrong by an analogy. Imagine that the state attempted to regulate only those "fighting words" directed at Republicans or at whites. Or imagine that the state made it a felony to engage in "incitement" if and only if the incitement was directed against people of a certain political view. It seems clear that such regulations would be impermissible. The reason is that laws discriminating on the basis of viewpoint are generally impermissible, because they are unacceptably motivated by government favoritism, and because they have skewing effects on the system of free expression.

This is a principal argument by the Supreme Court in the *R.A.V.* case: "Thus, the government may proscribe libel; but it may not make the further content discrimination of proscribing *only* libel critical of the government."[23] The principle apparently emerging from these analogies is that the state may not regulate unprotected speech if it selects, from the class of unprotected speech, material chosen on the basis of point of view. Viewpoint discrimination is unacceptable even in the context of otherwise unprotected speech. Hence it seems clear that:

V. *Unprotected acts of expression may not be regulated on the basis of viewpoint.*

The next question then becomes whether our hypothetical law violates the prohibition on viewpoint discrimination. In a critical sense, the ordinance is different from those in the clear cases of viewpoint discrimination. The locality has not drawn a line between prohibited and permitted points of view. It has not said that one view on an issue—race relations, for example—is permitted, and another proscribed. If cross-burning were all that it banned, we might well have a case of viewpoint discrimination, since cross-burning has a particular viewpoint. But here the class of prohibited speech ("symbols that arouse anger or resentment on the basis of race, color, or creed") is far broader. Antiwhite and antiblack statements are both allowed. The locality allows speech opposed to men and speech opposed to women; it does not distinguish between the two. In this respect, the law is viewpoint-neutral.

The locality has thus built on existing public reactions to certain kinds of speech, within a subset of the categories of "incitement" and "fighting words." It has not singled out a particular message for prohibition. It has regulated on the basis of subjects for discussion, not on the basis of viewpoint.[24] The final proposition to be evaluated is this:

VI. *If government singles out unprotected acts of expression for regulation when they cause "anger or resentment on the basis of race, color, or creed," it does not discriminate on the basis of viewpoint or otherwise on any impermissible ground.*

Is VI true? In the end, this was the central issue that divided the justices in the *R.A.V.* case. It is indeed a difficult question.

The analogous cases, involving "fighting words," are a helpful start here, for they show that regulation of "fighting words" is not by itself impermissibly viewpoint-based or otherwise objectionable. The "fighting words" doctrine is acceptable even though the listeners' reaction is indeed caused by an idea. The doctrine is deemed permissibly neutral because any regulation of fighting words fails to single out for legal control a preferred point of view. It depends instead on whether the average addressee would fight.[25] The viewpoint of the speaker is relevant in the sense that addressees will be reacting in part to the speaker's viewpoint; but the government has not endorsed a particular idea or a point of view. So long as the "fighting words" doctrine has any viability, this is a crucial difference.

As the *R.A.V.* majority emphasized, however, the hypothetical ordinance is not a broad or general proscription of fighting words. It reflects a decision to single out a certain category of "fighting words," defined in terms of audience reactions *to speech about certain topics.* Is this decision constitutionally illegitimate? The category of regulated speech—involving race, color, and creed—is based on subject matter, not on viewpoint. The question is then whether a subject matter restriction of this kind is acceptable. In *R.A.V.,* the Court, by a five-to-four vote, concluded that it is not. As we will soon see, the disagreement had everything to do with status quo neutrality.

Subject matter restrictions are not all the same. We can imagine subject matter restrictions that are questionable ("no one may discuss homosexuality on the subway") and subject matter restrictions that seem legitimate. As a class, they appear to occupy a point somewhere between viewpoint-based restrictions and content-neutral ones. Here too the analogies are revealing. Frequently subject matter restrictions are indeed upheld as a form of permissible content regulation. The Court has, for example, permitted a prohibition on political advertising on buses.[26] It has permitted a ban on partisan political speech at army bases.[27]

These cases show that there is no per se ban on subject matter restrictions. When the Court upholds subject matter restrictions, it does so either because the line drawn by government gives no real reason for fear about viewpoint discrimination, or (what is close to the same thing) because government is able to invoke neutral, harm-based justifications for treating certain subjects differently from others. Thus, for example, the restriction in the buses was justified as a means of preventing what would inevitably be a kind of governmental selectivity in choosing among political advertisements. The restriction in the army base was said to be a plausibly neutral effort to prevent political partisanship in the military.

If the subject matter restriction is acceptable in the cross-burning case, it must be so because the specified catalogue is sufficiently neutral and does not alert the judge to lurking concerns about viewpoint discrimination; or because (again a closely overlapping point) it is plausible to argue that the harms, in the specific covered cases, are sufficiently severe and distinctive to justify special treatment. This was the issue that in the end divided the Supreme Court.

In his dissenting opinion, Justice Stevens argued that the harms were indeed sufficiently distinctive. He wrote that "race based threats may cause more harm to society and to individuals than other threats. Just as the statute prohibiting threats against the President is justifiable because of the place of the President in our social and political order, so a statute prohibiting race based threats is justifiable because of the place of race in our social and political order." In his view, "Threatening someone because of her race or religious beliefs may cause particularly severe trauma or touch off a riot . . . ; such threats may be punished more severely than threats against someone based on, for example, his support of a particular athletic team."[28] Thus there were "legitimate, reasonable, and neutral justifications" for the special rule.

In its response, the Court said that this argument "is word-play." The reason that a race-based threat is different "is nothing other than the fact that it is caused by a distinctive idea, conveyed by a distinctive method. The First Amendment cannot be evaded that easily." [29] Who is right?

An initial response to the Court is that the "fighting words" doctrine itself shows that the state can ban speech even if the relevant harms are "caused by a distinctive idea, conveyed by a distinctive method." At first glance, moreover, it seems that a legislature could reasonably decide that the harms produced by this narrow category of speech are sufficiently severe to deserve separate treatment. Surely it seems plausible to say that cross-burning, displaying swastikas, and the like are an especially distinctive kind of "fighting word"—distinctive because of the objective and subjective harm they inflict on their victims and on society in general. An incident of cross-burning can have large and corrosive social consequences; a government could plausibly decide that the same is not true for a hateful attack on someone's parents or political convictions. A harm-based argument of this kind suggests that the legislature is responding not to an ideological message but to real-world consequences.

It turns out that the key issue here is the appropriate conception of neutrality. The debate over a version of status quo neutrality accounts for the disagreement within the Court. According to Justice Stevens, a state is indeed acting neutrally if it singles out cross-burning for special punishment, because this kind of "fighting word" has especially severe social consequences. According to the Court, a state cannot legitimately decide that cross-burning is worse than (for example) a vicious attack on your political convictions or your parents. A decision to this effect violates neutrality. But the Court's conception of neutrality, appearing here in a powerfully argued contemporary opinion, is highly reminiscent of (though of course not nearly as bad as) that in *Plessy v. Ferguson* itself. In *Plessy,* the Court upheld racial segregation in part on the ground that the view that segregation was distinctly stigmatizing had been created by black people, and was not really to be credited. In *R.A.V.,* the judgment that racial hate speech is distinctly stigmatizing was similarly thought to violate neutrality.

This is not an argument for broad bans on hate speech. As discussed above, such bans would indeed violate the First Amendment because they would forbid a good deal of speech that is intended and received as a contribution to public deliberation. But here we are dealing with hate speech that is limited to the exceedingly narrow category of admittedly unprotected "fighting words." The argument on behalf of the restriction is helped by an analogy, Justice Stevens' reference to the especially severe legal penalties directed toward threats against the President. Everyone seems to agree that this restriction is permissible because threats against the President cause distinctive harms. But if the government can single out one category of threats for special sanction because of the harm that those threats cause, why is not the same true for fighting words of the sort at issue here?

Justice Scalia's response is perhaps the best that can be offered: "[T]he reasons why threats of violence are outside the First Amendment (protecting individuals from fear of violence, from the disruption that fear engenders, and from the possibility that threatened violence will occur) have special force when applied to the President." [30] But very much the same thing could be said of the hate speech ordinance under discussion. Here, as in cases involving threats against the President, we are dealing with a subcategory of unprotected speech challenged as involving impermissible selectivity, and we have a justification for the selectivity made out in terms of the particular harms of the unprotected speech at issue.

The argument to this effect depends critically on the fact that the subject matter classification occurs on the context of speech that is, we are supposing, without First Amendment protection. A subject matter restriction on unprotected speech should probably be upheld if the legislature can plausibly argue that it is counteracting harms rather than ideas. An analogy is helpful here as well. Supplemental criminal penalties for racially motivated "hate crimes" seem to be a well-established part of current law, and it seems clear that those penalties do not violate the First Amendment (although the outcome in R.A.V. might draw this conclusion into doubt). The governmental motivation for the additional penalty—the distinctive subjective and objective harm produced by these crimes, in part because of their symbolic or expressive nature—is the same as in the cross-burning case. So long as we are dealing with otherwise unprotected speech, that motivation should not be fatal to the cross-burning enactment if it is not fatal to the "hate crimes" measures.

I conclude that, contrary to the outcome in R.A.V., proposition VI is true. A restriction on cross-burning and other symbolic speech is, in this context, a permissible subject matter classification, so long as the restriction is narrowed in the way described. In any event, the R.A.V. case helps show the interactions among the two-tier First Amendment, status quo neutrality, and the categories of viewpoint-based, content-based, and content-neutral restrictions.

Notes on Foundations: Deliberative Democracy and the Free Speech Principle

At this point a few remarks are in order about the functions of the free speech guarantee and the conception of democracy that it should be taken to embody.

We have seen that the American constitutional system is emphatically not designed only to protect private interests and private rights. Even more emphatically, its purpose is not to furnish the basis for struggle among self-interested private groups. That notion is anathema to American constitutionalism.

Instead a large point of the system is to ensure discussion and debate among people who are differently situated, in a process through which reflection will encourage the emergence of general truths. A distinctive feature of American republicanism is hospitality toward heterogeneity rather than fear of it. Recall here the words of the prominent antifederalist Brutus, speaking for those who lost the debate over the ratification of the Constitution: "In a republic, the manners, sentiments, and interests of the people should be similar. If this be not the case, there will be a constant clashing of opinions; and the representatives of one part will be continually striving against those of the other."[31] Recall too Alexander Hamilton's response that in a heterogeneous republic, discussion will be improved; "the jarring of parties . . . will promote deliberation."[32] The Federalists did not believe that heterogeneity would be an obstacle to political discussion and debate. On the contrary, they thought that it was indispensable to it.

In the American tradition, politics is not a process in which desires and interests remain frozen, before or during politics. The protection given to free speech should be understood accordingly. Its overriding goal is to allow public judgments to emerge through general public discussion and debate. This view does not depend on a sharp distinction between public interest and private interest, or on an insistence that private interest is not and should not be a motivation for political action. It is necessary only to claim that the provision of new information or alternative perspectives can lead to new understandings of what interests are and where they lie.

It is in this sense that conceptions of politics as an aggregation of interests or as a kind of "marketplace" inadequately capture the American system of free expression. Aggregative or marketplace notions disregard the extent to which political outcomes were supposed to depend on discussion and debate, and on the reasons offered for or against the various alternatives. The First Amendment is the central constitutional reflection of these ideas. It is part and parcel of the constitutional commitment to citizenship. And this commitment must be understood in light of the American conception of sovereignty, placing governing authority in the people themselves.

The proposals set out here flow directly from this conception of the First Amendment. The belief that politics lies at the core of the amendment is of course an outgrowth of the more general commitment to deliberative democracy. The concern for ensuring the preconditions for deliberation among the citizenry is closely associated with this commitment. It is in this respect that the proposals suggested here fit with the highest aspirations of the constitutional principles of which the First Amendment is the most tangible expression.

We have come far from the basic ideas that characterize current thinking about free speech. The familiar aversion to line-drawing with respect to speech seems to lead to insoluble problems. It is far better to be candid about the matter and to recognize that as far as the First Amendment is concerned, all speech is not the same. Threats to free speech do indeed come from government, but the general understanding of what this means is far off the mark. Such threats take the form not only of conventional, highly visible censorship but also of what is in some respects the same thing, that is, the allocation by government of rights of property, ownership, and exclusion that determine who can speak and who cannot, and that involve the use of civil and criminal law to carry out the rights of exclusion.

Government neutrality is the right aspiration, but, properly understood, neutrality does not require respect for rights of speech as these can be vindicated in light of the existing distributions of rights and entitlements. It is thus necessary to reform all the commitments that have, with respect to speech, come to represent the conventional wisdom.

Over the last forty years, the American law of freedom of speech has experienced nothing short of a revolution. The revolution has accomplished enormous good. It would be hard to argue that a return to the pre-1950 law of free speech would provide a better understanding of the free speech principle. In the aftermath of the bicentennial of the American Bill of Rights—a period in which an appreciation for freedom of speech seems to be exploding throughout the world—we should indeed celebrate our tradition of liberty and recognize the extent to which it is an extraordinary and precious achievement.

At the same time, a crucial part of that achievement involves the dynamic and self-revising character of the free speech tradition. Our existing liberty of expression owes its origins to the capacity of each generation to rethink and to revise the understandings that have been left to it. To the economists' plea that "the perfect is the enemy of the good," we might oppose John Dewey's suggestion that "the better is the enemy of the still better." [33] The conception of free speech in any decade of American history is often quite different from the conception twenty years before or after.

Moreover, it is increasingly clear that current understandings are inadequate to resolve current controversies, and that they threaten to protect both more and less free speech than they should. They are inadequate for current controversies because they are poorly adapted to the problems raised by campaign finance regulation, scientific speech, regulation of broadcasting, content-neutral restrictions on speech, hate speech, commercial advertising, and pornography. They protect more than they should because they include, within the category of protected expression, speech that serves few or none of the goals for which speech is protected, and that promises to cause serious social harms. They protect less than they should because current law does not adequately serve the central goal of producing a deliberative democracy among political equals.

Ironically, the existing system owes many of its failures to the supposed mandates of contemporary conceptions of the First Amendment. These failures often stem from status quo neutrality. They apply pre–New Deal understandings about existing distributions to contemporary problems of free expression. They do not see "regulation" when it actually exists; they disfavor as "regulation" governmental efforts to promote the system of free expression.

I have suggested two changes in existing understandings. Both of them derive from the American contribution to the theory of sovereignty. First, some forms of apparent government intervention into free speech processes can actually improve those processes, and should not be understood as an objectionable intrusion into an otherwise law-free social sphere. Such intervention should not always be taken as an impermissible abridgment of the free speech right. Efforts of this sort do not represent "positive" government action intruding on constitutionally protected "negative" liberty. They should not be taken to argue for a "positive" understanding of free speech in lieu of the heretofore dominant belief in "negative" liberty.

Instead these efforts would entail a democratic recognition of the dangers to free speech posed by market-constructing, content-neutral restrictions that limit access to arenas in which expression should be allowed to occur and might make a difference. The risks posed by content-neutral restrictions are generally recognized in the law. The gap lies in the unwillingness to see that the speech "market" is a product of law subject to legislative improvements and in any event to First Amendment constraints.

A healthy recognition that decentralized markets generally are indispensable to promote liberty—for both products and for speech—is not inconsistent with the basic claim. Nor is that recognition inconsistent with the view that the creation of markets might, on some occasions and in some settings, itself amount to an abridgment of free speech.

Second, the free speech principle should be understood to be centered above all on political thought. In this way the free speech principle should always be seen through the lens of democracy. Other forms of speech may be regulated not on a whim, and not for illegitimate reasons, but on the basis of a showing of lesser harm.

Taken together, these principles would bring about significant changes in the legal treatment currently given to electoral campaigns, electronic broadcasting, and the assertion of ownership rights in order to exclude political speech. In their most modest form, the principles would provide a major step toward resolving current free speech controversies without making serious changes in existing law. Rightly understood, these principles might well counteract the novel, sometimes invisible, and often serious obstacles that now lie in the path of free speech in America, and that threaten to do so in an increasingly severe way in the twenty-first century.

CHAPTER 9

Pornography, Abortion, Surrogacy

In recent years, legal controls on sex and reproduction have raised some of the most intense controversies in all of law. Pornography, abortion, and surrogacy are in the forefront of current debate. A moment's reflection shows that the three areas raise common questions.

Legal treatment of these issues is pervaded by the now familiar conception of neutrality. That conception rules out of bounds, as partisan, an argument that is at least highly plausible and that might indeed deserve ultimate support. Use of that argument would dramatically alter the legal and political discussion of all three areas.

Much of the debate involves a conflict between two well-known positions. On one view, the government should not repress or interfere with sexual drives. These drives have a special claim to freedom from government intrusion—a claim arising out of the need to permit intimacy with respect to practices that are central both to individual development and to mutual recognition between human beings. The law should respect the privacy of those who wish to see or read sexually explicit material, enter into surrogacy arrangements, or terminate pregnancies, and all for essentially the same reason, having to do with the individual's right to self-determination in matters of sexuality and reproduction.[1]

On the second, opposing view, the government should be allowed to control sexual and reproductive behavior. Government should act to ensure that sexuality and reproduction, in their best, current, or natural forms, are not polluted, altered, or debased through artificial external influences. Sexual services should not be sold for cash, and sexuality should be protected against dehumanization. On this view, the law properly ensures the separation of the private sphere of sexuality from the public sphere of the marketplace, by controlling obscenity; properly protects against abortion, most fundamentally to protect the interest in fetal life but also to ensure that sexuality is for purposes of reproduction; and properly protects reproduction and sexuality from the degrading economic trading involved in surrogacy arrangments.

For all their differences, these two positions have much in common. Both of them tend to assume that the current realm of reproduction and sexuality is just or even natural. The first position stresses the need to free sex from state repression. The second position, with its neoreligious roots, usually relies on the need to protect sex from harmful external influences.[2] The two views usually share a favorable view toward current sexual drives, whether they are deemed natural or good for some reason independent of nature.

It is because of this commonality that advocates of both positions are critical of a third, which they deem impermissibly partisan or selective. This third position does not stress privacy, a broad or acontextual "right to choose," or control over one's body. Nor does it focus on the interest in promoting traditional or conventional morality with respect to sex. Instead it invokes the need to ensure that *women's sexuality and reproductive functions are not turned into something for the use and control of others.*

This principle is grounded in a familiar conception of equality. It was set out long ago by John Stuart Mill: "[T]he principle which regulates the existing social relations between the two sexes—the legal subordination of one sex to the other—is wrong in itself, and now one of the chief hindrances to human improvement; and . . . it ought to be replaced by a principle of perfect equality, admitting no power or privilege on one side, nor disability on the other." Mill's comments on his own argument remain highly relevant: "And there are so many causes tending to make the feelings connected with this subject the most intense and deeply-rooted of all those which gather round and protect old institutions and customs, that we need not wonder to find them as yet undermined and loosed than any of the rest by the progress of the great modern spiritual and social transition; nor suppose that the barbarisms to which men cling longest must be less barbarisms than those which they earlier shake off."[3]

At a minimum, this principle means that a legislature may prevent society from turning morally irrelevant characteristics—most conspicuously race and sex—into systemic sources of social disadvantage. A systemic disadvantage is one that operates along standard and predictable lines in multiple important aspects of social life such as education, freedom from violence, wealth, political representation, and political influence (see Chapter 11). The claim that women's sexual and reproductive capacities may not be turned into objects for the control and use of third parties is simply a particular application of this general idea. Women's differences from men are morally irrelevant; that is, those differences are not a good reason to treat women worse than men. It follows that the law may not make women's differences into a source of systemic social harm for women, much less attribute the harm to "nature."

A legislature might, for example, attempt to counteract the disproportionate subjection of both blacks and women to private violence. Restrictions on rape, sexual assault, sexual harassment, and pornography containing violence against women (assuming that the free speech amendment objection has been overcome) can be justified on this general ground. These measures are part and parcel of a commitment to equality on the basis of gender. Legislative regulation of surrogacy arrangements (and prostitution) might be urged on the related idea that such arrangements contribute, even if mildly, to discrimination against women, by allowing women's reproductive capacities to be objects owned and used by others.

This general conception of equality has strong roots in the history of the Fourteenth Amendment. For the most part, however, the principle is for legislative and executive enforcement. Courts are quite ill suited to undertake any general attack on the translation of morally irrelevant characteristics into systemic sources of social disadvantage (see Chapters 5 and 11). But the equality principle, thus understood, will on occasion call for a judicial role under the equal protection clause. At a minimum, the principle requires a powerful gender-neutral justification for laws that are aimed, on their face or in their motivation, at women. For this reason laws restricting abortion, which contain a gender-based classification, do raise a serious equal protection problem.

If the abortion issue is seen in these terms, we can rethink a dilemma that has puzzled many lawyers, indeed that has served as one of the principal conundrums of the last generation of constitutional thought: How can one approve of *Roe v. Wade*, recognizing the abortion right, while disapproving of *Lochner v. New York?* The question seems hard to answer if *Lochner* is understood as a case in which the Supreme Court interpreted the due process clause to protect "fundamental rights." *Roe* used the due process clause in this very way. The cases might therefore be thought to stand or fall together.

But as we have seen, this is a crude and ahistorical approach to the *Lochner* period. To a nonlawyer who simply reads the text of the Constitution, it would seem odd indeed to suggest that if we think that maximum-hour laws are constitutionally valid, we must also accept laws restricting abortion. The two problems appear to have little to do with each other. Maximum-hour laws plausibly promote human liberty, or so a reasonable legislature might decide. At the very least, abortion restrictions raise a set of wholly different questions.

The notion that disapproval of *Lochner* requires disapproval of *Roe* is a singularly odd feature of the current legal culture. It is simply an artifact of a particular way of thinking about *Lochner.* More specifically, it is an artifact of the view that *Lochner* was a case fully and properly understood through the blunt notion that "the Court gave substantive protection to liberty." It is this rather strange way of thinking that makes people ask: If you reject *Lochner,* how can you accept *Roe?*

But if we shift our field of vision a little bit, we might as reasonably ask: If you approve of *Brown*'s invalidation of segregation, how can you disapprove of *Roe?* On this view, *Brown* represented a judicial invalidation of a law contributing to second-class citizenship for a group of Americans defined in terms of a morally irrelevant characteristic (race)—and *Roe* represented exactly the same thing (with respect to gender). Of course *Roe* can be distinguished from *Brown;* of course approval of *Brown* need not imply approval of *Roe.* But it is probably more fruitful to think of *Roe,* not as a rerun of *Lochner,* but as raising many of the same sorts of questions at issue in *Brown.*

Taken most generally, the sexual and reproductive status quo should be seen as, sometimes, a locus of inequality. It is for this reason that the restrictions on abortion, surrogacy arrangements, and free availability of pornography are troublesome. Legal and social control of women's sexual and reproductive capacities has been a principal historical source of sexual inequality. Even under current conditions, such control remains a vehicle for creating inequality. Now, as before, the inequality is often justified as a response to "real differences" or to nature. (Recall the segregation controversy and the discussion in

Chapter 2 of the "real differences" argument, invoking nature itself, offered by the Supreme Court in *Plessy*.) In fact, however, legal practices often help create the very differences by reference to which they are supposed to be justified. Consider laws ensuring that women will not be rewarded as well as men in the workplace, and that thus encourage women but not men to engage in the care of children. Even when the differences are biological, and not a product of law, it is legal practices that turn biological differences into a source of social disadvantage. Even biological differences need not have large social consequences unless society decides that they should. Here an objection to the relevant laws, from the standpoint of equality, is perfectly plausible. The objection should not be obscured by references to "nature."

To apply these ideas to the contexts at hand: A restriction on access to abortion turns women's reproductive capacities into something to be used by fetuses. Surrogacy arrangements do much the same, but in these cases the users are strangers seeking a child, and the vehicle is the market. (Of course the market is legally constituted.) Finally, the production and consumption of pornography are troublesome because and to the extent that they allow women's sexuality to be used by strangers, often through violence.

I do not mean to oppose equality to liberty and to declare that the former has precedence over the latter. Indeed, we should question the conception of liberty adopted by those who think that the liberty principle, rightly understood and standing by itself, entails free availability of pornography, abortion, and surrogacy (see Chapter 6). Liberty does not entail respect for all "choices" viewed acontextually and made pursuant to existing distributions of wealth and entitlements. Rather than attempting a broad new conception of liberty, however, we might focus more narrowly on the equality dimension of these problems. An approach defined in terms of gender equality better captures central aspects of all three of them.

Pornography

With respect to the question of pornography, two positions have captured the current constitutional landscape. According to the first, some categories of expression are simply excluded from the category of protected "speech." In the well-known formulation, "obscenity" is defined to include materials that appeal to the prurient interest, are patently offensive by contemporary community standards, and lack serious social value.[4] Obscenity does not count as speech. The Supreme Court treats it as sex rather than as expression.

The exclusion of obscenity from the category of protected expression is sometimes associated with the idea that sexuality is private or sacred. For this reason, it ought not to be permitted to intrude into the public space, and the public space should not intrude into it.[5] Separated, sexuality and the public space are unobjectionable in their current or traditional forms. The problem is their intermingling, which debases both. Sexuality and reproduction should be immunized from the effects of commercialization and, in particular, from the exploitative and degrading depictions of the marketplace. These depictions can easily spill into and harm the private realm. In a democratic society, the public should be permitted to police this process.

On this view, legal enforcement of the division between public and private spheres—aiming to protect the current or traditional versions of the two—is hardly wrong. Indeed, it represents a form of impartiality. To be sure, a decision to regulate obscenity is not entirely neutral, since it makes regulation turn on the content of the speech and even on existing social norms. But so long as contemporary community standards serve as the basis for regulation, controls on obscenity are at least neutral with respect to point of view. They are therefore nonpartisan in the crucial sense that the views of the speaker are not the trigger for the imposition of governmental controls.[6]

The opposing view is that all speech stands on the same ground and that government has no business censoring speech merely because some people or some officials are puritanical or offended by it.[7] On this view, obscenity is speech, not sex—just as a movie filled with violence is a representation rather than the thing itself. And on this view, government must remain neutral among different conceptions of the good—above all, among those conceptions as they are expressed through words and pictures. A decision to single out obscenity for special treatment, and to censor it, is a conspicuous violation of the neutrality requirement of the First Amendment.

In some of its incarnations, this position has relatively straightforward neo-Freudian roots. It rests on the perceived naturalness of sexual drives, and it emphasizes the need to liberate those drives from the constraining arm of the state. It could and sometimes does, of course, have different foundations. It need not rest on any form of naturalism, and might put Freud to one side, instead invoking the need to respect divergent conceptions of the good, whatever the source of those conceptions. We might believe that current sexuality is partly or even largely a product of current society, and not in all ways natural—but nonetheless insist that sexuality is an important human good entitled to immunity from government. Especially in the area of sexuality, government should respect people's diverse choices and not impose its own views or a sectarian morality.

The foundations of the opposing position, in many of its incarnations, can be found in some religious teaching. It also tends to depend on a belief in the naturalness of sexual drives, here understood as unpolluted by obscenity, which, on this account, depicts sexuality in a debased and unnatural way. The link between the two positions lies in their shared reliance on a private sphere of sexuality, taken as natural and in any case as neutral and just, that is to be the starting point for assessing proposed legal controls.

In some contexts there is much to be said on behalf of both of these positions. For both men and women, suppression of sexuality through law or social norms has been an important vehicle for injustice and for the infliction of extremely serious personal harms. The liberation of such drives from law or from certain social constraints can be an important individual and collective good. There is of course room for much dispute about exactly when this is so, but the general proposition is hard to doubt.

The point suggests that the creation of a realm of protected erotic life is an exceptionally important goal for a free nation. In order to support this proposition, it is altogether unnecessary to think that sexuality is prepolitical or independent of social forces. The case for a protected sphere of sexual life need not depend on a belief that sexuality is natural. It need only rest on an understanding that under appropriate conditions, sexuality is an important human good.[8]

In addition, the debasement of sexuality through distorting influences is a real phenomenon, one that can produce individual and collective harm. Here too the content of the category is disputable, and here too the general proposition seems unexceptionable. I do not deny the truth of both claims in some settings, but instead suggest that neither of them captures all the dimensions of the problem posed by the free availability of sexually explicit materials.

In the last decade a third position has emerged on the question of legal control of pornography.[9] On this view, sexually explicit speech should be regulated not when it is sexually explicit (the problem of obscenity) but instead when it merges sex with violence (the problem of pornography).[10] The problem of pornography does not stem from offense, from free access to sexually explicit materials, from an unregulated erotic life, or from the violation of community standards. Instead it is a result of tangible real-world harms, produced by the portrayal of women and children as objects for the control and use of others, most prominently through sexual violence.

The goal of regulation is to recognize and counteract the fact that in some cases sexual practices are a vehicle for sex discrimination. Materials that eroticize rape and other forms of violence should be treated as sex discrimination. On this view, the existing private sphere is sometimes the problem rather than the solution. Legal controls that draw attention to and help change that fact are to be approved for that very reason.

It is notable that under this approach, the category of regulable speech might be relatively broad or extremely narrow. We might, for example, ensure protection for all material with serious social value, or refuse to regulate speech unless it not only combines sex with violence, but also has no real cognitive content. In any case it is fully possible that the category would include far less speech than is subject to regulation under the current antiobscenity approach. The difference lies not in greater breadth, but in the emphasis on discrimination and harm to women rather than on contemporary community standards.

It is often suggested that the antipornography position raises especially serious free speech questions and that the antiobscenity and "no regulation" positions are far preferable. In fact, however, there is a quite straightforward argument for regulating at least some narrowly defined class of pornographic materials. The first point, made by traditional obscenity law as well, is that much pornographic material lies far from the center of the First Amendment concern. We might think of the First Amendment as, generally speaking and first and foremost, a safeguard against governmental suppression of points of view with respect to public affairs (see Chapter 8).

On this view, at least some forms of pornography are far from the core of constitutional concern. Under current doctrine and under any sensible system of free expression, speech that lies at the periphery of constitutional concern may be regulated on the basis of a lesser showing of government interest than is required for speech that lies at the core.

To say this is hardly to say that the definition of the core and the periphery will be simple. With nearly any standard, however, at least some pornographic materials will be easily classified in the periphery. Such materials fall in the same category as commercial speech, libel of private persons, conspiracies (which are, after all, words), bribes, perjury, threats, and so forth. The reason is that these forms of speech do not amount to part of an appeal to deliberative capacities about public matters, or about matters at all—even if this category is construed quite broadly, as it should be, and even if we insist, as we should, that emotive and cognitive capacities are frequently intertwined in deliberative processes.

The second point is that pornographic material causes sufficient harms to justify regulation under the more lenient standards applied to speech that does not fit within the free speech core. Of course it is possible to question the extent of the relevant harms. For present purposes, it is enough to suggest that those harms make for a stronger case for regulation that underlies the antiobscenity position, which relies on less tangible aesthetic goals, and which is said for that reason to be preferable from the standpoint of neutrality.

The harms fall in three categories. First, the existence of the pornography market produces a number of harms to models and actresses.[11] Many women, usually very young, are coerced into pornography. Others are abused and mistreated, often in grotesque ways, once they have entered the pornography "market." It is tempting to respond that government should adopt a less restrictive alternative. Rather than regulating speech, it should ban the coercion or mistreatment, as indeed current law does. Usually this is indeed the better strategy. But in this setting, such an alternative would also be a recipe for disaster, since it would be simply a means of allowing existing practices to continue.

It is hard enough to bring an action for rape and sexual assault. The difficulty becomes all the greater when the victims are young women coerced into and abused during the production of pornography. Often those victims will be reluctant to put themselves through the experience and possible humiliation and expense of initiating a proceeding. Often they will have extremely little credibility even if they are willing to do so. In this light, the only realistically effective way to eliminate the practice is to eliminate or reduce the financial benefits.[12] To be sure, some or most participation in pornography may well be voluntary in the relevant sense, and a regulatory approach would therefore ban more material than should be regulated if the argument is based solely on coercion in the production. But it appears that if we really want to stop such coercion, we must accept regulation than is overly broad in this way.

Second, there is a causal connection between pornography and violence against women.[13] The extent of the effect and the precise relationship between exposure to pornographic and sexual violence are sharply disputed. No one suggests that sexual violence would disappear if pornography were eliminated, or that most consumers of violent pornography act out what they see or read. But a review of the literature suggests that pornography does increase the incidence of sexual violence against women. The real question is not the existence of a causal connection but its degree. In light of current information, it is plausible to think that there would be significant benefits from regulation of violent pornography.

Third, and more generally, pornography reflects and promotes attitudes toward women that are degrading and dehumanizing and that contribute to a variety of forms of illegal conduct, prominent among them sexual harassment. The pornography industry operates as a conditioning factor for some men and women, a factor that has consequences for the existence of equality between men and women.[14] Of course it is more symptom than cause; but it is cause as well. One need not believe that the elimination of violent pornography would bring about sexual equality, eliminate sexual violence, or change social attitudes in any fundamental way, in order to agree that a regulatory effort would have an effect in reducing violence and other unlawful acts.

These considerations suggest a quite conventional argument for regulation of violent pornography, one that fits well with the rest of free speech law. Misleading commercial speech, for example, is regulable because it is not entitled to the highest form of protection and because the harms produced by such speech are sufficient to allow for regulation. The same is true of libel of private persons, criminal solicitation, unlicensed legal or medical advice, and conspiracy. Certain forms of pornography should be approached similarly. At least some form of regulation seems fully consistent with the treatment accorded to many other categories of speech. Indeed, the argument for regulation—in view of the nature of the material and the evidence of harm—is far more powerful than the corresponding argument for many forms of speech now subject to government control.

Moreover, the antipornography approach has significant advantages over the two more prominent approaches to the subject. As compared with the "speech is speech" position, the antipornography approach recognizes that it is extremely difficult to run a system of free expression without distinguishing among different categories of expression in terms of their centrality to the First Amendment guarantee. It also recognizes, as that position does not, that violent pornography is a serious problem, probably at least as serious as many of the problems that have been found sufficient to call for governmental controls on speech.

As compared with the "moral consensus" position, the antipornography approach has the advantage of concentrating on real-world harms rather than on the less tangible, more aesthetic problems captured in the use of contemporary community standards. Moreover, it sees that the private realm of sexuality might sometimes be the problem rather than the solution insofar as that realm can be a place of discrimination and violence. In this sense there is a close alliance between the effort to regulate violent pornography and the effort to reduce domestic violence.

Strikingly, however, the antipornography position is the least well-represented of the three in current constitutional law. Its present legal status has everything to do with prevailing conceptions of neutrality. What has made the antipornography approach so controversial is that it is rooted in a belief that the reproductive status quo, in terms of the relations between men and women, is sometimes itself a place for inequality, that women are not treated the same as men, that sexual violence by men against women is a greater social problem than sexual violence by women against men, and that social inequality can be both expressed and perpetuated through sexuality. The rejection of this belief—a refusal to recognize existing inequality, transmuted into a claim of partiality—has turned out to be critical to constitutional law. The objection is that the antipornography position is selective (especially compared with the antiobscenity approach), and that in its selectivity lies its partisanship, which is what makes it fatally inferior to its competitors. This objection accounts for the weakness of the antipornography position in current law.

In the leading decision on the subject, the U.S. Court of Appeals for the Seventh Circuit, in a case affirmed summarily by the Supreme Court,[15] invalidated an antipornography ordinance. The court reasoned that an argument that would allow regulation of pornographic materials by reference to the harms referred to above is worse, not better, than the obscenity approach. Indeed, it would be worse than the obscenity approach even if the category of speech suppressed turned out to be far narrower than the category that can be suppressed under existing law. According to the court, any statute that imposes penalties on a subcategory of obscene speech, defined by reference to these harms, would be unconstitutional.

For the court, the key point is that such an approach would constitute impermissible "thought control," since it would "establish[] an 'approved' view of women, of how they may react to sexual encounters, [and] of how the sexes may relate to each other." Under the antipornography approach, depictions of sexuality that involve rape and violence against women may be subject to regulation, whereas depictions that do not are uncontrolled. It is the non-neutrality of antipornography legislation—its focus on violence against women—that is its central defect. People with the approved view can speak; people with the disapproved view cannot. That, in the court's view, is what the First Amendment centrally prohibits.

But the category of neutrality turns out to be far more difficult to understand than appears at first glance; and the problem lies in the fact that any claim of non-neutrality rests on a controversial baseline. An initial way to make the point is to suggest that First Amendment law contains several categories of speech that are subject to ban or regulation even though they are non-neutral in precisely the same sense as antipornography legislation.

Consider, for example, the area of labor law, where courts have held that government may ban employers from speaking unfavorably about the effects of unionization in the period before a union election if the unfavorable statements might be interpreted as a threat.[16] Regulation of such speech is unquestionably non-neutral, since employer speech favorable to unionization is not proscribed. Similarly, the state may prohibit truthful television and radio advertisements for casinos and cigarettes.[17] This is so even though speech that takes the opposite side is freely permitted, in advertisements or elsewhere. Securities laws regulate the speech that may occur in proxy statements. Restrictions on viewpoint can be found here too, since favorable views about a company's prospects are banned, while unfavorable views are permitted and perhaps even encouraged.

In these cases, the partisanship of the regulation is not apparent, because there is so firm a consensus on the presence of real-world harms that the objection from neutrality does not even have time to register. The specter of partisanship does not arise, because a decision to control the speech in question has obvious legitimate justifications,

and an extension of the prohibition to other areas appears not compelled by neutrality but instead an unnecessary form of censorship.

More fundamentally, the existing law of obscenity might readily be
regarded as non-neutral. It is not a bit less partisan than antipornography legislation. The line drawn by existing law makes it critical
whether the speech in question departs from contemporary community standards. Those standards are the trigger for regulation. But if
contemporary community standards are, with respect to offensiveness
and prurience, themselves partisan and reflective of a particular viewpoint (and it would be most surprising if they were not), then a decision to make contemporary standards the basis for regulation is impermissibly partisan. (Imagine if the government said that contemporary community standards would be the basis for regulating depictions of race relations.) On what theory, then, can antiobscenity law be
treated as neutral and antipornography law as impermissibly partisan?

The answer lies in the fact that antiobscenity law takes existing social consensus as the foundation for decision, whereas antipornography law is directed against that consensus. Existing practice is the target of the antipornography approach, or what that approach seeks to
change; existing practice is the very basis of the antiobscenity approach, or what that approach seeks to preserve. Obscenity law, insofar as it is tied to community standards, is therefore deemed neutral,
but only because the class of prohibited speech is defined by reference
to existing social values. Antipornography legislation is deemed impermissibly partisan because the prohibited class of speech is defined
by less widely accepted ideas about equality between men and
women—more precisely, by reference to a belief that equality does not
always exist even in the private realm, that sexual violence by men
against women is a greater problem than sexual violence by women
against men, and that the sexual status quo is an ingredient in gender
inequality.

Along the axis of neutrality, however, the distinction between
antiobscenity and antipornography law cannot be sustained. That distinction would be plausible only if existing norms and practices themselves embodied equality. Since they do not, the distinction fails. Indeed, one could imagine a society in which the harms produced by
pornography were so widely acknowledged and so generally condemned that an antipornography ordinance would not be regarded as
viewpoint-based at all.

I conclude that the argument for regulation of materials that combine sex with violence is more powerful than the corresponding argument for regulating obscenity. Since perfectly conventional measures regulating speech are similarly partisan and have properly been upheld, the objection from non-neutrality is unpersuasive here as well.

To say this is not to say that it will be easy to design regulation with sufficient clarity and narrowness. But it is those questions that we should be addressing—not the question of neutrality. So long as any emerging law has the requisite clarity and narrow scope, the appropriate forum for deliberation is the democratic process, not the judiciary. There should be no constitutional barrier to a narrowly defined prohibition on material that combines sex with violence against women.

Nothing I have said here argues in favor of regulation of sexually explicit writing in general or of, say, the work of Robert Mapplethorpe, which depicts (among other things) homosexual relations and was recently subject to criminal prosecution. The antipornography argument is far more specific in its aims. Indeed, it is an exceedingly strange artifact of current legal thinking that an attack on material featuring sex and violence against women should be believed simultaneously to endanger art relating to homosexuality. The antipornography argument, rightly understood, calls for fierce protection of speech that complains of discrimination against homosexuals—because that speech is "high value" in the relevant sense and contains precisely none of the harms that call for regulation of pornography.

The notion that those who seek to regulate pornography, as defined here, must also regulate other sexually explicit speech is reminiscent of the idea that those who favor *Roe* must also favor *Lochner*. A better understanding of these various problems reveals that they raise questions that have little to do with one another. Of course it is always necessary to guard against the possible real-world abuses of any argument for restrictions on speech; but that practical concern is quite different from what I am discussing here. As a matter of principle, the argument for restrictions on pornography containing violence against women does not require restrictions on all sexually explicit speech.

Abortion

With abortion, as with pornography, two positions now dominate the constitutional territory. On the first view, the fetus has the status of a human life, for religious or other reasons. Because it has that status, nearly any governmental burden on the pregnant mother, if necessary to protect the fetus, is adequately justified.[18] This view is often closely identified with the idea—which is not a part of it as a logical or necessary matter—that sexual activity should be exclusively for purposes of reproduction. At least some of the controversy over abortion results from this idea, with many critics of abortion concerned that its free availability will promote promiscuity, remove a built-in check on sexual self-discipline, and encourage sexual activity for nonreproductive purposes.[19] Not all members of the antiabortion movement share these concerns; but as a matter of current fact these ideas lie close to the conceptual heart of the movement.

In some respects, this view closely resembles the idea that obscenity should be kept out of the marketplace. People who hold that view tend also to believe that abortion is impermissible, and for overlapping reasons. Both views usually assume a private, natural, and perhaps sacred sphere of sexuality and reproduction, and treat the appropriate goal of government as the protection of that sphere and of (what seems the same thing) traditional or conventional morality. Both views are often connected with the idea that sexuality is for purposes of reproduction and with fears about the debasing intrusion of external forces into the sexual realm. Of course the antiabortion position relies as well on the interest in protection of fetal life, and this interest is not present in the antiobscenity context. But the two positions are allied, in the sense that participants in the antiabortion movement also have sympathy for the attack on obscenity.

On the second view, the right to abortion is part of a capacious right of privacy, understood as a right to control one's own body without governmental restriction, especially with respect to matters of sexuality and reproduction. For those who believe in the right to abortion, the right to privacy calls first and foremost for control of the body. But it bears on sexuality more generally as well. Just as the antiabortion position is linked with the view that sexuality is for purposes of reproduction, the opposing view is deeply rooted in a belief that the abortion right is part and parcel of sexual freedom, which is said to be important for men and women. (It is not a coincidence that *Playboy* magazine is an important advocate of both abortion and elimination of legal controls on sexually explicit materials.)

On this view, the abortion right is necessary partly in order to ensure that nonreproductive sexuality will continue to be possible. One of the harms caused by antiabortion laws is the severe practical restrictions they impose on sexuality. Different evaluations of nonprocreative sexual activity thus help to explain the disagreement between the pro-life and pro-choice movements.

Many people who believe that the right to abortion is part of constitutionally protected privacy also believe that sexually explicit speech should always receive constitutional protection. Both views reflect a pro-choice position. Both views stem from the belief that government ought not to interfere with private liberty. Both views suggest that the private realm of sexuality and reproduction ought to be placed off-limits to the state. Rights of access to pornography and abortion are protected for closely analogous reasons.

There are serious difficulties, however, in treating the abortion right as one of privacy, not least because the Constitution does not refer to privacy and because the abortion decision does not involve conventional privacy at all.[20] Perhaps the right should be understood as involving liberty or autonomy. Liberty is of course protected by the due process clause, and the notion that this clause provides substantive protection to human liberty—though textually and historically controversial—is established in American law. But if the argument that follows in the text is correct, that understanding fails to capture the real nature of the abortion question. There are important equality dimensions to that question, and the notion of liberty is too abstract and general to encompass those dimensions. In any case, the competing views on abortion seem to have reached stalemate, with no possibility of developing criteria for mediating between them that might be acceptable to both sides. Moreover, those who stress "liberty" seem to have no way to respond to those who believe that abortion involves the death of a human being.

We might therefore explore another argument on behalf of the abortion right, one that is grounded in principles of equal protection.[21] This argument sees a prohibition on abortion as invalid because it involves an impermissibly selective co-optation of women's bodies. It claims that abortion restrictions turn women's reproductive capacities into something for the use and control of others. Unlike the privacy view, this argument does not and need not take a position on the status of the fetus. It acknowledges the possibility that fetuses are in important respects human beings. It does not disparage the good-faith moral convictions of those who believe that fetuses are vulnerable creatures deserving respect and concern. It is entirely comfortable with the claim that the destruction of a fetus is at least a morally problematic act. But it asserts that under current conditions, the government cannot impose on women alone the obligation to protect fetuses by co-opting their bodies through law. A key point here is that in no context does the law intrude on men's bodies in any comparable way.

On this view, abortion should be seen not as murder of the fetus but instead as a refusal to continue to permit one's body to be used to provide assistance to it. The failure to see abortion in this way is simply a product of the perceived naturalness of the role of women as childbearers—whether women want to assume that role or not. And even if a general legal obligation of bodily assistance to the vulnerable might be constitutionally acceptable or morally good, such an obligation cannot be permitted if it is imposed solely on women. It is akin to a law requiring blacks, but not whites, to given blood donations. This is so especially because of the close real-world connection between selective impositions of this sort and constitutionally illegitimate stereotypes about the appropriate role of women.

One last general note. Even the firmest defenders of abortion believe that the procedure is a tragic event, and far from a good way to prevent unwanted children. A far better approach is to use education campaigns, contraception, and the criminal law of rape and sexual assault so as to prevent unwanted pregnancies. If the argument to follow is correct, a woman should be allowed to choose abortion; but it would be far better if that choice were never necessary.

In its fullest form, the argument from equality is supported by four different points. Standing alone, some of these points may be insufficient. They derive force from their cumulative effect.

The first point is that restrictions on abortion should be seen as a form of sex discrimination. The proper analogy here is to a law that is targeted solely at women, and thus contains an explicit distinction on the basis of gender. A statute that is explicitly addressed to women is of course a form of sex discrimination. A statute that involves a defining characteristic or a biological correlate of being female should be treated in precisely the same way.[22] A law stating that "no woman" may obtain an abortion should readily be seen as a gender-based classification; a law stating that "no person" may obtain an abortion has an identical meaning.

The fact that some men may also be punished by abortion laws—for example, male doctors—does not mean that restrictions on abortion are gender-neutral. Laws calling for racial segregation make it impermissible for whites as well as blacks to desegregate, and this fact does not make such laws race-neutral. Nor would it be correct to say that restrictions on abortion merely have a discriminatory impact on women, and that they should therefore be treated in the same way as weight and height requirements with disproportionate effects on women. With such requirements, men and women are on both sides of the legal line; but abortion restrictions explicitly target women. A law that prohibited pregnant women, or pregnant people, from appearing on the streets during daylight would readily be seen as a form of gender-based discrimination. A restriction on abortion has the same gender-based characteristics.

It is important to recall here that the biological capacity to bear children, frequently taken as the basis for women's natural role, has the social consequence of involuntary childbearing only as a result of governmental decisions—significant among them the legal prohibition of abortion. The question at hand is whether government has the power to turn that capacity or difference, limited as it is to one gender, into a source of social disadvantage. The recognition of the abortion right might be rooted in a belief that in individual cases the biological capacity has no necessary social consequences, and that in the absence of a powerful justification, the role of motherhood for women should be seen as chosen rather than as given.

If we suppose that a restriction on the abortion right is a form of sex discrimination, the problem is hardly resolved. The question remains whether the interest in protecting the life of the fetus allows the state to compel women to bring the fetus to term. The second point in defense of an equality right to abortion would not devalue that interest or refer generally to the right to control one's body, but stress instead the selectivity of the compulsion. The basic problem is that an act of abortion should be viewed not as an ordinary killing, but instead as a refusal to allow one's body to be devoted to the protection of another. Government never imposes an obligation of this sort on its citizens—even when human life is uncontroversially at stake. A father is not compelled to devote his body to the protection of his children even if, for example, a risk-free kidney transplant is necessary to prevent the death of a child—and even though it could be said, in such cases, that the father "assumed the risk" of the bodily imposition by helping conceive the child in the first instance.

Indeed, it seems clear that a proposal to impose on the bodies of parents or others would currently be treated as a frightening and unacceptable intrusion on personal autonomy, even when life is at stake, even when death would result from refusal to carry out the relevant duty, and even when the person to be protected owes her or his existence and vulnerability to the people on whom the imposition would be placed. It is striking that no American legislature has imposed such an obligation and that courts have refused to do so as well.[23] The fact that similar impositions are not imposed in cases in which men are involved—the existence of discrimination in the imposition of the burden—suggests that the prohibition of abortion is a form of impermissible selectivity. It indicates that a discriminatory purpose is ultimately at work.

The point is not that the government is right to avoid imposing on people's bodies when other people's life is at stake. Perhaps government should do so more often, at least when the burden is small and the need is great. But government must be even-handed in its choices. An imposition on women but not on men violates the equal protection clause even if a more general imposition would be unobjectionable or highly desirable.

To be sure, nothing is quite like pregnancy. It is plausible that there are relevant differences between a prohibition on abortion and other forms of legally compelled use of bodies for the protection of others; I take up some of these differences below. In any case, my argument works most simply with pregnancies produced by rape and incest. It is more complex with pregnancies resulting from sexual relations that are voluntary. Indeed, the simple facts of abortion—which involves a certain death resulting from someone's voluntary choice—are often taken to make the procedure morally analogous to murder rather than refusal to aid. But the simple facts cannot settle the moral question. An abortion is indeed different from an ordinary refusal to aid in the sense that it involves a physical operation as a result of which a living being will be removed from its habitat in a way that will produce its death. It is in this sense that abortion really is not like anything else. But it is also true that the person seeking abortion is refusing to allow her body to be conscripted for the use of another. It is here that the parallel to refusal to aid becomes very close, and the assimilation of abortion to murder becomes very puzzling.

The fact that the burden of bodily use is imposed by law in this setting alone at least suggests that the interest in protection of human life is found adequate only as a result of impermissible sex role stereotypes. The fact that an abortion is treated as a killing, whereas the law treats other refusals to allow one's body to be used to save others as mere refusals to protect, suggests precisely the same thing.

More particularly, we might speculate that an abortion is seen as a murder rather than a failure to allow conscription only because of the perceived naturalness of the role of women as childbearers, whether they seek that role or not. The distinction between murder and failure to aid is a special case of the general distinction between acts and omissions, a distinction that generally turns on the identification of a baseline, that is, the natural or desirable state of affairs. For those who consider abortion to be murder, the carrying of the child to term is the implicit (but undefended and reflexive) baseline. An abortion is thus seen as a murder for the same reason that a trespass law is seen as government inaction (see Chapter 2). Consider here Mill's remarks: "But was there any domination which did not appear natural to those who possessed it? . . . So true is it that unnatural generally means only uncustomary, and that everything which is usual appears natural. The subjection of women to men being a universal custom, any departure from it quite naturally appears unnatural."[24]

A plausible counterexample to the argument here is the military draft, from which women have traditionally been excluded. The existence of a male-only draft seems to suggest that the state does indeed impose on the bodies of both men and women when the state deems this necessary. The draft even suggests that there is a kind of equality in the imposition of this burden. Women's compulsory role in the protection of unborn children might be thought to find a close parallel in men's compulsory role in the protection of the nation. It might even be said that the draft shows that men and women are treated the same after all.

In fact, the male-only draft does require a more precise statement of my basic claim, but when so restated the example turns out not to be a counterexample at all. The draft is in an important sense less or at least differently invasive than a prohibition on abortion, because the imposition on the body is wholly external. But the more fundamental problem is that legal requirements that only men be drafted are part of a system of sex role stereotyping characterized by a sharp, in part legally produced split between the domestic and public spheres—with women occupying the domestic and men occupying the public. In this light, legal restrictions on abortion and a male-only draft serve similar functions. Restrictions on abortion are an element in the legal creation of a domestic sphere in which women occupy their traditional role, and principally or only that role. Male-only drafts are part of the legal creation of a public sphere in which men occupy their traditional role, and principally or only that role. Discrimination against women is inextricably a part of social and legal structures that produce this form of role differentiation, which is in turn part of a system with persisting castelike features. When laws contribute to that differentiation, and thus to discrimination, they are constitutionally vulnerable.

From the standpoint of equal protection, then, the problem with restrictions on abortion is not merely that they impose on women's bodies but also that they do so in a way that is intertwined with the impermissible prescription, by the law and thus the state, of different roles for men and women. These different roles are part of second-class citizenship for women. Far from undermining it, the fact that only men are drafted helps to confirm the claim that abortion laws represent a form of unacceptable selectivity.[25] My claim is not that different social roles for men and women are constitutionally imper-missible or that men and women would in some other world be "the same." It is only that the state may not foreordain the conclusion.

The third point, buttressing the second, is that the notion that women should be compelled to carry fetuses to term is a product of constitutionally unacceptable stereotypes about the proper role of women in society. The history of abortion restrictions unambiguously supports the claim that in fact such restrictions are closely tied up with traditional ideas about women's proper role. This is of course an em-pirical claim; but it is one with ample support.[26] Consider, for ex-ample, the finding that those involved in antiabortion activities "con-cur that men and women, as a result of . . . intrinsic differences, have different roles to play: Men are best suited to the public world of work, whereas women are best suited to rearing children, managing homes, and loving and caring for husbands. . . . Mothering, in their view, is itself a full-time job, and any woman who cannot commit her-self fully to mothering should eschew it entirely. In short, working and mothering are either-or choices; one can do one or the other, but not both."[27]

I do not deny that it may well be logically possible to oppose with equal fervor both abortion and these traditional ideas. But the restric-tions that do or could exist in our world would not have been able to pass without the involvement and support of people holding and re-lying on unacceptable stereotypes. There is in this sense an analogy between restrictions on abortion and seemingly neutral tests for police officers whose existence is partly attributable to a racially discrimina-tory motive, or seemingly neutral height and weight requirements that would not have existed without gender-based discrimination. The existence of a discriminatory motivation is sufficient to invalidate the law, even if there is an independent neutral justification for it. It is enough to show that discrimination was a "but for" cause of enactment.

The fourth and final factor is that in the real world, the consequence of a restriction on abortion is not to save as many fetal lives as one would think or hope, but instead to force women to seek dangerous abortions, with increased risks to women themselves. Even the rate of legal abortions increased more in the three years before *Roe* than in the three years after that decision.[28] Indeed, some estimates suggest that before *Roe*, 5,000 to 10,000 women died per year as a result of incompetently performed abortions, and thousands more were admitted to hospitals for the same reason.[29] Since *Roe*, abortion-related maternal deaths have dropped by no less than 90 percent, falling by 40 percent in the year after *Roe* alone. Moreover, the abortion rate appears not to have increased dramatically as a result of the decision in *Roe*. Indeed, some studies show that nearly as many abortions were performed before *Roe* as are performed now. The abortion rate has increased from between 20 and 25 percent to about 28 percent; the total annual number has gone from between 1 million and 1.5 million to between 1.5 and 1.6 million.[30]

These figures are contested. But even if the statistics are overstated, and even if the number and rate of abortions have significantly increased as a result of *Roe*, at least it seems clear that the principal effect of the decision was not to increase fetal deaths, but instead to produce a shift from dangerous to safe abortions. If this is so, restrictions on abortion do not really protect life in the way that their proponents hope. Instead they increase maternal deaths without decreasing the termination of fetal lives nearly as much as one might anticipate.

I do not suggest that ineffective laws are unconstitutional. Instead the argument—a conventional one—is that those laws that intrude on fundamental interests or discriminate on the basis of gender must actually promote their legitimate goals.[31] It is possible, of course, that new abortion restrictions would be more effective or less dangerous than old ones because of technological changes and greater enforcement activity. But the severe difficulties of policing the practice without unacceptable costs suggest that this is probably too optimistic. Moreover, the technological changes that might decrease the danger of unlawful abortions—to those who have access to the relevant technology—would simultaneously tend to decrease the efficacy of the legal prohibitions.

The evidence on the futility of antiabortion restrictions also suggests, though it certainly does not demonstrate, the presence of a discriminatory purpose. The failure of critics of abortion to come to terms with that evidence suggests the possibility that at least a part of the antiabortion movement stems from punitive goals rather than an interest in protecting fetal life. Those goals may include the punishment and deterrence of nonreproductive activity, goals that appear to play a large role in producing antiabortion laws.

The argument for an abortion right built on principles of sex equality is thus straightforward. Restrictions on abortion burden only women and are therefore impermissible unless persuasively justified in gender-neutral terms. Adequate justifications might be available for gender-based discrimination in some settings; but in our world they are not in light of the fact that the burden of bodily use, properly understood, is imposed only on women, could not be enacted in the absence of unacceptable stereotypes about women's appropriate role, and does not operate in practice to save fetal lives.

Such arguments do not rely on an abstract right to privacy or to control of one's body. I do not mean to suggest that this alternative view is necessarily unpersuasive or that it is impossible to argue that an interest in autonomy or in freedom from bodily invasion justifies an abortion right. But one of several difficulties with those arguments is that they must come to terms with the moral or political status of the fetus, a problem that the equality argument successfully avoids. And of course the presence of a strong claim from liberty joins with the equality argument to increase the power of the basic position: It is not as if the abortion context involves an inequality with respect to something trivial. Indeed, there is some artificiality in completely separating the equality and liberty claims in this setting, since the matter treated unequally—control over reproductive processes—is so central an ingredient in a denial of both liberty and equality to women, and simultaneously so. The social and legal control of women's reproductive capacities is the defining characteristic of systems of caste based on gender; and a serious commitment to both liberty and equality calls for a legal attack on those systems in all their various forms.

In any event, no one is likely to be in a good position to answer the question whether abortion should be available in a world of gender-based equality. It may be that the biological difference creates a relevant inequality that would be at stake in *any* restriction on abortion. It may be that the autonomy interest is sufficient no matter how much there is in the way of sexual equality. Nonetheless, movements in the direction of sexual equality—before, during, and after conception, including after birth—unquestionably weaken the case for an abortion right by removing one of the factors that support its existence.

Ironically, it is the privacy argument, not the argument from equality, that forces proponents to ask bizarre and unresolvable counterfactual questions. The argument from equality stresses the context, wellsprings, and consequences of abortion restrictions; it is solidly anchored in existing practices. Nor does the equality argument depend on the counterfactual question: How would abortion be treated if men could become pregnant? The question has the usual problem of counterfactuals: It can be answered only if one isolated part of current reality is changed and the rest held constant—an extremely artificial strategy, since the change of that one isolated part of reality changes the rest of it as well.

It is tempting to think that abortion would be freely available if men could become pregnant, because mostly male legislatures would be unlikely to support a law that would so severely constrain them in the event that sexual intercourse produced an unwanted child. But advocates of the abortion right should not be so confident in asserting that abortion would, in that event, be freely available. If men could become pregnant, they would not be men (indeed no one would be a man as we understand that term). To ask how abortion would be treated in so fundamentally different a world is to ask a question that is not subject to meaningful evaluation. Similarly, the autonomy argument requires an assessment of how abortion would or should be treated if social practices were fundamentally changed. We are not in a position to make that assessment.

Moreover, it is a large advantage of equality arguments that unlike privacy or liberty arguments, they do not devalue the legitimate interest in protecting the fetus, and indeed make it unnecessary to take any position on the moral and political status of unborn life. Even if the fetus has all the status of human life, the bodies of women cannot under current conditions be conscripted in order to protect it. The (admittedly imperfect) analogy here would be to a case in which black people were required to become blood donors to ensure that certain people needing blood did not die. Even if the protection of those who needed blood was a compelling state interest, selectivity of this sort could not be tolerated. It does not matter if people's lives are at stake, since a selective imposition on one class of people, even to protect others who need them, is unacceptable under the equal protection clause.

There are two possible responses to the line of argument thus far. The first would be that pregnancy is a voluntary state; the woman is responsible for the very existence of the fetus. Because the existence and vulnerability of the fetus result from a voluntary choice, a special duty is properly placed on the woman to protect it, even if that duty calls for co-optation of her body through law. When the fetus exists by virtue of voluntary actions and cannot live without bodily co-optation, the proper analogy is to murder rather than to failure to assist. Moreover, and relatedly, what makes the abortion context distinctive is that selectivity in the imposition of the burden on human bodies is the only available option for those concerned about fetal life. Because of biology, government cannot make men bear this burden even if it wants to do so. If fetuses are to survive, it must be a result of impositions on women. Selectivity is foreordained by the brute facts of human physiology.

Even if this argument is accepted on its own terms, it would not work in cases in which pregnancy has resulted from involuntary intercourse, such as rape and incest. Certainly the argument from equality is secure in such cases.

Moreover, the fact that individualized proof of rape or incest is so difficult even in criminal cases reveals that it is extraordinarily hard to make pleading and proof of rape or incest a predicate for abortion. If the right exists in rape or incest cases, the only realistic way to protect the right, even in such cases, seems to be to create a general right to abortion. It is significant, of course, that such protection would be far too broad in the sense that it would protect abortions to which there is (on the argument offered thus far) no constitutional right. But it remains true that overprotection is necessary to allow those abortions that are constitutionally safeguarded.

More generally, the fact that intercourse was voluntary hardly means that pregnancy is. Voluntary intercourse does not mean, as a matter of simple fact, voluntary pregnancy, any more than the decision to walk at night in a certain neighborhood means voluntary mugging, or a failure to lock one's door means voluntary theft. Reasonable efforts at contraception frequently fail. The question is instead that raised by any claim that people have voluntarily assumed a risk: whether the decision to engage in certain activity justifies the state or society in imposing a correlative burden on them. This is a normative question; it is not successfully answered by saying that people have voluntarily run a certain risk.

In the context at hand, the question is whether intercourse, when voluntary, should be taken to allow the state to impose on women a duty of bodily co-optation in cases of pregnancy. It is insufficient to answer that question by emphasizing that the intercourse was voluntary.

If the argument thus far is correct, the answer must be negative. As we have seen, the imposition of that duty is deeply implicated in violations of the equality guarantee in terms of its wellsprings. Moreover, it remains impermissibly selective despite the genuine fact that the state cannot, as a biological matter, conscript men to protect fetuses. The reason is that even in cases in which men's bodies *could* be conscripted to protect children, the state imposes no such obligations. This is so even with respect to children for whose existence they are in part responsible, and for whom they therefore could be said to have assumed the risk. The selectivity comes in the state's across-the-board failure to impose on men a duty of bodily use to protect children. Finally, antiabortion restrictions serve their own purposes too poorly to be acceptable. For all these reasons, the fact that the fetus may owe its existence to the woman's voluntary action does not justify a ban on abortion.

The second response would be that the argument I have made fails to come to terms with the legitimate claims of the fetus. Few groups are as politically weak or generally vulnerable as unborn children; they cannot vote at all. Perhaps they themselves have a claim of inequality sufficient to override the imposition on women. On this view, any objection from inequality or selectivity in this context comes even more powerfully from fetuses than from women. It may even be the absence of a prohibition on abortion that most conspicuously denies "the equal protection of the laws." Without such a prohibition, fetuses are uniquely vulnerable to destruction at the hands of other human beings, and uniquely deprived of legal protection against that destruction.

This response properly points to the fact that politically vulnerable groups are on both sides of this question. Indeed, it suggests that in some contexts the government may be under a constitutional duty to protect the unborn, at least to the extent that it can do so without co-opting the body of the mother. It is not, however, a persuasive rejoinder to the claim of impermissible gender-based discrimination.

Even if fetuses are a vulnerable group, and even if they are entitled to special protection against discrimination, they do not have a claim on another vulnerable group to conscript bodies on their behalf. The closest analogy here would be to a law requiring Hispanic people to devote their bodies (through blood donations and compulsory kidney transplants, for example) to the protection of vulnerable black children, or imposing such a duty on the parents of black children alone. Even if the group to be protected has a special claim to protection, the state cannot impose the relevant duty on another vulnerable group.

An argument from sex equality seems preferable to one that claims a general or acontextual privacy right, and also to the view that restrictions on abortion simply do not raise constitutional questions. In particular, the equality argument has a large advantage over the pro-choice position in that it does not rest on privacy, freely acknowledges and indeed insists on the strength of the interest in protecting fetal life, and stresses rather than disregards the facts that women alone become pregnant and that discrimination and coercion exist in the realm of reproduction. The reasons for these advantages are parallel to those in the antipornography context.

The equality argument has advantages over the antiabortion position as well insofar as it stresses both the inadequacy of restrictions on abortion to protect life and the selectivity of the imposition on women. Indeed, it seems reasonable to conclude that an argument from sex discrimination is not merely a worthy competitor to the two alternatives, but on balance correct.

As far as current constitutional law is concerned, however, the argument from sex discrimination is the least well represented. In *Roe* itself there was no mention of equality, and the same has been true of the abortion issue for most of its history in American law. A claim of sex equality appeared for the first time in 1992, when a badly divided Supreme Court reaffirmed *Roe* in the *Casey* case.[32] One of the extraordinary features of the decision was the novel emphasis on equality. Justice Blackmun, the author of *Roe,* relied most explicitly on the equality principle: "By restricting the right to terminate pregnancies, the State conscripts women's bodies into its services, forcing women to continue their pregnancies, suffer the pains of childbirth, and in most instances, provide years of maternal care." Justice Blackmun urged that abortion restriction rest on the assumption "that women can simply be forced to accept the 'natural' status and incidents of motherhood," an impermissible conception of women's role. Justice Stevens similarly asserted that the abortion right "is an integral part of a correct understanding of . . . the basic equality of men and women."

In the principal opinion reaffirming *Roe,* Justices O'Connor, Kennedy, and Souter also emphasized issues of sex equality. "The ability of women to participate equally in the economic and social life of the nation has been facilitated by their ability to control their reproductive lives." These justices voted to strike down a law providing for notification of the husband in large part on the ground that a state "may not give to a man the kind of dominion over his wife that parents exercise over their children." Thus the Court found that the notice requirement ran parallel to old ideas about paternal control over the family unit, ideas that are "repugnant to our present understanding of marriage and the nature of the rights secured by the Constitution. Women do not lose their constitutionally protected liberty when they marry."

Notwithstanding these suggestions, the right to abortion is not now protected by the equal protection clause. The reason is that even after *Casey* there is a crisp answer to the equality argument, one that is strikingly reminiscent of the answer in the case of pornography. On the Supreme Court's view, laws restricting abortion cannot amount to discrimination, because only women can become pregnant.[33] A denial of equality involves a refusal to treat people who are "similarly situated" similarly. With respect to the capacity to become pregnant, women and men are not similarly situated. An equality argument is therefore unavailable.

This conception of equality turns out also to be a conception of neutrality. According to that conception, the government's duty of impartiality is violated when, and only when, it distinguishes between those who are the same—by, for example, treating blacks differently from whites, or women differently from men. But this conception of neutrality rules out of bounds perfectly plausible claims of inequality. It does so precisely because it embodies a controversial substantive baseline. Here the baseline is not existing distributions of wealth and opportunities; it is not as if the social status quo, in that sense, is taken as prepolitical and just. Something quite similar is, however, at work.

Women's biological differences "from the norm" are treated as a social given, and legal rules directed at those differences are said not to raise equality problems.

The problem here is that the norm itself is defined as the physical capacities of men. Sex discrimination is perceived when, and only when, women are the same as men. As currently understood, the equality principle requires only that women must be treated the same as men insofar as they *are* the same as men.

The difficulty with this approach is that it takes male biological capacities as the baseline against which to assess the equality issue. This is the parallel in the abortion context to the use, in other contexts I have discussed, of existing social practices as the baseline from which to assess deviations from neutrality. In fact it is a version of the same phenomenon. Of course there is no obvious reason to ask the equality question in this way. Indeed if one does so, one will both fail to see inequality in cases in which it plausibly exists, and see equality in cases in which it is plausibly absent. (See Chapter 11.) Surely a law that turns a biological capacity into a social and legal disability for a part of the population, and for only that part, should be seen as raising questions of discrimination. If a biological capacity limited to one gender is made a basis for social disadvantage through law, one might think that the relevant law creates a problem of inequality.

The failure to see this point in the context of abortion is a product of a peculiar notion of neutrality and a derivative, and similarly peculiar, notion of what equality means. I conclude that laws restricting abortion raise a question of sex discrimination, and that the response from neutrality embodies an unjustified baseline. Laws that prohibit abortion may not violate the due process clause or invade constitutionally protected privacy; but they do violate the constitutional commitment to equal protection of the laws.

Surrogacy

Many courts and state legislatures are in the process of deciding whether and how to regulate arrangements by which women sell their reproductive capacities, and the children who result, to couples who are infertile or otherwise unwilling to adopt children or to have a biological child between them. Thus far, the Constitution has played little role in this setting. But freedom of choice, and indeed contractual liberty, is the rallying cry for advocates of surrogacy agreements. At least one lower court has suggested that constitutional liberty forbids government restrictions on such agreements.[34]

On this view, surrogacy arrangements are acceptable for the same reason that *Roe v. Wade* is right. Freedom of choice, and control over one's body and reproductive processes, are the governing principles. What matters is not that the choice be correct, but that it be remitted to individuals rather than to the state. This view is set out by many who believe that *Roe* was correctly decided, and who support surrogacy arrangements for the same reason that they accept *Roe*.

As in the cases of abortion and pornography, there is a familiar competing position. On the competing view, reproductive capacities and babies should be considered sacrosanct in the sense that they cannot be purchased and sold. To trade reproductive capacities or people for money is to diminish and degrade them. Sexuality and reproduction should be protected from hedonism and profitmaking. On this view, surrogacy arrangements are wrong for the same reason that *Roe* is wrong. Both are insufficiently respectful of the special claims of sexuality and reproductive processes, in their traditional forms, to protection from various forms of debasement. Similar ideas of course underlie the antiobscenity position.

Advocates of surrogacy arrangements might well be prompted to ask (perhaps tendentiously) why women ought not to be permitted to sell babies if, under *Roe,* they are permitted to kill them. They might well be prompted to add that it is plausible to be for *Roe* and for surrogacy, or against *Roe* and against surrogacy, but impossible or even hypocritical to be, as some are, both for *Roe* and against surrogacy. If the abortion right finds its justification in a right to control one's body, then it follows that surrogacy arrangements are unobjectionable. They are similarly a result of individual control over reproductive choice.

In either case, it is often said to be extremely ironic that some advocates of a right to abortion are disturbed by free markets in reproduction. If the right is one to autonomy—or to control over one's own affairs with respect to issues of reproduction—surely the right to sell gestational services stands on at least as firm ground as the right to have an abortion.

As in the contexts of pornography and abortion, the most plausible response turns to principles of equal protection rather than privacy. We have seen that the problem with pornography is that it treats one group of people as objects for the sexual use of another or, more particularly, for sexual violence. In the case of abortion, the problem is similar: the reproductive capacities of one class of people are turned, by law, into something for the use of others. If surrogacy is troublesome, it is so for largely the same reason.[35] The practice of surrogacy also turns the reproductive capacities of one group of citizens into objects for other people's use. The problem arises even if the bargains that result are in an important sense voluntary. The problem is especially severe in light of the fact that social and legal institutions have frequently turned women's reproductive capacities into something for other people's use and control, and that this process is closely associated with the use, by those institutions, of women's reproductive capacities as a basis for creating second-class citizenship for women.

In the context of surrogacy, this argument faces some serious difficulties. A decision to constrain surrogacy might itself be seen as a mechanism for social control of the reproductive choices of women. Surrogacy agreements are (by hypothesis) voluntary and thus provide benefits for the women involved. A surrogate mother is choosing to sell her reproductive capacities; no one is compelling her to do so. In this sense, she is not an object of legal controls in the same sense as the involuntary mother in the abortion case. It is therefore necessary to explain why a government decision to allow this voluntary choice should be seen as a form of harmful discrimination.

It is plainly inadequate to invoke the term *exploitation* or (what may be the same thing) to refer to the sometimes harsh background conditions faced by women who participate in such agreements. Disallowance of the agreement does nothing to eliminate those conditions. It simply eliminates one mechanism by which women might try to counteract them. Elimination of the most-preferred option—even one that seems harsh to observers—is hardly a sensible way of dealing with background injustice. It is often tempting to think that we protect people from difficult circumstances by preventing them from selecting a difficult course of action; but it is hardly clear that this will help them at all.

The basic problem with the sale of reproductive capacities is not the background conditions, but the fact that the sale may have adverse consequences for those who participate in these arrangements and for women and children in general. The first difficulty is that notwithstanding what the woman may think before the fact, the process of selling reproductive capacities can be harmful for her. It may be hard to understand, in advance, exactly what it means to hand over a child that one has brought to term. Many examples, some highly publicized, can be found.[36]

The second problem is that there will be inevitable social effects from legal legitimation of the practice of exchanging women's reproductive capacities, and the children who result, for cash. A choice to allow these to be treated as objects for sale and use will affect how men perceive women, how women perceive themselves, and how both perceive children. Here the questions of surrogacy and prostitution become closely allied. Prostitution has effects on social perceptions of women; the institution of surrogacy could have similar consequences. Both of these are tied up with inequality.[37]

In particular, a world in which female sexual and reproductive services were freely traded on markets would legitimate and reinforce a pervasive form of inequality—one that sees the social role of women as that of breeders, and that uses that role to create second-class citizenship. Surrogacy arrangements, if widespread, could affect attitudes, on the part of both men and women, about the appropriate role of men and women. Social stigmatization of the sale of those services might therefore be justified on antidiscrimination grounds. In view of the social (and to some extent biological) differences between men and women, a decision to allow male reproductive capacities to be bought and sold has no such consequences. To treat the sales of male and female reproductive capacities in the same way is thus not required by neutrality.

I have not offered anything like a complete argument against surrogacy arrangements. The issue ultimately depends on a range of factors not mentioned here. Many such factors argue against such arrangements. There are possible adverse effects on children. To know that one has been or might have been sold could have harmful consequences for the children involved. It would be necessary to evaluate this view in order fully to come to terms with the surrogacy problem. Moreover, issues of race and poverty are important in this setting. There is a shortage of white children for purposes of adoption, and a large number of unwanted black children. The appeal of surrogacy must be understood in this context.

There are important competing considerations as well, and these considerations argue in favor of allowing surrogacy. It is possible that the effects I have described will occur only a little or not at all. It is possible that many or most women who participate in these arrangements would be pleased to have done so, and this is surely relevant (though not decisive). It is possible that a prohibition on surrogacy would involve an unacceptable form of protectionism, one that would help erase the fact that the process of carrying a fetus to term is actually a form of work. It is possible that the external effects of allowing such arrangements will be small; in any case an assessment of their magnitude is quite speculative, and social attitudes about the appropriate roles of men and women are affected by numerous factors, of which surrogacy arrangements might well be a quite minor one. It is possible that there are sufficient countervailing benefits to infertile couples and the women involved.

The problems involved in enforcing a prohibition on surrogacy argue powerfully against that route. A refusal to enforce such agreements when the birth mother declines to hand over the child seems far preferable to a criminal ban. In any case, much will depend on the details.

In light of these considerations, surrogacy arrangements probably should not be banned. If such arrangements are troublesome, however, they are troublesome for reasons that argue for rather than against the outcome in *Roe v. Wade*. And if those reasons are persuasive, there is no inconsistency in simultaneous approval of the abortion right and concern about surrogacy arrangements. That position will seem inconsistent only to those who have already set forth the premises on which the discussion is to be conducted. Those premises have everything to do with a certain conception of neutrality.

The right to an abortion can be securely founded on principles of equal protection. Laws restricting abortion embody a form of gender-based discrimination. They also impose on women a disability not imposed on men in the only parallel cases. The parallel cases are seen as irrelevant only because of a perception of the naturalness of the conscription of women as mothers. That perception is part of a system of sex role stereotyping; it grows out of ideas thought to be impermissible in other areas of the law.

I have not resolved the questions raised by pornography and surrogacy, which turn in part on complex considerations that I have been unable to discuss here. Taken together with the discussion in Chapter 8, the approach here does suggest that an appropriately narrow and clear restriction on pornography should be upheld. In any event, both issues raise serious problems of discrimination. The case for regulating pornography, founded on principles of sexual equality, is more powerful than the case for regulating obscenity, founded on traditional values. Under current conditions, the purchase of women's reproductive capacities poses issues of sex discrimination. To the extent that it is grounded on neutrality, the objection to regulation is unpersuasive in both settings.

CHAPTER 10

"It's the Government's Money": Funding Speech, Education, and Reproduction

Many of the most vexing questions in constitutional law arise from the fact that modern government affects constitutional rights not only through criminal penalties but also through spending, licensing, and employment. May the government refuse to hire people with unpopular political views? May it fund only artistic projects of which it approves? May it pay for childbirth but refuse to fund abortion, or speech on the subject of abortion? May it fill libraries with books of only a certain viewpoint? May it fund campaigns against smoking cigarettes but refuse to fund other sorts of campaigns?

It may well be in these areas that constitutional law is least developed. It is here that the Supreme Court and the Constitution will receive their most serious tests in the next generation.

Under current law, the "unconstitutional conditions" doctrine sets out the boundary between constitutional rights and government prerogatives in the areas of spending, licensing, and employment. The purpose of the doctrine is to limit the power of government to affect constitutional rights by using its resources to pressure people to do what it wants. The doctrine operates as a shorthand response to the view that those who voluntarily participate in government programs have "waived" their constitutional objections, and also to the claim that the government's power not to create a regulatory program necessarily includes the lesser power to impose on that program whatever conditions it chooses.

The various puzzles in the doctrine have produced considerable confusion and a wide range of commentary.[1] It is notable that for all their differences, participants in the debate treat the unconstitutional conditions doctrine as the appropriate vehicle for approaching disputed questions. The differences come in the description of the scope and nature of the doctrine.

In this chapter I argue that the unconstitutional conditions doctrine should be abandoned. The doctrine grows out of the same ideas about neutrality and action that predated the New Deal, and it is hopelessly ill suited to modern government. During the difficult transition from the common law system to the modern state, the doctrine represented an awkward and never fully explicated effort to protect constitutional rights in a dramatically different environment. Current approaches to the problem of unconstitutional conditions are pervaded by outmoded notions that reflect this peculiar legacy. The idea that the system of common law and criminal prohibition provides the basic, even natural state of affairs, and that regulatory and spending programs are occasional and somewhat jarring additions, affects all sides of the debate.

Indeed, the very idea of a unitary unconstitutional conditions doctrine is a product of the view that the common law is the ordinary course and that governmental "intervention"—the regulatory state—is exceptional. Despite its pervasiveness, this view is misconceived. It embodies status quo neutrality. It is inconsistent with both the realities of contemporary government and the principles that gave rise to it. Instead of an unconstitutional conditions doctrine focused on the issue of whether there has been "coercion" or "penalty," what is necessary is a model of reasons: an approach that asks whether the government has constitutionally sufficient justifications for affecting constitutionally protected interests.

This model draws on much of the analysis provided in Chapter 1. It is of a piece with the founding generation's effort to create a republic of reasons. Indeed, we might see this new focus as an effort to develop, for our government, a system of limitations carrying forward those imposed by the framers on their very different institutions.

I attempt to give content to these general claims by exploring the constitutional issues raised in several areas of selective government funding. My goal is to show the sort of analysis that would be used in a legal system that has abandoned the unconstitutional conditions doctrine. I conclude that government may constitutionally fund public but not private schools; that government has broad though not unlimited discretion to be selective in funding art and other projects involving speech; and, perhaps most controversially, that government is under a constitutional duty to fund abortion in cases of rape and incest, at least if it is funding childbirth in such cases.

A very general claim follows from and helps motivate the discussion. In a crucial sense, all constitutional cases are unconstitutional conditions cases. Ordinary property rights are created by a government—in the words of Justice Holmes, "as a matter of fact." (See the discussion in Chapter 2.) When the government says that it will take your property if you do something, it is, in essence, imposing a condition on a right that it has conferred. There is no fundamental or metaphysical difference between the unconstitutional conditions case (welfare benefits will be eliminated for those who criticize the government) and the ordinary constitutional case (people who criticize the government must pay a fine). The sharp distinction between ordinary cases and unconstitutional conditions cases depends on status quo neutrality. Once we repudiate that conception of neutrality, we will be able to reconstruct constitutional principles on a much sounder basis.

Spending, Licensing, Liberty

To make the analysis as concrete as possible, I will focus on three cases involving selective funding. In the first, government decides to fund public but not private schools. It does so even though there is a constitutional right to send one's children to private schools and even though public schools are funded through general revenues.[2] In the second case, government funds some artistic projects but not others— excluding, for example, projects containing nudity, criticizing the government, or proclaiming the virtues of Nazism or Communism. In the third, government funds childbirth but not abortion in cases in which pregnancy results from rape or incest.

I have said that the unconstitutional conditions doctrine is an artifact of the collision of the regulatory welfare state with the preexisting common law framework. We saw in Chapter 2 that in the early days of the regulatory state, legislation that is now generally taken as constitutionally uncontroversial—for example, minimum wage and maximum-hour laws—was subject to attack as an impermissible "taking" from one person for the benefit of another. The distribution of wealth and entitlements under the common law was treated as a part of nature, or at least as the baseline from which to assess whether government had violated its obligation of neutrality. We have also seen that before and during the New Deal period, this framework came under assault. The common law system appeared to be a set of collective choices, not a natural or impartial order. The rise of the regulatory state represented a general understanding that the common law and private markets were regulatory systems and that sometimes they produced both inefficiency and injustice.

At its inception, the unconstitutional conditions doctrine was a product of *Lochner*-like, pre–New Deal understandings. It was founded on status quo neutrality, and its original purpose was to protect common law rights in the face of threats to them created by the rise of the regulatory state. The doctrine arose when it became clear that regulatory and spending activities might produce impermissible redistribution of the kind condemned in *Lochner*, and that legal principles could be designed to control these novel intrusions on what had previously been regarded as a private sphere.

In 1917, for example, the Supreme Court dealt with a state's effort to allow companies to use the public highways only after obtaining a permit certifying that the business was for the "public convenience and necessity." The Court struck down the effort as an unconstitutional condition. The Court claimed that "the act . . . is in no real sense a regulation of the use of the highways," but instead "regulation of the business of those who are engaged in using them."[3] This form of business regulation was impermissible even if attempted as a condition on the grant of government benefits.

From its inception, then, the unconstitutional conditions doctrine grew out of a system that treated the regulatory state as an artificial and occasional supplement to the ordinary repertoire of legal controls. The doctrine was an effort to protect common law interests and market ordering from novel threats. The roots of the doctrine in the uneasy encounter of constitutional courts with the regulatory state are revealed by the three principal positions about its scope and nature.

HOLMESIANISM

The first position is traceable to Justice Oliver Wendell Holmes. It finds classic expression in Holmes's response to a claim by a police officer that he had been unlawfully discharged for his political views: "The petitioner may have a constitutional right to talk politics, but he has no constitutional right to be a policeman. . . . The servant cannot complain, as he takes the employment on the terms which are offered him."[4]

Holmes's view has several modern incarnations, and it has a prominent place in the work of Chief Justice William Rehnquist.[5] On this view, courts should never, or almost never, invalidate arguably unconstitutional conditions. The government's supposedly greater power not to create the program at all includes the supposedly lesser power to impose the condition.

The Holmesian view begins by acknowledging that an important lesson of the *Lochner* period was that courts should not treat the status quo, or existing distributions of entitlements pursuant to the common law, as sacrosanct. Justice Holmes saw the rejection of the *Lochner* framework—the basic ordering principle for the unconstitutional conditions doctrine—as entailing the abandonment of the doctrine as well. On this view, the only logical replacement for the doctrine is unlimited governmental discretion in the areas of employment, licensing, and funding. When citizens have participated in a program to which they have no constitutional entitlement, the Constitution imposes no constraints on such conditions as government imposes. It would follow, for example, that the government might award grants to whatever artists it wishes. Indeed, the Holmesian position has quite dramatic consequences. All three of the cases with which I started become simple ones: The government wins.

This position represents an extreme reaction to the rise of the regulatory state. It is unsurprising that many observers took the New Deal repudiation of common law baselines as a reason to abandon baselines, and to this (significant) extent constitutionalism, altogether. We should be not at all surprised to see this position in Holmes, whose *Lochner* dissent (discussed in Chapter 2) spoke in just these terms. But the rise of the regulatory state should hardly be taken as a reason to eliminate constraints on governmental activities that pressure constitutional rights.

If government may, for example, limit welfare programs to people who speak favorably of the party in power, there will be a serious distortion of free speech in a way that creates very much the same dangers, in terms of both purposes and effects, against which the First Amendment is supposed to guard. If that amendment is taken above all as a limit on governmental interference with political views, there is no exemption from its strictures for funding decisions. Governmental conditions on the receipt of licenses or funds may have powerful distorting effects on (for example) the system of freedom of expression or on racial equality. (Imagine a welfare program limited to white people.) All this suggests that in its broadest forms, the Holmesian position is unacceptable.

More fundamentally, and perhaps surprisingly, the Holmesian position turns out to be a legacy of status quo neutrality and of precisely the pre–New Deal understandings that it purports to repudiate. Many people with sympathy for the Holmesian view think that "coercive" governmental interference with the realm of private autonomy, defined in common law terms, may well raise constitutional objections. Spending and benefit programs do not. This view implements constitutional principles by reference to the (discredited) early twentieth-century distinction between a prepolitical sphere of common law autonomy and a postpolitical sphere of governmental action. After the New Deal, governmental benefit and spending programs cannot plausibly be seen as a regulatory system superimposed upon a set of spontaneous or natural arrangements. This is a central lesson of the demise of *Lochner.*

If this is so, the sharp line drawn by the Holmesian position between the common law and the regulatory sphere depends on assumptions and values that are inconsistent with those of modern government. It treats the world of common law rights as fundamentally different from the world of governmentally created benefits. (I do not deny that conditions on licensing and funding may raise issues different from those of criminal punishment. See below.)

A more interesting position, also with resonances in Holmes, would go a full step further. It would suggest that because common law rights are state created, all cases turn out to be unconstitutional conditions cases; and government wins all of them. Interference with constitutional rights in the old-fashioned sense—as through the criminal law—is merely interference with rights that government itself created and may therefore eliminate at its pleasure. The refusal to allow an unconstitutional conditions doctrine for spending might therefore be seen as simply a special case of a large-scale, post–New Deal abandonment of constitutionalism. We might speculate that something of this kind was indeed behind the thought of Justice Holmes. At least this position has the advantage of consistency. But since it would eliminate constitutional limits on government, there is little else to be said in its favor.

ANTIREDISTRIBUTION

The second position was prominent in the early twentieth century. Although it has echoes in many places, Richard Epstein is perhaps its only full-fledged defender today.[6] Here the connection between the unconstitutional conditions doctrine and its earliest manifestations is perhaps clearest.

On this view, the basic goal of the doctrine is the preservation and protection of *Lochner*-like rights—property and contract—under new circumstances. As elaborated at length by Epstein, the unconstitutional conditions doctrine operates as a second-best substitute for the outright prohibition, on constitutional grounds, of spending and taxing programs. Sometimes the doctrine applies for the same reason that the underlying program is itself unconstitutional as "redistribution," that is, because it upsets existing distributions of property. Sometimes the doctrine applies because even if the redistributive program would be upheld, courts can minimize the redistributive consequences through control of the "indirect" constraints imposed by the conditions. In its early twentieth-century incarnation and in Epstein's own version, this idea grows out of the same framework that accounted for *Lochner* and various other decisions invalidating modern legislation.

How would this understanding apply in the cases at hand? To take just one example, it would require that a government that funds public schools must also fund private schools. Some version of a voucher system for education is constitutionally compelled. The reason is that if government funds public schools alone, it will be working an impermissible redistribution from one group of taxpayers to another. It is redistribution against which the Constitution guards.

Under modern conditions, however, this approach is hard to accept. First, no constitutional provision generally forbids "redistribution."[7] Since the *Lochner* period,[8] the Constitution has been construed to authorize a wide range of changes benefiting some groups and burdening others, largely on the understanding that existing distributions of wealth and property are not sacrosanct. When a redistribution is found unconstitutional, it is judged to be so not because of any general constitutional disability, but because particular constitutional provisions rule off-limits particular government acts, some of them admittedly redistributive. For example, a welfare program limited to members of the Republican party is impermissible because of the constraints of the First Amendment; a decision to appropriate your house and to make of it a state building is unacceptable because of the takings clause. But an unconstitutional conditions doctrine rooted in an antiredistributive principle is simply too general a way to approach a constitutional system with quite concrete prohibitions.

x298   THE PARTIAL CONSTITUTION

More fundamentally, the second position depends on ideas about the purpose of the state that have been roundly repudiated in the twentieth century, and for good reasons.[9] At first there seem to be substantial differences between Holmesianism, which is minimally intrusive on governmental power, and the antiredistributive position, which intrudes a great deal on such power. For all their differences, however, both positions draw a sharp distinction between the realm of private autonomy, which is thought to be law-free, and the realm of public law, which is thought to signal government "intervention." Both positions understand the unconstitutional conditions doctrine by reference to precisely this distinction.

But unless we are to return to *Lochner*, redistributive and paternalistic programs are no longer constitutionally out-of-bounds. An unconstitutional conditions doctrine built on status quo neutrality is inconsistent with the assumptions that underlie the regulatory state. To abandon those assumptions in the context of the unconstitutional conditions problem would be most peculiar.

SUBSIDY VERSUS PENALTY

The third position is represented by the current constitutional mainstream. Many people see the unconstitutional conditions doctrine as an effort to preserve legal requirements of governmental neutrality under modern conditions. It is in this basic idea that one finds the staples of the unconstitutional conditions doctrine: the government may not do indirectly what it may not do directly; government may not "penalize" the exercise of constitutional rights; government may not coerce people into relinquishing their rights through regulation, spending, and license, any more than it may do so through criminal sanctions.

These are conventional arguments in the Supreme Court.[10] They reflect some important truths, especially insofar as they recognize the possibility that spending decisions may affect constitutional rights in ways that government is unable to justify. Above all, these ideas operate as a valuable corrective both to approaches that see common law rights as the general baseline against which an unconstitutional conditions doctrine must operate, and to those who, following Holmes, suggest that courts should not limit the intrusions on constitutional rights that occur through spending decisions.

In many respects, however, this third approach is badly flawed, not least because it has far more in common with *Lochner*-like ideas—

finding the regulatory state a strange and intermittent intruder—than at first appears. There are several problems here.

The first problem is that it is exceptionally hard to come up with the right baseline from which to distinguish subsidies from penalties. To see why this is so, consider *Harris v. McRae,*[11] in which the Supreme Court upheld a government decision to fund childbirth but not to fund medically necessary abortions. The Court said that the decision to withhold funding for abortions was permissible because it amounted only to a "refusal to subsidize." The Court said that the government may refuse to fund activities in its discretion; but the Court freely acknowledged that a "penalty" on the abortion right would be unconstitutional. A penalty would be, for example, a government decision to withdraw welfare benefits from everyone who has had an abortion—a decision that, the Court noted, would raise serious constitutional doubts.

But how do we know whether the refusal to pay for medically necessary abortions is a subsidy or a penalty in the face of government funding of childbirth and almost all other medically necessary expenditures? Quite plausibly, government action should be deemed a penalty rather than a subsidy if the government is preventing someone from obtaining something to which she would otherwise be entitled.[12] It is thus a penalty to withdraw welfare benefits from people who have had abortions; those people are "otherwise" entitled to such benefits. But it is not a penalty to fund childbith but not abortion, since the people denied funds for abortions are not "otherwise" entitled to the funding.

This formulation makes the distinction between subsidy and penalty, like the very category of coercion, rely on a baseline defining the ordinary or perhaps desirable state of affairs. We have to decide what people are "otherwise" entitled to. But this leads to crucial ambiguities. Is not a poor woman seeking an abortion, in a post-Medicaid world, "otherwise" entitled to payment for medically necessary abortions? Without the abortion limitation, she would indeed be entitled to such funding. The *Harris* dissenters made precisely this argument. The majority replied that there had never been a general right to funds for all medically necessary treatments. The dissenters might have answered that the existence of a Medicaid program altered the baseline to one containing such a general right. But the majority might have responded by asking in turn: Why?

All of this suggests that the development of the relevant baseline, specifying the ordinary state of affairs, is enormously difficult. In *Harris*, the Court appeared quite reflexively to use a common law, pre-Medicaid baseline; but in light of the creation of the Medicaid program and other similar statutes, the common law may no longer be appropriate in these cases. Once the common law touchstone is abandoned, it is not at all clear what is to replace it. This is the pivotal question, but it is one on which the unconstitutional conditions doctrine and the subsidy-penalty distinction, standing by themselves, have absolutely nothing to say. The doctrine and the distinction are thus unhelpful in resolving the very question they seem to make crucial.

The problem goes deeper. Sometimes, perhaps, the government indeed can "penalize" the exercise of constitutional rights through selective funding. Perhaps some constitutional provisions permit regulation through funding but not through criminal penalties. Not all penalties need be unconstitutional. At the very least, any claim to that effect requires an argument.

This point leads to the broader conclusion that the development of a baseline to distinguish between penalties and subsidies is neither necessary nor sufficient. It is not clear that there is any general protection, in the Constitution, against penalties on rights. The question the Constitution ordinarily makes it necessary to ask is whether government has intruded on a right in a way that is constitutionally troublesome and, if so, whether government can justify its intrusion under the appropriate standard of review. The view that there is a unitary category of intrusions called "unconstitutional conditions" is the product of a belief that in a certain set of cases, this question is displaced by another inquiry—into "subsidy/penalty"—altogether. But it is not at all clear why this displacement should occur.

Even more fundamentally, the very notion that we should approach these cases with a distinction between penalties and subsidies has a great deal in common with the two positions that appear to be its adversaries. Here, too, status quo neutrality turns out to be at the fore. The distinction between the subsidy and the penalty appears to depend (yet again) on the notion that the regulatory state is an artificial supplement to an otherwise well-defined status quo. One cannot sort out that distinction without positing such a status quo; we need to describe such a status quo to decide what people are otherwise entitled to. In the cases, the status quo is typically the world of common law rights. But in light of the omnipresence of government spending and funding, and its dramatic expansion and curtailment in relatively short periods, this approach seems poorly adapted to modern government. Our status quo is no longer the common law at all.

Any set of legal principles that assumes that spending programs are an artificial supplement to a system of common law ordering will be inconsistent with the values and operation of modern politics. So far we do not know what a better set of doctrines would look like. But we know enough to see that the distinction between subsidies and penalties will not do the job.

All three of the general approaches to the subject thus seem to be anachronisms. And they are anachronisms in precisely the same sense: They treat common law ordering as the usual state of affairs. They see governmental funding as a perhaps questionable interference with an otherwise well-defined status quo.

Why the Unconstitutional Conditions Doctrine Is an Anachronism

So far I have suggested that the unconstitutional conditions doctrine was able to take its shape only under distinctive historical conditions. The point can be made more vividly by imagining a society in which legal limits had been, from time immemorial, carried out through licensing, funding, and regulatory decisions. In such a society, the criminal law would be absent, and constitutional safeguards would be applied against the familiar kinds of penalties. Suppose that after many generations, the society created a new set of penalties—call them criminal fines and confinement—as a supplement to its basic regulatory system. Such a society might well find it necessary, at first, to create a new set of principles to control this novel kind of intrusion. Once the society matured, however, the category of criminalization would not be tested under a unitary doctrine, but would instead take its place alongside the more familiar principles. These principles would take account of the nature of the burden on the relevant rights and the available government justifications.

For modern observers, then, the question is whether the unconstitutional conditions doctrine provides any genuine help. It is possible to identify three functions for the doctrine. Two of them are anachronisms. The third is of considerable importance, but we do not need an unconstitutional conditions doctrine in order to carry it out. The unconstitutional conditions doctrine should be abandoned.

IDENTIFYING A TECHNIQUE OF BURDENING

The first function performed by the unconstitutional conditions doctrine is to identify a technique by which government burdens constitutional rights. The doctrine alerts courts to the fact that a spending decision—for example, conditioning the receipt of welfare benefits on a decision not to speak in favor of Republicans—may well affect a constitutional right in a way that calls for persuasive justification or perhaps invalidation.

This function of the doctrine is an important one. It would be quite wrong for courts to disregard the fact that spending decisions may affect constitutional rights. But this fact should hardly be thought surprising or unusual. A reminder of the possibility that government can impose constitutionally troublesome burdens through spending, licensing, or regulation is necessary only for those who hold an outmoded view of what it is that modern government does.

RESPONDING TO PERSISTENT ARGUMENTS

The second function of the unconstitutional conditions doctrine is to provide a shorthand response to two familiar arguments. The first is that if government need not create a program at all, it may create that program with certain conditions. The "greater power" not to have the program at all necessarily includes the "lesser power" to impose whatever conditions government chooses.

The second argument invokes the language of freedom and voluntary choice. If, for example, a person has freely chosen to forgo rights of free speech in order to work for the government, on what possible basis should he be heard to complain about the arrangement, and on what basis may the courts intervene? Surely the individual is bound by his free choice.

Unpacking what is right and what is wrong in these two arguments requires substantial work. The unconstitutional conditions doctrine serves as a brief response to these arguments in their crudest forms. It responds to the (implausible) idea that the government's power not to create the program necessarily includes the power to impose whatever conditions it chooses, and to the (equally implausible) idea that there can never be a constitutional obstacle to a voluntary individual choice.

But the implausibility of these arguments, in their broadest forms, should be self-evident under modern conditions. It is often irrelevant that the government need not create a program at all, or that the recipient freely accepted the condition. The Constitution limits the reasons for which government may act and the effects of its actions. A welfare program limited to Democrats is unconstitutional because of the First Amendment. To be sure, the government need not create the welfare program in the first instance, but from this it does not follow that all conditions are permissible. Some conditions will compromise the system of free expression, by pressuring people in the direction of the government's preferred point of view. That pressure is impermissible even if the program need not be created at all. Indeed, the power not to create the program is irrelevant to the legal issue.

Nor is it decisive that the citizen chose to accept the pressure as the price for participation in the program. The citizen's choice does not eliminate the key fact that government has acted for unconstitutional reasons and with impermissible effects on the system of free expression. For these reasons, claims about voluntary participation and the "greater power" are simply a diversion.

To make these points is not to deny the need to develop some detailed arguments, which will vary with context. For example, a citizen might voluntarily agree to waive her right to free speech in return for government employment, and consider herself better off as a result. The constitutional question, however, is not whether she is better off in the abstract, but instead whether she is better off, or equally well off, with respect to the constitutional right in question. The possibility that an offer to purchase the right to free speech in return for a job might help the recipient on balance—under some criteria—hardly disposes of the constitutional question, at least not if the right is to freedom from government pressure on your point of view. A system with no program at all creates far less pressure than a program accompanied by free speech "strings." It is the pressure imposed by the strings that is constitutionally troublesome. The fact that the program may be entirely eliminated is no answer to this objection.

To take another example: Waivers of constitutional rights by citizens who participate in government programs may be in the interest of the individual citizen, but they may also have large and harmful consequences for the system of expression as a whole. Government's "purchase" of the right to vote or the right to free speech undermines the First Amendment's broad protection not simply of individual autonomy, but also of a system of democratic governance. Individually voluntary "waivers" might well be invalidated on this ground. It may be reasonable for participants in a job training program to waive their right to free speech, if this is the price for participation in the program at all; but the program would be constitutionally unacceptable because of its large structural harm to the system of free expression.

(Imagine if a private or public organization were permitted to buy a large number of votes and to cast them all for its preferred candidate.)

Courts do not need an unconstitutional conditions doctrine in order to make these sorts of arguments. Whether the greater power includes the supposedly lesser, and whether there is a constitutional obstacle to an apparently free choice, depend on a complex range of considerations that shorthand phrases cannot capture.

SUBSTANTIVE RIGHTS AND GOVERNMENT JUSTIFICATIONS

The third function of the unconstitutional conditions doctrine is to reveal something true, important, and perhaps surprising about the character of some substantive rights and the nature of government justifications. In short: Some constitutional rights are not rights to government neutrality at all. In some contexts, government can indeed offer justifications that allow it to be selective in funding, employing, or licensing.

The point is a bit obscure in the abstract, but it emerges quite simply from a glance at some cases. Consider, for example, a statute under which the government provides medical benefits only to those who agree to speak for a Democratic presidential candidate and against the Republican candidate. Such a statute would be unconstitutional. The right to free expression is indeed a right to government neutrality as among competing points of view. It does not matter whether the neutrality requirement is violated through criminal prohibition or through cash payments.

By contrast, imagine a case in which the government pays for secondary education only in public schools. We have seen that the Supreme Court interprets the Constitution to include a right to send one's children to private schools. But under current law, that right operates only against criminal penalties, and not against the financial pressures that come from governmental funding of public but not private education.

This understanding of the relevant right may be controversial, but it is perfectly coherent. The reason is that plausible justifications are available to a government that is attempting to defend itself here. The government can justify its selectivity by the need to ensure that public funds are not spent on religious activities. From this point we can offer the proposition that in the spending context, the government may be able to invoke justifications that are tightly connected to, and become legitimate because of, the very fact that it is spending and employing.

There are many examples. In the *Snepp* case,[13] the Supreme Court upheld the use of secrecy agreements—including prepublication review by the government—to regulate speech by employees of the Central Intelligence Agency. The best argument for this result is that in its capacity as manager of an intelligence agency, the government has legitimate interests that justify restrictions on the speech of those who have access to sensitive information. Similarly, a possible argument, taken up below, for the outcome in *Harris* would be that in deciding what sorts of medically necessary operations should be federally funded, the government can properly consider the fact that many taxpayers have religious and other moral objections to abortion.

As a final example, consider the *Lyng*[14] case, in which the Supreme Court upheld an amendment to the food stamp act prohibiting striking workers from receiving food stamp benefits. A plausible argument for this outcome would start with the proposition that even if the government cannot forbid strikes through criminal punishment, it may limit scarce resources to people who are genuinely in need. Perhaps the government may legitimately conclude that strikers are not in need in the same sense as other unemployed people.

These points do not supply a decisive argument in favor of *Snepp, Harris,* or *Lyng.* They do, however, suggest that the fact that the issue is one of funding, licensing, or employment may allow the government to justify what are by hypothesis constitutionally troubling burdens on protected rights. It is in this point that one can find a core and unavoidable insight of current law, which continues to treat funding, regulating, and licensing decisions as different from criminal punishment.

Here, too, however, it is far from clear that an unconstitutional conditions doctrine is necessary in order to accomplish this task. It would be far more straightforward to ask whether the government has special justifications because of the context in which the burden is imposed. Nothing in the unconstitutional conditions doctrine is helpful in answering that question, or even in suggesting the need to ask it. The doctrine should be abandoned.

After the Demise of the Unconstitutional Conditions Doctrine

Thus far my discussion has been quite general. I have argued in favor of a shift in the law: away from an emphasis on whether there has been "coercion" or "penalty," and toward an inquiry into the nature of the interest affected by government and the reasons offered by government for its intrusion. The inquiry into both interests and reasons is not unconstrained. The Constitution identifies a restricted category of protected rights and limits the category of justifications that government may offer.

It is now time to give more specific content to these suggestions. But the goal of the discussion will be to structure inquiries rather than to come up with final answers. Thus one might accept my claims about the anachronistic character of the unconstitutional conditions doctrine, and about the need to shift from coercion to reasons, without at the same time accepting my particular recommendations.

Two major themes will run throughout the discussion. The first and most important is the need for attention to the specific constitutional provision at issue. In all the cases considered, the question is whether the measure at issue interferes with a constitutional right, properly characterized, and, if so, whether the government has a sufficient justification. These questions cannot be answered in the abstract or through a unitary doctrine. Different conclusions will be appropriate under different provisions.

The second theme involves the relevance of moral or conscientious objections of segments of the taxpaying public. In general, such objections are a legitimate reason for funding decisions. What is the status of those objections in connection with funding that involves constitutionally troublesome areas? Perhaps surprisingly, I argue that for the most part, moral objections ought to play no role. When the right at issue is not a right to genuine governmental neutrality, moral objections are of course sufficient, but they can almost always be translated into some other reason for government selectivity, one that has nothing to do with the mere fact of moral objections. And when the right is indeed to neutrality, the existence of a moral objection is inadequate. In both cases, the moral objection is an unimportant part of the constitutional analysis.

Instead the issue is one of reasons: Does the government have a legitimate justification for intruding on a constitutionally protected interest? In posing this question, we carry forward the original commitment to deliberative democracy, and insist on applying that commitment to the status quo.

PUBLIC SCHOOLS, PRIVATE SCHOOLS

We have seen that under current law, government is constitutionally obliged to permit people to send their children to private schools; but it is under no obligation to fund private schools, even if it pays for public schools. Neutrality between public and private schools is not a constitutional imperative.

The fact that the Constitution permits non-neutrality here is something of a puzzle. But for two reasons, the conventional wisdom is probably correct. The right to send one's children to private schools is based on the free exercise clause of the First Amendment. The right to free exercise of religion includes a right to provide religious instruction to one's children. But this right is a highly unusual one in light of the other fundamental guarantee of religious liberty, the establishment clause. That clause provides that there shall be no law "respecting an establishment of religion." By requiring a measure of separation between church and state, the Constitution imposes a special and even unique disability on religion. The establishment clause forbids the government from sponsoring religion even though the government is permitted to sponsor almost everything else.

In that sense, the Constitution is not neutral as between religion and nonreligion. Under the establishment clause, the government is prohibited from benefiting religion, although benefits to others are perfectly acceptable. If this distinction is to be justified, it must be based on the idea that a financial exaction from the taxpayers for the support of religious organizations is a distinctive social harm, one that is likely to lead to religious divisions and factional strife. The establishment clause creates a secular, liberal democracy in a way that is intended to minimize religious tensions. The decision to create that system is hardly neutral; it takes a controversial stand. That same stand informs the establishment clause, which imposes, for non-neutral but good reasons, a special burden on government funding of religious institutions.

It follows that governmental neutrality as between public and private schools is not a constitutional imperative. Many taxpayers would have severe objections to public funding of religious schools. Those objections are an inextricable part of the rationale behind the establishment clause. An interpretation of the right to educate one's children that would compel governmental neutrality between religious and nonreligious schools would be inconsistent with the logic of the Constitution's religion guarantees. Governmental neutrality would probably not violate the establishment clause, but it would raise sufficient problems, under the logic of that clause, to justify government in its selective funding.

A possible response to this argument is that private schools are not necessarily religious schools. Perhaps a decision not to fund private schools is therefore unsupportable by the desire to prevent taxpayer funding of religion. But it is probably sufficient, for these purposes, that the vast majority of private schools are religious. It would of course follow that there would be no constitutional problem if the government decided to fund only secular schools, whether public or private.

The second reason for permitting government to fund public but not private schools is that any government has strong and legitimate reasons to favor public over private education, in order (for example) to foster the development of an integrated national (or state) polity, to promote citizenship, and to break down barriers of race, religion, and class. In light of the constitutional guarantee of free exercise of religion, these reasons are insufficient to permit a governmental prohibition on private schools. But the same reasons do have considerable force; they are fully available to permit government to fund public but not private schools, and through that route to encourage attendance at public schools. Government is constitutionally authorized to be neutral as between the two, but it is under no obligation of neutrality.

A system in which government may fund public schools but not private schools, and must allow citizens to opt out of public schools at their own expense, seems to be the best reconciliation of the competing constitutional interests—understood through the lens of the constitutional structure generally and the First Amendment in particular. In this context, then, governmental selectivity is permitted, not because of the absence of "penalty," but because of the presence of legitimate justifications.

GOVERNMENTALLY FUNDED SPEECH

Governmentally funded speech has become especially controversial in recent years. Government has shown a good deal of selectivity in its funding decisions, and it has tried to withdraw money from controversial projects. These include depictions of Chicago Mayor Harold Washington dressed in a bra and panties, Jesus Christ in urine, the American flag on the floor to be stepped on, art involving AIDS, and sexually explicit scenes, including sex between gay men. The most controversial set of issues has grown up around the National Endowment for the Arts (NEA) and its decisions to fund, or not to fund, controversial artistic work.

The general issue is likely to become even more heated in the future. Government is quite generally involved in the funding of the arts and indeed of speech as a whole. It funds speech related to medical procedures, including those related to reproduction. It runs large grant programs for education. It is itself a speaker, equipped with taxpayer money. There are both legitimate and illegitimate reasons for refusing to fund or for withdrawing funds from certain programs. Some of these cases are exceptionally difficult, and my conclusions should be regarded as tentative. Here I will focus on funding of the arts because this is a helpful exemplary case, and because it involves the important current issues relating to the NEA.

It will be useful to begin with some permissible funding decisions. The central point here is that government has limited resources with which to fund the arts, and its allocation is necessarily selective. Full funding for all applicants is simply inconceivable. At least three conclusions seem to follow.

First, government may refuse to fund speech that it can ban through the criminal law. A refusal to fund obscenity, libelous speech, or incitement to crime is therefore unobjectionable. The only qualification is that there must be procedural safeguards to ensure that the relevant speech is actually unprotected by the First Amendment.

Second, funding decisions that are based on judgments about quality or aesthetics should, at least in most cases and at least as a presumption, be entirely legitimate. The government is permitted to fund projects that it considers to be of high caliber. Indeed, such judgments are inescapable for those who must allocate limited resources, at least short of a randomized lottery procedure.

Third, decisions to fund projects on the basis of subject matter should generally be uncontroversial. If the government wants to fund projects related to American history, Chaucer, World War II, the civil rights movement, Egypt, or the film industry, there seems to be no basis for complaint. In these cases, government is not discriminating on the basis of point of view. It is simply choosing to sponsor art relating to certain subjects. Here, too, the fact that funds are limited makes any alternative approach unrealistic.

Taken together, these conclusions will be sufficient to authorize most of current practice with respect to funding of the arts. In all these cases, government has legitimate reasons for selectivity. If government may make decisions by reference to subject matter, and if decisions about quality are allowed, existing policies will generally be upheld.

Under what circumstances might serious First Amendment objections arise? The most obvious come when government discriminates against people because of their point of view. Suppose that government decides to fund projects by Democrats but not by Republicans, or only by people who have voted for the current President. The case is an easy one for invalidation. As we saw in Chapter 7, the prohibition on discrimination based on point of view lies at the heart of the First Amendment. In this case, both the purpose and the effects of governmental action are objectionable. Government cannot provide a justification that shows why the special context of funding allows it to act in this way. Here the problem lies not in the absence of "coercion," but in the absence of legitimate reasons for the relevant form of selectivity.

The only possible justification for allowing discrimination here would rest on the taxpayers' unwillingness to subsidize art that they find abhorrent. But this justification would allow funding decisions to skew artistic creation in accordance with prevailing political convictions, especially the convictions of government. This would allow government to give money only to people of whose point of view it approved. Such a skewing effect could not plausibly be tolerated. It would run afoul of the core of the free speech guarantee.

Only slightly harder are cases in which government decides to limit funds to projects that contain a particular, approved viewpoint. Imagine, for example, a law to the effect that the NEA will fund only projects that deal favorably with the current performance of the American government, or only projects involving the Civil War that portray the relevant actors in a certain light. The government cannot justify selectivity in constitutionally acceptable terms; it is plainly discriminating on the basis of viewpoint. An across-the-board ban on the funding of projects critical of government or embodying governmentally disapproved views would at least usually be impermissible.

We saw in Chapter 7 that in *Rust v. Sullivan*[15] the Supreme Court upheld the so-called abortion gag rule, forbidding clinics receiving federal funds to provide abortion-related counseling to poor people. The Court seemed to suggest that government can establish a funding program limited to the government's preferred point of view. So taken, *Rust* has ominous implications. The case would allow government to fund people only if they promise not to criticize the government itself. The decision should probably be seen as limited to the context of private counseling, where the First Amendment interest is less substantial, and where the government's justifications are especially weighty.

It should not be applied to funding decisions relating to public discussion of public issues.

I say that viewpoint discrimination is "at least usually" impermissible, because even here there will be some counterexamples. Suppose that the government decides to fund programs for the celebration and possible export of democracy; or suppose that it says that portrayals of the Civil War cannot advocate slavery. For reasons to be explored shortly, even viewpoint discrimination may be acceptable in some narrow circumstances.

From these claims we can offer some tentative conclusions. The clearest constitutional violation consists in discrimination on the basis of point of view. Most other decisions will be permissible, for they will generally involve judgments involving subject matter or aesthetics. It follows that some of the hardest cases will arise when the relevant discrimination seems to involve subject matter or aesthetics but is in fact an effort to control a particular point of view.

The problem with these conclusions is that the line between the key two categories is an elusive one. This is so, first, in the relatively uninteresting sense that there will be hard intermediate cases, that is, cases that are at the borderline and for that reason difficult to decide. But it is also true in the far more troubling sense that the distinction is difficult to draw even as a conceptual matter. Judgments about aesthetics or quality often depend, at root, on ideas having a political or ideological component. This is most obvious for people who think that art celebrating Nazism or Communism cannot qualify as good art; but the point is very general.

The idea that yellow marks smeared on a page, a sentimental drawing of a cat, or American flags marked with swastikas should not qualify for government funding may well be rooted in views, broadly speaking political in nature, about the appropriate character and aims of the arts. The claim seems to find confirmation in the numerous recent debates about the possibly inevitable role of point of view in evaluating artistic creations.[16]

In these circumstances, the available options for law are few, and none of them is appealing. Realistically there are only three possibilities. The first is a constitutional principle that would forbid even aesthetic or subject-matter judgments on the ground that they, too, are rooted in politics and in a sense in point of view. But this principle would be intolerable. Such a principle would forbid selective funding of any sort, which is to say that it would forbid government funding entirely. This solution would hardly be desirable in a system in which public funding is an important individual and collective good. Public funding removes some of the distortions of private funding of the artistic process; it is not as if the elimination of governmental resources for the arts would return the system to a natural or just state. Indeed, government funding may make it more possible for dissident causes, or those disfavored by the wealthy, to have a chance to emerge. (Consider the discussion of the speech "market" in Chapter 7.)

The second route would be to permit even the most conspicuously partisan funding decisions on the ground that sensible lines cannot be drawn between politically and aesthetically motivated decisions. This approach would also be intolerable. It would authorize egregious governmental interference with expression for the state's own partisan purposes.

The third and only sensible solution is to apply the constitutional prohibition only in the most straightforward cases of viewpoint discrimination, and to permit aesthetic or qualitative judgments so long as they are not conspicuously based on partisan aims. Of course anyone who accepts this approach must recognize that it rests on some conceptually shaky ground.

There are two final hard cases. The first involves a legal restriction that does not clearly discriminate on the basis of viewpoint but that nonetheless is an attempt to impose conventional morality on art. The second involves "hate literature" or art that offends a significant portion of the community because it attempts to degrade them.

With respect to the first problem, suppose, for example, that government says that it will refuse to fund projects containing profanity or sexually explicit scenes. One concern is that in such cases, government will be distorting artistic processes by imposing financial pressures that incline people toward officially sanctioned views about what is fitting in art. In a system containing some public funding, this problem cannot be altogether avoided. But it can be minimized rather than increased. Probably the right approach is to refuse to permit across-the-board efforts by government to deny funding to art that offends conventional morality. Courts should strike down a nationwide statutory ban on funding projects with profanity or sexually explicit scenes.

But restrictions might be permissible if they are limited in time and space. A decision by the NEA to forbid the funding of all art containing nudity would be far more objectionable than a decision not to allow nudity in one or two governmentally funded projects. The latter would have some of the characteristics of time, place, and manner restrictions. If there is no express discrimination on the basis of point of view—and if restrictions on profanity and sexuality explicit speech are viewpoint-neutral—restrictions based on content may, in the funding context, be acceptable if they are only occasional.

Indeed, government might even be able to discriminate on the basis of point of view if it is doing so in the context of sharply limited, discrete initiatives. A fund for democracy may plausibly promote only democratic causes. An anticigarette campaign may fund people who will work against cigarette smoking and its attendant health risks. But an across-the-board form of viewpoint discrimination would be much harder to justify. Of course it is not obvious what is across-the-board and what discrete; there will be room for disagreement here.

The second category is at least equally troublesome. What if the government decides not to fund Nazi art, proslavery art, art of the Ku Klux Klan, or art glorifying rape and sexual violence, on the ground that the relevant causes are filled with hatred, are abhorrent, or are perceived as abhorrent by most of the community? The basic problem here is that conventional morality cannot be permitted to be the arbiter of governmental funding of expression. A system in which conventional morality played that role would be inconsistent with the First Amendment guarantee, which is designed precisely to protect views that do not reflect conventional morality. What would be required, in the cases at hand, is a principle of sufficient generality to reflect any legitimate concerns related to the use of taxpayer money in these areas, without at the same time amounting to impermissible dictation of point of view.

It is not easy to come up with any such principle. Surely government should not be permitted to decline to fund any project to which a significant number of taxpayers have a conscientious objection. Such a proposition would enshrine conventional morality as the basis for funding decisions. Perhaps, however, government should be permitted to decline to fund projects that fuel hatred of social groups. To be sure, such an approach would embody a form of viewpoint discrimination, and it would allow more room for government control than is permitted for criminalization. (Recall from Chapter 8 that most hate speech is protected against the criminal law.)

There is, however, at least a plausible argument for an exception to the ban on viewpoint discrimination in funding. Speech of the sort at issue is not merely offensive but also produces a distinctive set of harms. Perhaps government has sufficient reason to refuse to fund such speech even when it may not criminalize it. Surely this issue requires further attention.

However the hardest cases may be resolved, it follows from all of this that government has broad power to allocate funds to art, even if it does so on a highly selective basis. The only clear prohibition is on funding based on a straightforwardly partisan motive, as in the case of discrimination against a particular point of view; and even here there are some exceptions. A similar prohibition may apply when a subject-matter restriction embodies what some people might see as a form of viewpoint discrimination, as in the exclusion of art containing profanity. A constant question is whether any form of viewpoint or content discrimination is limited in time and place. Difficult cases will of course remain. But such an approach would resolve the vast majority of cases and help orient treatment of the rest.

One final note. There are lurking questions here about the government's own speech. It is generally agreed that government has broad authority over what it will say; public officials are allowed to speak as they wish without raising First Amendment issues. Some people think that it follows that government has similarly broad authority over all people whom it pays. The government, after all, consists solely of human beings who are its agents. When government is paying out money, perhaps all the recipients have become government agents or government employees, and therefore have no legitimate basis for constitutional complaint. This might follow from the conceded fact that government has broad authority to speak as it wants.

It would, however, be unacceptable to say that for this reason government funding decisions are unconstrained. There are important differences between government speech and government funding. Part of the difference lies in the fact that when government is speaking, the people know who the speaker is. The same cannot be said when the government is paying a private person to say what it wants. A further difference lies in the serious risk of government co-optation of the private sphere, a problem that conspicuously arises when speech-limiting conditions are attached to spending. This fear retains full authority even in a post–New Deal era. Indeed, the fear of government co-optation is all the more urgent in a period in which it is a constant threat. The fact that the private sphere is publicly constituted does not mean that the threat is irrelevant.

If government wants a certain point of view to be heard, it should require government officials to advocate that point of view. It should not bribe ordinary citizens to do its work for it.

FUNDING ABORTIONS IN CASES OF RAPE OR INCEST

The Supreme Court has held that the right to have an abortion does not imply a right to public funding of abortion, even if the government is also funding childbirth.[17] The right to have an abortion stands on the same footing as the right to send one's children to public schools. In neither case is government required to be neutral as between exercise and nonexercise of a constitutional right.

I want to explore the question whether the government is required to fund abortions in cases of rape or incest, at least when government is funding childbirth in such cases. I draw here on the general treatment of abortion in Chapter 9. I do not explore whether the relevant considerations might also support a right to funding for abortions even in cases not involving rape or incest. That broader question raises more difficult problems.

Under current law, government is almost certainly under no obligation to pay for abortion in cases of rape or incest. No matter what produced the pregnancy, taxpayers are not required to foot the bill for abortions. The Court has not been altogether clear about its reasoning. It has said that government need not remain neutral as between abortion and childbirth. It has said that there is a legitimate interest in protecting fetal life. As in the private school setting, the government has a reason for non-neutrality that lacks sufficient force to justify criminalization but does allow selectivity in funding.

In the context of private schools, we have seen that this line of argument is correct, largely because of the authority of the establishment clause. That clause is best taken as a protection against the use of taxpayer funds to pay for religious institutions. This rationale seems unavailable in the abortion context. There would be no tension with the establishment clause if people with religious or other objections to abortion were forced to pay for that procedure. Indeed, taxpayers are often forced to pay for things—national defense, welfare, certain forms of art, and others—to which they have powerful moral and even religious objections. There is no constitutional problem with this result. If government is to be relieved of its obligation to be neutral as between abortion and childbirth in cases of rape and incest, the argument must take a different form.

Perhaps one could generalize from the establishment clause, and from the structure of constitutional democracy more generally, a justification for non-neutrality in our desire not to force taxpayers to pay for practices that a significant number consider to be abhorrent for reasons of conscience. In most democratic countries, governments are permitted and indeed encouraged to take account of the conscientious objections of its citizens. Perhaps such objections provide a legitimate reason for selective funding.

Perhaps, too, conscientious objections could not be invoked to allow government to violate obligations of neutrality that seem an obvious inference from the relevant right—such as the First Amendment right to neutrality among points of view, or the equal protection right to neutrality between blacks and whites. But perhaps some rights are best understood as non-neutrality rights in the sense that they are not violated if funding decisions are selective because taxpayers have an objection from conscience. And since many taxpayers consider abortion to be murder of defenseless human beings, perhaps they can refuse to pay for it, even in cases of abortion and incest.

At least as a general rule, it seems not merely correct but obvious to say that government funding may take into account the desires of the citizenry. Those desires include conscientious objections,[18] of which government regularly takes account. It is not clear, however, what weight such objections should have in hard constitutional cases.

If the governing constitutional provision forbids selectivity of any sort—if government must be neutral between the exercise and nonexercise of the right—the existence of conscientious objections is probably illegitimate and in any case insufficiently weighty. Consider a decision to fund Christian but not Jewish art, a decision that could not be justified by reference to conscientious objections. And in cases in which the right does not call for neutrality, conscientious objections can easily be translated into moral justifications independent of what people currently think. The key question is whether the right at issue does or does not require neutrality.

To evaluate the conscientious objection argument in the context of abortion, it is therefore necessary to understand the nature of the abortion right. If the right is seen as one of privacy, it seems plausible to say that governmental neutrality is not required, and that government may fund childbirth but not abortion regardless of the cause of pregnancy. Indeed, if the right is one of privacy, it is plausible to say that the conscientious objections of a significant segment of the population provide a sufficient justification for selectivity.[19]

As we saw in Chapter 9, however, the best argument for the abortion right invokes sex discrimination rather than privacy. On this view, a prohibition on abortion is an involuntary co-optation of women's bodies in the service of third parties. I have argued that this argument applies to all such prohibitions, but it seems especially plausible in the context of abortions resulting from rape or incest.

If this argument is accepted, might government fund childbirth but not abortions in cases of rape or incest? If *Roe* is treated as a case in which government is not permitted to turn biological capacities into social disadvantages, it is hard to see why the abortion right, at least limited to such cases, should not be a right to governmental neutrality in funding. A selective funding decision has the precise consequence of turning women into involuntary incubators.[20] It takes biological capacities and poverty and uses these as a basis for requiring poor women to be breeders against their will.

Neither biology nor poverty justifies this decision, which is a legal and social one, and is hardly a product of nature. The Supreme Court has treated the translation of biology and poverty into the status of involuntary motherhood as not involving a governmental choice at all. But this understanding is based on the indefensible conception of neutrality that we have encountered throughout this book.

To be sure, the protection of potential life is a legitimate state interest. But if the interest is insufficient to outweigh the right in the criminal context, it is not clear why it suffices in the setting of funding. The abortion right, understood in equal protection terms, is akin to the First Amendment right to neutrality with respect to point of view. Indeed, it seems to follow that a refusal to fund abortion in cases of rape and incest might raise serious constitutional questions even if childbirth is not similarly funded. Such a refusal would require poor women to be breeders, thus creating a presumptive violation of the equal protection clause. Under current conditions the government has no sufficient justification for that action.

At least this view will seem right if funding decisions are not treated as an artificial supplement to a natural or spontaneous social order—the central instinct behind the Supreme Court's decisions in *Rust v. Sullivan* and *Harris v. McRae*—and if the ideas that gave rise to the regulatory state are taken seriously. Viewed through the lens of the New Deal period, the failure to fund is not inaction at all. It represents a conscious social choice, one that conscripts women in the cause of incubation. It does not simply let "nature" take its course.

*   *   *

The unconstitutional conditions doctrine is an anachronism. It is a product of conceptions of neutrality and action that are ill suited to modern government. There is no need to ask whether government has subsidized rather than penalized, or threatened rather than offered. We should substitute for that unhelpful and probably unanswerable question a more direct inquiry into, first, the nature of the incursion on the relevant right and, second, the legitimacy and strength of the government's justifications for any such incursion.[21] On this view, there will be not one unconstitutional conditions problem, but a varied set of results depending on the nature of the constitutional prohibition.

This reformulation of the problem raised by licensing, employment, and spending programs departs from a model of coercion in favor of a model of reasons. That model of reasons carries forward the antiauthoritarian impulse of the principle of impartiality discussed in Chapter 1. It is continuous with the effort, central in the framing generation, to create a republic of reasons. But the reformulation does not by any means solve particular cases. In order to accomplish that task, it will be necessary to decide what sorts of rights the Constitution protects, and what sorts of justifications are legitimate and sufficiently weighty. But an unconstitutional conditions doctrine could never be helpful on those issues. The doctrine is neither necessary nor sufficient for their resolution.

The reformulation suggested here need not imply more or fewer occasions for judicial invalidation of legislation. Whether the reformulation leads to more invalidation depends on the particular understandings that are brought to bear in the cases. It would be singularly odd to take the existence of the regulatory state as a reason for courts to allow all spending measures that burden what might otherwise be seen as constitutional rights. The regulatory state merely provides new and different occasions for constitutional scrutiny.

I have also argued that the Constitution permits government to pay for public but not private schools; allows government to be highly selective in funding art and other expression, subject to serious but only occasional limits; but forbids government from refusing to pay the expenses of abortion in cases of rape and incest, at least if government pays for childbirth in such cases. Whether or not these conclusions are persuasive, the broader point remains. In a mature legal system, one that has adapted to the functions and goals of the modern state, we will not need, and therefore we will not have, an unconstitutional conditions doctrine.

CHAPTER 11

The Limits of
Compensatory Justice

Principles of compensatory justice are the staple of Anglo-American legal systems. One person harms another; the purpose of the lawsuit is to ensure that the victim is compensated by the aggressor. Drawing from this basic understanding, principles of compensatory justice are organized around five basic ideas.

1. The event that produced the injury is both discrete and unitary.
2. The injury is sharply defined in time and in space.
3. The defendant's conduct has clearly caused the harm suffered by the plaintiff. The harm must be attributable to the defendant, and not to some third party or to "society."
4. Both plaintiff and defendant are easily identifiable.
5. Apart from the goal of compensation, narrowly defined, existing rights—and the status quo—are held constant. The purpose of the remedy and of the legal system is to restore the injured person to the position that he or she would have occupied if the unlawful conduct had not occurred. The law is not to engage in any kind of social reordering or social management except insofar as those functions are logically entailed by the principle of compensation. Noncompensatory disruption of the existing distribution of wealth and entitlements is barred. Losses to innocent bystanders are barred as well.

Principles of compensatory justice are the defining feature of the common law of tort, contract, and property. In all these areas, those principles are usually thought to perform reasonably well, in the sense that they capture ideas that underlie diverse conceptions of the role of the legal system in settling disputes and in remedying illegality. In particular, compensatory principles can be associated with approaches to law that draw on utilitarian and rights-based conceptions deriving from such otherwise diverse thinkers as Locke, Bentham, and Kant. These principles might serve to protect a realm of private autonomy— reflecting principles of both entitlement and desert—and at the same time to promote economic efficiency in the form of optimal deterrence of socially undesirable activity.

It is especially important for present purposes that compensatory principles also embody status quo neutrality. The legal system restores the status quo. It does not attempt to change anything.

In numerous areas of public and private law, however, traditional principles of compensatory justice are unattractive, or at least serve to rule out plausible alternatives. The basic problem is that in ways large or small, those principles are poorly matched to the best theories that underlie the legal claim. In these contexts, the relevant harm is not sharply defined, and it cannot be connected to a discrete event. The problem involves a shared, collective risk rather than an individual right. The defendant is not easily identifiable or has a highly ambiguous relation to the harm. Causation itself is doubtful and complex; we do not really know whether the defendant was responsible for the plaintiff's harm. The injured party cannot be specified in advance. The notion of restoration to a status quo ante seems logically incoherent, unworkable, or based on fictions. Perhaps most important, the status quo should itself be questioned, or taken as unjust and non-neutral, or as a product of the legal rule or the decision at issue.

In this chapter I make two basic claims. The first is explanatory. A number of confusions in both private and public law, I argue, are produced by the use of principles of compensatory justice when those principles are highly contested. Status quo neutrality lies behind such principles.

Indeed, the rise of administrative agencies and the dramatic displacement of the common law courts in the twentieth century are partly attributable to dissatisfaction with compensatory ideas and with the underlying notion of neutrality. In both the New Deal period and the "rights revolution" of the 1960s and 1970s—producing protection against environmental degradation, occupational injury, poverty, and discrimination on the basis of race, gender, and disability—there were self-conscious legal responses to the inadequacy of compensatory principles. The rise of new administrative institutions, foreign to the original system of checks and balances, reflects departures from compensatory thinking. An extraordinary anomaly of American public law is the continued use of compensatory principles in defining the content and reach of the very initiatives that were created to displace them.

My second claim is that we should undertake a large-scale shift in the role of law, a shift that has marked the twentieth century in general and will be increasingly important in the twenty-first. Legislatures and administrative agencies, I suggest, should sometimes abandon compensatory principles, and courts should be receptive to the abandonment. In many contexts, the judicial engrafting of compensatory principles onto programs built on quite different premises has produced results that are incorrect, even nonsensical. In particular, two conceptions provide superior accounts of the disputed territory.

The first conception replaces compensatory justice with a principle of *risk management*. Many modern legal standards are designed to diminish and manage risks, not to vindicate individual rights or furnish compensation to injured parties. Under risk management, social ordering is indeed the goal of legal rules, in the form of systematic, before-the-fact restructuring of the incentives faced by private actors.

The second conception, departing from compensatory justice in distinct ways, is based on *opposition to caste*. This principle is not simple to define, and I will have to be somewhat tentative about it. In discrimination law, the judgment underlying the legal claim is poorly captured when put in terms of compensatory principles. At least some of the time, blacks, women, the disabled, and others bringing discrimination suits do not claim that they have been injured by a discrete actor at a specific time. Nor are their claims connected in any simple way with past discrimination, and certainly not with acts of discrimination that can be tightly connected with their particular complaint. Nor are they seeking to hold the status quo and existing entitlements constant. On the contrary, the status quo is the precise object of attack. Their argument is that a difference that is irrelevant from the moral point of view has been turned, without sufficient reason, into a social disadvantage in important spheres of life.

Principles of risk management and opposition to caste provide better understandings of a number of disputes currently conceived in terms of compensatory justice. Indeed, a large part of the shift from private to public law consists of the progressive abandonment of traditional principles of compensatory justice. The shift consists in turn of a rejection of status quo neutrality.

This shift is one of both basic principle and institutional design. The dramatic twentieth-century movement from adjudication to administration; the New Deal reformation of the 1930s and the rights revolution of the 1960s and 1970s; the design of programs, especially in the environmental area, to redress individually small but collectively large injuries; dramatic softening of traditional requirements of causation; recognition of "rights" against risks, especially in the law of the environment, the workplace, and consumer products; substitution of public for private initiative and enforcement; various civil rights movements; the deterrence of injuries that are probabilistic and systemic in character—all these are part of the basic movement I wish to describe.

Compensatory Principles in Surprising Places

My goal in this section is to outline areas in which principles of compensatory justice are used even though they are highly contested. Many of these disputes arise from compensatory principles as they were understood in nineteenth-century private and public law. In Chapter 2 we saw that on this view, regulatory legislation—minimum wage or maximum-hour laws, for example—was often ruled unconstitutional because it represented an impermissible taking from one group for the benefit of another. "Redistribution" was constitutionally out of bounds; with few exceptions, the legal system could take wealth or property from one person only in the service of compensatory goals. Existing distributions of wealth and entitlements were off-limits to law. Unless changes were in the interest of compensatory justice, narrowly defined, they were barred.

We have also seen that this framework came under attack with a recognition that existing distributions were themselves a product of law rather than an aspect of "the state of nature." Thus Franklin Roosevelt argued for social security by pointing to harms that could not be wholly avoided in this "man-made world" of ours, and urged, "We must lay hold of the fact that the laws of economics are not made by nature. They are made by human beings." [1]

These ideas helped fuel the rise of the regulatory state, which frequently redistributes property among social groups and no longer treats existing distributions as sacrosanct. These same ideas were accompanied by a recognition, especially in the 1960s and 1970s, of the various problems that often make reliance on private markets inadequate.

This is so especially in the area of environmental controls. The compensatory capacities of the common law are outstripped by virtue of the enormous difficulties in aggregating individually small injuries through judicial processes. In these circumstances, regulatory programs, interfering with freedom of contract, find multiple justifications. Occasionally they respond to market failure. There may be a collective action problem, in which individual people cannot organize to stop shared injuries; people may have insufficient information with which to evaluate risks to safety and health; or some people may be imposing external harms on others. Sometimes these programs attempt to redistribute resources from one group to another. As we saw in Chapter 6, sometimes they reflect public aspirations or considered judgments, departing from private consumption choices. Sometimes they respond to the perception that private choices are based on limited opportunities or on unjust background institutions, both to be counteracted through law.[2]

In their entirety, the resulting shifts in substantive principle and institutional design make compensatory principles a partial and often anachronistic feature of the legal system. A legal system originally founded on these principles has an exceedingly difficult time in adapting itself.

THE SMALL-CLAIM CLASS ACTION

Since the Federal Rules of Civil Procedure were amended in the late 1960s, there has been an enormous increase in the use of the class action device, which allows many people to join together in a lawsuit. One of the purposes of this device is to ensure vindication of legal claims that are too small to be viable on their own. Small injuries must be aggregated if the suit is to be made feasible. If they must be redressed separately, they will not be redressed at all.

Assume, for example, that a defendant engages in fraudulent advertising, cheating several thousand purchasers of fifty dollars each. For each injured person, the expense of bringing suit dwarfs the damages. No one who is alert to cost will initiate litigation. Harms of this sort will have to be amalgamated in a class suit to be remedied at all. The class action device therefore helps ensure that the relevant wrongs will be punished and deterred.

In a number of ways, the small-claim class action, collecting individually small but collectively large injuries, strains compensatory principles.

Notice. It is not unusual for small-claim class actions to carry extremely high costs of notice to class members. Rule 23 of the Federal Rules of Civil Procedure says that in class actions, courts should give "the best notice practicable, including individual notice to all class members who can be identified through reasonable effort." Does this provision require the class representative to provide individual notice to all class members in the small-claim class action?

In *Eisen v. Carlisle & Jacquelin,*[3] the Supreme Court concluded that it does. The Court's holding is a straightforward adaptation of compensatory ideas. On this view, any person whose legal rights are at stake has a right to be notified before the case is adjudicated. But in the small-claim class action, claims are not viable individually. The case will go forward as a class action or not at all. The expense of giving notice to a huge group of members will usually be so high as to prevent the action from proceeding. In these circumstances, a requirement of individual notice—destroying the lawsuit—seems perverse.

Distribution of damages. How should damages be distributed in small-claim class actions? Suppose, for example, that a company has engaged in securities fraud against many millions of purchasers, that the average purchaser was defrauded of between $50 and $100, and that the total damages amount to nearly a billion dollars. Suppose also that the court has tried to permit purchasers to recover their damages, by providing notice in the newspapers and elsewhere; but that after these efforts, several million dollars remain in the fund produced by the extraction from the defendant of its ill-gotten gains.

The problems here are similar to those that arise in the context of notice. If the court is required to ensure that the money is actually distributed to class members, the fund will be depleted. The costs of identification and distribution will take a huge chunk out of the total. It is exceptionally expensive to identify all class members. Even exhaustive efforts may fail.

In these circumstances, there are several possibilities for distributing damages. First, the damages might go back to the defendant, on the ground that compensatory goals cannot be satisfied by any sensible system of distribution. If the injured parties cannot be identified, it might be best to allow the defendant to keep the money. Second, the court might allow for a system of "fluid class recovery." Under this approach, the defendant's illegal profits could be applied to reduce the prices charged by the defendant in future transactions—so that people who are securities purchasers, even if not necessarily injured parties, will benefit. Under another approach, the damages might go to various good works, including, for example, an antipoverty program or an institute for the study of the securities market. Yet another possibility would be to give the damages to the government.

In general, federal courts are hostile to fluid class recovery and to noncompensatory remedies. They think that damages should remain with the defendant if they cannot be used for the benefit of injured parties. But attitudes of this sort seem to misconceive the aim of the small-claim class action, which is not primarily to compensate the plaintiffs, but instead to deter and punish harmful behavior. Nothing is gained by allowing the defendant to keep funds that have been unlawfully obtained.

PROBABILISTIC TORTS

Often regulatory schemes, and sometimes modern litigation, are designed to respond to risks of injury that cannot be tightly connected with any specific harm to any individual. Any particular harm, such as incidence of cancer, may or may not be attributable to any particular act, such as exposure to any particular substance.

Prominent recent illustrations are lawsuits over the harms caused by substances such as Agent Orange. It is possible that some identifiable carcinogen was responsible for the death of someone who died of cancer after exposure, or for someone's infertility. But it is also possible that the person would have had the same problems in any event. No one can be certain that the injury was produced by an identifiable seller of the risk-creating substance.

In these circumstances, judicial treatment of the problem is murky. Standards have yet to be developed.[4] One possibility, rooted in traditional compensatory principles, is to deny recovery altogether unless and until the injury has occurred and has been proved to result from the conduct of the defendant. But if that route is followed, it is unclear that the plaintiff will be able to recover at all. The difficulties in establishing causation may prove insuperable; there are extraordinary evidentiary problems.

Another possibility would be to allow people to be compensated, either before or after the harm, in dollar equivalents for increased risks of disease. But there are problems with this approach as well. The legal system does not ordinarily compensate people for increased risks as opposed to "actual harms." Moreover, when the harm has occurred, compensation for the risk alone might seem, to many observers, to be far too low.

Whether or not the harm has occurred, the problem of valuation remains. This problem is especially troublesome where assessment of probabilities is so difficult. Use of principles of compensatory justice has made it extremely difficult to develop sensible solutions to the problem of probabilistic torts.

REGULATORY HARMS

Courts have frequently been confronted with regulation that is designed to prevent harms that are probable or systemic in nature. These harms consist of risks rather than concrete injuries. Usually the size of the risks is highly disputed; no clear relation can be established between an injured party and an alleged harm-causing agent. The goal of the program is to manage social risks rather than to vindicate individual rights. In numerous respects, the decision to create a system redressing regulatory harms represents a rejection of traditional compensatory principles.

Consider, for example, the decisions of the National Traffic Safety Administration to require passive restraints in automobiles, of the Occupational Safety and Health Administration to reduce levels of benzene in the workplace from 10 to 1 parts per million, and of the Environmental Protection Agency (EPA) to impose fuel efficiency requirements on new automobiles. Some courts are hostile to measures of this sort. They require agencies to demonstrate that discrete harms to identifiable actors have occurred or will occur. For this reason, courts have invalidated agency rules on the ground that the harms are simply too speculative.[5]

The judiciary tends to be skeptical when the government is unable to show a tight causal connection between legal requirements and discrete injuries, or when the injuries would occur in the future and are uncertain. The government is seeking to "reorder society" by demanding measures from someone who has not been shown to have committed any particular harm, and whose behavior may not in fact produce future injury. Here compensatory ideas and status quo neutrality move to the fore.

By contrast, courts are hospitable to administrative proceedings that fit compensatory principles more neatly. Backward-looking, remedial measures are treated with far less suspicion. In the context of automobile regulation, courts tend to approve of the recall proceeding, in which defective cars sold to identifiable people are taken off the market. In the area of automobile regulation, the result of the courts' simultaneous hostility to prospective rulemaking and endorsement of recalls is to press national policy into a system of safety regulation almost entirely through recalls. But this is a thoroughly irrational way to reduce automobile accidents and injuries. It would be far better to make prospective regulation than to control automobile risks with episodic, after-the-fact recalls.[6]

In a variety of areas, courts require administrators to satisfy the requirements of the traditional compensatory model. This is so even though that model is awkwardly adapted to systemic or regulatory harms and likely to produce a singularly ineffective system of law.

STANDING: ACCESS TO COURTS

Who is entitled to seek review of the action or inaction of a regulatory agency? The problem arises when the beneficiaries of government programs—victims of pollution, discrimination, securities fraud, toxic substances in the workplace—attempt to bring suit against regulatory inaction, or action on their behalf that they think inadequate.

In Chapter 3, we saw that the Supreme Court has held that plaintiffs challenging administrative decisions must show that their injury is a result of the conduct of which they complain and that their injury is likely to be redressed by a judicial decree in their favor. These requirements are described as involving "redressibility" or "causation." In fact they are clear holdovers from compensatory principles.

Notions of this sort are used to support a variety of important judicial conclusions: that parents of children attending schools undergoing desegregation may not challenge the grant of tax deductions to segregated private schools; that poor people may not challenge the change of tax regulations so as to reduce hospitals' incentives to provide medical services to the indigent; that prospective purchasers of fuel-efficient cars may not challenge the EPA's decision to give retroactive benefits to automobile manufacturers.[7]

In all these cases, denial of standing is based squarely on principles of compensatory justice. If plaintiffs cannot show that a discrete harm to them is a result of the government's action, courts are unavailable. The harm must take the form of those recognized at common law; they must not be merely probabilistic, or involve an "opportunity" to live in a world with restructured incentives. The basic model for the lawsuit consists of discrete injury and discrete remedy. If the suit does not fit that format, no legally recognizable harm exists at all.

The problem with these ideas is that in the cases at issue, the plaintiffs' injury is regulatory or systemic in character. The relevant harm is an increased risk, not a discrete injury. If the injury is recharacterized to involve an increased risk or a systemic harm, there is no doubt that some genuine harm has been suffered. For example, people might urge that their injury consists in an impairment of the opportunity to obtain medical services under a regime undistorted by unlawful tax incentives; that they have been deprived of the opportunity to undergo desegregation in school systems unaffected by unlawful tax deductions; that their opportunity to purchase fuel-efficient cars has been constrained. The question for the courts is whether increased risks are a legitimate basis for judicial intervention.

When the administration of governmental programs becomes an issue in court, it is frequently because of harms that are regulatory rather than tightly connected to a discrete plaintiff and a discrete defendant. From Congress' point of view, the programs exist precisely because the compensatory capacities of the courts have been outstripped. The problem raised by the standing cases is whether the courts ought to allow lawsuits that attempt to prevent harms that statutes were written to redress, but that do not fall within compensatory principles.

RACIAL DISCRIMINATION

In some of its most important recent decisions on racial discrimination, the Supreme Court concluded that plaintiffs alleging a violation of the equal protection clause must plead and prove "discriminatory purpose" on the part of the governmental actor.[8] A showing of discriminatory effects is insufficient. We have seen that these decisions have had enormous consequences, immunizing from attack a wide range of practices that have disproportionate discriminatory effects on blacks, women, and other disadvantaged groups.

The requirement of discriminatory purpose is a clear outgrowth of compensatory principles (and we have seen, not coincidentally, that they reflect status quo neutrality). Indeed, it defines the constitutional concept of equal protection by reference to the common law. In this respect, it attests to the tenacity of those principles in the legal culture. The basic notion is that the government violates the equality principle when it acts like a private wrongdoer, intentionally harming someone. When there is no identifiable act by an identifiable actor who intends to cause harm, legal redress is not forthcoming.

Equality, on this view, is itself rooted in traditional compensatory ideas. To be treated unequally is to be treated "differently" by a particular actor at a particular time. The equality principle is understood in terms of discrete rights and responsibilities, owed by identifiable perpetrators to identifiable victims.

A possible response would be to suggest that if traditional private law principles were taken seriously, discriminatory purpose would not be required. Reasonably foreseeable harmful effects are usually sufficient in private law; if I toss a bomb into the sky, I am liable even if I do not intend to hurt anyone. It is surely foreseeable that (for example) verbal tests will have racially discriminatory effects. On one version of the compensatory model, then, discriminatory effects would indeed be sufficient to raise a legal question.

In fact, however, the Court has rejected the "reasonably foreseeable effects" test for reasons that are ultimately connected to the compensatory model. If such effects were sufficient to draw government action into doubt, the compensatory model would itself be thrown into severe question insofar as it attempts to promote its own central goals: holding existing entitlements constant, avoiding social reordering or redistribution, and preventing injuries to innocent parties. More particularly, disproportionate effects along lines of race and gender are almost always foreseeable. If we said that such effects raise constitutional issues, we would be calling for wholesale reallocation of social benefits and burdens as between blacks and whites and between men and women. The burden of such a reallocation would have to be borne by people who played little or no role in "causing" the current inequalities of blacks and women.

It is here that the deeply substantive foundations of the compensatory model fit well with a requirement of discriminatory purpose. Above all, the compensatory model tries not to change the status quo—this is where it is committed to neutrality—and a discriminatory effects test would be incompatible with that central aspiration. Such a test would also require courts to engage in tasks for which they seem quite ill suited.

But the problem with the compensatory model and with the underlying principle of neutrality is that current distributions of benefits and burdens as between blacks and whites and between women and men are not part of the state of nature but a consequence of past and present social practices. The fact that a verbal test has a disproportionate racial impact results in part from the legacy of slavery, school segregation, and discrimination in the provision of public services. In any case the use of that test is what guarantees discriminatory outcomes. The test may have sufficient independent justifications to overcome this consideration. It may be an excellent test. But to embark on an inquiry of that kind is to abandon compensatory principles.

Similar issues arise in the context of sex discrimination. Consider, for example, *Personnel Administrator v. Feeney*,[9] in which the Supreme Court dealt with a veterans' preference program, which relegated to clerical positions most women in the Massachusetts civil service. The Court held that there was no violation, because the plaintiff was unable to show discriminatory intent. In the Court's view, the plaintiff must show that a particular measure was enacted "because of rather than in spite of" its effect on a disadvantaged group.

But perhaps an intent requirement, properly understood even under compensatory principles, would have required the Court to ask: Would the Massachusetts legislature have enacted the veterans' preference law if men, rather than women, had been hurt by it? That question seems to be the right one; unfortunately, it is probably impossible to answer. An effort to ascertain what the treatment of veterans' preference laws would have been in a world unaffected by sexism leads to insoluble logical conundrums. It requires people to ask questions that involve an imponderable counterfactual universe.[10] In any case, the controversy over the discriminatory intent requirement results from the difficulty of using traditional compensatory principles in this setting.

SCHOOL DESEGREGATION

Suppose that a school district segregated its schools until 1954, and that in 1958, 1968, or 1978 a judge issued a finding to that effect. What remedy ought to be imposed? The Supreme Court's cases are exceptionally complex on this issue.[11]

The Court's basic approach seems to involve an attempt to restore the status quo ante. The desegregation cases ask whether the remedy will restore the system to what it would have been without past acts of segregation. Under this rationale, the Court has invalidated "freedom of choice" desegregation plans, emphasizing that they will bring about less desegregation than would have occurred if there had been no segregation in the first instance.[12]

Principles of compensatory justice play a prominent, indeed central, role here. They define the very nature of the inquiry. Some justices, for example, stress the difficulty of finding that pre-1954 discrimination actually caused post-1970 outcomes. How do we know what role old practices played in current housing patterns, for example? For these justices, the weak causal connection with past illegality means that the law should not make people restructure present practices. By contrast, other justices emphasize the legacy of past discrimination and what they see as its undeniable connection with present injustice.

Both sides appear, however, to downplay the fact that issues of causation, and the compensatory principles that underlie them, have little coherence in this context. An inquiry into the amount of racial integration that would have occurred in a world unaffected by racial segregation is unlikely to have any empirical anchor. There is no real answer to that inquiry. Social scientists, let alone judges, are simply unequipped to resolve the problem—and not because of lack of appropriate tools, but because the question itself has no real answer. To try to resolve issues bearing on desegregation remedies in terms of compensatory principles is to invite confusion.

AFFIRMATIVE ACTION

In cases involving affirmative action, the Supreme Court has said that race-conscious measures are usually permissible only as a "remedy" for identifiable acts of past purposeful discrimination performed by the institution now engaging in affirmative action.[13] Affirmative action grounded in an effort to overcome "societal discrimination" is generally unacceptable.

In so holding, the Court has emphasized that the victims of affirmative action are either employers or, more frequently, white people or men who never engaged in discriminatory conduct. The harm to innocent victims is a principal concern behind the requirement of a showing of past discrimination. Under current law, affirmative action can be defended most easily as an effort to restore a status quo ante that has been unsettled by identifiable acts producing identifiable harms to identifiable actors. When the status quo is thus restored, the harm to innocent victims is acceptable. In such cases, the "victims" are where they are only because of past discrimination, to which they were hardly entitled.

This framework is a conspicuous outgrowth of the use of principles of compensatory justice. One could, however, imagine a different framework, with roots in the New Deal attack on compensatory principles. For example, "forward-looking" justifications for affirmative action might be brought into play. Such justifications would point not to remedies for discrimination by the affirmative actor in the past, but to other reasons for affirmative action: the need for race-conscious measures to promote diversity in the educational process, to ensure a balanced police force in the interest of community service, or to accomplish a range of other goals unrelated to compensation for past injustice.[14]

Affirmative action programs often stem from some such rationale. A prominent example is university admissions, where race consciousness might be part of an effort to ensure that the classroom benefits from having members of different social groups within it. Concepts of compensatory justice seem to miss, indeed to distort, some of the impetus behind affirmative action programs.

More generally, affirmative action might be understood not as a remedy for discrete acts by discrete actors, or as a response to identifiable breaches of past and present duty, but as an effort to overcome certain castelike features of contemporary society. On this view, it is not controlling and perhaps not even relevant that the harms that affirmative action attempts to redress cannot be understood in the usual compensatory terms. The purpose of the "remedy" is, to be sure, to respond to injustice. But the legal response cannot take the form of discrete remedies for discrete harms.

DISABILITY

For the most part, the disabled have nothing to gain from the Constitution as it is currently interpreted.[15] If the deaf and blind bring suit to challenge their exclusion from public jobs designed by and for people who hear and see, or if people using wheelchairs attack a transportation system to which they are denied access, the judicial answer is identical. The disabled have been treated "the same" as the able-bodied, and the equal protection clause imposes no "affirmative" obligation on government to restructure its business. Compensatory principles thus give content to constitutional equality principles. The use of stairs, of inaccessible buildings, or of practices established for the able-bodied does not violate a compensatory model of equality.

Advocates of legal rights for the handicapped are operating under a different conception of legal injury. Their complaint is that practices designed by and for the able-bodied predictably create a range of obstacles to the disabled. It is largely those practices, and not disability itself (a highly ambiguous concept), that produce the daily handicaps faced by the disabled. The objection from the standpoint of equality is that such systems turn a difference into a systemic disadvantage and must accordingly be justified or changed. Complaints of this sort have been unsuccessful in courts, but they have had a significant impact on Congress. Many recent statutes, including the Americans with Disabilities Act, respond to a principle of equality not rooted in compensatory ideas.

We have seen many different areas in which compensatory principles raise serious questions. It is now time to sort out those questions. In the small-claim class action, the problem simply involves the costs of notice and of distributing damages. The departure from the compensatory idea is required by the relatively trivial problem of high administrative costs in bringing about compensation itself. In the case of regulatory harms, the compensatory idea is tested more severely. Here the basic requirements of identifiable plaintiffs and defendants and of clear causation are drawn into doubt.

In the area of discrimination, the challenge to the compensatory model is most fundamental. The plaintiffs are seeking significant social reordering. They do not want to hold existing entitlements constant. They question the status quo.

There are of course similarities as well as differences. Above all, the courts' skepticism about speculative rulemaking, about discriminatory effects tests, and about probabilistic injuries has a similar foundation in status quo neutrality. More particularly, the foundation lies in the perception that the existing distribution of wealth and entitlements forms the neutral baseline against which to assess the propriety of legal intervention—and the associated belief that social reordering through law ought not to be permitted. This approach appears to be based on an understanding that existing distributions are not themselves unjust, are not the product of law, or at least are not to be challenged in the context of the issue at hand.

It is here that the compensatory model is rooted in a deeply substantive and controversial conception about the appropriate role of law. Is redistribution off-limits? Are existing distributions unjust or already a product of law? Should the legal system impose burdens on people who have not produced traditional legal injuries? How might those interested in social efficiency or social justice proceed, if compensatory principles are put to one side?

Substitutes for Compensatory Justice

The legal culture is permeated by compensatory ideas, from the first year of law school to the very structuring of adjudication. In part for this reason, compensatory principles have given content and shape to programs built on noncompensatory foundations. But there are many ways to understand the role of the legal system in these settings. Compensatory principles represent a controversial choice among competing possibilities.

The persistence of compensatory principles has had an important distorting effect on the law. More concretely, the legal issues that have been approached through compensatory principles might better be understood in terms of principles of *risk management* or *opposition to caste*. The risk management and anticaste principles do not require anyone to show that an identifiable actor has clearly caused a harm to an identifiable victim. They call for the redress of injuries that are systemic rather than sharply defined. They are intended to bring about a kind of social reordering rather than a restoration of some status quo ante. These principles are better implemented by legislatures and administrators than by courts. When the former have acted, courts should not define the reach of the relevant programs by reference to compensatory notions.

Thus far, the development of risk management and anticaste principles has been tentative. These principles can be found mostly in the work of Congress and administrative agencies. In the future, there can be few more important tasks than the elaboration of these principles. Indeed, the resulting shift—from judge-led reform to legislative and executive action—might well rival the New Deal reformation itself in scope and importance.

RISK MANAGEMENT

Many regulatory programs are designed not to prevent an ascertainable harm to an ascertainable actor, but instead to manage and diminish risks that affect whole classes of people. There is a close connection between principles of risk management and the understandings that underlay the New Deal and the rights revolution—especially insofar as the latter involved environmental degradation. The government is trying to change incentives, or even to restructure private behavior in some systemic way, rather than to compensate injured parties. The aim is the right level of deterrence of harmful conduct.

This aim is to be achieved in the presence of several problems: difficult issues of causation; victims and aggressors who are not readily identifiable; complex technical issues and scientific uncertainty; and severe collective action problems making it difficult to rely, as the common law system does, on the initiative of private persons. Statutes protecting the environment, consumers, and occupational safety and health are conspicuous examples. In these cases, the goal of law cannot realistically be understood in compensatory terms. No concrete event produced an identifiable harm stemming from an identifiable defendant to an identifiable plaintiff. The purpose of the regulatory system is not to restore a status quo ante. It is to change the status quo, above all by changing incentives.

These points have implications for a variety of issues. Consider, for example, the question of standing. We have seen that in recent cases some courts have suggested that to have access to judicial review, a plaintiff must show that he would suffer an identifiable harm as a result of the defendant's action. A "speculative" injury is not enough. But whether the harm is speculative depends on how it is defined. In the celebrated *Bakke* case, the rejected white medical school applicant, challenging an affirmative action scheme, was said to have standing because his injury consisted of deprivation of an "opportunity to compete." [16]

By characterizing his harm as an injury to an "opportunity," the Court was able to avoid the difficulties that would have been produced in terms of causation if the injury had been described as a failure to be admitted to medical school. It is by no means clear that Bakke would actually have been admitted if the affirmative action program did not exist.

The device of recharacterizing the injury as an "opportunity" is relatively rare in the cases. But we have seen that modern regulatory systems are typically designed to redress probabilistic or systemic harms—to alter "opportunities" or to change incentives rather than to mandate particular results. In these circumstances, the consequences for any single person are inevitably "speculative." The plaintiff attempts to redress an increased risk, not a discrete injury. In these cases, the question is whether a regulatory harm should be a sufficient basis for standing.

If Congress has granted standing to people trying to prevent such harms, the courts ought to be available. And when Congress has not spoken clearly, standing should also be granted, for this is the most reasonable view to attribute to the legislature in light of the purposes of the relevant regulatory program, which is precisely to reduce harms of this sort. Regulatory harms should quite generally be a sufficient basis for judicial review.

Principles of risk management would call for reformation of many of the doctrines described above. If compensatory principles were abandoned in favor of risk management, we would see a number of novel developments. One of our central goals should be to abandon the rigid, bureaucratized nature of New Deal law, and to create legal structures equipped with some of the decentralization, efficiency, and productive potential of market arrangements. Many of my proposals here are centered on that goal.

1. Most important, modern public law must develop strategies of risk management that control the most serious risks most cheaply. As a first step, it will be necessary for government to acknowledge that it will have to permit many risks, especially trivial ones. A system that bars trivial risks will create serious distortions in the allocation of public and private resources. To force an agency to eliminate small risks is to prevent it from focusing on large ones. It may also lead consumers to shift to substances that pose no risk of (say) cancer but that have a higher risk of producing (say) heart disease.

2. Government should rely not on banning substances but on providing information to ensure that citizens can make decisions for themselves, both in markets and in the ballot box. Markets cannot work if people do not have important information about products. Risk levels are important information. As a first step, then, government should attempt to complement the workings of markets by promoting public awareness of risk levels. Education of this sort is indispensable to democracy as well. People cannot decide about the appropriate nature of regulation unless they are given information about existing risks and the costs of eliminating them.

3. Government should also attempt to develop a system of priorities, putting its limited funds where they will do the most good. Administrative agencies and Congress alike have given too little attention to setting priorities. A major advance here would be to impose, in all regulatory programs, a proportionality principle, requiring regulators to look closely at, and to compare, the advantages and disadvantages of regulatory action in particular cases. Such a principle would encourage government to devote itself to the most serious problems.

4. As part of a system of risk management, government should en-

sure that people who produce harm must pay for it. Under current law, those who put pollution into the air and water need not pay at all. The same is true for those who use risk-creating pesticides or who dispose of garbage or toxic waste. A system of fines, taxation, or purchased permits is the best response to current dilemmas. Under this system, the government would refuse to specify the means of risk reduction; this should be left to the market, once costs are imposed on those who produce harm. "Green taxes" might be made an important part of environmental protection. Of course exceptionally dangerous substances such as DDT should be banned altogether.

A general shift in the direction of the idea that "polluters pay" would produce much greater efficiency in regulation. But an even larger advantage of this shift would be democratic: It would ensure that citizens and representatives would be focusing on how much pollution reduction there should be, and at what cost. The right question would be put squarely before the electorate. Moreover, a system of financial penalties allows far less room for interest-group maneuvering. Special favors cannot readily be provided through a system of economic incentives.

Under this general system, people who purchase permits or licenses for the right to produce (say) pollution should be able to trade the resulting permits. A trading system would increase efficiency in risk management and minimize the costs of achieving whatever goals we seek. Imagine, for example, that those who emit sulfur dioxide into the atmosphere must pay for a license to do so, and that the resulting license can be traded to others. Under this system, an economic reward is provided to those who devise a system for emitting less sulfur dioxide than the license allows. This economic reward creates powerful incentives for innovation in pollution control technologies, and this is an enormous gain. And if we want to reduce harm-producing conduct, the solution is not to ban trading, but to reduce the number of licenses.

5. Risk management principles will also call for coordination of regulatory systems now diffused over many statutes and agencies. The division of problems of cancer regulation among multiple agencies has produced regulatory irrationality, as has the failure to coordinate problems of air and water pollution.

6. It is also necessary to recognize the high potential costs of both action and inaction in the face of incomplete information. Often government cannot be expected to prove, in advance, that a substance is

extremely dangerous. If courts bar agency action in such circumstances, many lives will be lost.

7. Courts should be far more hospitable to agencies trying to counteract regulatory or systemic harms. Use of compensatory principles has distorted several regulatory programs, especially automobile regulation. The judicially mandated shift from rulemaking to recalls—founded in compensatory notions—has led to irrational regulation. Courts should permit regulatory controls to redress harms that cannot be confidently described before the fact. Particularly in the environmental area, but also in all other programs attempting to manage and reduce risks, it is especially appropriate for courts to defer to agencies, giving them the benefit of the doubt.

8. The legal system should abandon compensatory principles in dealing with the small-claim class action. The *Eisen* case, mandating notice in such cases, should be overruled by statute or rule. In the small-claim class action, courts should not insist that the damages be transferred to the injured parties. The purpose of these actions is not compensation at all. Courts should be permitted to experiment with remedial strategies that include fluid class recovery. Above all, Congress should allow such recoveries.

9. Strategies should be developed to allow for damages or punishment in cases of probabilistic harms, as in the context of exposure to toxic substances. Exposure to risk should itself be a liability-creating event. The development of some sort of mixed public and private enforcement mechanism, supplementing the tort system, would be a natural development.

OPPOSITION TO CASTE

We have seen that courts often approach equality questions by way of principles of compensatory justice, and that this approach produces serious conceptual problems in the identification of the relevant status quo. We might then start in another way. The legal claim might be understood not as an insistence on compensation for past wrongdoing, but instead on the elimination, in places large and small, of something in the nature of a caste system. The concept of caste is by no means self-defining, and I will have to be tentative about it. I do not suggest that the castelike features of current American practices are the same, in nature or extent, as the features of genuine caste societies. I do mean to say that the similarities are what make the current practices a reason for collective concern.

The motivating idea behind an anticaste principle is that differences that are irrelevant from the moral point of view ought not without good reason to be turned, by social and legal structures, into social disadvantages. They certainly should not be permitted to do so if the disadvantage is systemic. A systemic disadvantage is one that operates along standard and predictable lines in multiple important spheres of life, and applies in realms that relate to basic participation as a citizen in a democracy. These realms include education, freedom from private and public violence, wealth, political representation, and political influence. The anticaste principle might suggest that with respect to basic human capabilities and functionings, one group ought not to be systematically below another.[17] We might well understand the Civil War amendments as an effort to counteract this form of disadvantage.

In the areas of race and sex discrimination, and of disability as well, the problem is precisely this sort of systemic disadvantage. A social or biological difference has the effect of systematically subordinating the relevant group—not because of "nature," but because of social and legal practices. It does so in multiple spheres and along multiple indices of social welfare: poverty, education, political power, employment, susceptibility to violence and crime, and so forth. That is the caste system to which the legal system is attempting to respond.

Differences are usually invoked as the justification for disadvantage. It is often said, for example, that women are different from men, or blind people different from those who see, and that different treatment in law is therefore perfectly appropriate. The claim is tempting; but it will not do (see Chapters 2 and 9). The question for decision is not whether there is a difference—often there certainly is—but whether the legal and social treatment of that difference can be adequately justified. Differences need not imply inequality, and only some differences have that implication. When differences do have that implication, it is a result of legal and social practices, not the result of differences alone. Since they are legal and social, these practices might be altered even if the differences remain.

The problems faced by the handicapped, for example, are not a function of handicap "alone" (an almost impenetrable idea), but instead of the interaction between physical and mental capacities on the one hand and a set of human obstacles made by and for the able-bodied on the other. It is those obstacles, rather than the capacities taken as brute facts, that create a large part of what it means to be handicapped. It would be implausible, for example, to defend the construction of a building with stairs, and without means of access for those on wheelchairs, on the theory that those who need wheelchairs are "different." The question is whether it is acceptable or just to construct a building that excludes people who need an unusual means of entry. That question may not be a simple one, but it cannot be answered by merely pointing to a difference.

There is a further point. Originally the Fourteenth Amendment was understood as an effort to eliminate racial caste—emphatically not as a ban on distinctions on the basis of race.[18] A prohibition on racial caste is of course different from a prohibition on racial distinctions. A ban on racial distinctions would excise all use of race in decisionmaking. By contrast, a ban on caste would throw discriminatory effects into question and would allow affirmative action. In any case the question for the anticaste principle would be: Does the practice at issue contribute to a system with castelike features? It would not be: Have the similarly situated been treated differently? This is the key feature of the shift that I propose.

Originally it was also understood that Congress, not the courts, would be the principal institution for implementing the Fourteenth Amendment. The basic idea was that Congress would transform the status of the newly freed slaves, engaging in a wide range of remedial measures. It was not at all anticipated that federal judges—responsible for the *Dred Scott* decision, establishing slavery as a constitutional right—would be enforcing the amendment. Indeed, the notion that judges would play a major role in helping to bring about equality under law was entirely foreign to the Civil War amendments.

At some stage in the twentieth century, there was an extremely dramatic change in the legal culture's understanding of the notion of constitutional equality under the Constitution. The anticaste principle was transformed into an antidifferentiation principle. No longer was the issue the elimination of second-class citizenship. Instead it was the entirely different question whether those similarly situated had been treated similarly. This was a fundamental shift. Its occurrence remains one of the great untold stories of American constitutional history.

So long as the courts were to be the institution entrusted with enforcing the equal protection clause, the shift was fully intelligible, notwithstanding its inconsistency with the original understanding of the Fourteenth Amendment. An anticaste principle is simply beyond the capacities of the judiciary, which lacks the necessary tools. The transformation in the understanding of what equality meant is therefore understandable in light of what came to be, under the Fourteenth Amendment, the astonishing institutional importance of courts and the equally astonishing institutional insignificance of Congress. But the transformation of an anticaste principle into a prohibition on differentiation has badly served the constitutional commitment to equal protection of the laws. It has ensured that little will be done about the second-class citizenship of blacks (and women and the handicapped). We should now return to the roots of the constitutional commitment. These roots call for an emphasis on the legislature rather than on the courts, and on the question of caste rather than on the question of difference.

A few qualifications are necessary. The anticaste principle, if taken seriously, would call for significant restructuring of social practices. For this reason it must be emphasized that the principle is better set out and implemented by legislative and administrative bodies, with their superior democratic pedigree and fact-finding capacities, than by courts. Moreover, it is important to acknowledge that a wide range of differences among people are indeed morally arbitrary, in the sense that the difference does not by itself justify more resources or greater welfare. In a market economy, those morally irrelevant differences are quite frequently translated into social disadvantages. Consider educational background, intelligence, strength, existing supply and demand curves for various products and services, even willingness to work hard. In a market economy all these factors affect resources and welfare, and all or most of them are arbitrary from the moral point of view. Is someone really entitled to more money because he was born into a family that stressed education, because he has high intelligence, or because he happened to produce a commodity that many people like?

Markets thus reward qualities that are irrelevant from a moral point of view. But it would be difficult indeed to justify an anticaste principle that would attempt, through law, to counteract the factors that markets make relevant. The reason is precisely the fact that in general, the recognition of such factors is inseparable from the operation of a market economy. It should always be remembered that a market economy is a source of important human goods, including individual freedom, economic prosperity, and respect for different conceptions of the good. Any legal solutions that call for major intrusions on markets must be evaluated in light of the many possible human goods that those solutions will compromise. If legal remedies produce more unemployment, greater poverty, higher prices for food and other basic necessities, they are, precisely to that extent, a bad idea.

The implementation and reach of any anticaste principle should be defined by reference to considerations of this kind. My point is not that human equality should be "traded off" against the seemingly sterile and abstract notion of market efficiency. I do not claim that unjustified equality is justified by some intrinsic good called "efficiency." I argue only that intrusions on markets may defeat valuable human goods, and that all such goods should be taken into account. Economic efficacy and free markets thus have instrumental value. They tend to produce appropriate prices, a range of socially valued commodities, high unemployment, and good incentives for productive work.

To be more precise: The use of the factors that ordinarily underlie markets is at least sometimes in the interest of the most disadvantaged, in the sense that lower prices and higher employment are especially important for the poor, who are peculiarly vulnerable to unemployment and price increases. When this is so, any government program that would bar use of those factors—intelligence, production of socially valued goods, and so forth—seems extremely perverse. Moreover, an anticaste principle that would override all morally irrelevant factors would impose extraordinary costs on society, both in its implementation and administrative expense and in its infliction of losses on a wide range of people.

I do not set out a full program for government action here. But the anticaste principle seems to have greatest appeal in discrete contexts in which gains from current practice to the least well-off are hard to imagine; in which second-class citizenship is systemic and occurs in multiple spheres and along easily identifiable and sharply defined lines; in which there will be no major threat to a market economy; and in which the costs of implementation are most unlikely to be terribly high. Ideas of this sort fully justify a legal assault on the castelike features of the status quo with respect to race, sex, and disability— though there is much room for discussion about the precise nature, and the likely effectiveness, of any such assault.

Although anticaste principles and risk management ideas have a degree of overlap, they depart from compensatory thinking in very different ways. Risk management has clear connections to long-standing compensatory goals, and it is rooted in broadly analogous notions of individual entitlement, individual desert, and deterrence of harmful activity. Above all, risk management is supported by a belief that compensatory principles are inadequate in light of difficulties in establishing causation, in identifying perpetrators and victims, and in overcoming collective action problems in cases involving individually small but collectively large harms. Because the departures are not radical, people who start from the compensatory tradition, broadly conceived, can often be led, without serious reluctance, to endorse risk management.

The anticaste principle is not so easily defensible in these modest terms. Because it represents a conspicuous rejection of the status quo as non-neutral and unjust, those who accept the anticaste principle are not bothered if some people are made worse off by the results for which it calls. For example, affirmative action does not appear an impermissible taking of any real entitlement held by whites and men. Because the existing distribution of benefits and burdens between blacks and whites and between men and women is not natural and sacrosanct, and because it is in part a product of current laws and practices having discriminatory effects, it is not so bad if some whites and men are disadvantaged as a result. This idea is a direct application of the New Deal attack on status quo neutrality. (I do not claim that as a matter of policy, affirmative action programs are preferable to those that are not race- or gender-conscious.)

Moreover, the anticaste principle offers a different and competing conception of individual entitlement. The idea that differences are systematically, and illegitimately, turned into disadvantages by law is entirely foreign to the compensatory scheme. And although an anticaste principle does have a compensatory feature—past and present discrimination is of course an ingredient here—its foundations will seem foreign or objectionable to many who are schooled in the compensatory tradition.

The anticaste principle suggests a norm of equality that cannot be captured by standard ideas about compensation. If accepted, the principle would also have a series of consequences for present law. All these consequences are connected with a reading of the Civil War amendments that is not limited to the capacities of courts.

1. The most important and general step is to shift attention from the question whether members of one group have been treated differently from members of another to the question how to eliminate second-class citizenship.

On this view, civil rights policy should concern itself first and foremost with such problems as lack of opportunities for education, training, and employment; inadequate housing, food, and health care; vulnerability to crime, both public (through the police) and private; incentives to participate in crime; and teenage pregnancy and single-parent families. In resolving these problems, the traditional claims of civil rights law offer little or no help. Far better models are provided by targeted educational policies, including Head Start, and by recent initiatives designed to reduce violence against women—through education, additional government resources for crime prevention and punishment, and new legal remedies for victims of gender-related violence.

2. Disabled people should have a legal claim of unacceptable inequality when standards are used that exclude them from important areas of public and private life. Inequality is produced when people who need wheelchairs cannot enter buildings; when blind people are not given the means to read materials that the sighted take for granted; when deaf people cannot hear fire alarms or act on equal terms in the courtroom. A system that turns differences into social disadvantages embodies an objectionable form of inequality.

This is not to suggest that a world designed for the able-bodied must be redesigned to create equality in all areas for the handicapped. The costs of social change are relevant, and they would be very high. But some justification in terms of cost or other values must always be made; and frequently no adequate justification is available.

3. At the very least, people should be permitted to engage in voluntary race-conscious efforts even when the requirements of compensatory justice cannot be satisfied, that is, when no identifiable defendant has "caused" the plaintiff's injury. Past social discrimination is a sufficient reason for affirmative action. Measures designed to overcome the effects of discrimination by advantaging members of minority groups should not be treated the same as ordinary discrimination. Above all, race-conscious measures designed to reduce castelike features of current society are supported by purposes and effects clearly opposite to those designed to bring it about.

4. "Forward-looking" reasons for race-conscious measures provide a legally sufficient justification for them—quite apart from the backward-looking reasons that the Supreme Court has generally required.[19] Race-conscious efforts to promote diversity in education, or otherwise to improve the performance of public institutions, ought to be permitted.

5. A showing of discriminatory effects should in some settings be sufficient to trigger a requirement that government justify its behavior in persuasive, race- and gender-neutral terms. If a law has a disproportionate impact on members of minority groups or on women, the state should demonstrate that the law is well supported by nondiscriminatory considerations. A test that excludes more blacks than whites, or a veterans' preference law excluding women from high-level civil service jobs, should be invalidated unless shown to be substantially related to an important state interest.

Probably a standard of this sort should be set out by legislatures rather than by courts, because of the superior democratic pedigree and fact-finding competence of the former. Many civil rights laws do indeed reject compensatory criteria in favor of standards that rely on discriminatory effects. They point in the right direction.

Anglo-American legal systems are comfortable with principles of compensatory justice. Those principles provide the foundation for the common law of property, tort, and contract. They are emphasized throughout law school, particularly in the influential first year. They are well adapted to what courts are actually able to do. And even in a heavily industrialized nation with a large administrative apparatus, they must continue to play an important role. In many areas of modern law, however, compensatory thinking produces real confusion.

But the problem goes deeper than confusion. Substance and not mere form is at the heart of compensatory thinking. Such thinking embodies status quo neutrality. It holds existing entitlements constant, and it sees revision of the status quo or the infliction of costs on third parties as impermissible partisanship or "redistribution" unless in the service of compensation, narrowly defined. The result is administrative, legislative, and judge-made doctrine that misconceives the most persuasive basis for the legal claim—producing decisions that are sometimes positively perverse and that shut off exploration of alternatives.

Regulatory programs introduced by legislative and executive officials have frequently rejected compensatory thinking and associated ideas about neutrality. But the shift from private to public law—partly a recognition of this problem—remains tentative and halting. Courts continue to invoke compensation to define the nature and scope of programs developed in self-conscious repudiation of status quo neutrality. And although courts generally ought not to undertake significant social restructuring on their own, no such barriers apply to legislative and administrative officials.

New conceptions, already evident in public law, are based on emerging principles of risk management and opposition to caste. These principles reveal the limitations of compensatory justice and status quo neutrality as understandings of the role of the legal system in alleviating social harm. In the future, legislative and administrative action should be directed toward the management of social risks and the elimination of social castes. Successful performance of these tasks will take the legal system far from its focus, so damaging in the last generation, on courts and on compensation. It should greatly improve democratic governance as well.

Conclusion:
The Impartial Constitution

At its inception, the genius of the American Constitution consisted in its effort to combine political accountability with a large measure of public deliberation. The framers devised a system that was democratic, in the sense that it ensured popular responsiveness, but that was also deliberative, in the sense that it promoted public-spirited deliberation among both government officials and the public at large. All the basic institutions—national representation, federalism, checks and balances, judicial review—should be understood in this light.

Many of our most important rights are part and parcel of this system of deliberative democracy. The right of freedom of speech is the most conspicuous example. But we can point as well to the rights to equal protection of the law, to due process, to religious liberty, even to private property and freedom of contract. At the very least, the system of constitutional rights requires a public-regarding justification whenever government dispenses social benefits and imposes social burdens. This general principle of impartiality lies at the center of our constitutional heritage. The impartiality principle reflects the effort of the founding generation to eliminate the monarchical legacy, based on "nature" and "authority," and to replace it with a republic of reasons.

Rightly understood, this principle should be applied not simply to new governmental initiatives, but also to the status quo. Existing practice and its legal underpinnings should be subject to both deliberation and democracy. They should not be seen as a given or as necessarily natural and just.

The Constitution and the Status Quo

In contemporary constitutional law, however, there is a persistent tendency to take the status quo as the baseline for distinguishing between neutrality and partisanship or between action and inaction. Status quo neutrality can be found in some surprising places. In many areas, existing ownership rights are treated as the state of nature, when they are actually a product of law.

Status quo neutrality affects the debate over the reach and nature of the free speech guarantee, even the conception of when government is "abridging" free speech. It influences the description of what it means to discriminate on the basis of race and gender. It affects legal thinking about the role of the government in redistributing resources and opportunities. It influences the issue of control of reproduction, seen, incorrectly, as an issue of privacy rather than as one of gender discrimination. It even helps resolve the question whether government is involved in the case and thus answerable to the Constitution at all. It would not be an overstatement to say that the most serious issues involving constitutional rights are influenced by use of the status quo as the baseline for decision.

To use the status quo in this way is not always a mistake. In some contexts, and for various reasons, existing distributions should indeed be the baseline (see Chapter 5). A system with private property and market ordering promotes both liberty and prosperity. Such a system depends for its very existence on a decision to treat existing distributions as a given. Indeed, this is part of what we mean by describing a system as one of private property.

The problem arises when the status quo is used without adequate justification or merely by reflex. In constitutional law, the status quo is indeed used in this way. It is treated as part of the state of nature, when it is not; it is treated as neutral and just, when it is neither. Often the legal rules that produce existing distributions or opportunities and even preferences are not recognized as law at all. We have seen this problem in numerous areas.

In the end, the use of status quo baselines may well be attributable to ideas about law that build on principles of compensatory justice. If one person has harmed another, the law requires compensation. The compensatory notion takes existing distributions as given. It is designed to restore the status quo ante, that is, distributions before the occurrence of the particular act in question. It is admirably well suited to the limited capacities of common law (and constitutional) courts. But compensatory ideas about law describe only one of law's functions; and they are a product of the odd view that the role of law in society should be defined by reference to the capacities of the judiciary.

President Roosevelt's New Deal marked a fundamental change in American legal and political culture. Above all, it deepened and extended the original constitutional commitment to deliberative democracy. The New Deal reformers saw the status quo as defensible only to the extent that reasons could be offered on its behalf. This idea has helped facilitate a number of governmental initiatives. Numerous functions for law have become conspicuous; these include reflecting social aspirations, reducing poverty, managing environmental and occupational risks, providing opportunity and information, and eliminating social caste.

When legislative and executive officials reject compensatory principles, the Supreme Court and the Constitution should not be obstacles. Most generally, the legal culture should adjust to the new foundations of law in the modern state. Such adjustments would call for large-scale revisions in current understandings. Discrimination on the basis of race, gender, and disability would raise a concern, not because it involves irrational distinctions between people who are really the same, but because the law should not translate differences into a source of social disadvantage—in short, because it creates something like a caste system. The management of social risks and the elimination of social caste should be the overriding principles of much of contemporary law. High-quality and roughly equal educational opportunity—spurred by the anticaste principle and the aspiration to equal life prospects, ideas that undergird the Civil War amendments—is a central part of the American constitutional heritage. It would also be necessary to reformulate the problems raised by governmental funding that is accompanied by conditions that affect the exercise of constitutional rights.

Free speech principles would have to be revised in some dramatic ways. Such principles should focus on the distinctive American conception of sovereignty, and thus on democratic self-governance. The law should be alert, as it currently is not, to the ways in which free markets in speech sometimes disserve that overriding goal. There should be no constitutional obstacle to governmental efforts to improve existing markets by promoting greater attention to public issues and by ensuring more diversity of view. Moreover, there should be greater room for government regulation of "lower-tier," nonpolitical speech, including libel of celebrities, commercial advertising, scientific speech with potential military applications, violent pornography, and narrowly defined categories of hate speech.

On this general view, existing private "preferences" do not always provide an appropriate foundation for law. Those preferences are sometimes a result of an unjust status quo, including limited information and opportunities. They are sometimes a product of law, and therefore cannot, without circularity, work to justify law. In their capacity as citizens, people often have aspirations that diverge from their purchases and expenditures in their capacity as consumers. The economic notion of "consumer sovereignty" should not be confused with the Madisonian ideal of sovereignty in "We the People." It is the latter ideal that marks our constitutional tradition.

Most of these recommendations are aimed at legislative and executive officials, not at the judiciary. Indeed, a persistent theme of this book has been that the identification of constitutional law with the decisions of the Supreme Court is a damaging and ahistorical mistake. This identification, fueled by the Warren Court, is inconsistent with the democratic goals of the American constitutional tradition. Those goals call for nonjudicial actors—Congress, the President, state officials, ordinary citizens—to engage in deliberation about the meaning of the Constitution's broad guarantees. The meaning of the Constitution is, in this sense, not identical with the interpretations of the Supreme Court, which should be seen as a mere part of a long and complex dialogue. A large part of my goal here has been to refocus attention toward other institutions, in the interest of recovering the original constitutional commitment to deliberative democracy.

Institutions to one side, my seemingly disparate recommendations are united by their general rejection of status quo neutrality. But the argument I have offered should not be taken as a general challenge to the commitment to neutrality in law. In recent years it has become common to treat that commitment as an unfortunate disguise for controversial substantive theories, so that neutrality in any form is something that judges and lawyers should attempt to avoid.[1] But this does not follow. We should agree that neutrality is a futile aspiration if the term is intended to refer to legal decisions uninformed by value judgments or commitments. In questions involving the proper organization of human affairs, that form of neutrality is obviously unavailable.

Every approach to social life depends on some importantly non-neutral view about the right or the good. This point need not, however, be taken to suggest that all conceptions of neutrality are impossible goals.

Conceptions of Neutrality

I conclude by outlining several possible uses of the notion of neutrality in law. None of them is wedded to existing distributions or the status quo. All of them recognize the role of human beings in creating the background against which principles of neutrality must operate. In fact, all of them have played a major role in the arguments I have made here.

First: The requirement of neutrality is unobjectionable insofar as it is a call for internal consistency.[2] It is often thought that people should order their convictions through a kind of internal Socratic dialogue, in which their original judgments about the case at hand are corrected through encounter with many of their other views about both the particular and the general. In a similar vein, Rawls famously describes our efforts to reach reflective equilibrium—consistency between our general theory and our considered views about particular problems.[3] These ideas are hardly to be disparaged. They are part of the rule of law. They embody methods of reasoning that affect substantive outcomes in many settings.

In fact the process of reasoning by analogy—central to legal interpretation—is best understood as a method of producing the necessary consistency across cases.[4] The effort is to develop principles that cohere with one another. We have seen this process at work in many settings. Often lawyers test a principle said to be decisive in one context by seeing whether they could live with it in another context. Through this testing, it is possible to see which of our beliefs are actually most fundamental, and to carry those beliefs into areas to which they were originally thought inapplicable. The general application of basic rights—given to new groups and in new contexts—has often occurred through this process.

The method of reasoning by analogy has recently come under severe attack.[5] But this form of reasoning is a critical vehicle for political and legal thought. It corrects initial judgments in numerous settings. It also embodies an important and perfectly intelligible principle of neutrality.

Second: Neutrality is an important goal insofar as it is a requirement of public-regarding justifications for legal outcomes or for the distribution of social benefits and burdens. Sometimes the demand for neutrality is actually a demand for justifications that can be phrased in public terms—the impartiality principle described in Chapter 1. As a means of flushing out pure political power or unarticulated, illegitimate, or unarticulable considerations, there is everything to be said in defense of that conception of neutrality. We have seen that much of constitutional law consists of a requirement of public-regarding justifications for what might otherwise be seen as naked preferences.

This requirement helps distinguish deliberative democracy from authoritarianism, whether through majority rule or otherwise. The distinctive response to authoritarianism is a call for reasons for the imposition of social burdens or the denial of social benefits. The antiauthoritarian impulse, thus understood, plays a major role in constitutional law; in one respect, it *is* constitutional law.

Third: The ideal of neutrality is unobjectionable insofar as it imposes, in certain contexts, a requirement of impersonality or abstraction on certain decisionmakers. Thus understood, neutrality restricts the kinds of considerations to which people in authority may point. It is part of a system of role differentiation. A judge in an accident case ordinarily pays no attention to the religion or race of the parties. If she does, she is violating her duty of impartiality. So, too, a legislator distributing defense department grants should pay no attention to attempted bribes, personal friendships, political affiliation, or even campaign contributions.

Neutrality might therefore entail a form of institutional division of labor, that is, a principle that certain officials must be indifferent to certain considerations. The often controversial division between law and politics can be understood in these terms. If that division is to be accepted, as it should be, it can only be for straightforwardly political reasons. The division is thus justified when we can decide that distinctly legal actors should not look to certain factors that have been deemed irrelevant for them. It is highly revealing that in most well-functioning legal systems, judges cannot consider factors that are properly part of the day-to-day work of administrators and legislators. For example, a contracts case cannot ordinarily turn on the relative wealth of the parties, even though relative wealth is important for other government officials in other settings.

The content of this constraint must of course be justified, and there is a risk that role differentiation or generality, like neutrality, will sometimes conceal an indefensible theory. But the notion that in some contexts certain considerations will be deemed irrelevant is a perfectly uncontroversial conception of neutrality. It is also one that a free society cannot easily do without.[6]

Fourth: Neutrality might refer to decisions made in accordance with a suitable social point of view[7] or, in the terms used here, the right baseline. For example, an employer's decision to exclude from the workplace people who require wheelchairs or who care for children would be objectionable because it turns morally irrelevant differences into a source of systemic social disadvantage (see Chapter 11). Objections about selectivity and bias are a familiar and indispensable part of legal and political argument. In this usage, the development of the appropriate baseline is doing the serious work. Notions of neutrality are derivative in the sense that they depend on that baseline. But to say this is not to disparage the use of those notions, which capture the problem of illegitimate partiality in various contexts.

In many areas of American constitutional law, however, a quite different conception of neutrality is at work. According to that conception, the status quo—existing practices, existing distributions of wealth, opportunities, preferences, and natural assets—is the baseline from which judgments about partiality will be made. A departure from those practices and distributions signals both action and partisanship; adherence signals inaction and neutrality. Status quo neutrality is unobjectionable if the status quo can be defended in substantive terms or if it does not itself embody injustice, whether social, biological, or otherwise. But sometimes existing practice is biased or at least the subject of controversy, and here a conception of neutrality that takes it as natural or just is at best reflexive and often serves as a mask for substantive theories that conceal injustice and cannot be defended if brought into the open. That conception of neutrality is surprisingly pervasive. We would be better off without it.[8]

Toward Deliberative Democracy

An abandonment of status quo neutrality would be consistent with the deepest aspirations of the American constitutional tradition. Those aspirations have been expressed not only in the New Deal rejection of common law baselines, and not only in the Civil War repudiation of supposedly natural racial differences, but also in the founding generation's insistence on the "man-made" quality of both law and culture. In the American legal tradition, government cannot rely on authority or nature.

The rejection of these sources of law, and of status quo neutrality itself, does not lead in any particular direction. It remains necessary to develop principles with which to give meaning to the Constitution's broad phrases, which are not self-interpreting. But in this enterprise we are not entirely at sea. The commitment to deliberative democracy implies not only a rejection of status quo neutrality, but also a series of substantive commitments that help give content to constitutional guarantees.

Those commitments—including political equality, citizenship, deliberation, and agreement as an ideal for politics—inform the meaning of such diverse provisions as the First Amendment, the equal protection clause, the due process clause, and the guarantee against takings of private property without just compensation. To be sure, constitutional commitments described at so high a level of generality will not resolve concrete cases. We will not find any formula or algorithm by which to circumscribe the exercise of practical reason in constitutional interpretation. On such matters a heterogeneous society will have room for disagreement and uncertainty. But this is no cause for embarrassment. On the contrary, it is extremely healthy, as the framers themselves insisted.

It is important to recall here two of the most distinctive yet overlooked features of the American constitutional tradition: its remarkable lack of complacency, and its extraordinary capacity for self-revision. Ours is the oldest written constitution in the world, but its longevity has everything to do with its flexibility over time. Even on fundamental matters, the meaning of the Constitution's broad guarantees is often quite different, in any given year, from what it was as little as thirty years before. Sometimes the revision occurs through the judiciary; usually it happens elsewhere. And it would be exceedingly odd to think that as the twentieth century draws to an end, we have finally reached closure. Perhaps we can hope for newly reinvigorated deliberation about constitutional commitments—deliberation that will occasionally take place in the courtroom, but more often, and far more fundamentally, through democratic channels.

Notes
Index

Notes

Introduction

1. Consider these words from a classic essay on private law: "When a loss is left where it falls in an auto accident, it is not because God so ordained it. Rather it is because the state has granted the injurer an entitlement to be free of liability and will intervene to prevent the victim's friends, if they are stronger, from taking compensation from the injurer. . . . [A]n entitlement to a good or to its converse is essentially inevitable. We either are entitled to have silence or entitled to make noise in a given set of circumstances. We either have the right to our own property or body or the right to share others' property or bodies. We may buy or sell ourselves into the opposite position, but we must start somewhere." Guido Calabresi & A. Douglas Melamed, "Property Rules, Liability Rules, and Inalienability: One View of the Cathedral," 85 *Harv. L. Rev.* 1089, 1091, 1100–01 (1972).

2. Ackerman's views are best elaborated in Bruce A. Ackerman, *We the People,* vol. 1: *Foundations* (1991); see also idem, *Reconstructing American Law* (1981). For Laurence Tribe's views, see, e.g., both editions of his *American Constitutional Law* (1st ed. 1978; 2d ed. 1988) and *Constitutional Choices* (1985). Related views in the area of discrimination law include Owen Fiss, "Groups and the Equal Protection Clause," 5 *Phil. & Pub. Aff.* 108 (1976); and Catharine MacKinnon, *Feminism Unmodified* (1987). On the "state action" issue, see Paul Brest, "State Action and Liberal Theory," 130 *U. Pa. L. Rev.* 1296 (1982). See also the related discussion of private law in Duncan Kennedy, "Form and Substance in Private Law Adjudication," 89 *Harv. L. Rev.* 1685 (1976).

3. In my view, for example, the New Deal is not a constitutional amendment, as Ackerman describes it. Nor do I see constitutional interpretation as a matter of "synthesizing" what Ackerman treats as the three crucial constitutional moments, the founding, the Civil War, and the New Deal. See Chapters 4 and 5. I

am also more skeptical about an intrusive judicial role than are Tribe and Fiss, for reasons discussed in Chapters 5 and 11. And I do not believe that the challenge to status quo neutrality entails a challenge to "individualism" of the sort set out in Kennedy, or a commitment to his "altruist" alternative. Many such differences will emerge as the discussion proceeds.

4. See *The Mind of the Founder* 156–160 (Marvin Meyers ed. 1981).

5. 14 *The Papers of James Madison* 162–163 (R. Rutland & W. Rachal eds. 1975). For a helpful discussion, see Jack Rakove, "Parchment Barriers and the Politics of Rights," in *A Culture of Rights* 98, 124–142 (Michael J. Lacey & Knud Haakonssen eds. 1992). Rakove writes that "Madison placed his greatest hopes for the Bill of Rights in its educative value," id. at 142, and notes that the historian and political scientist Herbert Storing concluded that "the fundamental case for a bill of rights is that it can be a prime agency of that political and moral education of the people on which free republican government depends." Herbert Storing, *What the Antifederalists Were For* 69–70 (1981).

To say this is not to say that nothing was expected of the judiciary. Jefferson referred to "the legal check which [the bill] puts into the hands of the judiciary." Madison, influenced by Jefferson, also hoped that "independent tribunals of justice will consider themselves in a peculiar manner the guardians of those rights; they will be an impenetrable bulwark against every assumption of power in the legislative or executive; they will be naturally led to resist every encroachment upon rights expressly stipulated for in the constitution by the declaration of rights." See the references and discussion in Rakove, "Parchment Barriers," at 141.

6. Notable exceptions include Paul Brest, "The Conscientious Legislator's Guide to Constitutional Interpretation," 27 *Stan. L. Rev.* 585 (1975); Tribe, *American Constitutional Law* (2d ed. 1988); Laurence Sager, "Fair Measure: The Legal Status of Underenforced Constitutional Norms," 91 *Harv. L. Rev.* 122 (1978). I am indebted to these discussions here. See also Louis Fisher, "The Curious Belief in Judicial Supremacy," 24 *Suffolk L. Rev.* 85 (1991), for a discussion of the long tradition of nonjudicial deliberation on the meaning of the Constitution.

1. A Republic of Reasons

1. See Gordon Wood, *The Radicalism of the American Revolution* (1992), which is a sustained elaboration of the American attack on monarchy, and on which I draw here; see also Stephen Macedo, *Liberal Virtues* 38–77 (1990).

2. Wood, *The Radicalism of the American Revolution* 19, 272.

3. Madison to Jefferson, Oct. 17, 1988, in 11 J. Madison, *The Papers of James Madison* 298 (R. Rutland & C. Hobson eds. 1977).

4. See *The Federalist* No. 10 (Madison); William Bessette, "Deliberative Democracy: The Majority Principle in American Government," in *How Democratic Is the Constitution?* 102 (Robert Goldwin & William Schambra eds. 1980).

5. Gordon Wood, *The Radicalism of the American Republic* 167 (1992). Thus the influential Archbishop Tillotson, writing in the early eighteenth century, noted that "He who would persuade a man or prevail with him to do anything must do it one of three ways, either by entreaty or authority or argument." In the modern era, it would be "preposterous to entreat men to believe anything or to charge them to do so" until they "were convinced . . . by sufficient arguments that it is reasonable to do so." See id. at 158.

6. *The Federalist* No. 10.

7. *The Federalist* No. 63.

8. The leading historical sources include Gordon Wood, *The Creation of the American Republic* (1972); idem, *The Radicalism of the American Republic;* J. G. A. Pocock, *The Machiavellian Moment* (1975); Bernard Bailyn, *Ideological Origins of the American Revolution* (1967). In law, see Frank Michelman, "Foreword: Traces of Self-Government," 100 *Harv. L. Rev.* 4 (1986); idem, "Law's Republic," 97 *Yale L. J.* 1493 (1988); Cass R. Sunstein, "Beyond the Republican Revival," 97 *Yale L. J.* 1539 (1988); idem, "Interest Groups in American Public Law," 38 *Stan. L. Rev.* 29 (1986); Suzanne Sherry, "Civic Virtue and the Feminine Voice in Constitutional Adjudication," 72 *Va. L. Rev.* 543 (1986). The extent of the republican influence is of course sharply disputed. For various views, see, in addition to the sources cited above, Joyce Appleby, *Liberalism and Republicanism* (1992); Thomas Pangle, *The Spirit of Modern Republicanism* (1988); John Diggins, *The Lost Soul of American Politics* (1986).

9. The "rights" view can be found in Richard Epstein, *Takings* (1985); the interest-group view appears in Robert Dahl, *A Preface to Democratic Theory* (1959).

10. Letter to Jefferson, Oct. 3, 1785, reprinted in 8 *The Papers of James Madison* 374 (Robert Rutland & William Rachal eds. 1975); Remarks on Mr. Jefferson's Draft of a Constitution, in *The Mind of the Founder* 35 (Marvin Meyers rev. ed. 1981).

11. 1 *Annals of Cong.* 733–745 (Joseph Gales ed. 1789) (emphasis added).

12. Letter from Jefferson to John Adams, Aug. 1, 1787, reprinted in 1 *The Adams-Jefferson Letters* 194, 196 (Lester J. Cappon ed. 1959).

13. 3 Max Farrand, *The Records of the Federal Convention of 1787,* 479 (1911).

14. See *The Federalist* No. 78.

15. See id.; Bruce Ackerman, *We the People* (1991), for a detailed exposition of this idea.

16. 2 *The Complete Antifederalist* 369 (Herbert Storing ed. 1980).

17. *The Federalist* No. 70.

18. See Jeremy Waldron, "Theoretical Foundations of Liberalism," 37 *Phil. Q.* 127 (1987); Stephen Macedo, *Liberal Virtues* (1990); William Galston, "Defending Liberalism," 76 *Am. Polit. Sci. Rev.* 621 (1982).

19. See, e.g., Robert Dahl, *A Preface to Democratic Theory* (1956); Arthur Bentley, *The Process of Government* (1908); George Stigler, "The Theory of Eco-

nomic Regulation," 2 *Bell J. Econ. & Mgmt. Sci.* 3 (1971); Gary Becker, "A Theory of Competition among Pressure Groups for Political Influence," 98 *Q. J. Econ.* 371 (1983).

20. See, e.g., Daniel Farber & Philip Frickey, "The Jurisprudence of Public Choice," 65 *Tex. L. Rev.* 873 (1987).

21. See Wood, *The Radicalism of the American Revolution,* at 252–259, 288.

22. As we will see, the prohibition is not vigorously policed by the judiciary, a phenomenon that probably reflects the Court's sensitivity to its own institutional position. The prohibition is thus part of a category of "underenforced" constitutional norms—norms that have constitutional status but that courts, precisely because they are courts, enforce less aggressively than they might. I take up this issue in more detail later. For general discussion, see Laurence Sager, "Fair Measure: The Legal Status of Underenforced Constitutional Norms," 91 *Harv. L. Rev.* 1212 (1978).

23. On this question, the influential treatment in John Hart Ely, *Democracy and Distrust* (1980), is untrue to the original constitutional structure or to current law.

24. See Wood, *The Radicalism of the American Revolution,* at 325.

25. Williamson v. Lee Optical, 348 U.S. 483 (1955).

26. And in the light of relevant interpretive principles. See Chapter 4.

27. See the powerful analysis in Einer Elhauge, "Does Interest-Group Theory Justify Aggressive Judicial Review?" 101 *Yale L. J.* 31 (1991), arguing that interest-group theory, to be a basis for judicial review, must rely on some substantive evaluations of different states of affairs, including the status quo.

28. See, e.g., Palmore v. Sidoti, 466 U.S. 429 (1984).

29. See Washington v. Davis, 426 U.S. 229 (1976).

30. See Roe v. Wade, 410 U.S. 113 (1973).

31. See Geoffrey Stone, L. Michael Seidman, Cass R. Sunstein, & Mark Tushnet, *Constitutional Law* ch. 9 (2d ed. 1991).

32. See Manigault v. Springs, 199 U.S. 473 (1905).

33. 290 U.S. 398 (1934).

34. See generally Alison Dunham, "*Griggs v. Allegheny County* in Perspective: Thirty Years of Supreme Court Expropriation Law," 1962 *Sup. Ct. Rev.* 63, 65–71.

35. Hawaii Hous. Auth. v. Midkiff, 465 U.S. 1097 (1984).

2. The Revolution of 1937

1. 163 U.S. 537 (1896).

2. 198 U.S. 45 (1905).

3. 208 U.S. 412 (1908).

4. 347 U.S 483 (1954). This basic view of *Plessy* is also set out in Planned Parenthood v. Casey, 60 U.S.L.W. 4795, 4803 (1992) (opinion of Justices O'Connor, Kennedy, and Souter).

5. 198 U.S 45 (1905).

6. 261 U.S. 525 (1923).

7. 300 U.S. 379 (1937).

8. Three qualifications are in order here. First, the tax system, at least at the state level, could be used to redistribute resources. Second, not every common law right was, by virtue of its status as such, immunized from collective control. Some adjustments were permissible. Nonetheless, the basic framework of the common law formed the baseline from which to decide cases. Indeed, one can trace to this period the idea that legislative elimination of "core" common law rights was permissible only if the legislature furnished an adequate alternative remedy. See, e.g., New York Cent. R.R. v. White, 243 U.S. 188 (1917) (upholding workers' compensation in part because of quid pro quo); see also Duke Power Co. v. Carolina Envtl. Study Group, 438 U.S. 59, 88 & n. 32 (1978) (upholding liability-limiting provisions of Price-Anderson Act against due process challenge but suggesting relevance of quid pro quo).

Third, the protection of common law rights depended not merely on the fact that the rights at issue were protected by the common law, but also on the (unsurprising) fact that the common law corresponded to a widely held theory about the proper role of government. The interests protected at common law thus tracked the category of natural rights. For a modern statement, see Richard Epstein, "A Theory of Strict Liability," 2 *J. Legal Stud.* 151 (1973); idem, *Takings* (1985).

9. Note that at most it is only an attempt. Maximum-hour laws do not simply transfer resources from employers to employees. Some employees are hurt by such laws—those who wish to work for longer hours and more money. The incidence of benefits and burdens is difficult to predict in advance. Indeed it has been plausibly suggested that maximum-hour legislation is sought by large, unionized firms, in an effort to stem competition from small, nonunionized employers. See Bernard Siegan, *Economic Liberties and the Constitution* (1980). If this is right, such legislation might well be seen as a naked preference.

10. See Gary Becker, "A Theory of Competition among Pressure Groups for Political Influence," 98 *Q. J. Econ.* 371 (1983) (making this argument). On Holmes, see Yosal Rogat, "Some Modern Views—The Judge as Spectator," 31 *U. Chi. L. Rev.* 213 (1964).

11. 198 U.S. at 76.

12. Herbert Spencer, *Social Statics* (1882).

13. See, e.g., Rogat, "Some Modern Views"; Yosal Rogat & James O'Fallon, "Mr. Justice Holmes, a Dissenting Opinion—The Speech Cases," 36 *Stan. L. Rev.* 1349 (1984).

14. See, e.g., Nebbia v. New York, 291 U.S. 502 (1934); Bunting v. Oregon, 243 U.S. 426 (1917); Muller v. Oregon, 208 U.S. 412 (1908).

15. Jeremy Bentham, *Principles of the Civil Code*, in 1 *Collected Works of Jeremy Bentham* 308 (Timothy Sprigge ed. 1968).

16. See Robert Hale, "Coercion and Distribution in a Supposedly Non-

Coercive State," 38 *Pol. Sci. Q.* 470 (1923); Morris Cohen, "Property and Sovereignty," 13 *Cornell L. Q.* 8 (1927).

17. Robert Hale, 8 *ABAJ* 638 (1922).

18. International News Service v. Associated Press, 248 U.S. 215, 246 (1918) (Holmes, J., concurring).

19. Robert Hale, "Rate Making and the Revision of the Property Concept," 22 *Colum. L. Rev.* 209, 214 (1922) (emphasis added).

20. Id. at 214; Robert Hale, unpublished manuscript, quoted in Barbara Fried, "Robert Hale and Progressive Law and Economics," ch. 3 (unpublished manuscript); Robert Hale, 8 *ABAJ* 638, 639.

21. Hale, 8 *ABAJ* at 639. A similar point was made by Gerald Henderson in 1920; see Henderson, "Railway Valuation and the Courts," 33 *Harv. L. Rev.* 902 (1920). (I owe the citation to the useful discussion in Morton Horwitz, *The Transformation of American Law, 1870–1960,* at 162–163 [1992].) Henderson describes a situation in which a company lawyer argues to a ratesetting commission that the company should "be allowed always a certain percentage on the value of the property. If value goes up, rates should go on proportionately." But an economist, Henderson notes, could respond "that the only accepted and sensible meaning of the word 'value' is 'value in exchange.'" And "value in exchange" is in turn a function of "what we allow you gentlemen to charge the public. If we reduce your rates, your value goes down. . . . Obviously we cannot measure rates by value, if value is itself a function of rates." In this way Henderson made the point—prevalent throughout the legal culture in the period—that property rights and economic values were creatures of regulatory decisions.

22. Note, 35 *Colum. L. Rev.* 1090, 1091–92 (1935) (emphasis added).

23. Lester Ward, "Plutocracy and Paternalism," 20 *Forum* 304–309 (November 1885), quoted in Sidney Fine, *Laissez Faire and the General Welfare State* 262 (1919). An excellent discussion of this period is Fried, "Robert Hale and Progressive Law and Economics." The same point is made about hunger in Amartya Sen, "Ingredients of Famine Analysis: Availability and Entitlements," in *Resources, Values and Development* 452, 458 (1984).

24. See William James, *Pragmatism* (1907).

25. John Dewey, *The Philosophy of John Dewey* 370, 366 (John J. McDermott ed. 1981).

26. John Dewey, *The Public and Its Problems* 102 (1927).

27. Dewey, *The Philosophy of John Dewey,* at 366.

28. See William James, "The Meaning of Truth," in *Pragmatism and the Meaning of Truth* 169 (A. J. Ayer ed. 1978).

29. I am indebted in the discussion in this section to Bruce Ackerman, *We the People,* vol. 1: *Foundations* (1991), and Laurence Tribe, *American Constitutional Law* 567–586 (2d ed. 1988).

30. 276 U.S. 272 (1928).

31. Id. at 279 (emphasis added).

32. Home Building Loan Ass'n v. Blaisdell, 290 U.S. 398 (1934).

33. 304 U.S. 64 (1938). Observers of the *Erie* decision usually emphasize the understanding of federalism that underlies *Erie*. The Court did indeed contend that the Constitution provides for state rather than federal regulation of intrastate commercial interactions; and it saw *Swift* as unconstitutional in part for that reason. But the emphasis on federalism disregards an equally important factor: the view, irresistible in the late 1930s, that a judicially administered national system of common law principles based on the (entirely misleading) principle of laissez-faire was inconsistent with the needs of an integrated economy.

34. 41 U.S. (16 Pet.) 1 (1842).

35. 334 U.S. 1 (1948).

36. 2 *The Public Papers and Addresses of Franklin D. Roosevelt* 5 (1938). For an argument that the New Deal should be seen as a structural amendment to the Constitution, see Ackerman, *We the People.* I do not accept this characterization. But one need not go so far as Ackerman in order to agree that the developments associated with the New Deal are relevant to interpretive practices. See Chapters 4 and 5.

37. 1 *Public Papers of Franklin D. Roosevelt* 657 (1938); Franklin D. Roosevelt, "Message to Congress," June 8, 1934, reprinted in *Statutory History of the United States: Income Security* 61 (Robert B. Stevens ed. 1970). See also Morris Cohen, "Property and Sovereignty," 13 *Cornell L. Q.* 8 (1927), which makes similar points.

38. 29 U.S.C. § 151 (1982) (emphasis added).

39. Amartya Sen, *Poverty and Famines* (1981), is a striking contemporary illustration of similar ideas, demonstrating that famines are a result not of a decrease in the supply of food, but of social choices, prominent among them legal ones, deciding who is entitled to what. See especially id. at 165–166: "Finally, the focus on entitlement has the effect of emphasizing legal rights. Other relevant factors, for example market forces, can be seen as operating *through* a system of legal relations (ownership rights, contractual obligations, legal exchanges, etc.). The law stands between food availability and food entitlement. Starvation deaths can reflect legality with a vengeance." This claim can be seen as a special case of the New Deal understanding of "laissez-faire." See also Jean Dreze & Amartya Sen, *Hunger and Public Action* (1991), demonstrating that both famines and entrenched hunger are artifacts of identifiable social policies rather than consequences of "nature."

40. Robert Hale, unpublished manuscript, quoted in Fried, "Robert Hale and Progressive Law and Economics," ch. 3; Cohen, "Property and Sovereignty," 8, 14. The basic view of the *Lochner* period that is set out here is strongly endorsed by the important leading opinion in the 1992 *Casey* case, affirming *Roe v. Wade.* A chief argument in that opinion is that the *Lochner* Court's understanding of liberty did not truly serve human needs. Thus the justices write that the key

problem with the *Lochner* era's "interpretation of contractual freedom" is that it "rested on fundamentally false factual assumptions about the capacity of a relatively unregulated market to satisfy minimal levels of human welfare." Planned Parenthood v. Casey, 60 U.S.L.W. 4795, 4803 (1992) (opinion of Justices O'Connor, Kennedy, and Souter). In this way, these justices rejected the view, elaborated in Justice Scalia's dissenting opinion, that the problem with the *Lochner* era rested solely in the aggressive use of the due process clause.

41. 2 *Public Papers of Franklin D. Roosevelt* 72. See also Rex Tugwell, *The Struggle for Democracy* (1935), which emphasizes experimentation on nearly every page.

42. Franklin D. Roosevelt, "Message to the Congress on the State of the Union," Jan. 11, 1944, in 13 *Public Papers and Addresses of Franklin D. Roosevelt* 41 (1969).

43. See Gordon Wood, *The Radicalism of the American Revolution* 272 (1991).

44. I will not be evaluating New Deal institutions here. In important respects, however, I believe that the new arrangements have failed. See Cass R. Sunstein, "Democratizing America through Law," 20 *Suffolk L. Rev.* 221 (1992); idem, "Constitutionalism after the New Deal," 101 *Harv. L. Rev.* 421 (1987); idem, *After the Rights Revolution* (1990).

45. 208 U.S. 412 (1908).

46. Id. at 421, 420 n. 1, 422–423. Compare this description of attitudes in prerevolutionary America: "So distinctive and so separated was the aristocracy from ordinary folk that many still thought the two groups represented two orders of being. . . . Ordinary people were thought to be different physically, and because of varying diets and living conditions, no doubt in many cases they were different. People often assumed that a handsome child, though apparently a commoner, had to be some gentleman's bastard offspring." Wood, *The Radicalism of the American Revolution* 27.

Note also the suggestion in the post–Civil War debates that "God himself has set His seal of distinctive difference between the two races, and no human legislation can overrule the Divine decree." *Congressional Record,* 43rd Cong., 1st sess., vol. 2 at 22 (1873–74) (remarks of Rep. Southard). See the related suggestion that civil rights legislation put the two races in "*unnatural relation* to each other," *Congressional Record,* 43rd Cong., 2d sess., vol. 3 at 983 (1875) (remarks of Rep. Eldredge). See generally Carol Horton, "Constitutional Equality and Racial Difference: The Political Construction of African American Citizenship, 1870–1900" (Paper delivered at the 1992 Annual Meeting of the American Political Science Association).

47. See Chapter 3.

48. See Catharine MacKinnon, *Feminism Unmodified* ch. 2 (1987).

49. See Dreze & Sen, *Hunger and Public Action;* Sen, *Poverty and Famines.*

3. Status Quo Neutrality in Contemporary Law

1. See J. S. Mill, "Nature," in 10 *The Collected Works of John Stuart Mill* 373 (J. M. Robson ed. 1967). See also the remarks on the role of "nature" in the production of famines, in Jean Dreze & Amartya Sen, *Hunger and Public Action* 46–47 (1989): "[E]ven when the prime mover in a famine is a natural occurrence such as a flood or a drought, what its impact will be on the population would depend on how society is organized. For example, a country with an extensive irrigation network is much less influenced by a drought than one without it. . . . Furthermore, even the occurrence of droughts, floods, and so on is not independent of social and economic policies. Many deserts have been created by reckless human action, and the distinction between natural and social causation is substantially blurred by the impact that society can have on the physical environment. . . . Blaming nature can, of course, be very consoling and comforting. It can be of great use especially to those in positions of power and responsibility. Comfortable inaction is, however, typically purchased at a very high price—a price that is paid by others, often with their lives."

2. See, e.g., David Currie, "Positive and Negative Constitutional Rights," 53 *U. Chi. L. Rev.* 864 (1986); Frank Michelman, "Welfare Rights in a Constitutional Democracy," 1979 *Wash. U. L. Q.* 659; Ralph Winter, "Poverty, Economic Equality and the Equal Protection Clause," 1972 *Sup. Ct. Rev.* 41.

3. See, e.g., Deshaney v. Winnebago County, 109 S.Ct. 998 (1989).

4. 448 U.S. 297 (1980).

5. Thus "protection by the government" is part of the social contract, a point noted in no less an authority than Marbury v. Madison, 5 U.S. 137 (1903). A detailed historical discussion with multiple references is Steven Heyman, "The First Duty of Government: Protection, Liberty and the Fourteenth Amendment," 41 *Duke L. J.* 507 (1991).

6. See the helpful discussion in Jeremy Waldron, "Homelessness and Freedom," *UCLA L. Rev.* (1991). A similar point appears in Amartya Sen, "Ingredients of Famine Analysis," in *Resources, Values, and Development* 452, 458 (1984).

7. I am indebted here to the valuable discussions in Laurence Tribe, *American Constitutional Law,* ch. 15 (1st ed. 1978); idem, *Constitutional Choices* (1985); Paul Brest, "State Action and Liberal Theory," 130 *U. Pa. L. Rev.* 1296 (1982).

8. 447 U.S. 74 (1980).

9. On abolition of trespass laws as state action, see id. at 82–85; on antidiscrimination law, see Reitman v. Mulkey, 387 U.S. 369, 374–377 (1967) (suggesting that a "mere" repeal is not state action).

10. 424 U.S. 507, 512–521 (1976).

11. 334 U.S. 1 (1948).

12. 387 U.S. 369 (1967).

13. 347 U.S. 483 (1954).

14. 23 *Harv. L. Rev.* 1 (1959).

15. City of Richmond v. Croson Co., 488 U.S. 469 (1989); Johnson v. Transportation Agency of Santa Clara County, 107 S.Ct. 1442 (1987); Wygant v. Jackson Bd. of Educ., 476 U.S. 267 (1986); Fullilove v. Klutznick, 448 U.S. 448 (1980); Regents of the Univ. of Calif. v. Bakke, 438 U.S. 265 (1978).

16. This is so for the pragmatic arguments as well. Both affirmative action and minimum wage legislation may hurt the people one intends to help. I do not address these pragmatic concerns. They present forceful counterarguments, but they seem best addressed to the political process, not to courts.

17. William James described this phenomenon as "vicious abstractionism": "We conceive a concrete situation by singling out some salient or important feature in it, and classing it under that; then, instead of adding to its previous characters all the positive consequences which the new way of conceiving it may bring, we proceed to use our concept privatively; reducing the originally rich phenomenon to the naked suggestions of that name abstractly taken, treating it as a case of 'nothing but' that concept, and acting as if all the other characters from out of which the concept is abstracted were expunged. Abstraction, functioning in this way, becomes a means of arrest far more than a means of advance in thought. It mutilates things. . . ." William James, "The Meaning of Truth," in *Pragmatism and the Meaning of Truth* 302 (A. J. Ayer ed. 1978; originally published 1909).

18. John Dewey, "The Future of Liberalism," in John Dewey, 11 *Later Works* 291 (1935).

19. See Geoffrey Stone, L. Michael Seidman, Cass Sunstein & Mark Tushnet, *Constitutional Law* 558–559, 567–575 (1986).

20. See Mississippi Univ. for Women v. Hogan, 458 U.S. 718 (1982); Reed v. Reed, 404 U.S. 71 (1971).

21. 430 U.S. 199 (1977); 429 U.S. 190 (1976); 458 U.S. 718 (1983); 453 U.S. 57 (1981).

22. It is not necessary to ask to what degree gender differences have a biological component. Even if there is such a component, it hardly justifies the measures at issue in most cases; it is by no means clear that the legal system should turn biological differences into social disadvantages. See Chapter 11.

23. See generally Violence against Women: Victims of the System, Hearings before the Committee on the Judiciary, U.S. Senate, 102d Cong., 1st sess., on S. 15 (1991).

24. See Cleveland Bd. of Educ. v. Loudermill, 470 U.S. 532 (1985); Arnett v. Kennedy, 416 U.S. 134 (1974); Board of Regents v. Roth, 408 U.S. 564 (1972).

25. See Goldberg v. Kelly, 397 U.S. 254 (1970); Charles Reich, "The New Property," 73 *Yale L. J.* 733 (1963).

26. See 470 U.S. at 538–542.

27. See, e.g., Ingraham v. Wright, 430 U.S. 651 (1977) (bodily integrity). See also Frank Easterbrook, "Substance and Due Process," 1982 *Sup. Ct. Rev.* 85,

which draws a sharp distinction between common law and statutory interests and which understands the distinction in *Lochner*-like terms, as responding to the differences between interests created by government and interests from some other source.

Sometimes, however, the statutory entitlement approach has been used to remove even common law interests from the category of liberty and property. See Paul v. Davis, 424 U.S. 693 (1976) (reputation as a property interest). Note also that it would be possible to treat common law interests as protected only because and to the extent that they can be classified as "entitlements"; under this view, the statutory entitlement and common law cases are closer than they might at first appear. But this sort of positivist approach to liberty and property misconceives the intended function of the due process clause, which was to protect important interests from procedural irregularity, regardless of whether there was a state-created right.

28. 363 U.S. 603, 608–611 (1960).

29. See United States R.R. Retirement Bd. v. Fritz, 449 U.S. 160 (1980).

30. See Thomas v. Union Carbide, 473 U.S. 568 (1984).

31. 424 U.S. 1 (1976).

32. Id. at 48–49.

33. See Sherbert v. Verner, 374 U.S. 398 (1963); Shapiro v. Thompson, 394 U.S. 618 (1969); Snepp v. U.S., 447 U.S. 507 (1980); Harris v. McRae, 448 U.S. 297 (1980).

34. See Doyle v. Continental Insurance Co., 94 U.S. 535 (1876); William Van Alstyne, "The Demise of the Right–Privilege Distinction in Constitutional Law," 81 *Harv. L. Rev.* 1239 (1968).

35. McAuliffe v. Mayor of New Bedford, 155 Mass. 216, 220, 29 N.E. 517, 517–518 (1892).

36. See Barron v. Burnside, 121 U.S. 186 (1887); Frost & Frost Trucking Co. v. Railroad Commission, 271 U.S. 583 (1926).

37. 448 U.S. 297 (1980).

38. Lyng v. Int'l Union, 485 U.S. 360 (1988).

39. 111 S.Ct. 1759 (1991).

40. See Joseph Vining, *Legal Identity* (1978); Richard Stewart, "The Reformation of American Administrative Law," 88 *Harv. L. Rev.* 1667, 1672–73 (1975).

41. See, e.g., Alabama Power Co. v. Ickes, 302 U.S. 464, 478 (1938); Vaca v. Sipes, 386 U.S. 171, 181–183 (1967).

42. See, e.g., Dunlop v. Bachowski, 421 U.S. 560 (1975); Adams v. Richardson, 480 F.2d 1159 (D.C. Cir. 1973); EDF v. Ruckelshaus, 439 F.2d 584 (D.C. Cir. 1971).

43. 470 U.S. 821 (1985).

44. See Alabama Power Co. v. Ickes, 302 U.S. 464 (1938); Stewart, "The Reformation of American Administrative Law," at 1723–24.

45. See Chicago Junction Case, 264 U.S. 258 (1924).

46. 397 U.S. 150, 153–157 (1970).

47. See Allen v. Wright, 468 U.S. 737, 750–752 (1984).

48. See id.; Eastern Kentucky Welfare Rights Org. v. Simon, 426 U.S. 26 (1976); Worth v. Seldin, 422 U.S. 490 (1975); Lujan v. Defenders of Wildlife, U.S. (1992).

49. See cases cited in notes 47 and 48 above.

50. See Robert Bork, "Neutral Principles and Some First Amendment Problems," 47 *Ind. L. J.* 1, 2–3 (1971); Robert Dahl, *A Preface to Democratic Theory* (1956); Richard Posner, *Economic Analysis of Law* (3d ed. 1986).

51. Green v. County School Bd., 391 U.S. 430 (1968). See Paul Gewirtz, "Choice in the Transition: School Desegregation and the Corrective Ideal," 86 *Colum. L. Rev.* 728 (1986).

52. See Gewirtz, "Choice in the Transition," at 745–748.

53. 466 U.S. 429 (1984).

4. Interpreting the Constitution: Method

1. This idea is identified and criticized in Ronald Dworkin, *Law's Empire* (1986); see also idem, *Taking Rights Seriously* (1976). As will be apparent, I am much indebted to Dworkin's work on this point, but there are some differences in our approaches.

2. Robert Bork, *The Tempting of America* (1990).

3. Id. at 4, 5, 9.

4. Id. at 6–7, 8, 10–11.

5. See Ronald Dworkin, "Bork's Jurisprudence," 57 *U. Chi. L. Rev.* 657 (1990).

6. Bork, *The Tempting of America* at 176.

7. See Jefferson Powell, "The Original Understanding of Original Intent," 98 *Harv. L. Rev.* 885 (1985).

8. Bork, *The Tempting of America* at 201.

9. See Frank Easterbrook, "Abstraction and Authority," 59 *U. Chi. L. Rev.* 349 (1992).

10. Bork, *The Tempting of America* at 258–259.

11. Some important qualifications are necessary here. Sometimes semantic principles are not easily distinguished from substantive ones. At a certain level of generality, every semantic principle must operate in the context of substantive principles; these principles seem invisible or absent, but this is only because everyone accepts them. The notion that the President must be at least thirty-five years of age is clear not merely because of syntax and dictionary meaning, but also because of agreed-upon substantive ideas about how to interpret the constitutional text. In this context, for example, we do not think that changed circumstances—involving education or longevity—ought to be taken to authorize courts to abandon the literal meaning of the words. This is so even though

changed circumstances do call for such abandonment in other settings. Consider the fact that we have an air force even though the Constitution does not allow for one. Congress is allowed to create an air force only through an abandonment of literalism. Substantive principles having to do with changed circumstances and other matters are thus at work even in the easiest of cases. It follows that meaning seems purely a matter of semantics only when we agree on substance. But substance—in the form of interpretive principles that must rest on a political foundation—is always there. In some cases, however, substantive disputes are on the surface, and here a moral or political argument is conspicuously necessary.

W. V. Quine, "Two Dogmas of Empiricism," 60 *Phil. Rev.* 20 (1951), famously argues that a familiar version of the distinction between semantic and substantive principles turns out to be untenable. For the legal context, the argument may be described in the way suggested in this note. The distinction between semantic and substantive principles should be understood as one of convention.

12. Paul Brest, "The Misleading Quest for the Original Understanding," 60 *B. U. L. Rev.* 204 (1980), and Ronald Dworkin, "The Forum of Principle," in *A Matter of Principle* (1985), are especially helpful here. For a powerful discussion of the problem of "translating" legal texts in new conditions, see Larry Lessig, "Fidelity and Restraint," *Texas L. Rev.* (forthcoming 1993).

13. John Ely, *Democracy and Distrust* (1980), is an extended argument to this effect.

14. I do not deal here with a different conception of formalism, powerfully defended by Frederick Schauer. See Schauer, *Playing by the Rules* (1991); idem, "Formalism," 97 *Yale L. J.* 509 (1988). Schauer understands formalism as a willingness to be bound by the literal meaning of legal terms even though an inquiry into their purposes, or into the reasonableness of particular applications, would suggest that we should not be so bound. Literalism, in law, might well be defended in this way. The argument for this kind of formalism would be self-consciously political; it would rest on the need to limit judicial discretion. A willingness to follow "plain meaning," or dictionary definitions, might produce absurdity in some individual cases; but it might also bind the judges in a way that leads, on balance, to a better legal system. This conception of law might be understood as a healthy part of the rule of law. It should not be confused with formalism of the sort I criticize here.

15. John Hart Ely, *Democracy and Distrust* (1980).

16. Id. at 72, 73, 88.

17. The point has been noted in many places. See, e.g., Dworkin, "The Forum of Principle"; Laurence Tribe, "The Puzzling Persistence of Process-Based Theories of Constitutional Law," 89 *Yale L. J.* 1063 (1980).

18. Laurence Tribe & Michael Dorf, *On Reading the Constitution* (1991).

19. 478 U.S. 186 (1986).

20. A constitutional attack on the New Deal is urged in Richard Epstein, *Takings* (1985).

21. Formalism can be found in some surprising places. Bruce Ackerman argues in *We the People* (1991) that we should understand constitutional interpretation as an effort at synthesis among three constitutional moments: the founding, the Civil War, and the New Deal. This is an intriguing effort to give some historical depth to constitutional interpretation. A detailed discussion of the proposal would take me far beyond the scope of the present discussion. But for the moment, it should be clear that there are competing possible views about how to "synthesize" the three moments, and that any particular view about the right synthesis will have to partake of the judgments of the synthesizer. This is hardly a decisive objection to Ackerman's approach. But it suggests that the task of interpretation, as he describes it, will have a large, nonhistorical dimension. At least in his account thus far, that crucial dimension is not addressed.

22. See Richard Epstein, "Property, Speech, and the Politics of Distrust," 59 *U. Chi. L. Rev.* 41 (1992).

23. See the brief discussion in David Estlund, "Book Review," 102 *Ethics* 871–874 (1991), citing John Rawls's doctoral dissertation, "A Study in the Grounds of Ethical Knowledge" (Princeton University, 1950), pp. 1–2. See also idem, "Making Truth Safe for Democracy," in *The Idea of Democracy* (David Copp, Jean Hampton, & John Roemer eds. forthcoming 1993).

24. Bork, *The Tempting of America* at 14. It is ironic that Bork attributes this idea to Madison, who would have found it most puzzling. See Chapter 1.

25. Quoted in Mark D. Howe, *Justice Oliver Wendell Holmes: The Proving Years* 40–41 (1963). See generally Yosal Rogat, "The Judge as Spectator," 31 *U. Chi. L. Rev.* 213 (1964).

26. See, e.g., Brandenburg v. Ohio, 395 U.S. 444 (1969) (Black, J., concurring); Cohen v. California, 403 U.S. 15 (1971); Cox v. Louisiana, 379 U.S. 536, 575–578 (Black, J., dissenting).

27. See John Austin, *The Province of Jurisprudence Determined* (1832); H. L. A. Hart, *The Concept of Law* (1961).

28. See Dworkin, *Taking Rights Seriously.*

29. See Stanley Fish, *Doing What Comes Naturally* (1989).

30. Alan Hutchinson, "Reading Rorty Radically," 103 *Harv. L. Rev.* 555, 569–573 (1989); Anthony Cook, "Beyond Critical Legal Studies," 103 *Harv. L. Rev.* 985, 1042–44 (1990).

31. See Fish, *Doing What Comes Naturally;* Stanley Fish, book review, 57 *U. Chi. L. Rev.* 1447 (1991).

32. See Hilary Putnam, *Renewing Philosophy* 123–128 (1992); Martha Nussbaum, "Sophistry about Conventions," in *Love's Knowledge* (1990); and idem, "Skepticism about Practical Reason" (unpublished manuscript 1991); see also the sources cited in notes 33 and 34 below.

33. The point is made in various forms in William James, *Pragmatism* (1907); John Dewey, *Experience and Nature* (1926); Ludwig Wittgenstein, *Philosophical Investigations* (1953); Hilary Putnam, *Reason, Truth, and History* (1981).

34. For discussion from various angles, see, e.g., Putnam, *Renewing Philosophy* 176–179, 186–200; John Rawls, "Constructionism in Moral Theory," 77 *J. Phil.* 515, 554–572 (1980); idem, "Outline of a Decision Procedure for Ethics," 60 *Phil. Rev.* 177 (1951); Donald Davidson, "On the Very Idea of a Conceptual Scheme," in *Inquiries into Truth and Interpretation* 183 (1984); T. M. Scanlon, "Contractualism and Utilitarianism," in *Utilitarianism and Beyond* (Amartya K. Sen & Bernard Williams eds. 1982). Thus Dewey complained that "we oscillate between a theory that, in order to save the objectivity of judgments of values, isolates them from experience and nature, and a theory that, in order to save their concrete and human significance, reduces them to mere statements about our own feelings." For him, there was no need to "alternate between sending us to a realm of eternal and fixed values and sending us to enjoyments [or beliefs] such as actually obtain." See John Dewey, *The Philosophy of John Dewey* 582, 598 (John J. McDermott ed. 1981).

35. For conventionalists, including Stanley Fish, this is thought always to be the case. Thus the category of semantic interpretive principles is identified, wrongly, with that of substantive interpretive principles—and this because the fact that the latter must be developed in this world makes them, for Fish, purely semantic or rhetorical after all. See Fish, *Doing What Comes Naturally*.

A related problem can be found in Richard Rorty's influential work. I cannot discuss the many complexities of Rorty's view. But he sometimes seems to suggest that if human beings do not have unmediated access to the world—if what they think is only that, what they think—universalism, essentialism, theory, philosophy, and perhaps even good arguments as that notion is ordinarily understood all go out the window. Hence, Rorty sometimes suggests, we must have a kind of ironic distance from our own views or dispense altogether with "philosophy" and "theory." See, e.g., Richard Rorty, "Feminism and Pragmatism," 30 *Mich. Q. Rev.* 231 (1991).

But none of this follows. It may be universally true, for example, that the subordination of women to men is a bad thing; or it may be essential to all human lives that people have air, food, and drink; or there may be universally good arguments that people with black skin and those with white skin should be treated the same way in the workforce; or theory may show us that people live better lives if they are able to reflect critically on different conceptions of the good. The fact that anything people think is a human product is not inconsistent with any of these claims. Sometimes Rorty seems surprisingly if covertly wedded to a transcendental or foundational conception of truth; sometimes he writes as if the failure of that conception has large negative implications for the possibilities of philosophy or theory in general. Dewey and Rawls, whom Rorty greatly admires, are only two of many counterexamples to any such claim.

36. See Charles Black, *Structure and Relationship in Constitutional Law* (1965); Laurence Tribe & Michael Dorf, *On Reading the Constitution* (1991).

37. See Richard Posner, "Bork and Beethoven," 42 *Stan. L. Rev.* 1365 (1990).

5. Interpreting the Constitution: Substance

1. Learned Hand, *The Bill of Rights* (1958); James Landis, *The Administrative Process* (1938); West Virginia State Bd. of Educ. v. Barnette, 319 U.S. 624, 646 (1943) (Frankfurter, J., dissenting).

2. See Chapter 4; Barbara Herrnstein Smith, *Contingencies of Value* (1988); Stanley Fish, *Doing What Comes Naturally* (1989); Gary Peller, "The Metaphysics of American Law," 73 *Calif. L. Rev.* 1151 (1985).

3. See Mancur Olson, *The Logic of Collective Action* (1965); Russell Hardin, *Collective Action* (1982).

4. See Kenneth Arrow, *Social Choice and Individual Values* (1963); see also Brian Barry & Russell Hardin, *Rational Man and Irrational Society?* (1982).

5. The claim is defended in Chapter 6. See also Robert Goodin, "Laundering Preferences," in *Foundations of Social Choice Theory* (Jon Elster and Aanund Hylland eds. 1986).

6. For related discussion, see Martha Nussbaum, "Sophistry about Conventions," in *Love's Knowledge* 220–228 (1991).

7. See, e.g., Michel Foucault, *Power/Knowledge* (1981) (power); Fish, *Doing What Comes Naturally* (conventions); Jacques Derrida, *On Grammatology* (Gayatri Spivak trans. 1976) (play).

8. Jurgen Habermas, *The Philosophical Logic of Modernity* 294 (1986).

9. See, e.g., Roberto Unger, *False Necessity* (1987), whose enthusiasm for "context-smashing" appears, in this light, most puzzling.

10. Different versions of this view can be found in John Dewey, *Experience and Nature* (1926); William James, *Pragmatism* (1928); Ludwig Wittgenstein, *Philosophical Investigations* (1953); and Hilary Putnam, *Reason, Truth, and History* (1981).

11. Albert Hirschman, *The Rhetoric of Reaction* (1991), attacks these ideas.

12. See Jon Elster, "Introduction," in *Constitutionalism and Democracy* (Jon Elster & Rune Slagstad eds. 1988).

13. See Lon Fuller, *The Morality of Law* (1964).

14. Edmund Burke, *Reflections on the Revolution in France* (1790); Friedrich Hayek, *The Road to Serfdom* (1944).

15. A good example is Burnham v. Superior Court, 2105 S.Ct. (1990) (opinion of Scalia, J.).

16. See Aristotle, *Physics* B25–27 (Hippocrates G. Apostle trans. 1980).

17. For an account of democracy along these lines, see S. L. Hurley, *Natural Reasons* ch. 15 (1989). On the constitutional periods, see Bruce Ackerman, *We the People: Foundations* (1991). Ackerman understands America as having had three regimes following three distinctive constitutional "moments": the founding, the Civil War, and the New Deal. One need not agree with this claim in order to see the Civil War amendments and the New Deal as having continuing relevance for interpretation.

18. From this description it appears that the often-drawn opposition between liberalism and republicanism is, in the American tradition, a large mistake. The opposition tends to caricature both traditions. It sees liberalism as committed to interest-group pluralism or the protection of given private rights—a conception of liberalism rejected by nearly all important liberal thinkers, including Constant, Kant, Rawls, Madison, Mill, and Dewey. The opposition also treats republicanism as if it were committed to a rejection of rights entirely. It should be clear that ideas of this sort are unsuitable to modern democracy. The American tradition does not separate its liberalism from its republicanism.

19. See John Dewey, *The Public and Its Problems* 207–208 (1927). See also Hurley, *Natural Reasons* ch. 15.

20. See Gordon Wood, *The Radicalism of the American Revolution* 178–181, 234 (1992).

21. This is a familiar theme in the liberal tradition. See John Rawls, *A Theory of Justice* (1971); Habermas, *The Philosophical Logic of Modernity;* T. M. Scanlon, "Contractarianism and Utilitarianism," in *Utilitarianism and Beyond* (Amartya Sen & Bernard Williams eds 1982). Of course there are constitutional limits on what citizens may decide. In a constitutional system, however, these limits are themselves set down in advance by the citizenry. See Bruce Ackerman, "Constitutional Politics/Constitutional Law," 99 *Yale L. J.* 453 (1989) (criticizing "rights foundationalists" in their understanding of American constitutionalism). It is also true that genuine consensus will sometimes be impossible to achieve.

22. *The Federalist* No. 39 at 241 (J. Madison) (1961).

23. The inconsistency between egalitarianism and liberty is a major theme of *The Federalist* No. 10.

24. See Amartya Sen, *Commodities and Capabilities* (1985); Martha Nussbaum, "Aristotelian Social Democracy," in *Liberalism and the Good* 203 (R. Bruce Douglas, Gerald M. Mara, & Henry S. Richardson eds. 1990). Experimental evidence showing a significant effect of discussion on the content of preferences is offered in Norman Frohlich & Joe A. Oppenheimer, *Choosing Justice: An Experimental Approach to Ethical Theory* ch. 7 (1992).

25. Thomas Jefferson, 8 *The Papers of Thomas Jefferson* 681–682 (1953) (emphasis added).

26. James Madison, 14 *The Papers of James Madison* 197–198 (1983). This is a familiar theme in liberal thought. Thus Montesquieu wrote, in a passage that the American founders would have found familiar: "The riches of the state suppose great industry. Amidst the numerous branches of trade it is impossible but that some must suffer, and consequently the mechanics must be in a momentary necessity. . . . When this happens, the state is obliged to lend them a ready assistance, whether it be to prevent the suffering of the people, or to avoid a rebellion." Montesquieu, *The Spirit of the Laws,* vol. 2 at 26 (1949; originally published 1748). Mill wrote in a similar vein: "Apart from any metaphysical considerations respecting the foundation of morals or of the social union, it will be admitted to

be right that human beings should help one another; and the more so, in proportion to the urgency of the need: and none needs help so urgently as one who is
starving. The claim to help, therefore, created by destitution, is one of the strongest which can exist; and there is prima facie the amplest reason for making the
relief of so extreme an exigency as certain to those who require it, as by any
arrangements of society it can be made." J. S. Mill, *Principles of Political Economy* 468 (1899). The liberal view on the provision of welfare is well discussed in
Stephen Holmes, "The Paradox of Democracy" ch. 9 (unpublished manuscript
1992).

27. See Louis Hartz, *The Liberal Tradition in America* 3–32 (1960).

28. See Wood, *The Radicalism of the American Revolution* 233–238.

29. 411 U.S. 1 (1973).

30. See, e.g., Jonathan Riley, *Liberal Utilitarianism* (1988).

31. See the references in Chapter 6, note 28.

32. See Habermas, *The Philosophical Logic of Modernity*.

33. See J. S. Mill, *Considerations on Representative Government* (C. V. Shields
ed. 1861); John Rawls, "Kantian Constructivism in Moral Theory," 77 *J. Phil.*
515, 539, 538 (1980).

34. See, e.g., Jennifer Nedelsky, *Private Property and American Constitutionalism* (1990).

35. See Ronald Dworkin, *Law's Empire* 364 (1986), for a similar rejection of
the view that democracy entails a passive judicial role. Dworkin's powerful and
lucid account has influenced mine. That account does, however, pose several difficulties, and it will be useful to outline them here.

1. Dworkin's argument against judicial "passivism" seems too flat. On his
view, the passivist must "contend that over the long run legislatures are more
likely to develop a sounder theory of what rights justice does require than courts trying
to interpret the vague language of abstract constitutional provisions" (id. at
375). But the passivist might instead rely on the view that representative self-
government is an independent good or a part of the set of rights that people have,
and that its outcomes are therefore to be respected even if judges are apt to develop a sounder theory of rights. A full theory of judicial review should take into
account the potential independent values of representative government. In this
way, it will incorporate a good deal of the passivist creed. (A form of passivism is
defended later in this chapter and in Chapter 11.)

2. In his defense of a judicial role, Dworkin relies heavily on the view that we
have no reason to think that judges are "less competent political theorists than
state legislators or attorneys general." But on the question of competence as theorists, we have no decisive evidence from either theory or practice. The passivists'
failure to establish the comparative incompetence of the judges is hardly a weakness of the passivist approach, which might well rest on the very inconclusiveness
of the issue. A rejection of passivism cannot easily be defended on the ground that
this debate has not been concluded.

3. Dworkin's general approach—including his attack on use of the original understanding—does not address the various institutional deficiencies of the judiciary. Our account of what judges should do must be attentive to these deficiencies. These include the fact that the judiciary is composed of lawyers coming from a particular, narrow segment of society; the judges' lack of good fact-finding tools; their insulation from relevant groups and relevant events; their concentration on the details of particular cases; and their inability to process the systemic effects of their decisions. Dworkin rightly points to difficulties in our actual democratic practices, both in terms of their connection with democracy, properly conceived, and in terms of the limited capacity of those in such processes to deliberate on issues of principle. But this is only one side of the picture. It is vital to address the comparative deficiencies of the courts.

4. The principles Dworkin brings to bear on interpretation seem excessively free-floating. See, in particular, the discussion of race discrimination, where the relevant principles appear drawn from moral theory in the abstract and are set forth without attention to the history behind the Civil War amendments, and without engagement with the particular American conception of the evils of slavery and its aftermath. Id. at 381–387. Dworkin offers no clear sense of the role, in disputed cases, of history or of the major structural transformations in American history. I attempt here, by contrast, to root interpretive principles in the concrete constitutional commitment to deliberative democracy, and to explain how that commitment derives its content and its appeal from both history and independent political justifications. In the context of race discrimination, the relevant principle, a subpart of the general commitment, is an opposition to caste—a principle directly traceable to and emerging from close engagement with the Civil War amendments and, again, with considerable independent appeal.

36. See Cass R. Sunstein, "Constitutionalism, Prosperity, Democracy: Transition in Eastern Europe," 5 Constitutional Political Economy 450 (1991).

37. J. H. Ely, Democracy and Distrust (1980).

38. The common view that the Court's decisions helped to mobilize political actors and protest or to pave the way for King appears to have little empirical support. See Gerald Rosenberg, The Hollow Hope (1991).

39. See Ronald Dworkin, A Matter of Principle (1985).

40. See, e.g., Alexander Bickel, The Least Dangerous Branch (1958); Michael Perry, The Constitution, the Courts, and Human Rights (1982); Dworkin, A Matter of Principle.

41. See Donald Horowitz, The Courts and Social Policy (1977); R. S. Melnick, Regulation and the Court: The Case of the Clean Air Act (1983); Rosenberg, The Hollow Hope.

42. See Rosenberg, The Hollow Hope, on which I draw heavily for the discussion of Brown and Roe.

43. Id.

44. Webster v. Reproductive Services, 109 S.Ct. 3040 (1989).

45. See Eric Schnapper, "Affirmative Action and the Legislative History of the Fourteenth Amendment," 71 *Va. L. Rev.* 753 (1985).

46. See Shelby Steele, *The Content of Character* (1990); Stephen Carter, *Reflections of an Affirmative Action Baby* (1991).

47. See Richard Epstein, *Takings* (1985).

48. Lassiter v. Northampton Election Bd., 360 U.S. 45 (1959).

49. 384 U.S. 641 (1966). Helpful discussion of the points discussed in the text, from which I have benefited greatly, are Laurence Tribe, *American Constitutional Law* (2d ed. 1988); Laurence Sager, "Fair Measure: The Legal Status of Under-enforced Constitutional Norms," 91 *Harv. L. Rev.* 1212 (1978).

50. 449 U.S.

51. See Richard Stewart, "Madison's Nightmare," 57 *U. Chi. L. Rev.* 335 (1990).

52. For helpful related discussion, see Laurence Tribe, *Constitutional Choices* ch. 16 (1985); Paul Brest, "State Action and Liberal Theory," 30 *Stan. L. Rev.* 1296 (1982).

6. Democracy, Aspirations, Preferences

1. See the endorsement of "[t]he principle that, in deciding what is good and what is bad for a given individual, the ultimate criterion can only be his own wants and his own preferences." John C. Harsanyi, "Morality and the Theory of Rational Behavior," in *Utilitarianism and Beyond* 39, 55 (Amartya K. Sen & Bernard Williams eds. 1982). David Gauthier, *Morals by Agreement* (1986), contains arguments in this direction; for a representative example at the intersection of economics and law, see Richard Posner, *The Economics of Justice* 53 (1983).

It is notable that the great expositors of liberalism in the nineteenth and twentieth centuries are emphatic in their rejection of the view that existing preferences should be taken as given, for purposes of ethics or politics. See J. S. Mill, *Considerations on Representative Government* (1861) and *The Subjection of Women* (1869); John Rawls, *A Theory of Justice* (1971). Mill repudiates that view in his essay on Bentham, in which he criticizes Bentham for the view that "[t]o say either that man should, or that he should not, take pleasure in one thing, displeasure in another, appeared to him as much an act of despotism in the moralist as in the political ruler." Mill, by contrast, emphasized the need to explore the influences "on the regulation of . . . affections and desires" and pointed to "the deficiencies of a system of ethics which does not pretend to aid individuals in the formation of their own character." *Mill on Bentham and Coleridge* 68, 71, 70 (1950). Of course there is a difference between what a system of ethics and what a system of politics should say about that question, as Mill clearly believed. See also John Rawls, "Justice as Fairness," 68 *Phil. Rev.* 164, 166–177, 186–187, 192 (1958) (rejecting view that preferences "have value as such" and that preference-satisfaction is an adequate conception of justice); sources cited in note 27.

John Dewey spoke in similar terms, invoking the need for critical reflection on the "conditions under which objects are enjoyed" and "the consequences of esteeming and liking them," and arguing that *"judgments about values are judgments about that which should regulate the formation of our desires, affections and enjoyments."* John Dewey, *The Quest for Certainty: A Study of the Relation of Knowledge and Action* 259, 265, 272–273 (1929).

2. The basic idea appears in J. H. Ely, *Democracy and Distrust* (1980), and Robert Bork, *The Tempting of America* (1989).

3. See Kenneth Arrow, *Social Choice and Individual Values* (1963); Brian Barry & Russell Hardin, *Rational Man and Irrational Society?* (1982). Some of the problems with this approach for the theory of democracy are taken up in S. L. Hurley, *Natural Persons* (1989).

4. See Chapter 1; Gordon Wood, *The Radicalism of the American Revolution* (1992).

5. John Dewey, *The Philosophy of John Dewey* 597 (John McDermott ed. 1981); idem, *The Public and Its Problems* 103–104 (1927).

6. 3 M. Farrand, *Records of the Federal Convention of 1787* 479 (1911).

7. For a good collection, see *Interpersonal Comparisons of Well-Being* (Jon Elster & John Roemer eds. 1991).

8. For an early work in this vein, see David Mayhew, *Congress: The Electoral Connection* (1974); a more complex account can be found in R. D. Arnold, *The Logic of Congressional Action* (1990).

9. See Robert Ellickson, *Order without Law* (1991).

10. It was first so called in Richard Thaler, "Toward a Positive Theory of Consumer Choice," 1 *J. Econ. Behavior and Org.* 39 (1980). This essay, along with others of similar interest, can be found in Richard Thaler, *Quasi-Rational Economics* (1990).

11. Daniel Kahneman, Jack Knetch, & Richard Thaler, "Experimental Tests of the Endowment Effect and the Coase Theorem," 98 *J. Pol. Econ.* 1325 (1990). See also Jack Knetch, "The Endowment Effect and Evidence of Nonreversible Indifference Curves," 79 *Am. Econ. Rev.* 1277 (1989); Jack Knetch & Lawrence Sinden, "Willingness to Pay and Compensation Demanded: Experimental Evidence of an Unexpected Disparity in Measures of Value," *Q. J. Econ.* 507 (1984).

12. Knetch, "The Endowment Effect."

13. Dan Brookshire & Don Coursey, "Measuring the Value of a Public Good: An Empirical Comparison of Elicitation Procedures," 77 *Am. Econ. Rev.* 554 (1987); John Hammock & George Brown, *Waterfowl and Wetlands: Toward Bioeconomic Analysis* (1974); Robert Rowe, Ralph d'Arge, & Dan Brookshire, "An Experiment on the Economic Value of Visibility," 7 *J. Env. Ec. and Management* 1 (1980); Thaler, "Toward a Positive Theory of Consumer Choice."

14. A related survey showed similarly large status quo biases in willingness to pay for changes in risks. Thus only 39 percent of respondents would accept $700 to have their chance of a serious accident increased by 0.5 percent (from 0.5

percent to 1.0 percent). By contrast, only 27 percent would trade an identical decrease in accident risk (from 1 percent to 0.5 percent) for $700. In another study, people were willing to pay $3.78 on average to decrease the risk from an insecticide, but 77 percent refused to buy the product at any price, however reduced, if the risk level would increase by an equivalent amount. W. Kip Viscusi, Wesley Magat, & Peter Huber, "An Investigation of the Rationality of Consumer Valuations of Multiple Health Risks," 18 *RAND Journal of Economics* 465 (1987).

15. Such effects may come from experience; people who use a product or have an entitlement may learn to appreciate its value. The effects may be a product of strategic considerations; someone may be unwilling to give up a right because the concession would reveal weakness in bargaining. Sometimes endowment effects might be produced by the wealth effect of the initial allocation of the entitlement. Different allocations produce differences in wealth—someone with more entitlements is to that extent richer—and perhaps some allocations have wealth effects sufficiently large to affect the point to which people will bargain. Or such effects might derive from what we might call "anticipated after-the-fact regret." People who trade one good for another may fear that in the event of disappointment, they will be left not only with a good of uncertain value, but also with a feeling of responsibility for that very fact. Notably, some of these explanations do not depend on real preference change at all. They account for endowment effects while holding preferences constant. But these sorts of explanations do not appear sufficient.

16. See Daniel Kahneman, Jack Knetch, & Richard Thaler, "Fairness and the Assumptions of Economics," in *Rational Choice: The Contrast between Economics and Psychology* (1987), p. 101, esp. at pp. 113–114.

17. See, e.g., Roger Noll & James Krier, "Some Implications of Cognitive Psychology for Risk Regulation," 19 *J. Legal Stud.* 747 (1990).

18. See Shelley Taylor, *Positive Illusions* (1989).

19. See Ronald Coase, "The Problem of Social Cost," 3 *J. L. & E.* 1 (1960).

20. Richard Posner, *Economic Analysis of Law* (3d ed. 1986), contains many examples.

21. See Cass R. Sunstein, *After the Rights Revolution* (1990).

22. The endowment effect is not the only phenomenon that casts doubt on expected utility theory, that is, the view that people's decisions and desires are a product of rational efforts to maximize their utility. See Daniel Kahneman, Paul Slovic, & Amos Twersky, *Judgment under Uncertainty: Heuristics and Biases* (1982). It has been shown that people tend to assess probabilities by reference to certain heuristics, or rules of thumb, and that these heuristics produce predictable errors. It is highly likely that these heuristics help to explain government outcomes and political behavior. For example, people tend to think that the probability of an event increases as it becomes more "available" to them, in the sense that its occurrence comes readily to mind. Views about probabilities are for this

reason endogenous to the availability to the relevant groups of similar events. We might predict that regulation would be systemically affected by this heuristic. Regulation of highly visible risks—such as a nuclear power disaster—would therefore be more stringent than regulation of less visible events, such as increases in atmospheric ozone. Political actors might attempt to exploit the availability heuristic by attempting to keep certain events in the minds of the citizenry. The use of disasters as a device for mobilizing people is thus a familiar part of political debate. In the environmental area, shorthand phrases—Love Canal, Chernobyl, Three Mile Island, and so forth—are actively manipulated by those who seek aggressive regulatory controls.

A related phenomenon is that people tend to judge policies by reference to the traceability of their connection with real-world events. See Arnold, *The Logic of Congressional Action*. We might understand in these terms the government's failure to raise gasoline taxes in order to prevent environmental degradation. Command-and-control regulation, such as emissions limits for new cars or mileage requirements, tends to be both less efficient and less effective than gasoline taxes as a method of reducing automotive pollution. But it is simple for people to see the connection between emissions limits and environmental policy. The causal link between gasoline taxes and pollution reduction is more complex. It seems clear that the difference helps to explain the selection of unsatisfactory environmental policies.

23. See Jean Hampton, "Expected Utility Theory" (unpublished manuscript 1992), on which I draw for the discussion in this and the following paragraphs. A similar point is made in Donald Davidson, "Judging Interpersonal Interests," in *Foundations of Social Choice Theory* 195 (Jon Elster & Aanund Hylland eds. 1986); S. L. Hurley, *Natural Reasons* 121 (1989). See also Elizabeth Anderson, "Some Problems in the Normative Theory of Rational Choice" (unpublished manuscript 1992). On the impossibility of justifying social or legal systems by reference to preferences that they have produced, see Jon Elster, *Sour Grapes* 109–140 (1983); Rawls, *A Theory of Justice* 136–142, 251–257.

24. For a modern utilitarian account along these lines, see Richard Brandt, *A Theory of the Good and the Right* (1979). For a neo-Aristotelian view, see Amartya Sen, "Well-Being, Agency, and Freedom," 82 *J. Phil.* 169–221 (1985); idem, *Commodities and Capabilities* (1985); idem, *Inequality Reexamined* (1992).

25. See Amartya Sen, *The Standard of Living: Tanner Lectures on Lectures on Human Values, 1985* (G. Hawthorne ed. 1987). On various conceptions of welfare, see generally James Griffin, *Well-Being: Its Meaning, Measurement and Moral Significance* (1986).

26. See Chapter 5.

27. John Rawls, "Kantian Constructivism in Moral Theory," 77 *J. Phil.* 515, 539, 538 (1980). See also idem, "The Basic Structure as Subject," 14 *Am. Phil. Q.* 159, 160 (1977): "Consider the situation of individuals engaged in market transactions. We have seen that certain background conditions are necessary for

these transactions to be fair. But what about the nature of individuals themselves: how did they get to be what they are? A theory of justice cannot take their final aims and interests, their attitudes to themselves and their life, as given. Everyone recognizes that the form of society affects its members and determines in large part the kind of persons they want to be as well as the kind of persons they are. It also limits people's ambitions and hopes in different ways, for they will with reason view themselves in part according to their place in it and take account of the means and opportunities they can realistically expect. Thus an economic regime is not only an institutional scheme for satisfying existing desires and aspirations but a way of fashioning desires and aspirations in the future." To say that preferences can be endogenous is not, of course, to say that they are mere whim or fancy, or highly malleable. Some preferences are in fact relatively stable even if they are a function of legal rules, social pressures, or existing institutions. A high degree of stability, and great resistance to change, will counsel against efforts at changing preferences, certainly on welfare grounds, and perhaps on autonomy grounds as well (though stable preferences may be nonautonomous, as in the case of rigid adaptations to an unjust status quo). In the face of extremely stable preferences, democratic efforts at change will breed resentment and frustration on the part of its objects. But my claim here is that this is simply a subcategory of preferences, and does not capture a general truth.

28. John Dewey, "The Future of Liberalism," in *Dewey and His Critics* 695, 697 (Sidney Morgenbesser ed. 1977); idem, "Philosophies of Freedom," in *Freedom in the Modern World* 243 (H. Kallen ed. 1936). This theme appears throughout Dewey's work. John Dewey, *Freedom and Culture* 108 (1989): "The assumption that desires are rigidly fixed is not one on its face consistent with the history of man's progress from savagery through barbarism to even the present defective state of civilization"; id. at 22: "A certain complex culture stimulates, promotes, and consolidates native tendencies so as to produce a certain pattern of desires and purposes"; "The idea of a natural individual in his isolation possessed of full-fledged wants, of energies to be expended according to his own volition, and of a ready-made faculty of foresight and calculation is as much a fiction in psychology as the doctrine of the individual in possession of antecedent political rights is one in politics." Dewey, *The Public and Its Problems* 102.

See also Dewey, *The Quest for Certainty* 258–259, stating that his "objection is that the theory in question holds down value to objects antecedently enjoyed, apart from reference to the method by which they come into existence; it takes enjoyments which are causal because unregulated by intelligent operations to be values in and of themselves. The suggestion almost imperatively follows that escape from the defects of transcendental absolutism is not to be had by setting up as values enjoyments that happen anyhow, but in defining value by enjoyments which are the consequence of intelligent action. Without the intervention of thought, enjoyments are not values but problematic goods, becoming values when they re-issue in a changed form from intelligent behavior. The fundamental problem with the current empirical theory of values is that it merely formulates and justifies the socially prevailing habit of regarding enjoyments as they are actually experienced as values in and of themselves. It completely side-steps the question of regulation of these enjoyments. This issue involves nothing less than the problem of the directed reconstruction of economic, political and religious institutions."

29. See Sen, *Commodities and Capabilities* 82.

30. See Wood, *The Radicalism of the American Revolution.*

31. See id. at 232–243 (quoting Byrd and Rush).

32. See Mill, *Considerations on Representative Government.*

33. See Dewey, *The Quest for Certainty* 260. "In justifying our actions and our requests to one another we normally make our case by explaining why it is that we want a certain thing rather than merely by citing the fact that we do prefer it and indicating the strength of that preference. In a situation in which there is real disagreement over what is to be done, to be willing to say only, 'I prefer . . .' amounts to deliberate incommunicativeness or even imperiousness." See also T. M. Scanlon, "The Moral Basis of Interpersonal Comparisons," in Elster & Roemer, *Interpersonal Comparisons of Well-Being* 17, 37.

34. See Howard Margolis, *Selfishness, Altruism, and Rationality: A Theory of Social Choice* (1982); John Orbell, Alphons von de Fragt, & Robyn Dawes, "Explaining Discussion-Indexed Cooperation," 54 *Journal of Personality and Social Psychology* 811 (1988). See also the interesting empirical finding of cross-national judgments in favor of provision of decent minimal welfare guarantees in Norman Frohlich & Joe A. Oppenheimer, *Choosing Justice: An Experimental Approach to Ethical Theory* ch. 4 (1992).

35. For helpful discussion, see Jon Elster, *The Cement of Society* (1989).

36. See Charles Taylor, "The Diversity of Goods," in *Philosophy and the Human Sciences* 230, 243 (1985); Amartya K. Sen, "Plural Utility," 81 *Proceedings of the Aristotelian Society* 193 (1981); Elizabeth Anderson, "Values, Risks, and Markets Norms," 17 *Phil. & Pub. Aff.* 54, 57–59 (1987); Martha Nussbaum, "Plato on Commensurability and Desire," in *Love's Knowledge* (1991). Cf. Margaret Jane Radin, "Market Inalienability," 100 *Harv. L. Rev.* 1849 (1987).

37. This is the approach in Rawls, *A Theory of Justice* 395–399.

38. This is the approach in Sen, *Commodities and Capabilities;* Scanlon, "The Moral Basis of Interpersonal Comparisons"; Martha Nussbaum, "Aristotelian Social Democracy," in *Liberalism and the Good* 203 (R. Bruce Douglas, Gerald M. Mara, & Henry S. Richardson eds. 1990).

39. See Joshua Cohen, "Deliberation and Democratic Legitimacy," in *The Good Polity: Normative Analysis of the State* 27–34 (Alan Hamlin & Philip Pettit eds. 1989).

40. See Wood, *The Radicalism of the American Revolution* 190–191.

41. Dewey, *The Philosophy of John Dewey* 645; J. S. Mill, "Inaugural Address at the University of St. Andrews," in *John Stuart Mill on Education* 153–154 (William Garforth ed. 1971).

42. See citations in note 5 above.

43. Jon Elster, *Sour Grapes* (1983).

44. Ed. C. Poston (New York: Norton, 1975; originally published 1792) at 43. Similar points are made in Mill, *The Subjection of Women*, as against the claim that the existing desires of women are a product of consent.

45. "Should I call it a blessing of God, or a last malediction of his anger, this disposition of the soul that makes men insensible to extreme misery and often gives them a sort of depraved taste for the cause of their afflictions? Plunged in this abyss of wretchedness, the Negro hardly notices his ill fortune; he was reduced to slavery by violence, and the habit of servitude has given him the thoughts and ambitions of a slave; he admires his tyrants even more than he hates them and finds his joy and pride in servile imitation of his oppressors." Alexis de Tocqueville, *Democracy in America* 317 (1987). On cognitive dissonance, see Leon Festinger, *A Theory of Cognitive Dissonance* (1957); on some of its implications for social theory, welfare, and autonomy, see Elster, *Sour Grapes*.

Consider also the discussion of women's illiteracy in Bangladesh in Nussbaum, "Aristotelian Social Democracy." Drawing on Martha Chen, *A Quiet Revolution: Women in Transition in Rural Bangladesh* (1983), Nussbaum explores the fact that many women in Bangladesh did not demand or even want greater education or literacy, and indeed expressed satisfaction with their current educational status. Of course desires of this sort were a product of a lack of available opportunities and of social and cultural pressures.

46. See Melvin Lerner, *The Belief in a Just World: A Fundamental Delusion* (1980).

47. Rubin and Pepau, "Belief in a Just World and Reaction to Another's Lot," 29 *Journal of Social Issues* 73–93 (1973).

48. See Lerner, *Belief in a Just World*.

49. See Green v. County School Bd., 391 U.S. 430 (1968); Paul Gewirtz, "Choice in the Transition," 86 *Colum. L. Rev.* 728–798 (1986).

50. See George Akerlof & William Dickens, "The Economic Consequences of Cognitive Dissonance," 72 *Am. Econ. Rev.* 307–318 (1982).

51. See John Dewey & J. Tufts, *Ethics* 386 (rev. ed. 1936). See also Hilary Putnam, "A Reconsideration of Deweyan Democracy," 63 *So. Cal. L. Rev.* 1671, 1674–88 (1990); Nussbaum, "Princess Cassamassima and the Political Imagination," in *Love's Knowledge*.

52. See Eckstein, "Rationality and Frustration in Political Behavior," in *Economic Analysis of Politics* (K. Monroe ed. 1991). I do not, however, endorse Eckstein's suggestion that an absence of goals is an accurate description of the behavior of poor people; instead their goals may be scaled back so dramatically that they seem absent to those accustomed to think that people naturally seek more.

53. Menachem Yaari, "Endogenous Changes in Tastes: A Philosophical Discussion," in *Decision Theory and Social Ethics: Issues in Social Choice* 59–98 (1978).

54. Thomas Schelling, "Egonomics, or the Art of Self-Management," 68 *Am. Econ. Rev.* 290–294 (Papers and Proceedings) (1978); Jon Elster, "Weakness of Will and the Free-Rider Problem," 1 *Economics & Philosophy* 231–265 (1985).

55. Of course all consumption has an effect on preferences. For example, exposure to classical music usually increases appreciation. But the pattern under discussion is a rare one; it is that pattern, producing miserable lives, to which a democracy might respond. To be sure, in practice the response might make things worse rather than better.

56. See Robert Goodin, *No Smoking: The Ethical Issues* (1989).

7. Speech in the Welfare State: A New Deal for Speech

1. Indeed, the protection of free speech may have been originally thought principally to confer a ban against "prior restraints"—licensing systems and other means of requiring prepublication permission from government. See Leonard Levy, *The Emergence of a Free Press* 272–274 (1985). On this view, subsequent punishment for speech usually raises no constitutional problem at all.

Even if this extreme view is incorrect, it seems clear that during the founding period, much of what we now consider "speech" was thought to be unprotected, and that speech could be regulated if it could be shown to be dangerous. See Joseph Story, *A Familiar Exposition of the Constitution of the United States* §§ 445–457 at 316–318 (1986). In any case it is highly revealing that in the founding period the infamous Sedition Act—making it a crime to libel "the government," and in that sense criminalizing a wide range of criticism of government—was generally thought constitutional. See Philip Kurland & Ralph Lerner, 5 *The Founders' Constitution* 112–185 (1987).

2. James Madison, "Report on the Virginia Resolution," Jan. 1800, in 6 *Writings of James Madison* 385–401 (Caillard Hunt ed. 1906).

3. Geoffrey Tooth, "Why Children's TV Turns Off So Many Parents," *U.S. News and World Report*, February 18, 1985, p. 65.

4. Statement on the Children's Television Act of 1990, Government Printing Office 26, no. 2 *Weekly Compilation of Presidential Documents* 1611 (Oct. 17, 1990).

5. Some of this is stated in Robert Bork, "Neutral Principles and Some First Amendment Problems," 47 *Ind. L. J.* 1, 21–22 (1971).

6. Content-neutral restrictions are subject to a form of balancing. See generally Geoffrey R. Stone, "Content-Neutral Restrictions," 54 *U. Chi. L. Rev.* 46, 48–50 (1987).

7. Virginia State Bd. of Pharmacy v. Virginia Citizens Consumer Council, 425 U.S. 748, 770 (1976) (commercial speech); New York Times v. Sullivan, 376 U.S. 254, 265–266 (1964) (libel); Cox Broadcasting Corp. v. Cohn, 420 U.S. 469 (1975) (names of rape victims); Brandenburg v. Ohio, 395 U.S. 444, 447–448 (1969) (advocacy of illegality); Buckley v. Valeo, 424 U.S. 1, 22–23 (1976) (cam-

paign expenditures); First National Bank of Boston v. Bellotti, 435 U.S. 765, 776 (1978) (corporate speech).

8. See Valentine v. Christensen, 341 U.S. 52, 54–55 (1942).

9. Something of this general sort is suggested in Onora O'Neill, "Practices of Toleration," in *Democracy and the Mass Media* 155 (Judith Lichtenberg ed. 1990); T. M. Scanlon, "Content Regulation Reconsidered," in id. at 331; Owen Fiss, "Free Speech and Social Structure," 71 *Iowa L. Rev.* 1405 (1986); idem, "Why the State?" 100 *Harv. L. Rev.* 781 (1987); J. M. Balkin, "Some Realism about Pluralism," 1990 *Duke L. J.* 375.

Many of the concerns expressed here were set out long ago in Commission on Freedom of the Press, *A Free and Responsible Press* (1947). That commission, headed by Robert Hutchins and Zechariah Chafee, included among its members John Dickinson, Harold Lasswell, Archibald MacLeish, Charles Merriam, Reinhold Niebuhr, and Arthur Schlesinger. It did not recommend legal remedies for the current situation, but it suggested the need for private measures to control novel problems. "The press has been transformed into an enormous and complicated piece of machinery. As a necessary accompaniment, it has become big business. . . . The right of free public expression has therefore lost its earlier reality. Protection against government is now not enough to guarantee that a man who has something to say shall have a chance to say it. The owners and managers of the press determine which persons, which facts, which versions of the facts, and which ideas shall reach the public." Id. at 15–16.

10. Robert Hale, "Force and the State," 36 *Colum. L. Rev.* 149, 197 (1935).

11. 376 U.S. 254 (1964).

12. See Alexander Meiklejohn, *Free Speech and Its Relation to Self-Government* 14–19 (1948). The link is made explicitly in William J. Brennan, "The Supreme Court and the Meiklejohn Interpretation of the First Amendment," 79 *Harv. L. Rev.* 1 (1965).

13. New York Times v. Sullivan, 273 Ala. 656, 144 So. 2d 25 (1962). Unlike most cases in which First Amendment objections have been raised, in *Sullivan* the government was not a party. But to see this fact as meaning that there is no state action is simply another version of the problem discussed in the text.

14. 376 U.S. at 265.

15. It is sometimes so argued. See David A. Strauss, "Persuasion, Autonomy, and Freedom of Expression," 91 *Colum. L. Rev.* 334, 361–368 (1991).

16. Lloyd Corp. v. Tanner, 407 U.S. 551, 570 (1972); Hudgens v. NLRB, 424 U.S. 507, 519–521 (1976).

17. Columbia Broadcasting v. Democratic National Committee, 412 U.S. 94, 114–120 (1973). There only three justices said that there was no state action. But those three justices may now represent the majority view. See Flagg Bros. v. Brooks, 436 U.S. 149, 163 (1978).

18. To say this is not to say that the distinction itself is untenable. We can understand a positive right as one that requires for its existence some act by gov-

ernment, and a negative right as one that amounts merely to an objection to some such act. There is nothing incoherent about this distinction. The argument in the text is directed against the view that an objection to rights of exclusive ownership is a call for a positive right; in fact that objection is mounted against something that government is actually doing.

19. See, e.g., Kunz v. New York, 340 U.S. 290, 294–295 (1951); Edwards v. South Carolina, 372 U.S. 229, 231–233 (1963); Cox v. Louisiana, 379 U.S. 536, 550 (1965); Gregory v. City of Chicago, 394 U.S. 111, 111–112 (1969). See also Scanlon, "Content Regulation Reconsidered" at 338–339; and Fiss, "Free Speech and Social Structure," both discussing this point.

20. A qualification is necessary here. To decide whether there is a subsidy, one always needs a baseline. To see reputation as part of the initial set of endowments is to proceed under the common law baseline; and the social contract version of this idea (the state must protect certain rights in return for the decision of citizens to leave the state of nature) might support it. But it would of course be possible to say that on the right theory, people do not have such a right to reputation, and that therefore no subsidy is involved in the libel cases.

21. Red Lion Broadcasting Co. v. F.C.C., 395 U.S. 367 (1969).

22. See Robert Entman, *Democracy without Citizens* 104–106 (1989).

23. 295 U.S. at 375, 392, 289, 390 (citations omitted, including a reference to the Brennan article referred to earlier). See also Commission on Freedom of the Press, *A Free and Responsible Press* at 18: "To protect the press is no longer automatically to protect the citizen or the community. The freedom of the press can remain a right of those who publish only if it incorporates into itself the right of the citizen and the public interest."

24. Mark Fowler, former chairman of the Federal Communications Commission, quoted in Bernard D. Nossiter, "The FCC's Big Giveaway Show," *The Nation,* October 26, 1985, p. 402.

25. The key decision is Syracuse Peace Council, 2 F.C.C.R. 5043, 5055 (1987). See also L. S. Powe, *American Broadcasting and the First Amendment* (1987).

26. Phyllis Kaniss, *Making Local News* 110 (1991), on which I draw for the material in this paragraph and the next.

27. See James Fishkin, *Democracy and Deliberation* 63 (1991).

28. J. Max Robins, "Nets' Newscasts Increase Coverage of Entertainment," *Variety,* July 18, 1990, pp. 3, 63.

29. "Consumer News Blues," *Newsweek,* May 20, 1991, p. 48.

30. "Advertisers Drop Program on Logging," *New York Times,* Sept. 23, 1989.

31. Verne Gay, "NBC v. Sponsors v. Wildman RE: Telepic 'Roe v. Wade,'" *Variety* May 10, 1989, p. 71.

32. Statements of Bruce Christensen, president of the National Association of Public Television Stations, before the Hearing on Children and Television, 98th Cong, 1st sess. 36–37 (March 16, 1983).

33. See Tom Engelhardt, "The Shortcake Strategy," in *Watching Television*

(Todd Gitlin ed. 1986). See generally Amy Gutmann, *Democratic Education* 241–244 (1987), on the subject of children's television.

34. See George Gerbner & Nancy Signorielli, "Violence Profile 1967 through 1988–89: Enduring Patterns," 117 *Broadcasting* 97 (Dec. 4, 1989).

35. See Jerome Singer, Dorothy Singer, & Wanda Rapaczynski, "Family Patterns and Television Viewing as Predictors of Children's Beliefs and Aggression," 34 *J. of Communication* 73, 87–88 (1984).

36. Lana Rakow & Phyllis Kimberlie, "Women as Signs in Television News," 42 *J. of Communication* 8 (1991). Concerns about social stereotyping in the mass media were set out long ago in Commission on Freedom of the Press, *A Free and Responsible Press* at 26–27.

37. J. Lemon, "Women and Blacks on Prime-Time Television," 27 *J. of Communication* 70, 73 (1977).

38. Katha Pollitt, "The Smurfette Principle," *New York Times,* April 7, 1991, sec. 6, p. 22, col. 3.

39. John Corry, "Children's TV Found Dominated by White Men," *New York Times,* July 15, 1982, sec. C, p. 14, col. 4.

40. See Daniel Farber, "Free Speech without Romance: Public Choice and the First Amendment," 105 *Harv. L. Rev.* 554, 558–562 (1991). Information is not a pure public good, for it is often feasible to provide it only to those who pay for it, and copyright and patent laws can guarantee appropriate incentives for its production. But it does have much in common with pure public goods.

41. It might be thought that the distinctive characteristics of the broadcasting market provide at least a partial solution. Because advertisers attempt to ensure a large audience, viewers are commodities as well as or instead of consumers. In these circumstances, it is not as if individual people are purchasing individual pieces of information. Instead, advertisers are aggregating individual preferences in seeking popular programming and, in that sense, helping to overcome the collective action problem.

The problem with this response is that the advertisers' desire to attract large audiences does not adequately serve the goal of overcoming the public good problem with respect to information about public affairs. A program with a large audience may not be providing information at all; consider most of network television. As we have seen, advertisers may even be hostile to providing the relevant information. Their economic interests often argue against sponsorship of public-service or controversial programming, especially if the audience is relatively small, but sometimes even if it is large. The external benefits of widely diffused information about politics are thus not captured in a broadcasting market. The peculiarities of the broadcasting market do overcome a kind of collective action problem, by providing a system for aggregating preferences; but they do not overcome the crucial difficulty.

42. See Cass R. Sunstein, *After the Rights Revolution* (1990); David Osborne & Ted Gaebler, *Reinventing Government* (1992).

43. Consider Meiklejohn, *Free Speech and Self-Government* at 16–17: "Con-

gress is not debarred from all action upon freedom of speech. Legislation which abridges that freedom is forbidden, but not legislation to enlarge and enrich it. The freedom of mind which befits the members of a self-governing society is not a given and fixed part of human nature. It can be increased and established by learning, by teaching, by the unhindered flow of accurate information, by giving men health and vigor and security, by bringing them together in activities of communication and mutual understanding. And the federal legislature is not forbidden to engage in that positive enterprise of cultivating the general intelligence upon which the success of self-government so obviously depends. On the contrary, in that positive field the Congress of the United States has a heavy and basic responsibility to promote the freedom of speech."

44. 198 U.S. 45, 53 (1905).

45. Consider John Rawls, "Basic Liberties and Their Priority," in 3 *The Tanner Lectures on Human Values* 76 (S. McMurrin ed. 1982): "[T]he Court fails to recognize the essential point that the fair-value of the political liberties is required for a just political procedure, and that to insure their fair-value it is necessary to prevent those with greater property and wealth, and the greater skills of organization which accompany them, from controlling the electoral process to their advantage. . . . On this view, democracy is a kind of regulated rivalry between economic classes and interest groups in which the outcome should properly depend on the ability and willingness of each to use its financial resources and skills, admittedly very unequal, to make its desires felt." See also Scanlon, "Content Regulation Reconsidered" at 349–350: "It seems clearly mistaken to say that freedom of expression never licenses government to restrict the speech of some in order to allow others a better chance to be heard."

46. See the discussion of the failure "of the commercial radio" in Meiklejohn, *Free Speech and Self-Government* at 104–105: "The radio as it now operates among us is not free. Nor is it entitled to the protection of the First Amendment. It is not engaged in the task of enlarging and enriching human communication. It is engaged in making money. And the First Amendment does not intend to guarantee men freedom to say what some private interest pays them to say for its own advantage. . . . The radio, as we now have it, is not cultivating those qualities of taste, of reasoned judgment, of integrity, of loyalty, of mutual understanding upon which the enterprise of self-government depends. On the contrary, it is a mighty force for breaking them down. It corrupts both our morals and our intelligence. And that catastrophe is significant for our inquiry, because it reveals how hollow may be the victories of the freedom of speech when our acceptance of the principle is merely formalistic. Misguided by that formalism we Americans have given to the doctrine merely its negative meaning. We have used it for the protection of private, possessive interests with which it has no concern. It is misinterpretations such as this which, in our use of the radio, the motion picture, the newspaper and other forms of publication, are giving the name 'freedoms' to the most flagrant enslavements of our minds and wills."

47. Hale, "Force and the State" at 149, 199.

48. Food Employees Local 590 v. Logan Valley Plaza, 391 U.S. 308, 324–325 (1968); Lloyd Corp. v. Tanner, 407 U.S. 551, 567–570 (1972); Hudgens v. NLRB, 424 U.S. 507, 521–523 (1976).

49. Martin v. Struthers, 319 U.S. 141, 145–149 (1943) (door to door); Schneider v. State, 308 U.S. 147, 165 (1939) (leafletting).

50. This claim casts doubt on the outcome or at least the rationale in Miami Herald Publishing Co. v. Tornillo, 418 U.S. 241, 254–258 (1974).

51. Hague v. CIO, 307 U.S. 416, 514–518 (1939) (Roberts, J., writing for a plurality); Clark v. Community for Creative Non-Violence, 468 U.S. 288, 293–299 (1984).

52. Ikscon v. Lee, 112 S.Ct. 2701, 2718 (1992) (Kennedy, J., concurring).

53. Clark v. Community for Creative Non-Violence, 468 U.S. 288 (1984). For general discussion, see Geoffrey R. Stone, "Content Regulation and the First Amendment," 25 *William & Mary L. Rev.* 189, 202, 208–209, 217–218, 227–228 (1983).

54. Widmar v. Vincent, 454 U.S. 263 (1981); U.S. Postal Service v. Council of Greenborough, 453 U.S. 114 (1981); Heffron v. Intl. Society, 452 U.S. 640 (1981).

55. Stone, "Content-Neutral Restrictions."

56. See Strauss, "Persuasion, Autonomy, and Freedom of Expression."

57. 111 S.Ct. at 1759.

58. Id. at 1772. The Court added: "To hold that the Government unconstitutionally discriminates on the basis of viewpoint when it chooses to fund a program dedicated to advancing certain permissible goals, because the program in advancing those goals necessarily discourages alternate goals, would render numerous government programs constitutionally suspect. When Congress establishes a National Endowment for Democracy, it is not required to encourage other countries to fund a program to encourage competing lines of political philosophy such as Communism and Fascism."

8. Speech in the Welfare State: The Primacy of Political Deliberation

1. Alexander Meiklejohn, *Free Speech and Its Relation to Self-Government* 94 (1948): "The guarantee given by the First Amendment is not . . . assured to all speaking. It is assured only to speech which bears, directly or indirectly, upon issues with which voters have to deal—only, therefore, to the considerations of matters of public interest. Private speech, or private interest in speech, on the other hand, has no claim whatever to the protection of the First Amendment."

2. Here I depart from Meiklejohn, who originally believed that nonpolitical speech was not covered by the First Amendment at all. Much of the analysis in this chapter is devoted to an exploration of how to protect nonpolitical speech in a two-tier First Amendment. It is notable that late in his career, Meiklejohn came

to believe that a great deal of speech is relevantly political: "[V]oting is merely the external expression of a wide and diverse number of activities by means of which citizens attempt to meet the responsibilities of making judgments, which that freedom to govern lays upon them. . . . Self-government can exist only insofar as the voters acquire the intelligence, integrity, sensitivity, and generous devotion to the general welfare that, in theory, casting a ballot is assumed to express." Meiklejohn went on to include literature, the arts, and the achievements of philosophy and the sciences in the protected category. See Alexander Meiklejohn, "The First Amendment Is an Absolute," 1961 *Sup. Ct. Rev.* 245, 255–257. Meiklejohn's shift responds to real concerns; but I think that those concerns can be handled in a different way.

3. Central Hudson Gas v. Public Serv. Comm. of N.Y., 447 U.S. 557, 562–563 (1980); Posadas de Puerto Rico Associates v. Tourism Co., 478 U.S. 328, 340 (1986); Miller v. California, 413 U.S. 15, 23 (1973); compare New York Times v. Sullivan 413, U.S. 15 (1973), with Gertz v. Robert Welch, Inc., 418 U.S. 323, 342–348 (1974).

4. See T. M. Scanlon, "Freedom of Speech and Categories of Expression," 40 *U. Pitt. L. Rev.* 519 (1979).

5. T. M. Scanlon, "A Theory of Free Expression," 1 *Phil. & Pub. Aff.* 204, 214–215 (1972); David Strauss, "Persuasion, Autonomy, and Freedom of Expression," 91 *Colum. L. Rev.* 334, 353–360 (1991); Martin Redish, "The Value of Free Speech," 130 *U. Pa. L. Rev.* 591, 625 (1982). It is for this reason that Scanlon revised his own earlier position, see Scanlon, "Freedom of Speech and Categories of Expression" at 533–534 (1979); T. M. Scanlon, "Content Regulation Reconsidered," in *Democracy and the Mass Media* 346 (Judith Lichtenberg ed. 1990).

6. It would be possible, however, to have a more refined conception of autonomy—not a right to say and do what you "want," but to have the social preconditions for autonomy, a notion that may well allow distinctions among different forms of speech. See C. Edwin Baker, *Human Liberty and Freedom of Speech* 37–46 (1989). But it will be very hard to develop a full system of free expression from this foundation.

7. See R. George Wright, "A Millian View of the Free Speech Principle," 1985 *Sup. Ct. Rev.* 149.

8. See Leonard Levy, *Emergence of a Free Press* (1985). As discussed in Chapter 4, the fact of support in the original understanding is not decisive. The same support could be found for an unacceptably narrow view of the equal protection clause, whose history suggests validation of much discrimination on the basis of sex and even race. But a position that can draw on a good historical pedigree is surely strengthened by that fact.

9. See Scanlon, "Content Regulation Reconsidered" at 338; this is an application of the notion of reflective equilibrium as famously discussed in John Rawls, *A Theory of Justice* 48–51 (1971).

10. See Frederick Schauer, *Freedom of Speech: A Philosophical Inquiry* 35, 39, 45 (1982); Scanlon, "Content Regulation Reconsidered" at 338. As work in public choice theory has shown, there are possible bad incentives elsewhere too. For example, government restrictions on commercial advertising might well result from an effort by a selfish well-organized group to eliminate competition. But this does not distinguish regulation of speech from regulation of anything else; all regulation is vulnerable to interest-group pressures in this way. Hence this kind of bias provides no special reason to be suspicious of government regulation of speech; and post-*Lochner*, we are not suspicious, under the Constitution, of all government regulation. Regulation of political speech, by contrast, raises the distinctive specter of governmental efforts to suppress criticism of its own conduct.

11. See J. H. Ely, *Democracy and Distrust* 75–77 (1980).

12. This would be an Aristotelian approach, for which there is no clear defense in current legal writing. Cf. Baker, *Human Liberty and Freedom of Speech*.

13. See Meiklejohn, *Free Speech and Self-Government* at 99–100: "We have assumed that the studies of the 'scholar' must have, in all respects, the absolute protection of the First Amendment. But with the devising of 'atomic' and 'bacteriological' knowledge for the use of, and under the direction of, military forces, we can now see how loose and inaccurate, at this point, our thinking is. . . . It may be, therefore, that the time has come when the guarding of human welfare requires that we shall abridge the private desire of the scholar—or of those who subsidize him—to study whatever he may please. . . . As I write these words, I am not taking a final stand on the issue which is here suggested. But I am sure that the issue is coming upon us and cannot be evaded. In a rapidly changing world, another of our ancient sanctities—the holiness of research—has been brought under question."

14. See Central Hudson Gas & Elec. v. Public Serv. Comm'n., 447 U.S. 557 (1980).

15. Gertz v. Robert Welch, Inc., 418 U.S. 323, 342 (1974).

16. A possible response would be that many famous people have governmental associations of some sort, and that the notion of "public figures" is designed to overcome the difficulties of case-by-case inquiries into such questions. Note also that many people not involved in government are indeed involved in activities in which the public is legitimately concerned on democratic grounds; consider attempted bribery of public officials by corporate executives. Probably the best approach, suggested by Justice Marshall, would involve an inquiry into whether the issue is one of public importance. See Rosenbloom v. Metromedia, 403 U.S. 29, 78–87 (1971) (Marshall, J., dissenting).

17. 112 S.Ct. 2538 (1992).

18. Texas v. Johnson, 491 U.S. (1989); United States v. Eichman, 110 S. Ct. 2404 (1990).

19. Lloyd Corp. v. Tanner, 407 U.S. 551 (1972); Hudgens v. NLRB, 424 U.S. 507 (1976).

20. See Terminiello v. Chicago, 337 U.S. 1 (1949).

21. I am putting issues of overbreadth to one side, by assuming that with the narrowing construction, the law applies only to speech unprotected by the first amendment. In the *R.A.V.* case itself, four justices concluded that there had been no sufficient narrowing construction.

22. 112 S.Ct at 2550 (White, J., concurring).

23. Id. at 2543. The dissenters in *R.A.V.* argue that this is an equal protection principle, not a First Amendment principle. But it is surely sensible to think that the First Amendment of its own force prohibits government from acting on the basis of the motive of self-insulation.

24. The Court offers a tempting and clever response: "In its practical operation, moreover, the ordinance goes even beyond mere content discrimination to actual viewpoint discrimination. Displays containing some words—odious racial epithets, for example—would be prohibited to proponents of all views. But 'fighting words' that do not themselves invoke race, color, creed, religion, or gender—aspersions based upon a person's mother, for example—would be seemingly usable ad libitum in the placards of those arguing in favor of racial, color, etc. tolerance and equality, but could not be used by that speaker's opponents. . . . St. Paul has no such authority to license one side of a debate to fight freestyle, while requiring the other to follow Marquis of Queensbury Rules." Id. at 2547. The short answer to this point is that the distinction does not embody viewpoint discrimination as that term is ordinarily understood. Viewpoint discrimination occurs if the government takes one side in a debate, as in, for example, a law saying that libel of the President will be punished more severely than libel of anyone else. Viewpoint discrimination is not established by the fact that in some hypothetics, one side has greater means of expression than another, at least—and this is the critical point—if the restriction on means is connected to legitimate, neutral justifications. See the discussion of pornography in Chapter 9. If the argument offered on that point is unpersuasive, the Court may well be right in finding viewpoint discrimination.

25. See Chaplinsky v. New Hampshire, 315 U.S. 568 (1942). There are lurking difficulties here with quiescent or nonviolent victims of fighting words, e.g., pacifists, physically disabled people, or perhaps women.

26. Lehman v. Shaker Heights, 418 U.S. 298 (1974).

27. Greer v. Spock, 424 U.S. 828 (1976).

28. Id. at 2561 (Stevens, J., concurring).

29. Id. at 2548.

30. Id. at 2546.

31. 2 *The Complete Antifederalist* 369 (Herbert Storing ed. 1980).

32. *The Federalist* No. 81.

33. See *The Philosophy of John Dewey* 652 (John McDermott ed. 1981). The ideas in Chapters 7 and 8 are set out in much more detail in Cass R. Sunstein, *Free Speech Now* (forthcoming 1993).

9. Pornography, Abortion, Surrogacy

1. See Roe v. Wade, 410 U.S. 113, 152–156 (1973); Philip Heymann & Michael Barzelay, "The Forest and the Trees: Roe v. Wade and Its Critics," 53 *B. U. L. Rev.* 765, 769–775 (1973); David Richards, *Toleration and the Constitution* 269–280 (1986). The identification is made explicit in a statement by Kathy Keeton, the president of *Penthouse* magazine: "I think if a woman has a right to an abortion and to control her body, then she has the right to exploit her body and make money from it. We have had it hard enough. Why give up one of our major assets?" *Newsweek*, December 16, 1991, p. 15.

2. John Dewey emphasizes the same linkage in challenging the theory of "self-expression" in the political and economic spheres: "The theory assigns a certain intrinsic rightness in this original structure, rightness in the sense of conferring upon them a title to pass into direct action, except when they directly and evidently interfere with similar self-manifestation in others. The idea thus overlooks the part played by interaction with the surrounding medium, especially the social, in generating impulses and desires. They are supposed to inhere in the 'nature' of the individual when that is taken in a primal state, uninfluenced by interaction with an environment. The latter is thus thought of as purely external to an individual, and as irrelevant to freedom except when it interferes with the operation of native instincts and impulses. A study of history would reveal that this notion . . . is a 'faint rumor' left on the air of morals and politics by disappearing theological dogmas, which held that 'nature' is thoroughly good as it comes from the creative hand of God, and that evil is due to corruption through artificial interference and oppression exercised by external or 'social' conditions." John Dewey, "Philosophies of Freedom," in *Freedom in the Modern World* (H. Kallen ed. 1928).

3. See J. S. Mill, *The Subjection of Women*, reprinted in J. S. Mill, *On Liberty and Other Essays* 471 (J. Gray ed. 1991). This is an anticaste principle, defended as such in Chapter 11.

4. Miller v. California, 413 U.S. 15, 24 (1973).

5. I draw here on the careful exposition in Harry M. Clor, *Obscenity and Public Morality* (1969).

6. Some understanding of this sort must undergird the claim that viewpoint discrimination is impermissible but that contemporary community standards are a legitimate basis for regulation. See American Booksellers Assn. v. Hudnut, 771 F.2d 323, 328–330 (7th Cir. 1985) aff'd mem., 475 U.S. 1001 (1986).

7. See, e.g., Ronald Dworkin, "Do We Have a Right to Pornography?" in *A Matter of Principle* 335–372 (1985); Barry Lynn, "Civil Rights Ordinances and the Attorney General's Commission," 21 *Harv. Civ. Rights–Civ. Lib. L. Rev.* 27, 48–56 (1986).

8. Of course it remains necessary to spell out the appropriate conditions, and here there will be some difficulty in working out the relationship between the belief in a protected realm for sexual life and the commitment to eliminating sex-

based caste systems. The difficulty is likely to be much greater in the abstract, however, than in working with particular disputed cases. It is clear, for example, that the law should punish (though in most states it does not) rape within marriage, even though such punishment intrudes in some sense into (at least one person's) erotic life. On sexuality as postpolitical, see Catharine MacKinnon, *Toward a Feminist Theory of the State* (1989); David Greenberg, *The Construction of Homosexuality* (1989); Richard A. Posner, *Sex and Reason* (1992).

The opposition of some gay and lesbian groups to antipornography efforts seems to be rooted in a general fear of governmental control of sexuality and an insistence that sexual desires should be free from the constraints of the state. The fear and the insistence are easily understandable in light of the history of legal suppression of homosexuality. In view of that history, the notion that sexual desires should be freed from legal controls might seem irresistible.

One might doubt, however, whether the existence of legitimate fears about state suppression of homosexuality should so readily be taken to disable the state from controlling speech or acts that are closely connected to violence against women. To take the suppression of homosexuality as a reason to bar the state from controlling all sexually related behavior, even speech, perhaps seems plausible as a strategic matter, but no more than that. It may well be that an antipornography movement could be rooted in a kind of anticaste principle (see Chapter 11) that would be an inextricable part of any movement to eliminate regulation of homosexuality as well. More fundamentally, a decision—based on the history of suppression of homosexuality—to remove all state-produced limits on something called "sexuality" seems to collapse too many distinct problems into the same conceptual category.

9. See Catharine MacKinnon, *Feminism Unmodified* 146–162 (1987).

10. Not all of those who focus on this problem treat pornography as a problem of sex discrimination only because it is associated with violence. See, e.g., Rae Langton, "Whose Right? Ronald Dworkin, Women, and Pornographers," 19 *Phil. & Pub. Aff.* 311, 335–336 (1990). (MacKinnon's own position on this is complex. Subordination is her principal target, not violence; but violence underlies much of the argument and almost all the examples.) Instead the argument might deal far more broadly with the role of pornography in creating inequality, in part through its place in the sexual subordination or objectification of women. I deal here, however, with pornography as a subject of regulation only to the extent that it is associated with violence against women (an important ingredient in sexual inequality). The broader understanding of the harms that pornography produces raises even more severe First Amendment difficulties. This is especially so for the very large category of objectification—a category with which it is extremely difficult for a legal system to work. The category of subordination is also difficult when we are dealing with speech.

11. See the summary in U.S. Department of Justice, Attorney General's Commission on Pornography, *Final Report* 888–889 (1987).

12. The Court recognized this point in the context of child pornography in New York v. Ferber, 458 U.S. 747, 760 (1982).

13. See generally Edward Donnerstein et al., "The Question of Pornography on Sex Crimes," in *Handbook of Sexual Assault* (W. L. Marshall et al. eds. 1990); Murrin & Laws, "The Influence of Pornography on Sex Crimes," id. at 73; Edward Donnerstein, "Pornography: Its Effect on Violence against Women," in *Pornography and Sexual Aggression* 53–81 (Neil Malamuth et al. eds. 1984); Attorney General's Commission on Pornography, *Final Report*. On the problem of causation, see Frederick Schauer, "Causation Theory and the Causes of Sexual Violence," 1987 *Am. Bar. Found. Res. J.* 737.

It would probably be best to respond to this evidence by creating a private cause of action for those harmed through the production or use of pornography, rather than by creating a criminal action to be brought by prosecutors, whose incentives may not always be aligned with those of the injured parties.

It may be that these first two arguments suggest that antipornography legislation should be addressed only to movies and pictures, with the written word exempted, since it is only in movies and pictures that abuse of participants will occur. (One might support a law against child pornography in movies and print while allowing essays that amount to child pornography.) Moreover, the evidence on pornography as a stimulus to violence deals mostly with movies and pictures, and the immediacy and vividness of these media suggest a possible distinction from written texts. I do not discuss the exact breadth of an antipornography statute here. But the possibility of exempting written texts, no matter what they contain, suggests the weakness of the objection from neutrality. A statute that is directed at violent pornography but exempts written texts is very plausibly treated as harm-based rather than viewpoint-based.

Note also that the argument in the text makes it a necessary condition for regulation that the relevant material involves sexual violence against women. That is not a sufficient condition; very probably speech with serious social value should be exempted, in order to ensure that only "low-value" speech is regulated. Moreover, material that involves sexual violence against men, or gay or lesbian material, would not be regulable unless it could be shown to be connected with the harms discussed in the text.

14. It is revealing to consider in this connection the general reaction to the *Final Report* of the Attorney General's Commission on Pornography. The *New Republic*—a liberal journal priding itself on its belief in racial and sexual equality—gave the title "Big Boobs" to its response to the report. See Hendrick Hertzberg, "Big Boobs: Ed Meese and His Pornography Commission," *New Republic*, July 14, 1986, p. 21. It sought to ridicule the authors of the report by depicting them as parts of the female anatomy. On the cover, the *New Republic* carried a drawing of Attorney General Edwin Meese as an attractive woman, with the description, "Fast, Loose, and Stacked." The cover thus ridiculed the commission by describing the Attorney General as a woman and, more particularly, as a pornographic model. The *New Republic*'s coverage of the report quite inadvertently

confirmed much of the antipornography movement's argument about the relationships among sexuality, pornography, and inequality.

In this light, it is indeed plausible to think that pornography sometimes plays a part in "silencing women"—not by criminalizing their speech, but by discrediting it in a way that has consequences for the attitudes of men and women alike. The notion that "no means yes" in conventional attitudes about sexual availability has especially grotesque consequences in the context of the attack on pornography.

To say this is not to say that the argument from "silencing" properly plays a role in the First Amendment. This form of silencing is produced by social attitudes resulting from speech itself, and one cannot find that fact to be a reason for regulation without making excessive inroads on a system of free expression. The fact that many forms of speech do indeed have silencing effects is not a reason to regulate them. See Ronald Dworkin, "Two Forms of Liberty," in *Isaiah Berlin: A Celebration* 100, 107–109 (Edna Ullmann-Margalit & Avishai Margalit eds. 1991). The silencing effect is an important part of the political argument against pornography; but it probably should not be part of the First Amendment debate.

15. See American Booksellers Assn. v. Hudnut, 771 F.2d 323 (7th Cir. 1985), aff'd mem., 475 U.S. 1001 (1986).

16. See NLRB v. Gissel Packing Co., 395 U.S. 575, 618–619 (1969).

17. Posadas de Puerto Rico Associates v. Tourism Co. of Puerto Rico, 478 U.S. 328, 341 (1986).

18. See Richard Epstein, "Substantive Due Process by Any Other Name: The Abortion Cases," 1973 *Sup. Ct. Rev.* 159, 170–185.

19. See Kristin Luker, *Abortion and the Politics of Motherhood* 171–174 (1984).

20. See John Hart Ely, "The Wages of Crying Wolf: A Comment on *Roe v. Wade*," 82 *Yale L. J.* 920, 932 (1973).

21. There appears to be a mounting consensus that equality arguments are better than liberty arguments with respect to abortion generally. See Ruth Bader Ginsburg, "Some Thoughts on Autonomy and Equality in Relation to *Roe v. Wade*," 63 *N.C. L. Rev.* 375, 282–283 (1985); Kenneth Karst, "Foreword: Equal Citizenship under the Fourteenth Amendment," 91 *Harv. L. Rev.* 1, 57–59 (1977); Frederick Schauer, "Easy Cases," 58 *So. Cal. L. Rev.* 399 (1985); Sylvia Law, "Rethinking Sex and the Constitution," 132 *U. Pa. L. Rev.* 955 (1984); David Strauss, "Discriminatory Intent and the Taming of *Brown*," 56 *U. Chi. L. Rev.* 935, 970–992 (1989); MacKinnon, *Feminism Unmodified* at 93–102; Laurence Tribe, *American Constitutional Law*, 1353–56 (2d ed. 1988); Catharine MacKinnon, "Reflections on Sex Equality under Law," 100 *Yale L. J.* 1281, 1307–24 (1991). It will not have escaped notice that this argument itself depends on a baseline assumption that women's reproductive capacities are just that—women's. If this argument depends on a belief in a natural or prepolitical right of ownership, it may well run afoul of the considerations introduced in Chapter 2. The argument should be seen instead as rooted most straightforwardly in a norm

of equality on the basis of gender: a right on the part of women not to have their bodies used by others when men's bodies are not similarly used. It would be most surprising, however, if a general right of bodily ownership could not also be justified for both men and women.

An argument of the general sort set out here is made in Donald Regan, "Rewriting Roe v. Wade," 77 *Mich. L. Rev.* 1569 (1979); and Judith Jarvis Thomson, "A Defense of Abortion," 1 *Phil. & Pub. Aff.* 47 (1971), to whose discussions I am much indebted. Issues of sexual inequality are not, however, sufficiently emphasized there.

22. I am indebted to David Strauss for help with this point. The Supreme Court held otherwise in Geduldig v. Aiello, 417 U.S. 484 (1974), but the context involved a disability insurance program from which pregnancy was excluded. It is by no means clear that *Geduldig* would be extended to a case in which pregnant people were (for example) forced to stay indoors in certain periods or were subjected to some other unique criminal or civil disability.

An argument that discrimination on the basis of pregnancy should not be treated the same as discrimination on the basis of gender might stress that statutes directed at biological correlates of gender are less likely to reflect prejudice and stereotyping. There is, after all, a real difference here, and the legislation might be responding sensibly to it. But it is doubtful whether an approach to gender-based discrimination should be based on an inquiry into whether there are real differences. Whether a "real difference" justifies social disadvantage is the question to be decided. See MacKinnon, *Feminism Unmodified* at 32–45. And even if it does, pregnancy is a particular kind of real difference, one whose exclusive targeting is in fact likely to reflect prejudice or subordination.

23. See Curran v. Bosze, 566 N.E.2d 1319 (Ill. 1990); McFall v. Shimp, 10 Pa. D. & C. 3d 90 (1978).

24. Mill, *The Subjection of Women* at 482–484.

25. All of this does not mean that male-only registration or male-only combat necessarily violates the equal protection clause, a question that turns on issues of justification that I cannot discuss here.

26. See James Mohr, *Abortion in America: The Origins and Evolution of National Policy, 1800–1900* 168–172 (1978), demonstrating that the physicians largely responsible for bringing about abortion restrictions "were among the most defensive groups in the country on the subject of changing traditional sex roles. . . . To many doctors the chief purpose of women was to produce children; anything that interfered with that purpose, or allowed women to 'indulge' themselves in less important activities, threatened . . . the future of society itself. Abortion was a supreme example of such an interference for these physicians." Id. at 168–169. See also id. at 105, quoting a nineteenth-century doctor complaining that "the tendency to force women into men's places" was creating insidious "new ideas of women's duties" and including among such ideas the view "that her ministrations . . . as a mother should be abandoned for the sterner rights of voting and law making."

See also Linda Gordon, *Women's Body, Women's Right: A Social History of Birth Control in America* 3–25 (1976); and Carole Smith-Rosenberg, *Disorderly Conduct* (1985). Smith-Rosenberg quotes a statement by the American Medical Association's influential Committee on Criminal Abortion, describing the woman who sought an abortion: "She becomes unmindful of the course marked out for her by Providence, she overlooks the duties imposed on her by the marriage contract. . . . Let not the husband of such a wife flatter himself that he possesses her affection. Nor can she in turn ever merit even the respect of a virtuous husband." Id. at 236–237.

The best recent sources are Kristin Luker, *Abortion and the Politics of Motherhood* and "Abortion and the Meaning of Life," in *Abortion: Understanding Differences* 25, 31 (Sidney Callahan & Daniel Callahan eds. 1984), which deal with abortion laws passed within the last generation and bear on abortion laws likely within the next generation.

27. Luker, "Abortion and the Meaning of Life" at 31.

28. See Gerald Rosenberg, *The Hollow Hope* 179–180, 353–355 (1991).

29. See L. Lader, *Abortion* 3 (1966); R. Schwartz, *Septic Abortion* 7 (1968). See also H. Morgantaler, *Abortion and Contraception* 111 (1982).

30. See Rosenberg, *The Hollow Hope* 179–180, 353–355; and H. Rodman et al., *The Abortion Question* (1987). See also the useful discussion of the relevant facts in Posner, *Sex and Reason*. Facts of this sort are used in Mary Ann Glendon, *Abortion and Divorce in Western Law* (1987), in support of a powerful argument that America has used abortion as a prominent part of its solution to the problem of unwanted children, and even of (so to speak) its childcare policy. Glendon contrasts the far more attractive European approach, which is to use law and social supports to provide care for the mother and the child, with more restricted rights to abortion. On Glendon's view, the free availability of abortion in the United States is closely associated with the absence of social supports for women and young children.

Glendon's argument is important and persuasive. It shows that abortion should not be the principal focus of social policies protecting reproduction, women, and children. It is necessary instead to emphasize access to contraception, education, protection against unwanted sexual intercourse, and social supports for women who are unsure whether to have children. The general goal should be to make abortion both less necessary and less desirable. Under current conditions, however, Glendon's arguments should not be taken as a reason to reject an abortion right built on principles of sex equality.

31. For some, of course, the symbolic gain—the affirmation of human life produced by a prohibition on abortion—might be sufficient. But in a world of heightened scrutiny, that symbolic gain is probably inadequate. Cf. Griswold v. Connecticut, 381 U.S. 479 (1965) (refusing to invoke symbolic goals in cases in which a statute inadequately serves its other legitimate purposes).

I do not deal here with restrictions on the abortion right that fall short of prohibition, such as waiting periods, parental notification and consent requirements, or provision of information to pregnant women. These restrictions raise distinctive issues that cannot be discussed here.

32. Planned Parenthood of Southeastern Pennsylvania v. Casey, 60 U.S.L.W. 4795 (1992).

33. See Geduldig v. Aiello, 417 U.S. 484, 496 N. 20 (1974); Harris v. McRae, 448 U.S. 297, 322–323 (1980). This conception of equality is challenged in MacKinnon, *Feminism Unmodified* at 32–34; and Martha Minow, *Making All the Difference* 56–60 (1990). It might be useful to explore a legal system taking female biological capacities as the norm. Imagine, for example, a state's giving every citizen the choice of either bearing a child or giving the government nine months in salary. Such a law should readily be seen as a form of discrimination against men, even though it is a far weaker case for invalidation than laws burdening female reproductive capacity in light of (a) the fact that the burdened class consists of infertile women as well as men and (b) the fact that laws that burden female reproductive capacity are part of a system of subordination on the basis of gender, something that cannot be said for laws that burden male capacities.

34. In re Baby M, 217 N.J. Super. 313, 387–389, 525 A.2d 1128, 1165–1166 (N.S. Super. Ct. Ch. Div.) rev'd 537 A.2d 1227 (N.J. 1987), 109 N.J. 396 (1987).

35. There is also, perhaps, a distinctive autonomy concern here. A unique intrusion is imposed on people who are forced to give up a child that they have borne through pregnancy. That intrusion may be sufficient for allowing the relevant contracts to be voidable even without an equality dimension.

If the argument in the text is persuasive, it would not matter whether the surrogate mother's egg is involved. What is crucial is that she carried the baby to term. The problem with surrogacy arrangements consists in the commodification of gestational services, a problem that exists even if the fetus is biologically connected to both mother and father. I speculate that the view that the fetus "is" the father's, or "is not" the surrogate mother's, is connected in all cases with an old and still-pervasive view, notwithstanding its biological implausibility: that children are in a deep sense products of the father alone, and that the mother is a mere vehicle for the act of production. See Thomas Laqueur, *Making Sex* 57–59 (1990).

36. See Martha Field, *Surrogate Motherhood* 1–4 (1988).

37. See Margaret Jane Radin, "Market-Inalienability," 100 *Harv. L. Rev.* 1849, 1929 (1987).

10. "It's the Government's Money"

1. See Richard Epstein, "Foreword: Unconstitutional Conditions, State Power and the Limits of Consent," 102 *Harv. L. Rev.* 4 (1988); Kathleen Sullivan, "Unconstitutional Conditions," 102 *Harv. L. Rev.* 1413, 1419 (1989); Seth Kreimer, "Allocational Sanctions: The Problem of Negative Rights in a Positive State," 132 *U. Pa. L. Rev.* 1243, 1259 (1984); Laurence Tribe, *American Consti-*

tutional Law § 10-8 at 681–685, § 10-9 at 685–687 (2d ed. 1988); William Van Alstyne, "The Demise of the Right-Privilege Distinction in Constitutional Law," 81 *Harv. L. Rev.* 1439, 1448 (1968).

2. Pierce v. Society of Sisters, 268 U.S. 510 (1925).

3. Frost & Frost Trucking Co. v. Railroad Commission, 271 U.S. 583 (1926). Epstein, "Foreword," and Sullivan, "Unconstitutional Conditions," discuss some of the origins of the doctrine.

4. McAuliffe v. Mayor of New Hampshire, 155 Mass. 216, 220, 29 N.E. 517, 517–518 (1892). Holmes expressed the same basic position in many places. See, e.g., Myers v. U.S. 72 U.S. 52 (Holmes, J., dissenting); Western Union Tel. Co. v. Kansas, 216 U.S. 1, 53 (1910) (Holmes, J., dissenting).

5. For modern incarnations, see, e.g., Frank Easterbrook, "Insider Trading, Secret Agents, Evidentiary Privileges, and the Production of Information," 1981 *Sup. Ct. Rev.* 309, 344–352; Lyng v. International Union, 485 U.S. 360 (1988). For Chief Justice Rehnquist's view, see, e.g., First National Bank v. Bellotti, 435 U.S. 765, 822 (1978); Rust v. Sullivan, 111 S.Ct. 1759 (1991); Arnett v. Kennedy, 416 U.S. 134 (1974) (plurality opinion).

6. See Epstein, "Foreword," for the basic statement and defense.

7. The takings clause is of course antiredistributive, but it has never been and should not be taken as a wholesale assault on all governmental action with redistributive consequences.

8. And before *Lochner* as well; there was no general barrier to redistribution in the founding period. See Thomas Grey, "The Malthusian Constitution," 41 *U. Miami L. Rev.* 21 (1986).

9. John Rawls, *A Theory of Justice* (1971); and Bruce Ackerman, *Social Justice in the Liberal State* (1980), provide philosophical treatments within the liberal tradition; for an analysis along similar lines with particular focus on the appropriate scope of regulation, see Cass R. Sunstein, *After the Rights Revolution: Reconceiving the Regulatory State* (1990).

10. See, e.g., F.C.C. v. League of Women Voters, 468 U.S. 364 (1984); Arkansas Writers' Project v. Ragland, 481 U.S. 221 (1987); Harris v. McRae, 448 U.S. 297 (1980); Sherbert v. Verner, 374 U.S. 398 (1963); Shapiro v. Thompson, 394 U.S. 618 (1969).

11. 448 U.S. 297 (1980).

12. Robert Nozick, "Coercion," in *Philosophy, Science, and Method* 440, 447 (Sidney Morgenbesser, P. Suppes, & M. White eds. 1969); Sullivan, "Unconstitutional Conditions."

13. Snepp v. U.S., 444 U.S. 507 (1980).

14. Lyng v. International Union, 485 U.S. 360 (1988).

15. Rust v. Sullivan, 111 S.Ct. 1759 (1991).

16. See, e.g., *Canons* (Robert Von Hallberg ed. 1986).

17. Harris v. McRae, 448 U.S. 609 (1980).

18. Some such desires are of course constitutionally unacceptable; see Cle-

burne v. Cleburne Living Center, 473 U.S. 432 (1985) (prejudice against and fears of mentally retarded do not qualify as reasons for discrimination against them), but here the question to be decided is whether the objection to abortion is unacceptable in that sense.

19. See Michael McConnell, "The Selective Funding Problem: Abortions and Religious Schools," 104 *Harv. L. Rev.* 989 (1991).

20. The point is well discussed in Laurence Tribe, *Constitutional Choices* ch. 15 (1985), to which I am much indebted here.

21. A characteristic feature of the unconstitutional conditions doctrine—the inquiry into the germaneness of the condition to the program; see generally Sullivan, "Unconstitutional Conditions"—should be understood as a means of flushing out impermissible reasons and of ensuring that legitimate reasons are in fact at work. This task can readily be performed under the reformulation suggested here.

11. The Limits of Compensatory Justice

1. F. D. Roosevelt, "Speech Accepting the Nomination for the Presidency" (July 2, 1932), 1 *The Public Papers of Franklin D. Roosevelt: The Genesis of the New Deal* 657 (1938); idem, "Annual Message to Congress" (Jan. 3, 1936), 5 *The Public Papers and Addresses of Franklin D. Roosevelt: The People Approve* 13 (1938).

2. For a catalogue, see Cass R. Sunstein, *After the Rights Revolution: Reconceiving the Regulatory State* chaps. 1 and 2 (1990). One of my themes there is the need for more flexible, market-oriented strategies for satisfying regulatory goals. Endorsement of the New Deal attack on status quo neutrality should not be confused with enthusiasm for the often unsuccessful New Deal solutions. The following discussion of risk management is an effort to counteract some of the evident difficulties in those purported solutions.

3. Eisen v. Carlisle & Jacquelin, 417 U.S. 156 (1974).

4. See generally David Rosenberg, "The Causal Connection in Mass Exposure Cases: A 'Public Law' Vision of the Tort System," 97 *Harv. L. Rev.* 851–929 (1984).

5. See Industrial Union v. American Petroleum, 448 U.S. 607 (1980); see generally Jerry L. Mashaw & David L. Harfst, *The Struggle for Automobile Safety* (1990).

6. See Mashaw & Harfst, *The Struggle for Automobile Safety*.

7. Allen v. Wright, 468 U.S. 737 (1984); Simon v. Eastern Kentucky Welfare Rights Org., 426 U.S. 26 (1976); Center for Auto Safety v. Thomas, 847 F.2d 843 (D.C. Cir. 1988) (en banc). In the last case, the court divided five to five, and thus reinstated a previous decision granting standing. See also the important recent decision in Lujan v. Defenders of Wildlife, 112 S.Ct. 2130 (1992), in which the Supreme Court denied standing to people protesting a government decision

not to apply the Endangered Species Act to its funding activities outside the United States. Two of the plaintiffs claimed that they had visited sites having endangered species in the past, and that they planned to return in the future. The Court denied standing on the ground that no "injury in fact" had been shown; it was purely "speculative" whether the plaintiffs would actually return. Four justices added that the injury would not be redressed by a decree in their favor, since the relevant projects might go forward even if American funding were cut off. Most important, the Court held that Congress' explicit grant of standing to "citizens" was unconstitutional. If the following analysis is correct, Lujan was wrongly decided, for Congress does indeed have power to grant standing in cases of this kind. For more detailed and technical discussion, see Cass R. Sunstein, "Standing and the Privatization of Public Law," 88 *Colum. L. Rev.* 1432 (1988); idem, "What's Standing after *Lujan?*" 91 *Mich. L. Rev.* 163 (1992).

8. Washington v. Davis, 426 U.S. 229 (1976); Personnel Administrator of Massachusetts v. Feeney, 442 U.S. 256 (1979).

9. 442 U.S. 256 (1979).

10. David Strauss, "Discriminatory Intent and the Taming of *Brown*," 56 *U. Chi. L. Rev.* 935 (1989).

11. See Geoffrey Stone, L. Michael Seidman, Cass R. Sunstein, & Mark Tushnet, *Constitutional Law* (1986).

12. See Green v. County School Bd., 391 U.S. 430 (1968).

13. See City of Richmond v. Croson, 488 U.S. 469 (1989).

14. See Kathleen Sullivan, "Sins of Discrimination: Last Term's Affirmative Action Cases," 100 *Harv. L. Rev.* 78 (1986).

15. See Greater Los Angeles Council on Deafness v. Community Television of So. Calif., 719 F.2d 1017 (9th Cir. 1983) (rejecting suit by hearing-impaired persons claiming that television must be made accessible to them); Gallagher v. Pontiac School Dist., 807 F.2d 75 (6th Cir. 1986) (rejecting a claim from a deaf and mentally handicapped student for educational services on the ground that the "essence of his claim does not constitute a valid equal protection challenge. When a handicapped child does not allege that he has been singled out or treated differently from the nonhandicapped child, but rather needs additional special services, the fourteenth amendment is rarely implicated"); Pinkerton v. Moye, 509 F.2d 107 (W.D. Va. 1981) (same). See also Ferris v. Univ. of Texas at Austin, 558 F. Supp. 536 (W.D. Tex. 1983); Dopico v. Goldschmidt, 518 F. Supp. 1161 (S.D.N.Y. 1981), aff'd in part, rev'd in part, 687 F.2d 644 (2d Cir. 1982).

The exception is that the Court applies "rationality review" to measures disadvantaging the disabled. See, e.g., Cleburne v. Cleburne Living Center, 473 U.S. 432 (1985). Rationality review is, however, highly deferential and almost always results in validation, as we saw in Chapter 1. Note also that the problem facing handicapped people is rarely "classifications" directed against them. It is instead, as discussed in the text, a world made by and for the able-bodied.

16. Regents of the University of California v. Bakke, 438 U.S. 265 (1978).

17. The notion of morally irrelevant differences draws on John Rawls, *A Theory of Justice* (1972). We might understand systemic disadvantages in terms of the primary goods discussed in id. at 90–95, 433–439, including self-respect. The notion of capabilities and functionings—an alternative to primary goods— is set out in Amartya K. Sen, *Commodities and Capabilities* (1985).

There are important and revealing connections between discrimination on the basis of gender and discrimination on the basis of sexual orientation. The two forms of discrimination are closely related, indeed in some ways the same thing; both are connected with maintenance of a caste system based on gender. This is not the place for a full discussion of the point, but the treatment thus far of the issue of "differences" seems to raise it, and I therefore offer a few tentative speculations.

Consider the social and legal ban on same-sex marriages, a ban that can be found in one or another form in almost all nations. The ban on same-sex marriages is not thought to raise a problem of gender-based inequality in most legal systems. But might the legal ban (and the social taboo) not be crucially a product of a desire to maintain a system of gender hierarchy, a system that same-sex marriages tend to undermine by complicating traditional and still influential ideas about "natural differences" between men and women? There could well be differences between the reasons for stigmatizing/outlawing male homosexual relations on the one hand and female homosexual relations on the other. Might not the ban on male homosexual relations be an effort to insist on and to rigidify "natural difference," in part by ensuring firm and clear lines, defined in terms of gender, about sexual (and social) activity as opposed to sexual (and social) receptivity or passivity? Might not the ban on lesbian relations be at least in part an effort to ensure that women are sexually available to men? I speculate that considerations of this sort help to maintain the legal and social taboo on homosexuality, in a way that might well be damaging to both men and women, and to heterosexual and homosexual alike, though of course in very different ways and to quite different degrees.

If these points seem exotic, we might think about a close analogy, legal and social bans on racial intermarriage. It is certainly not exotic to insist that such bans are typically (though not always) an effort to maintain a system of racial caste. For example, the American legal system has come to see such bans as an effort to maintain white supremacy, or racial caste, by keeping racial lines firm and distinct. See Loving v. Virginia, 388 U.S. 1 (1967). This is so even though bans on racial marriage are formally equal: whites and blacks are treated "the same" by such bans. Bans on same-sex marriages might similarly seem to treat men and women "the same," and thus to involve discrimination on the basis of sexual orientation rather than on the basis of sex. But in terms of their purposes and effects, bans on same-sex marriage have very much the same connection to gender caste as bans on racial intermarriage have to racial caste. Related points are discussed in Sylvia Law, "Homosexuality and the Social Meaning of Gender,"

1988 *Wisc. L. Rev.* 187; and Cass R. Sunstein, "Sexual Orientation and the Constitution: A Note on the Relationship between Due Process and Equal Protection," 55 *U. Chi. L. Rev.* 1161 (1988).

18. See Charles Fairman, "Does the Fourteenth Amendment Incorporate the Bill of Rights?" 2 *Stan. L. Rev.* 5, 163–170 (1949).

19. See Sullivan, "Sins of Discrimination."

Conclusion

1. See, e.g., Ann Scales, "The Emergence of Feminist Jurisprudence: An Essay," 95 *Yale L. J.* 1373, 1385 (1986): "Feminism does not claim to be objective, because objectivity is the basis of inequality. Feminism is result-oriented. . . . [W]hen dealing with social inequality there are no neutral principles." See also Catharine MacKinnon, *Feminism Unmodified* 43–44 (1987): "When [sex inequality] is exposed as a naked power question, there is no separable question of what ought to be. . . . In this shift of paradigms, equality propositions become no longer propositions of good and evil, but of power and powerlessness, no more disinterested in their origins or neutral in their arrival at conclusions than are the problems they address."

2. This idea plays a role in Herbert Wechsler, "Toward Neutral Principles of Constitutional Law," 73 *Harv. L. Rev.* 1 (1959), as well; see Kent Greenawalt, "The Enduring Significance of Neutral Principles," 78 *Colum. L. Rev.* 982 (1978), which elaborates this conception of neutrality.

3. See John Rawls, *A Theory of Justice* 19–22, 48–51 (1971).

4. See Cass R. Sunstein, "On Analogical Reasoning," 106 *Harv. L. Rev.* 741 (1993).

5. See Richard Posner, *The Problems of Jurisprudence* 86–100 (1990); Mark Tushnet, "Following the Rules Laid Down: A Critique of Interpretivism and Neutral Principles," 96 *Harv. L. Rev.* 781 (1983).

6. See Don Herzog, *Happy Slaves* 171–175 (1989).

7. See the discussion of objectivity in John Rawls, "Kantian Constructivism in Moral Theory," 77 *J. Phil.* 515, 570–572 (1980).

8. For some qualifications, see Chapter 5.

Index

Abortion, 270–283, 289; ban on federally funded family planning services from counseling about, 229, 310–311; clinics giving advice on, 86–87; conditions imposed on receiving, 85, 86; effect of *Roe v. Wade* on, 147, 171; equal protection clause applied to laws restricting, 259, 272–285; government control of, 257–258; government funding of, 70, 293, 299, 315–317; Hyde Amendment on, 86; physicians' role in creating restrictions on, 396n26; privacy right as including right to, 271–272, 279, 280; restrictions on as sex discrimination, 270–283, 285, 317; in social policy, 397n30

Addictive behavior, regulation of, 175, 191, 192

Adkins v. Childrens Hospital, 45, 46, 65, 66

Administrative agencies, 320–321; compensatory model applied to, 326–327; risk management by, 334–338; standing to challenge, 88–90, 157, 327–328, 335–336; unlawful inaction by, 87–88, 157

Advertising: for casinos and cigarettes, 268; on children's television, 198; effects on free speech, 216–217; political, on buses, 250

Affirmative action, 77–78, 149–150, 151, 156–157, 331–333, 335, 344; New Deal and, 57–58

Affirmative rights, 69–71

Agent Orange lawsuits, 265

Agreement as regulative ideal, 137, 141

Aliens, and equal protection doctrine, 38

American Booksellers Association v. Hudnut, 267–268

American Civil Liberties Union, 200

Anticaste principle, 338–345

Aristotelianism, 141, 187

Arrow, Kenneth, 125

Art and literature: depicting homosexual conduct, 270; freedom of speech in, 239, 240, 241, 242, 244–245; government funding of, 292–293, 308–315

Article III tribunals, 83–84

Articles of Confederation, 19, 21

Association of Data Processing Service Organization v. Camp, 89

Austin, J. L., 110

Authoritarianism, 352; antiauthoritarian impulse, 352; antiauthoritarianism in constitutional law, 25; impartiality discouraging, 24

Automobile regulation, 326–327, 328, 338

Autonomy: in collective self-determination, 178; governmental interference with,

405

ACN 4594   6/10/93

KF
4549
S86
1993